# The Grotesque Dancer
# on the Eighteenth-Century Stage

STUDIES IN DANCE HISTORY

A Publication of the Society of Dance History Scholars

Titles in Print

*The Origins of the Bolero School*

*Carlo Blasis in Russia*

*Of, By, and For the People: Dancing on the Left in the 1930s*

*Dancing in Montreal: Seeds of a Choreographic History*

*The Making of a Choreographer: Ninette de Valois and "Bar aux Folies-Bergère"*

*Ned Wayburn and the Dance Routine: From Vaudeville to the "Ziegfeld Follies"*

*Rethinking the Sylph: New Perspectives on the Romantic Ballet*

*Dance for Export: Cultural Diplomacy and the Cold War*

*José Limón: An Unfinished Memoir*

*Dancing Desires: Choreographing Sexualities on and off the Stage*

*Dancing Many Drums: Excavations in African American Dance*

*Writings on Ballet and Music, by Fedor Lopukhov*

*Liebe Hanya: Mary Wigman's Letters to Hanya Holm*

*The Grotesque Dancer on the Eighteenth-Century Stage: Gennaro Magri and His World*

# The Grotesque Dancer on the Eighteenth-Century Stage

*Gennaro Magri and His World*

Edited by

## Rebecca Harris-Warrick and Bruce Alan Brown

THE UNIVERSITY OF WISCONSIN PRESS

The University of Wisconsin Press
1930 Monroe Street
Madison, Wisconsin 53711

www.wisc.edu/wisconsinpress/

3 Henrietta Street
London WC2E 8LU, England

Library of Congress Cataloging-in-Publication Data
The grotesque dancer on the eighteenth-century stage : Gennaro Magri and his world /
edited by Rebecca Harris-Warrick and Bruce Alan Brown.
p. cm. — (Studies in dance history)
Includes index.
ISBN 0-299-20354-9 (pbk.: alk. paper)
1. Magri, Gennaro, fl. 1779. 2. Ballet dancers — Italy — Biography.
3. Choreographers — Italy — Biography. 4. Ballet — Italy — History — 18th century.
I. Harris-Warrick, Rebecca. II. Brown, Bruce Alan.
III. Studies in dance history (Unnumbered)
GV1785.M2525G76 2004
792.8'092 — dc22
2004007796

This book is dedicated to the memory of Ingrid Brainard (1925–2000).

As a scholar and performer, Ingrid was instrumental in making dance history a legitimate area of study. Her own interests were extremely broad—including not only many centuries of music and dance but also costume history, theater history, and twentieth-century mime. Her writings in both English and German—called small jewels by some of her editors—leave an impressive legacy. While the bulk of her writing consisted of articles and reviews in scholarly journals and encyclopedias, Ingrid also wrote a much consulted "blue book," *The Art of Courtly Dancing in the Early Renaissance, Part 2: The Practice of Courtly Dancing,* and was at work on part 1, the theory, when she died. Ingrid was dedicated to the practical application of her scholarship—singing, playing keyboard and viola da gamba, creating dance reconstructions and new choreography—and her Cambridge Court Dancers opened many eyes to the beauties of early dance. A member of several scholarly organizations for musicology and dance research, Ingrid was particularly active in the International Congress on Medieval Studies in Kalamazoo, Michigan, and the Society of Dance History Scholars, of which she was a founding member. For her pioneering efforts on behalf of the discipline, all subsequent dance historians owe her a debt of gratitude. Our own memories of her guidance and friendship accompany these essays.

# Contents

# Illustrations, Musical Examples, and Tables

# Acknowledgments

This book has been a cooperative effort from the start, and many people were involved in its evolution from conference session to printed volume. We would like first to thank all those who participated, both formally and informally, in the Magri sessions at the 1996 conference of the Society of Dance History Scholars in Minneapolis, especially Letizia Dradi, Judith Chazin Bennahum, Chrystelle Bond, and Catherine Turocy, whose own experiences in dance reconstruction enlivened all the sessions. While the book was in preparation we consulted many other colleagues who generously lent us their own expertise, among them the late Irene Alm, Evan Baker, Michael Burden, Sibylle Dahms, Edmund Fairfax, Angene Feves, Nathalie Lecomte, Ken Pierce, Giannandrea Poesio, Eugénia Roucher, and Marian Smith. We would like to mention all those whose reconstructions of portions of the Ferrère manuscript helped explore its workings: Lisa Arkin and her students at the University of Oregon, Moira Goff, Madeleine Inglehearn, Kaspar Mainz, Carol G. Marsh and students from the dance and theater departments at the University of North Carolina at Greensboro, Ken Pierce, Jennifer Thorpe, and Linda Tomko and her students at the University of California at Riverside. We would also like to thank the staffs at the following institutions for their able assistance: Sidney Cox Library of Music and Dance at Cornell University, Ithaca; Doheny Memorial Library at the University of Southern California, Los Angeles; J. Paul Getty Museum, Los Angeles; Walter Clinton Jackson Library at the University of North Carolina, Greensboro; Harvard Theatre Collection, Cambridge; Dance Division of the New York Public Library for the Performing Arts; Music Division, Library of Congress, Washington, D.C.; Bibliothèque de l'Opéra, Paris; Biblioteca di Santa Cecilia, Rome; Archivio di Stato and Conservatorio di Musica San Pietro a Majella, Naples; Accademia Filarmonica, Bologna; and Státní Oblastní Archiv v Třeboni, Český Krumlov.

We are grateful for the support of the Society of Dance History Scholars and its edtorial board, especially Elizabeth Aldrich and Lynn Garafola, who oversaw this project on its way to publication. Above all we would like to thank Mary Ann O'Brian Malkin, without whose generous support this book would not have seen the light of day.

# Abbreviations

Library sigla adhere to those given in *The New Grove Dictionary of Music and Musicians*.

| | |
|---|---|
| *Grove Opera* | *The New Grove Dictionary of Opera*, ed. Stanley Sadie (London: Macmillan, 1992) |
| LMC | Meredith Ellis Little and Carol G. Marsh, *La Danse Noble: An Inventory of Dances and Sources* (Williamstown, MA: Broude Bros., 1992) |
| Magri, *Trattato* | Gennaro Magri, *Trattato teorico-prattico di ballo* (Naples: Orsino, 1779) |
| Magri/ Skeaping | Gennaro Magri, *Trattato teorico-prattico di ballo* (1779), trans. Mary Skeaping, with Anna Ivanova and Irmgard E. Berry, ed. Irmgard E. Berry and Annalisa Fox, as *Theoretical and Practical Treatise on Dancing* (London: Dance Books, 1988) |
| *New Grove* | *The New Grove Dictionary of Music and Musicians*, ed. Stanley Sadie (London: Macmillan, 1980) |
| *New Grove* (rev. ed.) | *The New Grove Dictionary of Music and Musicians*, rev. ed., ed. Stanley Sadie and John Tyrrell (London: Macmillan, 2001) |
| Noverre, *Lettres* | Jean-Georges Noverre, *Lettres sur la Danse et sur les Ballets* (Stuttgart and Lyon: Delaroche, 1760; facsimile ed. New York: Broude Bros., 1967) |

Noverre/          Jean-Georges Noverre, *Lettres sur la Danse et sur les*
Beaumont          *Ballets* (1760), trans. Cyril Beaumont, from the revised
                  and enlarged edition published at St. Petersburg,
                  1803, as *Letters on Dancing and Ballets* (London, 1930)

Winter,           Marian Hannah Winter, *The Pre-Romantic Ballet*
*Pre-Romantic*    (London: Pitman, 1974)
*Ballet*

# The Grotesque Dancer
## on the Eighteenth-Century Stage

# Introduction

REBECCA HARRIS-WARRICK

This book was inspired by another: Gennaro Magri's *Trattato teorico-prattico di ballo*, published in Naples in 1779, the only book from the eighteenth century that explains the practices of mid-century Italian theatrical dancing. Magri himself was an internationally known *ballerino grottesco* and choreographer, and his long experience on the stage gives his writings the ring of authority. Even though his book, written at the end of his performing career, addresses in its two parts the fundamental principles of dance as they apply to both social and theatrical dancing, it is particularly valuable for its attention to the grotesque style, which receives very little treatment in other dance manuals from the period. Given that Italian theatrical dance was performed all over Europe, notwithstanding the historiographic insistence on the primacy of French dancing, Magri's *Trattato* clearly represents a crucial source for understanding an important chapter in ballet history.

It has, however, received very little study. Marian Hannah Winter, in her groundbreaking book, *The Pre-Romantic Ballet*, devoted three pages to the *Trattato*, which she considered "a key to understanding the development of ballet technique." She was able to offer the encouraging news that Mary Skeaping, choreographer at the Swedish court theater,

3

Drottningholm, had undertaken a translation into English, which was subsequently published in 1988. Skeaping's book has the significant virtue of making Magri's work available to a wider audience, but it has relatively little to say about its contents. The most substantial work to date on Magri is the thesis by Salvatore Bongiovanni, only portions of which, however, have heretofore been published.[1] And whereas a number of contemporary dancer/choreographers have made use of Magri's *Trattato* in their stagings of eighteenth-century ballets, they have not written about what their study of his writings has taught them. As a sign of increased interest, however, an annotated edition of Magri's book has recently been published in Italy, and a facsimile of the original can be consulted on the Library of Congress's Web site.[2]

In defense of earlier scholars it must be said that Magri's *Trattato* does present difficulties: a focus on individual steps with only occasional explanation of how they combine with each other or when they are to be used; an organizational structure that distinguishes inadequately among different styles of dance; a certain opacity in the writing style — not to mention grammatical errors in the Italian — that leaves open many questions about the author's intentions. Dance movements are notoriously difficult to translate into words and Magri did not avail himself of any kind of dance notation, except for the diagrams of figures for the ballroom *contraddanze* in part 2, the section of the book devoted to social dances. Moreover, Magri makes very little mention of whole works or of the theatrical environments in which he spent his career. Nonetheless, the riches contained in the *Trattato* suggested that an approach from several different angles might provide the best means of resolving its ambiguities.

Our own book thus began life as a multipart session at the annual meeting of the Society of Dance History Scholars in Minneapolis, Minnesota, in 1996. Our idea was to bring together people with differing but related areas of expertise in pursuit of a common goal: an understanding

1. See Winter, *Pre-Romantic Ballet*, 149–52; Magri/Skeaping; Salvatore Bongiovanni, "Gennaro Magri e il *Trattato teorico-prattico di ballo*" (unpublished *tesi di laurea*, Università degli Studi "La Sapienza," Rome, 1991), and the same author's "Gennaro Magri e il 'ballo grottesco,'" *Creature di Prometeo: Il ballo teatrale dal divertimento al dramma* , ed. Giovanni Morelli (Florence: Olschki, 1996), 239–45.

2. *Trattati di danza in Italia nel Settecento: G. B. Dufort, "Trattato del ballo nobile," Napoli 1728; G. Magri, "Trattato teorico-prattico di ballo," Napoli 1779; F. Sgai, "Al signor Gennaro Magri," Napoli 1779*, ed. Carmela Lombardi (Naples: Istituto Italiano per gli Studi Filosofici, 2001). For the facsimile of Magri's *Trattato*, see "American Ballroom Companion" at the Library of Congress Web site: http://memory.loc.gov/ammem/dihtml/dihome.html.

of late-eighteenth-century theatrical dance as it was practiced by *grotteschi* such as Magri. Our collective approach involved eight speakers in two kinds of session: one sought to discover as much as possible about Magri's own artistic career and the theatrical environments in which he had operated, and the other supplemented practical papers by scholar/reconstructors with workshops in which participants could try out and discuss the movement vocabulary that forms the bulk of Magri's book. Conference attendees were invited in advance to bring their own ideas about interpreting Magri to the sessions and many of them did so; as a result, all the Magri sessions brimmed over with lively discussion, demonstration, and experimentation.[3] So much new material about eighteenth-century theatrical dance practices emerged from these sessions that a book pulling it all together seemed essential. Since the sessions took place, the authors represented here have continued to share ideas with each other and have extended their research; all the essays have been written afresh in order to reflect these broadened perspectives, and new chapters have been added. Transforming the manner of presentation from participatory sessions into prose has of necessity produced changes, most notably in the chapters regarding the practice of dancing, which have become more contextual and less focused on individual movements or phrases. In an ideal world, this book would include a video demonstration; however, the material realities of the underfunded world of early dance make such dreams impracticable. And although each chapter in this book is oriented more toward either the historical or the practical, all the chapters contribute to an understanding both of the performances and of their contexts, not just in Italy but across Europe.

In 1779 when Magri published his *Trattato,* the world of ballet was a turbulent place, with several competing aesthetic visions of what ballet should be. Magri himself got caught up in the polemics of one debate when his book was attacked in print by Francesco Sgai, a partisan of Jean-Georges Noverre, prompting him to add a defense ("Warning to the Courteous Reader") while the *Trattato* was still in press.[4] At issue for

---

3. For abstracts of the presentations, see Rebecca Harris-Warrick, organizer and chair, Salvatore Bongiovanni, Ingrid Brainard, Bruce Alan Brown, Letizia Dradi, Sandra Noll Hammond, Kathleen Kuzmick Hansell, and Carol G. Marsh, "In Search of the Ballerino Grottesco: Summary of the Panel on Gennaro Magri," *Proceedings of the Society of Dance History Scholars, Nineteenth Annual Conference, University of Minnesota, Minneapolis, Minnesota, 13–16 June 1996* (Riverside: Society of Dance History Scholars, 1996), 87–89.

4. Inserted in the *Trattato* between pp. 12 and 13; in Skeaping, 46–49.

Magri were the time-honored traditions of the *grotteschi*, in which vigorous athleticism and technical virtuosity were put to the service of pantomime ballets largely on light-hearted topics, as opposed to Noverre's type of serious ballets on mythological or historical subjects, in which the dancing style was considerably more restrained. Both these kinds of ballet could be seen on the same night — as, for instance, in Naples, at the end of Magri's dancing career (1773–74), when a tragic ballet by Noverre's disciple Charles Le Picq was performed between acts 1 and 2 of an *opera seria*, and a comic ballet by Magri between acts 2 and 3. But the "reformers" of ballet even argued with each other, the most visible polemic being the one between Gasparo Angiolini and Noverre; there was no single vision of what Noverre called the "ballet d'action" — and what Angiolini termed "danza parlante" — should be. Moreover, the Naples example serves to remind us that in the eighteenth century ballet did not exist as an independent art, the attempts of the reformers notwithstanding. Across Europe an evening which included ballet invariably also involved either an opera or a play; ballet could be integrated into the larger work, performed between its acts, or done as an afterpiece. These juxtapositions gave rise to other kinds of aesthetic controversies: should an evening's entertainment be an integrated whole — as had traditionally been the case at the Paris Opéra or in the reform operas Christoph Willibald Gluck composed for Vienna, where the ballet was a fundamental part of the opera — or could a disconnected entertainment, in which the ballet and the opera had nothing to do with each other, be aesthetically viable?

Although researchers today inevitably find themselves caught up in these aesthetic controversies as they seek to recover not only the milieu in which ballets of the past were performed but the dance movements themselves, Magri's *Trattato* largely ignores them. Only the hastily added "Warning to the Courteous Reader," in which Magri sounds hurt and baffled by what he sees as an attack on himself, offers a direct response. For the rest of his book, Magri remains a practicing dancer and pedagogue, eager to communicate the fundamentals of his art to other aspiring dancers. He appears to be very open-minded and even quotes approvingly some passages of Noverre's famous *Lettres sur la danse*. Magri assumes an audience of his own time, not of the future, and thus does not explain principles that he and his imagined readers take for granted, such as the distinctions between the three main styles of dancing of his tradition — *serio, mezzo carattere,* and *grottesco* — but only alludes to them from time to time. We today are left to construct our own picture of these styles, and to imagine Gennaro Magri's own dancing abilities as a *ballerino grottesco*, on the basis of the tantalizing but all too infrequent hints he distributes throughout his chapters. Similarly, we are left to reconstruct dance phrases or even entire works from the only tools he gives us, descriptions of individual steps, with occasional references to their uses on stage.

What does emerge very clearly from the chapter-by-chapter survey of dance steps in part 1 of Magri's book is the enormous stylistic, technical, and expressive range of his type of dancing. At its basis lies a movement vocabulary derived largely from French traditions, as Magri himself states ("We are obliged to the French for the precision which dancing shows today")[5] and which leads him generally to make use of French terminology — either translated (e.g., *fioretto* for *fleuret*) or spelled to reflect Italian pronunciation (e.g., *tordichamb* for the French *tour de jambe*). This basic movement vocabulary had international currency, as comparisons with other dance manuals from the eighteenth and early nineteenth centuries show, even though the execution of steps as Magri describes them often reflects temporal or stylistic differences (see chapter 5, by Sandra Noll Hammond). But from the "Spanish," false, and forced positions of the feet in Magri's chapter 7 to the twenty-three different varieties of caprioles, each with multiple variants, described in his chapter 60, we are given access to a realm of dance that other early ballet manuals barely touch on, the world of the virtuoso *ballerino grottesco* (see chapter 6, by Linda Tomko). Here the vocabulary becomes more Italian, and Magri sometimes comments on the type of character to which a movement is appropriate. In the following passage from the chapter on caprioles, we get a sense both of the technique required and of the effect the dancer is aiming to produce.

> The *salto dell'impiccato* called *saut empendu* is performed by the characters of Pulcinella or a Drunkard or other Dullard, and sometimes it is done for eccentricity, this being a difficult jump. It too is taken with legs and knees together: bend, and in taking the jump, straighten the whole body with the legs together, let the extended arms fall with the hands touching the thighs, and the head lolling towards one side, then coming down, just before touching the ground, detach one leg well into the air as much as possible, landing obliquely on the other foot.

5. Magri/Skeaping, 44; Magri, *Trattato*, 1:10: "Alli Francesi siam tenuti della lindura, in cui è posto il ballo al presente." On 1:31 (Magri/Skeaping, 66) Magri explains that he will be using the step names "by which they are ordinarily known, most of them being in French" (daremo loro quel nome, con cui si sentono per ordinario nominare, essendo di maggior numero in Francese).

The difficulty of this jump consists in the great height that it needs to draw the spectators' attention to this figure, otherwise it would be reduced to nothing, and he who has no ability to reach this height must on no account do this *capriole*.[6]

Elsewhere Magri shows that differences in style depended not only on the choice of steps but on how those steps were done.

[The *tordichamp*] is employed by all three categories of *Ballerini*, with the difference that in the *ballo grave* [i.e., in *serio* style] ordinarily it is done with all composure, in the *mezzo carattere* it is done with great velocity, in the *Grottesco* it is done on a grand scale. And all this according to the nature of the real characters, but then everyone must know how to do it in all three variants.[7]

The closest Magri comes to a definition of the three categories of *ballerino* takes a functional perspective that comes on the heels of a recommendation that dancers not try to perform too many jumps in a row.

A breathless *Ballerino,* utterly exhausted, can never land lightly or lift himself gracefully but he needs strength to give impetus for the elevation or to support himself in coming down from high to low on the ball of that foot on which he lands. Moreover, the *ballerino* who wishes to jump must not labour with the legs nor need to dance on the ground, otherwise the joints would be too tired and then they would not be strong enough to lift him; therefore it is necessary that the character must be all jumped or else all in mid-air or entirely on the ground, thus is there the division of the three characters and therefore no properly equipped theatre should lack the *Ballante serio* or that of *mezzo Carattere* or the *Grottesco* for the

---

6. Magri/Skeaping, 165; Magri, *Trattato,* 1:134–35: "Il *Salto dell'Impiccato* detto *Saut Empedù* si fa nel carattere di Pulcinella, di un'Ubbriaco, o d'altro Goffo, e talvolta si fa per bizzaria; per esser questo un salto difficile. Si prende pure a piedi pari con le ginocchia unite, si piega, e nello spiccar del salto si raddrizza bene il corpo con le gambe accoppiate, le braccia distese si lasciano cadere con le mani toccanti le cosce, e la testa abbandonata da un lato, nel cader poi, arrivato a fior di terra, si distacca bene in aria un piede, quanto più si puole, cadendosi obliquo su l'altro piede.

"La difficoltà di questo salto consiste in una gran levata, che ha di bisogno per far bene osservare quelle figura a Spettatori, diversamente a nulla ridurrebbesi, e chi non ha l'abilità di questa alzata, in verun conto deve fare sì fatta Capriola."

7. Magri/Skeaping, 76; Magri, *Trattato,* 1:42: "Si adopera da tutte le tre specie de' Ballerini, con tal differenza, che per ordinario nel ballo grave si fa con ogni posatezza, nel mezzo carattere si fa velocissimo, nel Grottesco si fa in grande; E tutto ciò secondo la proprietà de' veri caratteri, ma tutto poi han di mestiere saperlo fare in tutte le tre diversità, come spesso occorre di eseguirlo."

Heroic, the Comic and the Burlesque characters which ordinarily enter into the dances.[8]

This tidy three-part distinction notwithstanding, elsewhere Magri claims the comic, and even the pastoral, as within the purview of the *ballerino grottesco*.

Should the *Grottesco* be less skilled in the art of expressing through gestures the Pantomime and comic Action than the *Serio* to express the same in Tragedy? . . . Pastoral dancing, like that of the Artisans, has always been the *Grottesco*'s speciality and why should it not be in the future?[9]

In the absence of any clearer statements on Magri's part, these remarks invite us to look at the kinds of works in which Magri performed. Fortunately, a fair amount of documentation survives about Magri's career and works. Kathleen Kuzmick Hansell's chapter explores the Italian theatrical context in which dancers such as Magri operated and the extent to which the *grottesco*'s technique underlay all of Italian-style ballet. Magri's own career, summarized in chapter 2 by Salvatore Bongiovanni, took him from his native Naples not only to theaters all over Italy but even to Vienna, whose rich theatrical environment and Magri's role within it are explored by Bruce Alan Brown in chapter 3. Magri's peripatetic career is summarized in the form of a chronology prepared by Patricia W. Rader that is appended to chapter 2. At least twice in his career Magri returned to Naples, and his activities there, as choreographer, dancer, and writer, are discussed by Salvatore Bongiovanni in chapter 4. In chapter 7 Rebecca Harris-Warrick and Carol G. Marsh explore the extension of Italian dance practices to French theaters. From all these

8. Magri/Skeaping, 167; Magri, *Trattato*, 1:138: "Un Ballerino affannato, e del tutto lasso non può mai cader leggermente, e levarsi con lindura: ma bisogna della forza per aver impeto all'alzata, o sostenersi, nel piombare dall'alto a basso, su la punta di quel piede, sopra di cui cade. In oltre il ballerino, che voglia saltare, non deve travagliar di gamba, non bisogna ballar terreno, altrimente fatigasebbesi troppo le articolazioni, e stanchi poi non avran vigore all'elevarsi; onde fa di mestieri, che il carattere deve essere, o dell'intutto saltato, ovvero del tutto a mezz'aria, o intieramente a terra, perciò v'è la divisione de' tre caratteri, e perciò in ogni fornito Teatro non deve mancarvi nè il Ballante serio, nè quel di mezzo Carattere, nè il Grottesco, per l'Eroico, il Comico, ed il Bernesco carattere, che per ordinario entrano ne' balli."

9. Magri/Skeaping, 153; Magri, *Trattato*, 1:116–17: "E che forse l'arte di esprimere per mezzo de' gesti la Pantomima, l'Azione comica la deve avere il Grottesco meno di quella del Serio, per esprimer questi la sua Tragica? . . . Il ballar Pastorale, come quello dell'Artiggiano è stato sempre specifico del Grottesco, e perchè non puol' esserlo, per l'avvenire?"

chapters emerges a rich picture of Magri's professional associates, his repertoire, his choreographic activities, and the theaters within which he and his colleagues worked. Surviving scenarios of ballets from his orbit (see a representative sample in appendixes 2–5) show that he and his associates created Turkish pashas, Savoyard soldiers, characters from the commedia dell'arte, pirates, Irish sailors, rustic villagers, gypsies, shopkeepers, Moorish slaves, wigmakers, magicians — all within a loosely narrative context that blended pantomime with dance for its own sake. These roles embrace both the comic and the burlesque that Magri himself mentioned in the passage cited above; a *ballerino grottesco* had to be versatile. Moreover, as the list of *ballerini grotteschi* in appendix 1 shows, many Italian *serio* and *mezzo-carattere* dancers were originally trained as *grotteschi*. Their aerial style was, in fact, one of the hallmarks of Italian theatrical ballet.

Attempts to mediate between the scenarios that can be linked to Magri's career on the one hand and his technically grounded step descriptions on the other pose problems. Magri gives only a few hints regarding *enchaînements* of steps, writes only a little about the overall affect of a dance or of a scene, and provides no information whatsoever about choreography per se. He mentions the existence of dance notation, but chooses not to use it for notating steps because he doesn't find it capable of indicating all the movements involved.[10] And whereas he has several interesting things to say about the tempo and character of music appropriate to various steps, these remarks remain general. The problem is particularly vexing, in that the theatrical choreographies that survive in Feuillet or Favier notation from the period 1688–ca. 1725 (i.e., from Favier to L'Abbé) and coming mostly from within the realm of French-style opera, do not contain more than the occasional hint at gestures that might be called "pantomimic," whereas Magri's own works, which belong to the later genre of pantomime ballet, pose the thorny question of how the necessary mime gestures were incorporated into a danced context. Fortunately, a contemporaneous source — originating in France, but nonetheless drawing upon theatrical traditions related to Magri's — provides choreographed models of several comic pantomime ballets. This manuscript, compiled by Auguste Ferrère in 1782, is described in chap-

---

10. Magri/Skeaping, 66; Magri, *Trattato*, 1:31: "Non recherò segni di corografia; farò larga la spiega, senza metter agli occhi tante cifre, che recheran confusione anzi, che no; nè que' segni sono bastanti ad indicare tutti i movimenti, che fansi in un passo." Magri did, nonetheless, make use of diagrams showing floor patterns in the section on *contraddanze* in pt. 2 of the *Trattato*.

ter 7, then mined for the help it offers. In chapter 8 Moira Goff explores questions around combining gesture with steps within individual dances, drawing upon Ferrère and other sources, and in chapter 9 Carol G. Marsh and Rebecca Harris-Warrick use the Ferrère manuscript as the principal lens for looking at the issues involved in staging an entire ballet — from how the dance works with the music to the construction of *pas de deux* and group dances within a narrative framework.

One of the contributors to the original panel in Minneapolis, Ingrid Brainard, died suddenly while this volume was in preparation. Ingrid was a warm and supportive colleague to us all and a mentor to several among us; we deeply regret her loss. We are also saddened by the fact that it has not proved possible to recover the paper she presented at the conference, "Gesture in Eighteenth-Century Ballet." We refer our readers to a related publication of hers, "The Speaking Body: Gaspero Angiolini's *rhétorique muette* and the *ballet d'action* in the Eighteenth Century," which elegantly and thoroughly mines texts from dance and acting manuals to place Angiolini's own writings about gesture in the context of his time.[11] Our book is dedicated to Ingrid's memory.

The issues arising from Ingrid's article remind us yet again that the type of ballet that Magri represented was under attack in some quarters, even as it enjoyed European-wide popularity. As Angiolini wrote in 1765, in the introduction to his own tragic ballet *Sémiramis,* "I believe that the [grotesque] genre is the lowest of all. It can only arouse in spectators astonishment mixed with fear, as they see their fellows in danger of death at any moment."[12] Magri apparently felt sensitive to this kind of attack, and in one brief moment attached to the end of his chapter 59 ("Of the use of the arms"), he responded to the critics of his art, without naming anyone in particular.

> The true Ballerini, whether Seri or Comici must equally be in general possession of everything pertaining to dancing; no real distinction can be made between one Character and another, for if it is difficult to dance the *serio* it is no easier to dance the truly light comic. . . . Those who are biased and full of prejudice are mistaken in making distinctions between the merit of the one and the other character. Each one is

11. This article is published in *Critica Musica: Essays in Honor of Paul Brainard,* ed. John Knowles (Amsterdam: Gordon and Breach, 1996), 15–56.

12. "Je crois que ce genre [grotesque] est le dernier de tous. Il ne peut exciter dans les Spectateurs qu'un étonnement mêlé de crainte, voyant leurs semblables exposés à se tuer à chaque instant." *Sémiranis* program, f. [C6v], as cited in Brainard, "The Speaking Body," 39n92.

worthy of applause, each is skilful if he expresses his Action well, if he portrays his Character well. . . . The prudent Man, the wise Man, despises neither the former nor the latter and is only interested in whoever performs his duties well.[13]

Magri would undoubtedly have applauded the words of French commentator Ange Goudar, who in 1773 also came to the defense of Italian dancers: "He [Noverre] wishes that all grotesque dancers, whom he humiliates by consigning them to the lowest rank, were so many Polichinelles or Pierrots; they could well reply that it is better to be a genuine Pierrot than a false Pyrrhus."[14]

Unfortunately, even more than two hundred years later, the case in favor of grotesque dancing still needs to be made, although the more recent enemy has been simple neglect. It is our hope that this book will help redress the historiographic imbalance by providing a point of entry into the rich world of the *ballerino grottesco*.

A word about editorial policies in this book.

For English translations of the passages from Magri's *Trattato* cited in this book we have generally relied on Mary Skeaping's published translation (see above and note 1). We have, however, checked all quoted passages against Magri's original publication and sometimes modified the translation, in which case the modifications appear within square brackets. The original Italian is always supplied in a footnote. We have retained Skeaping's somewhat inconsistent capitalization policy (which mostly follows Magri's own practices), although within quoted passages we have silently corrected her misspelling ("grotesco") of the Italian word "grottesco" and its derivatives.

---

13. Magri/Skeaping, 153–54; Magri, *Trattato*, 1:116–17: "I veri Ballerini o sian Serj, o Comici devono avere egualmente il possesso generale di tutto quello, che si appartiene al ballo; nè distinzione veruna puol correre da un Carattere all'altro, che se difficile è il ballar serio, non è più facile il vero comico grazioso. . . . Male intendono, quei, che prevenuti, e pieni di pregiudizio, fan distinzione di merito tra l'uno, e l'altro carattere. Ognuno è degno di applauso, ognuno è bravo, se bene esprime la sua Azione, se bene eseguisce il suo Carattere. . . . L'Uomo prudente, l'Uomo savio non vilipende nè questo, nè quello e sol s'interessa di chi bene adempie il dovere."

14. Ange Goudar, *De Venise: Remarques sur la musique et la danse de Mr G. . . . à Milord Pembroke* (Venice: Palese, 1773): "Il veut que tous les danseurs grotesques, qu' il place humblement dans la derniere classe, soient des Polichinelles ou des Pierots: ceux-ci pourroient leur répondre qu' il vaut mieux être un vrai *Pierot* qu' un faux *Pyrrhus*." Goudar's pamphlet is available in an Italian translation: *Osservazioni sopra la musica ed il ballo, ossia Estratto di due lettere di Mr. G. . . . a Milord Pembroke* (Milan: Motta, [1773]), which has been edited, with introductory remarks by José Sasportes, in *La danza italiana* 5/6 (Autumn 1987): 35–76.

In referring to the steps Magri discusses, we have preferred Magri's own terminology, which uses both Italian and French (sometimes together), to Skeaping's translations, which sometimes add a third language (English) to the mix. For example, Skeaping renders Magri's "assemblè sotto al corpo" (Magri, *Trattato*, 1:23) as "jump *sur place*" (61). In order to offer access to both Skeaping's translation — which is difficult to use because it contains neither a table of contents nor an index — and Magri's original text, we have included a table of contents of both the original and the translation as appendix 6, and an index to Magri's steps and other dance terms as appendix 7.

In referring to steps or terminology from other sources, such as Feuillet's *Chorégraphie*, we have retained the source's own spelling. Titles of books or works, however, have been supplied with necessary accents when they occur in the main text.

When speaking of dancers in groups, we have retained the eighteenth-century terms "figuranti" or "figurants" (in Italian or French, depending on the context), rather than replace them with *corps de ballet*, both because the latter term was only beginning to come into use and had not yet acquired its modern meaning, and because the modern understanding of a *corps de ballet* calls forth an inaccurate mental image of the group dances in ballets such as Magri's.

Other terms are sometimes left in the original language for similar reasons.

# I

# Eighteenth-Century Italian Theatrical Ballet

## *The Triumph of the* Grotteschi

KATHLEEN KUZMICK HANSELL

"The opera with three ballets lasts six good hours: the ballets, however, are now going to be shortened for they last two good hours." It is 29 December 1770 in Milan, at the old Regio Ducal Teatro, shortly before the third performance of youthful Mozart's opera *Mitridate*, which had opened Carnival season three days before; his father, Leopold, complains here about the length of the show, since it obliged them to delay their supper, probably until after midnight.[1] Of course, he lays the blame on the three accompanying ballets rather than on Wolfgang's *opera seria* which, with its playing time of four hours for the three acts, was unusually prolix even by the standards of that day.

Leopold should have been well aware by then, however, that an evening's entertainment in any major Italian theater was not complete without at least two independent ballets staged in the intervals between the acts: this arrangement had been typical since the late seventeenth century and the Mozarts had witnessed a number of productions during

---

1. *Mozart: Briefe und Aufzeichnungen*, ed. Wilhelm A. Bauer and Otto Erich Deutsch, 7 vols. (Kassel: Bärenreiter, 1962–75), 1:411: "Die opera mit 3 balletten dauert seine 6 Starke stund: man wird aber itzt die Ballett abkürzen den sie dauern 2 Starke stund."

their long sojourn in Italy. Then too, having attended Carnival operas in Milan the preceding February, Leopold should have known that the Regio Ducal was one of the theaters that included as well a closing ballet following act 3. Starting at about 6:30 p.m., the evening's program was thus the following: act 1 of *Mitridate* (about one hour and ten minutes), followed by the heroic pantomime ballet *Il giudizio di Paride* (The Judgment of Paris),[2] probably fifty minutes to one hour; act 2 of *Mitridate* (one hour), succeeded by the lighter divertissement-style ballet *Il trionfo della Virtù a fronte d'Amore* (The Triumph of Virtue against Love), perhaps twenty-five to thirty minutes; act 3 of *Mitridate* (forty-five minutes), and finally a short ballet celebrating the protagonists of the opera, *Dame e cavalieri che applaudano alle nozze d'Aspasia e d'Ismene* (Ladies and Gentlemen Who Applaud the Wedding of Aspasia and Ismene), about ten to fifteen minutes. All three ballets were choreographed by Francesco Caselli, a noted *ballerino grottesco,* and in addition to himself his company featured five other prominent Italian grotesque dancers (Domenico Morelli, Angiola Lazzari, Bettina Stellato, Gaetano Cesari, and Elisabetta Morelli), as well as two Italian serious dancers (Clarici Bini and Giacomo Romolo). It is not known who wrote the music for any of the dances; certainly, that was not Mozart's obligation.[3] Leopold Mozart's reckoning of the program's duration was accurate, but the reason for abbreviating it was not its excessive length, for by the later 1760s most Carnival season ballets required about "two good hours" total. Instead, it was most likely their poor reception.

Although choreographer Caselli did not furnish a scenario for any of the ballets with *Mitridate,* several kinds of sources allow us a notion of the genres they represented and the style of dancing they would have incorporated. Among the most important for an understanding of any Italian theatrical ballet of the era is Gennaro Magri's seminal treatise of 1779, *Trattato teorico-prattico di ballo.* As the following chapters in this volume make clear, Magri, though noted as a *grottesco* especially for his prodigious leaps, knew all the genres of his day and stressed their equality — the grotesque dances being no less important than the serious *ballet noble.* And his treatise is one of the very few sources to reveal how theatrical

2. *Il giudizio di Paride* may have been an adaptation of Jean-Georges Noverre's 1751 ballet *Le Jugement de Pâris;* Caselli knew both Noverre and his noted disciple Charles Le Picq during the time they were all working in Vienna. See Winter, *Pre-Romantic Ballet,* 119.

3. Neither the opera libretto (a copy at the Biblioteca Nazionale Braidense, Milan, Racc. Dramm. 6013/1), which lists the ballets, nor a report on the productions in the newspaper *Gazzetta di Milano* (2 January 1771) indicates the ballet composer.

dancers performing in the three major styles—the serious, the *demi-caractère*, and the grotesque—though basing their technique on the same repertory of movements, differentiated them so as to achieve wholly diverse effects. Though unique among eighteenth-century Italian works, Magri's *Trattato* belongs to a long, shared tradition, as Sandra Noll Hammond's survey of dance treatises over a 150-year period makes eminently clear (chap. 5).

Increasingly, aspects of the eighteenth-century Italian tradition gradually became part of an international vocabulary, as dancers and choreographers traveled more widely. French performers appeared in Italy, on a limited scale before 1750 (confined mainly to Turin), but with greater frequency thereafter. Except in the case of ballets in the style of Jean-Georges Noverre, however, French dancers in Italy were hired mainly as *ballerini seri*. In this respect a segregation among performers according to type, which became yet more prominent in the nineteenth century, was operative already in Magri's time and earlier.[4] Certainly, a large part of the technical terminology Magri and other Italians used was French, but it needs to be recognized that the movements and usages they stand for extend well back into the seventeenth century, when Italian influence on the development of ballet in France was significant. In other important ways, however, eighteenth-century Italian dance productions differed from those in France, just as did the training Italian dancers received. The short survey that follows attempts to point up some of the most telling differences, beginning with the placement of the ballets themselves. It concentrates especially on those aspects that kept the art of the *grotteschi* at the forefront of Italian practice, even in the face of an onslaught in the 1770s from the Noverrian camp.

Until long into the nineteenth century, theatrical ballets in Italy were always produced together with operas. Nevertheless, they were considered a complement to rather than an integral part of the vocal entertainments. Though during the seventeenth century a tenuous connection to an opera's plot often served as a pretext for staging brief dances near the ends of the acts, such dances were gradually dispensed with in favor of more expansive, completely independent ballets that were performed between the acts of the opera. A remnant of an earlier tradition lingered

---

4. For more detailed discussed of categories of dancers, see my study "Theatrical Ballet and Italian Opera," in *Opera on Stage*, vol. 5, The History of Italian Opera (Chicago: University of Chicago Press, 2002), 177–308, esp. 210–11, 245–46, 261–63.

until the late eighteenth century at some theaters in northern Italy, which concluded the final act of an *opera seria* with a chaconne or "ballo nobile" glorifying the exalted personages represented in the vocal work. Otherwise, Italian audiences long maintained an antipathy toward the French custom of inserting divertissements of dance *within* the acts of an opera.

Opera librettos provide an important source of information regarding the growing prominence of theatrical ballets in Italy. During the later seventeenth century and up to about 1710, librettos from theaters in Italy's major centers, such as Venice, Milan, Turin, Florence, and Naples, increasingly included notices concerning the dances. These generally indicated the placement of the ballets, titles, and short descriptions of their themes, actions, or characters, sometimes together with comments on the scenery or stage machines employed. Names of choreographers appear very seldom and those of participating dancers never. Only rarely is there any indication even as to how many dancers were involved. Thus one must turn to other sources, such as archival records, for more detail. From these one may ascertain that at the beginning of the eighteenth century the average size of an Italian theatrical dance company was just four to eight dancers, with occasionally as many as a dozen. Twelve to fourteen performers indeed remained the norm for the next half century. And during this period — the first half of the eighteenth century — dancers' salaries remained quite static and far below those paid the opera singers. From around mid-century, however, a remarkable change was to occur, one that began very gradually in the 1740s and reached a climax in the 1770s.[5]

Before forging ahead into that period — the time of the first internationally renowned choreographers and dancers, the time of Magri — let us consider briefly two aspects of the situation in Italian theatrical dance during the *first* half of the eighteenth century, for they help us understand better the later developments. In the history of the Italian theater the period from the later 1710s to the mid-1740s was notable for two phenomena, both of which indirectly affected theatrical dance. These were the flowering of heroic opera, or *opera seria*, and the heyday of comic vocal intermezzos. Heroic opera, advocated by the Arcadian reformers at the turn of the seventeenth century and fully realized by the second decade of the eighteenth, eliminated all aspects of the "marvelous" as well as comic scenes from the vocal works — in other words, just those aspects

5. For payment statistics on dancers in Milan in the mid-eighteenth century see my dissertation, "Opera and Ballet at the Regio Ducal Teatro of Milan, 1771–1776: A Musical and Social History" (Ph.D. diss., University of California, Berkeley, 1980), 653–57.

that had been conducive to the dance. At the same time, this tendency served to establish the definite separation of the danced episodes from the vocal works. Although the dominant types of ballets were the same exotic, fantastic, character, and comic scenes that had once graced seventeenth-century operas, they were now performed independently. Three-act operas became the norm, as did the custom of staging two entr'acte entertainments, one after each of the first two acts.

The position of dominance that ballets had attained as entr'actes by the early eighteenth century was challenged for about twenty-five years by comic vocal *intermezzi*—those one- or two-act farces for just two or three singers and a small orchestra of which Pergolesi's *Serva padrona* is perhaps today the only one known to more than specialists. In what is otherwise a clearly traceable history of steady advances in the realm of theatrical dance, this period, approximately 1715–40, is an exceptional one in several respects. Apart from Turin, where the ballet enjoyed a special status, at all other major Italian centers the era when the vocal *intermezzi* flourished also saw the temporary elimination from opera librettos of nearly all information concerning the dances. It is nonetheless evident that, even with the rise of the *intermezzi buffi*, ballets continued to be staged throughout the peninsula, and by the mid-1730s at the latest ballets were once again the preferred entr'actes. In point of fact, the use of vocal *intermezzi* constituted but a short-lived historical parenthesis. If I emphasize here, it is because of the great—and I am tempted to say undue—importance accorded them in most studies of eighteenth-century Italian opera. Notwithstanding this long-lived bias among music historians, the weight of evidence proves overwhelmingly that the vocal *intermezzi* are properly regarded as the exception rather than the rule. And the rule for about two hundred years, even during the period 1710 to 1735, was that entr'acte entertainments with Italian opera consisted of ballets.[6]

That said, we must still reckon with the effects of the vocal *intermezzi* in Italy. The status of the dance and dancers within the overall theatrical panorama, and the kinds of works they performed, seem to have changed little during this period. It was only after the decline of the *intermezzi* that more resources of every type began to be allocated to theatrical ballets and they saw their tremendous growth. Although it is more difficult to gather information about specific productions of ballets for the first half of the eighteenth century, we do find descriptions of Italian

---

6. The present survey offers a very brief synthesis of developments in eighteenth-century Italian ballet which I treat at length in "Theatrical Ballet and Italian Opera," see esp. 192–241.

dancers and dancing, and these show a remarkable consistency. They help us to get a grasp on important characteristics that carry over to the 1770s and well beyond. Together with the details gleaned from librettos they strongly suggest that the style of dancing to come to the fore by the early eighteenth century must have incorporated an acrobatic technique and a considerable degree of mime.

Here are just a few examples of such descriptions, taking us from the early to the later eighteenth century. In 1715, Pier Jacopo Martello (after likening the French dancer to a swimmer who, "arms, always raised and supple, breaks the waves graciously") writes: "The Italian, no matter on what part of the stage, displays his spirited dance with great precision: he jumps in the air and there performs nimble caprioles. He comes down to the boards very lightly, on the points of his feet and barely touching the planks he reascends. . . . This type of dancing, which is displayed more in the air, is similar to flying."[7] Shortly afterward, Gottfried Taubert in Leipzig commented on the "Italian Dance-Art, which through harmonious cadences and motions of the feet, arms and entire body, symmetrically regulated throughout, could express manners, actions, passions, etc."[8] In 1739 Charles de Brosses visited the theater in Italy and expressed a typical French reaction: "If the Italians occasionally dance on the opera stage, it is not as though the ballets form a part of the drama. . . . These ballets are of the sorts of pantomimes that are very ridiculously placed in the intervals of a tragedy. The dancers, men and women, are lively, light, rising higher than la Camargo and as much as Maltère l'Oiseau."[9] And here is Francesco Algarotti in 1755, after years away from Italy: "This ballet of ours, though it delights people so much, is nothing more than a leaping about up to the point of exhaustion."[10]

Now we have the English musician and historian Charles Burney, visiting the Teatro San Carlo of Naples in 1770 and witnessing ballets choreographed by Onorato Viganò — in a year when Magri was away from Naples: "In the opera to-night there were three entertaining

7. Pier Jacopo Martello, *Della tragedia antica e moderna* (Rome, 1715); a modern edition is found in Pier Jacopo Martello, *Scritti critici e satirici,* ed. Hannibal S. Noce, vol. 225, *Scrittori d'Italia* (Bari: Laterza, 1963), 313.

8. Gottfried Taubert, *Rechtschaffener Tantzmeister, oder gründliche Erklärung der Frantzösischen Tantz-Kunst* (Leipzig, 1717), 962. A reprint edition by Kurt Petermann is found in the series *Documenta choreologica: Studienbibliothek der Geschichte der Tanzkunst,* 22 (Munich: Heimeran, 1976).

9. *Le Président de Brosses en Italie: Lettres familières écrites d'Italie en 1739 et 1740,* 5th ed. (Paris: Garnier, [1886]), 8:335–36.

10. *Saggio sopra l'opera in musica* (1755), in *Saggi,* ed. Giovanni da Pozzo (Bari: Laterza, 1963), 145–223: "Dei Balli," 173–75.

dances, but all in the lively way; the Italians are not pleased with any other. Indeed . . . all their dances are more pantomime entertainments than any thing else, in which the scenes are usually pretty and the stories well told. . . . The first man [Viganò] has great force and neatness, and seems to equal [the English dancer] Slingsby in his *à plomb*, or neatness of keeping time; and [Colomba] Beccari's many *twinkling feet* are not inferior in agility to those of Radicati."[11] The Italian theorist of the theater, Francesco Milizia, distressed about the present state of opera, opines just a year later: "Such a beautiful opera is cut up by two ballets, to which all the spectators remain most attentive and silent, as though they had to see it with their ears; and the performer who leaps more, who contorts his feet and torso more, wins the greater applause."[12] Finally, in 1777 an English physician, John Moore, during a sojourn in Florence: "In this city . . . little attention is paid to the music. . . . But the dancers command a general attention: as soon as they begin conversation ceases; even the card-players lay down their cards, and fix their eyes on the Ballette. Yet the excellence of Italian dancing seems to consist in feats of strength, and a kind of jerking ability, more than in graceful movement. There is a continual contest among the performers who shall spring highest."[13]

The negative comments come from foreigners more used to the French noble style of *terre-à-terre* dancing, in which the feet scarcely left the ground, or from Italians anxious about the state of contemporary heroic opera. There are numerous other eyewitness observations that could be added, even to the mid-nineteenth century, and they would all present a surprisingly consistent picture. Whether the reactions voiced are positive or negative, they all stress two main qualities about Italian ballet: it was decidedly acrobatic, featuring an aerial style, and it made use of a good deal of pantomime. Moreover, the pantomime was not a separate element, as it was to become in the ballets of Noverre and his disciples, but an integral part of the vigorous Italian style of theatrical dancing, which portrayed actions and passions "pantomimically diffused through the whole body" in motion, as the choreographer Giovanni-Andrea Gallini put it in 1762.[14]

These traits are of course those generally associated with the *grotteschi*,

---

11. Charles Burney, *The Present State of Music in France and Italy* (London: T. Becket et al., 1773; repr., New York: Broude, 1969), 354–55.

12. Francesco Milizia, *Trattato completo, formale e materiale del teatro*, 2nd ed. (Venice: Pasquali, 1794; repr., Bologna: Forni, 1969), 40.

13. *A View of Society and Manners in Italy*, 2 vols., 4th ed. (London, 1787), 1:397–98.

14. *A Treatise on the Art of Dancing* (London: Dodsley, 1762; repr., New York: Dance Horizons, 1967), 51.

as the English choreographer John Weaver had already noted in 1702.[15] But as we have seen in some of the observations just quoted, at least the non-Italians considered them characteristic not just of one class of Italian comic dancers but of Italian theatrical ballet as a whole. The interpenetration of the virtuoso technique of the Italian grotesque dancer into all aspects of Italian stage dancing remained a constant throughout the eighteenth century and beyond. As other chapters in this volume show, by the nineteenth century it had become the common currency taught and practiced throughout Europe, forming the basis for classical ballet as we know it today. That a majority of Italian ballet dancers were trained and performed for at least a part of their careers in the exuberant but difficult *danza alta*, or aerial style of the *grotteschi*, certainly had a profound influence on this development. While gathering information on the training of dancers and the types of works they performed is more difficult for the first half of the eighteenth century, the rapid expansion that the ballet enjoyed in Italy from the 1750s allows one to form an increasingly comprehensive picture as the century advanced.

Opera librettos and theater account books tell us where the priorities of audiences lay, and hence of the impresarios who depended on them for income. In the 1750s choreographers and then dancers once again began to be listed in librettos, in ever greater detail. Dance companies of the 1750s still numbered around a dozen, on the average, with eight principal dancers and four *figuranti*—the latter were dancers who participated only in the larger ensemble movements and are not to be confused with the *corps de ballet* of later decades. But records of expenses show that their salaries grew dramatically until at major centers like Turin and Milan by 1760 they had already reached a level on a par with all but the highest paid *primi uomini* and *prime donne* in the operas.

Titles of the ballets were by then regularly included in opera librettos, as well as descriptions of their scenery. These inform us, if we were not already aware of it, that the plots and scenery of the ballets had absolutely nothing to do with the opera which they served as entr'actes. In-

---

15. John Weaver (1673–1760) noted, for instance, that his earliest attempt at an action ballet, staged in 1702, "was performed in Grotesque Characters, after the manner of the Modern *Italians*," although at the same time he also claimed this work to be "the first Entertainment that appeared on the *English* Stage where the Representation and Story was carried on by Dancing, Action and Motion only." *The History of Mimes and Pantomimes* . . . (London: J. Roberts and A. Dod, 1728), 45. An annotated facsimile edition appears in Richard Ralph, *The Life and Works of John Weaver: An Account of His Life, Writings and Theatrical Productions, with an Annotated Reprint of His Complete Publications* (New York: Dance Horizons, 1985), 677–732.

deed, the ballets appear to have spurred many developments in stage design, since the dancers used increasingly larger portions of the stage with built-up stage units at different heights in more human-scale perspective, rather than the flats in monumental scale still characteristic of *opera seria*, using perspective that forced singers to perform near the proscenium.

The titles and scene descriptions also demonstrate that the ballets staged with an opera were generally of three main types. The ballet after the first act was usually the most complex and increasingly featured lengthy pantomime actions. Drawn from mythology rather than ancient history, the pantomime ballets promoted the use of fantastic or characteristic elements long discarded from heroic opera. Magical scene transformations and aerial entrances became fixtures of the more elaborate ballets. A good example is offered by the scenario for Vincenzo Galeotti's ballet *La favola di Phsiche* (Milan, 26 December 1768), given in appendix 2, particularly in the latter half, when the scene is transformed into a "horrid mountain in Lapland" which then opens up to reveal the god of the north wind, Boreas, followed by Psyche's leap into a ravine. It is possible that the dancers portraying both the gentle breeze Zephyrus, at the ballet's opening, and Boreas were flown on wires.

After the second act of an Italian opera, the most common practice was to stage what I term a *divertissement* ballet. Typically, these satirized nationalities or occupations, often using rustic, foreign, or exotic settings. As such they represented a genre found commonly throughout Europe. Whereas the first ballet might be *The Legend of Cupid and Psyche*,[16] the second would be along the following lines: *A Village in Germany with Its Inhabitants Occupied in Various Rustic Pursuits* or *An English Arsenal Showing the Actual Building of Every Type of Vessel* — titles of actual ballets staged in Milan in the 1750s.[17] Naturally, these too included the Italian style of pantomime. The rationale for the lighter *divertissement* ballet was to discourage tedium in the audience so that theatergoers would remain until the end of the show — which in some cases meant increasing revenues for the impresario because of the gambling facilities allowed in theaters.

16. See app. 2 for a transcription and translation of the scenario for Vincenzo Galeotti's ballet *La favola di Phsiche*, first performed at Milan's Regio Ducal Teatro on 26 December 1768; a copy of the relevant libretto is preserved at Milan, Biblioteca Ambrosiana.

17. *Un villagio nella Germania co' suoi abitatori occupati in varie opere contadinesche ec.*, choreographed by Luigi Biscioni, had its premiere at Milan on 14 January 1758 (a copy of the libretto is found at Milan, Biblioteca Nazionale Braidense, Racc. Dramm. 6067/7). *Un arsenale inglese con attuale fabbrica d'ogni sorte di vascella ec.*, choreographed by Giuseppe Salomoni *père*, first performed at Milan 26 December 1756 (a copy of the libretto is in the same collection, 6067/2).

The third ballet at the close of some operas was generally a *ballo no-bile*, often a grand chaconne, and in the theaters that included one it frequently alluded to the last scenes of the opera. These so-called analogous or related ballets were a particular feature of serious operas in Milan and Turin, and to some extent Naples, but elsewhere on the peninsula they figured only infrequently. With its rather old-fashioned celebratory form going back to the court entertainments of the Renaissance (when noble amateurs would have participated), the third ballet died out completely by the 1790s. The use of analogous ballets elsewhere than at the opera's close was even more anomalous from the Italian viewpoint. Thus, entirely unlike the situation at the Opéra in Paris and other major French houses, where integrated dances enhancing the action of the main work were a well-established practice, in Italy attempts to produce operas in the French manner, with *divertissements* of dancing within the acts, were always seen as experiments. And more often than not such audacities failed and had to be withdrawn.

The 1750s in Italy also saw the rise of full-length comic operas in two or three acts, generally performed in a different season or at other theaters than the heroic operas. They too had danced entr'actes — generally two — that were no different from those staged with serious operas. With either kind of spectacle, by about 1770 the overall length of an evening in the theater occupied five to six hours, as we have seen. For a serious opera the ballets required in total about two hours' performance time: perhaps one hour for the first ballet, forty minutes for the second, and fifteen or twenty minutes for the third. While Italian audiences felt cheated if an evening at the theater was much shorter, even they had limits. Thus in 1774 when the Teatro San Carlo in Naples staged Niccolò Piccinni's setting of Pietro Metastasio's old libretto *Alessandro nell'Indie*, a theatrical poet was hired to condense the text, and in a printed preface he explained that the decision had to do with the desire to accommodate long ballets, in this case Charles Le Picq's *Aminta e Clori* and Magri's *Pantomimo con maschere:* "But modern taste, so different from the past, and the great length introduced into the ballets obliges one to alter and condense his [Metastasio's] operas. . . . The present opera is a perfect instance; . . . for if one wished to present it in its entirety, together with the lengthy ballets, it would require no less than seven hours."[18]

18. Cited in Claudio Sartori, *I libretti italiani a stampa dalle origini al 1800*, 8 vols. (Cuneo: Bertola & Locatelli, 1990–95), 1:84: "Il moderno gusto assai diverso dal passato, e l'introdotta lunghezza de' Balli, n'obbligano a variare ed a ristringere il di lui Drammi. . . . Siane appunto un testimonio il

This distribution, of course, is far different from the short danced interludes of the earlier eighteenth century and was part of the reason for the complaints voiced by the apologists of the opera. The ballets had grown not only in length but in complexity and in the size of their companies. Whereas in 1765 the average complement at the major theaters was still just fourteen, by 1770 the troupes had grown to twenty-eight at Milan, twenty-seven at Turin, twenty-six at Venice, and so forth. Only five years later Naples and Milan headed the list with forty-eight and forty-four dancers respectively. Expenses for the ballet necessarily rose dramatically. According to my calculations, the danced portion of the spectacles eventually constituted about 35 to 40 percent of the budget of larger theaters. And as a glance at the *Indice de' spettacoli teatrali*—the annual index of offerings in Italian theaters—shows, theaters in cities of any size, even the smallest, endeavored to produce ballets accompanying the operas.[19]

At this time, too, librettos became more specific in classifying dancers according to rank and type, so that we can at last begin come to terms with the makeup of the companies. In the 1760s the principal dancers were categorized as serious or grotesque dancers; the remainder were the *figuranti*. At that time there was usually one couple termed *ballerini seri* and one or two couples who were *grotteschi*. Another frequently encountered term refers to dancers designated as *fuori dei concerti*. These were well-paid *ballerini* who were hired to perform exclusively "outside the company dances" and they could be either *seri* or *grotteschi*. In the 1770s, particularly in the ballets staged by French choreographers such as Noverre and his adherents, there were few or no dancers listed as *grotteschi*, but rather many of another category called *mezzo-carattere*, that is, *demi-caractère*. At houses that relied more on Italian choreographers, however, we find that the number of principals designated as *grotteschi* grew ever larger, up to as many as four couples, while there remained as before only a single couple of principal serious dancers. One explanation for the rising cost of dance productions was that outlay for the principal

presente Dramma; . . . onde se interamente presentar si volesse, unito a' prolissi balli, nulla men di sett'ore richiederebbe." For the scenarios of both ballets, see appendix 4.

19. The series *Indice de' spettacoli teatrali* was published annually (with slightly varying titles) in Milan from 1764 to 1800, and then irregularly from 1803 to 1809 in Venice and 1819–23 in Rome. These indexes list all singers and dancers performing at Italian theaters large and small, as well as at most of the principal houses throughout Europe. They are now available in their entirety in a collective facsimile edition: *Un almanacco drammatico: L'indice de' teatrali spettacoli 1764–1823*, ed. Roberto Verti, 2 vols. (Pesaro: Fondazione Rossini, 1996).

*grotteschi* was higher not only because they were more in evidence but because their salaries were eventually on a par with those of the "noble" or serious dancers. Ample evidence for both the increasing number of principal grotesque dancers and their rising salaries is readily at hand from the account books and other documents exhaustively mined for the multivolume study of Turin's Teatro Regio.[20]

Such denominations of dancers tell us far from the whole story, however. Almost all of those who studied in Italy received a grounding in the difficult techniques of the aerial style and a schooling in the art of pantomime. But because in Italian librettos formal classification of dancers is not generally found before the late 1760s, this aspect is not immediately apparent from printed sources of the earlier part of the century, apart from eyewitness observations such as those given above. With information available from later decades, however, we can come to some conclusions at least as far back as 1750.

The list of "Grotteschi in Italy, 1750–1800" in appendix 1 is a preliminary enumeration of those dancers who are actually named *grottesco/-a* in one or more Italian printed librettos or other documents of the period 1750–1800. Far from exhaustive, it is likely to call for further updating. But by using a simple tabulation of this sort, in conjunction with listings of dancers in both librettos that do *not* provide categorizations and rankings—such as those of the 1750s—and those that do, we can draw several conclusions, which other evidence then substantiates.

In the first place, we see how many dancers indeed had the kind of training to qualify them to perform as *grotteschi*. Taking this list and comparing it to the roster given in any theatrical libretto from 1750 onward, we find that at least half of all the dancers named in a libretto, whether ranked or not, have at one time or another performed as *grotteschi*. No doubt this percentage will only increase as we are able to make the tabulation more comprehensive.

Secondly, the list substantiates the notion that Italian dancers performed in a variety of styles and did not remain confined to a single category, thus confirming an aspect stressed by Gennaro Magri throughout his treatise. Every performer included here danced in one or more productions as a *grottesco,* but a great majority may also be found named as *mezzo-carattere* or even serious dancers in other ballets. One example among many is Onorato Viganò, a direct contemporary of Magri and the

---

20. *Storia del Teatro Regio di Torino,* ed. Alberto Basso, 5 vols. (Turin: Cassa di Risparmio, 1976–88); see in particular vol. 1: Marie-Thérèse Bouquet, *Il teatro di corte dalle origini al 1788.*

father of the renowned choreographer Salvatore Viganò. In the earlier part of his career Onorato performed exclusively as a *grottesco,* then took on serious roles, and thereafter devoted himself to choreography, finally becoming an impresario. His name and those of all the others on my list shown in boldface type were choreographers as well as dancers. (Among the female dancers on the list, there is no evidence that any were ever entrusted with choreography.) The works they created, and the dancers they employed, include nearly the whole spectrum of eighteenth-century theatrical ballet and not merely comic or so-called characteristic dances.

I say "nearly" the whole spectrum because there was a prominent exception: the pantomime ballets of Jean-Georges Noverre, which in their "purest" form made little or no use of Italian dance technique or performers. Noverre exalted French "noble" dance with its *terre-à-terre* style. Indeed, Magri described such a preference as characteristic of French dance on the whole: "They do not care to make much use of the caprioles, preferring to dance *terre à terre.*"[21] Furthermore, Noverre devised a kind of pantomime that observers called more walking than dance.[22] In his ballets these two aspects were used in alternation; the pantomime was not integrated within the danced episodes as was characteristic of Italian ballets, and was to be found as well in the less "exalted" sorts of French dance works represented by the ballets that Auguste Ferrère notated in 1782.[23] Noverre even went so far as to advocate the total cessation of

21. Magri/Skeaping, 119; Magri, *Trattato,* 1:82: "Presso i Francesi è più in costumanza, che presso noi Italiani, perchè quelli non si curano del troppo uso delle Capriole, servendosi più tosto del ballar terreno."

22. Baron Grimm described his impression of Noverre's ballets thus: "One walks much more in them than one dances. One sees in them much less of steps and symmetrical dances than of gestures and groups." (On y marche bien plus qu'on danse. On y voit bien moins de pas et de danse symétriques que de gestes et de groupes.) "In the ballets of Noverre dance and measured walking are very distinct; one dances only in the great movements of passion, in decisive moments; during the scenes one walks in time, it is true, but without dancing. This transition from measured walking to dance and from dance to measured walking is as necessary in this spectacle as the transition from recitative to aria and from aria to recitative is in opera; but dancing for the sake of dancing cannot occur except when the danced drama is over." (Dans les ballets de Noverre la danse et la marche cadencée sont très distinctes; on ne danse que dans les grands mouvements de passion, dans les moments décisifs; dans les scenes, on marche en mesure à la verité mais sans danser. Ce passage de la marche mesurée à la danse et de la danse à la marche mesurée est aussi nécessaire dans ce spectacle que, dans celui de l'opéra, le passage du récitatif à l'air et de l'air au récitatif; mais danser pour danser ne peut avoir lieu que lorsque la pièce en danse est finie.) Friedrich Melchior von Grimm, Diderot, Raynal, Meister, et al., *Correspondance littéraire, philosophique et critique* (Paris: Garnier, 1879), 6:300 (letter of November 1765) and 11:237 (letter of January 1771).

23. See Moira Goff, 217f., and Rebecca Harris-Warrick and Carol G. Marsh, 247ff. and 265ff.

dance in scenes of despair and the like: "The dancer in these sorts of scenes is never so excellent as when he is no longer dancing."[24] Above all Noverre disparaged the Italian *grotteschi* and their pantomime as fit only for children.[25]

For a few years in the late 1760s and early 1770s, during the ascendancy of this best known of eighteenth-century choreographers, some prominent Italian theaters mounted the works of Noverre either under his direct supervision—this at Milan only—or through the offices of his disciples, such as Charles Le Picq.[26] As Salvatore Bongiovanni notes, when Le Picq began staging his master's ballets in Naples, one critic pointed to what he considered to be excesses in the grand Noverrian tragedies, singling out the lack of pure dance: "Everything is the work of the pantomime: *the feet dance very little* [italics added], and every plot is a new [danced] drama three times the length of the principal [sung] drama."[27] These productions generated hot discussions and sparked a pamphlet war very unusual in Italian theatrical annals.[28]

Noverre's most visible opponent was the Italian choreographer Gasparo Angiolini, who at one time professed adherence to ideas similar to those of his rival. When Angiolini returned to Italy from Vienna in 1773 and became reacquainted with his Italian legacy, however, he soon turned against Noverre, both in published works and in his staged presentations.[29] Angiolini's changed attitude appears to have been influenced in part by the first of several critical "letters" on the Italian theater

---

24. Noverre, *Lettres*, 277: "Le Danseur dans ces sortes de Scenes ne sera jamais si excellent que lorsqu'il ne dansera pas." Noverre's treatise was reissued in Vienna in 1767 and many times subsequently. An English translation by Cyril W. Beaumont, *Letters on Dancing and Ballets* (London, 1930; repr. 1966), was made from the first volume of the 1803–4 St. Petersburg edition of Noverre's works, which was a revised and enlarged version of the original treatise.

25. Noverre, *Lettres*, 263 (my translation): "Let beginning dancers not confuse this noble pantomime of which I am speaking with that low and trivial form of expression that the Italian *bouffons* have brought to France and which bad taste seems to have embraced." (Que les Danseurs qui commencent ne confondent pas cette *Pantomime* noble, dont je parle, avec cette expression basse & triviale que les Bouffons d'Italie ont apporté en France & que le mauvais goût semble avoir adopté.)

26. For further information on Le Picq's life and works see my entry on him in *Grove Opera*, 2:1152.

27. Bongiovanni, 98 and n17, citing a 1781 commentary to a Neapolitan edition of Metastasio's works.

28. For details on the controversy see my "Theatrical Ballet and Italian Opera," 215–41.

29. The longest and most important of Angiolini's surviving writings is his major treatise, the two *Lettere a Monsieur Noverre sopra i balli pantomimi* (Milan [colophon]: "Appresso Gio. Batista Bianchi Regio Stampatore," 1773), which takes Noverre to task on many issues. Although Angiolini had earlier adopted a stance similar to Noverre's regarding the *grotteschi*, from this time forward he once again stood on the side of his more eclectic countrymen.

put out in 1773 by the irascible Frenchman Ange Goudar. In *De Venise: Remarques sur la musique et la danse de Mr. G. . . . a Milord Pembroke*,[30] Goudar devotes two-thirds of the contents to ballet, satirically confronting impressions of dance productions staged in Venice and Padua in 1772–73 with the high-flown rhetoric of Noverre, as well as of Angiolini's earlier Viennese writings. For example, he finds the acrobatic style associated with the Italian *grotteschi* to be no less worthy of esteem than the posturing of French heroic dancers, contrasting the affected Le Picq ("dead to nature") with Onorato Viganò portraying a peasant ("a living picture"): "I will say that everything which has any realism about it in modern pantomime is found in good grotesque dancing."[31] Goudar urges other issues that Angiolini subsequently took up, disparaging lengthy ballets based on plots too complicated to be expressed in pantomime, along with the resulting "humiliating" use of printed ballet scenarios to explain them and the reliance on spectacular effects to sustain audience interest.

Angiolini developed these ideas further and expounded on many others as well, both in his major treatise and in printed addresses to his audience in Milan in 1773–74. Among other concerns were adherence to the Aristotelian unities, the use of simple, unified plots, the utility of developing choreographic notation, and the need to make ballet music more responsive to the action portrayed. He now veered away from his earlier stance on the superiority of the *la haute danse*, stating, "We do not recognize as a real ballet dancer one who only dances the serious style to perfection, since a part does not constitute the whole."[32] Indeed, he went so far as to recognize the legitimacy and parity of all genres if well executed: "As for me, I know no gesture nor movement that be not dance, when all is subjected to those rules through which the art is formed."[33] In this respect he anticipated Magri's remarks in the same vein.

Noverre brushed aside almost all of his rival's concerns as irrelevant

---

30. Venice: Palese, 1773. Appearing in Italian translation not long afterward under the title *Osservazioni sopra la musica ed il ballo, ossia Estratto di due lettere di Mr. G . . . a Milord Pembroke* (Milan: Gaetano Motta, [1773]), it is the first in a series of eleven such "letters" that Ange Goudar published either anonymously or under the name of his almost equally infamous wife, Sara, between 1773 and 1776. A modern edition of the Italian translation appears in *La danza italiana* 5–6 (Autumn 1987): 35–76. Francis L. Mars describes Goudar's extraordinary career in "Ange Goudar, cet inconnu (1708–1791): Essai bio-bibliographique sur un aventurier polygraphe du XVIIIe siècle," *Casanova Gleanings* 9 (1966): 1–64.

31. Goudar, *Remarques*, 131: "Je dirai que s'il reste quelque chose de vrai dans la pantomime moderne, c'est dans le bon grotesque."

32. Angiolini, *Lettere a Monsieur Noverre*, 78.

33. Ibid., 95–96.

for a creative choreographer, but he did defend the use of printed ballet programs, having come to the conclusion that pantomime ballet was "a restricted and languishing art that needs help" and thus "a scenario can serve as an interpreter."[34] Angiolini, unfazed by Noverre's ineffectual response, for the rest of career, both in Italy and in Russia, produced works at La Scala and elsewhere based solidly on his Italian training, which was becoming international currency in the later eighteenth century, even in Paris. Noverre, on the other hand, was to fail when he finally attained his life-long goal as choreographer at the Paris Opéra in 1776. Audiences there preferred his lighter, more decorative works over the grand tragedies in dance, which they found enigmatic. These reactions mirrored to some extent those of the Milanese during Noverre's two-year engagement there (1774–76), when he had specifically brought in seven principal dancers from Vienna in order to have performers, as he phrased it, "all trained in my style of composition."[35] This qualification meant excluding all Italian grotesque dancers, whom Noverre always denigrated: five of the eight principals were French and all belonged to the categories of "serious" or "demi-caractère" dancers. Thus the Noverre canon in its most extreme form implicitly discredited the education not only of the grotteschi but of practically the entire corps of Italy's dancing elite. While Noverre left Milan disgruntled, in Paris he was forced to resign.

Through the efforts of Le Picq, Paolo Franchi, Sébastien Gallet, and other students of Noverre, works nominally in the style of their master continued to play at certain Italian theaters, particularly at the San Carlo of Naples in the 1770s and '80s, but in the end their effect was limited. As Salvatore Bongiovanni speculates, the Neapolitan theater's rehiring of Magri in 1773, after an absence of several years, may have been an attempt to counter or cushion the effects of the new taste introduced by Le Picq by alternating with ballets upholding the traditional Italian character.[36] While some aspects of Noverre's works, such as his ability with large, massed scenes and his instinctive taste for more effective music, certainly did influence Italian ballets of all sorts for the better, his mode

---

34. Jean-Georges Noverre, *Introduction au ballet des Horaces, ou Petite réponse aux grandes lettres du Sr. Angiolini*, cited here in the edition published in Milan in the spring of 1774 (along with a counter-reply) as *Discussioni sulla danza pantomima*, which faithfully reproduces Noverre's original essay, 13.

35. See Noverre's letter to David Garrick of 13 January 1775, cited in Winter, *Pre-Romantic Ballet*, 121.

36. Bongiovanni, 99.

of pantomime and above all his dismissal of the native aerial style of highly acrobatic dancing made famous by the *grotteschi* had no long-standing influence. Even during its heyday, the Noverrian grand ballets had succeeded best in the hothouse environment of autocratic courts — Stuttgart, Vienna, and thereafter Naples — where tastes were more easily imposed.[37]

By the later 1780s and '90s, a younger generation of Italian dancers and choreographers, such as the Neapolitan Gaetano Gioia[38] and others schooled in the rigors of the difficult, highly acrobatic techniques of the *grotteschi,* dominated the scene, and this not only in Italy. Even at that bastion of conservatism, the Paris Opéra, Noverre's successors Maximilien and Pierre Gardel, in forcing adherence to the old order, essentially stifled all creative efforts. The finest French talents fled to more favorable climes, above all to the mecca of La Scala, while Italian dancers gradually conquered European stages from London to St. Petersburg. The dance techniques described by the most noted nineteenth-century theorists and teachers, from Carlo Blasis to Enrico Cecchetti, while they may rightly be called international in scope and the basis for what we now know as classical ballet, have far more to do with the kinds of dance performances that dominated Italian theaters of the previous century than they do with French *danse noble* and static Noverrian pantomime.

Italian theatrical ballet was first and foremost pure dance. The pantomimic element made its best effect when it was simple, even exaggerated, and achieved not merely through attitudes struck but through the vocabulary of steps and figures, leaps, and other exhilarating physical exploits that were part of every Italian dancer's training but particularly the realm of the *grotteschi.* Yet except for the efforts of Gennaro Magri, these would remain for us today only in the realm of distant, all-too-general amateur descriptions and static pictorial representations. With the 1779 treatise of Magri, however, we may begin to comprehend the actual practices of Italian theatrical dancing. Magri's work, grounded in his experiences as a performer on stage, not only offers a tutor in abstract

37. Bruce Brown points out how the environment for ballet in Vienna from the mid-1750s on was critically affected by Count Durazzo's preference for more rationally conceived works (see 64, 72–73).

38. For details on Gioia's life and works see my entry on him in *Grove Opera,* 2:423–24. A more thorough treatment, which includes a complete listing of all his ballets, is my article "Gaetano Gioia, il ballo teatrale e l'opera del Primo Ottocento," in *Creature di Prometeo: Il ballo teatrale. Dal divertimento al dramma: Studi offerti a Aurel M. Milloss* (Florence: Olschki, 1996), 191–238.

techniques but repeatedly relates his instructions to enhancing the over-all theatrical effects of the dances they create. And it is these effects, after all, which allowed eighteenth-century Italian ballet to achieve the over-whelming popularity it enjoyed in its day and which encouraged the adoption of its vocabulary on an international scale.

# 2

# Gennaro Magri

## *A Grotesque Dancer on the European Stage*

SALVATORE BONGIOVANNI

(TRANSLATED BY BRUCE ALAN BROWN)

The career of Gennaro Magri is notable not only for its excellent artistic quality and international dimensions but also because it demonstrates some of the more significant and exemplary aspects of the entire panorama of theatrical dance in the eighteenth century.

While we have no information about Magri's artistic training, we know that his birth and professional apprenticeship occurred in Naples: all the sources call him Neapolitan and also use the dialect stage name Gennariello. If (as seems presumable) Magri made his theatrical debut during the 1750s—when one of the main sources of documentation, opera librettos (and Neapolitan ones in particular), did not yet regularly include the names of dancers — then we can infer that he was born sometime during the 1730s.[1]

The first evidence of Magri's presence in a ballet company dates from 1758.[2] (For an overview of Magri's entire career, see the chronology

---

1. The difficulties one generally encounters in examining eighteenth-century Neapolitan theatrical life are augmented by the near-total destruction of its documentary sources; see also n8, below.

2. Some secondary sources contain information that I have not been able to confirm through my own research. According to Winter (*Pre-Romantic Ballet*, 150), the name Magri is found in a

compiled by Patricia Rader that follows this chapter.) According to indications in the libretto for Tommaso Traetta's opera *L'Olimpiade*, given that autumn at the Teatro Nuovo dell'Accademia filarmonica in Verona,[3] Magri performed in the capacity of "primo ballerino grottesco," dancing in the ballets produced between the acts of the opera. These ballets were choreographed by Pierre Alouard, an important French dancer of the time who was very active in Italy (his name is listed in Italian sources in wildly disparate forms, such as Aloardi, Alovar, Aleardi, Alnardi, Allouar). Alouard devoted his talents particularly to a type of ballet that went beyond the scope of pure *divertissement*, also incorporating narrative elements and ever more extended pantomimic sequences. Confirmation of this is found in the ballet he produced at the Teatro Argentina in Rome, for Carnival 1762, at the end of the second act of Traetta's *Zenobia*—a ballet in which Magri participated as one of the dancers. Its narrative plot is in fact quite considerable — and with a literary pedigree besides, being a staging of an episode from Ariosto's *Orlando furioso* (Canto VII): it depicts Ruggiero's arrival at the enchanted palace of the sorceress Alcina, who by means of her witchcraft then causes the knight to fall in love with her. Magri was to meet up with Alouard not only in Verona and Rome, but also in Reggio Emilia and Padua in 1762.

By the date of this first available source (1758), then, Magri was already a successful *primo ballerino* in a prestigious company; his engagements immediately thereafter would give his fame an international dimension. In fact, already during the next year (1759–60) Magri spent the first of two separate seasons in Vienna. (See chap. 3 of this volume, by Bruce Alan Brown, for Magri in Vienna.)

After this initial Viennese experience, Magri's activities were concentrated principally on the theaters of Padua and Venice, where he pro-

---

theatrical roster in Lisbon in 1754, along with those of other choreographers, such as Andrea Alberti and Giuseppe Salomoni. Mary Skeaping (Magri/Skeaping, 10), on the other hand, citing Benedetto Croce (*I teatri di Napoli* [Naples: Pierro, 1891]), and Winter ("Venice: Proving Ground and Arbiter for Italian Choreographers," in *Venezia e il melodramma nel Settecento*, ed. Maria Teresa Muraro [Florence: Olschki, 1978], 79–87 [86]), signals Magri's presence at the Teatro San Carlo in Naples during the 1755–56 season. This indication finds no confirmation in Croce, however; Skeaping probably confused these dates with 1765–66. Likewise I can find no record of Magri's presence in Venice for the 1762–63 season, as Skeaping implies. For further information, see my "Gennaro Magri e il *Trattato teorico-prattico di ballo*" (unpublished *tesi di laurea*, Università degli Studi "La Sapienza," Rome, 1991) and my "Gennaro Magri e il 'ballo grottesco,'" in *Creature di Prometeo: Il ballo teatrale dal divertimento al dramma*, ed. Giovanni Morelli (Florence: Olschki, 1996), 239–45.

    3. See Claudio Sartori, *I libretti italiani a stampa dalle origini al 1800: catalogo analitico con 16 indici* (Cuneo: Bertola & Locatelli, 1990–95). (See also chronology in this volume.)

duced his first works as a choreographer. These two cities of the Veneto were linked by a continual exchange of artists, who moved freely from one to the other, and archival studies reveal that, despite the rich and intense activity at the Venetian theaters, the provincial houses did not limit themselves simply to importing Venetian works but also contributed new productions, sometimes expressly commissioned. As Maria Nevilla Massaro has noted, "The activity of some choreographers and dancers present in Padua or in Venice demonstrates that the Paduan theater was not considered simply a testing ground for a given work, and . . . it is impossible to claim that the more important artists only arrived there after having worked in Venetian theaters."[4] And yet Venice, with its many opera houses, each also having a ballet company, acted during the entire eighteenth century as the principal launching pad for dancers and aspiring choreographers — as a sort of showcase watched by all the European courts. A success in Venice opened the doors to an international career. As Marian Hannah Winter has observed, nearly all Italian choreographers of a certain international stature passed through Venice during their youths: Gasparo Angiolini (1747), Vincenzo Galeotti (1759), Onorato Viganò (1766–67), Salvatore Viganò (1789). These were the personalities, together with Magri and Giuseppe Salomoni Junior (Winter claims), "who defended Italy's share in ballet development in the face of what had become French primacy."[5] And it was to these artists — including Magri — that Count Giacomo Durazzo turned, during his tenure as director of Vienna's theaters, in order to assist Christoph Gluck, the librettist Ranieri de' Calzabigi, and the choreographers Franz Hilverding and Gasparo Angiolini in realizing their celebrated works of those years.

Between 1760 and 1764 Magri worked four times in Padua's Teatro Nuovo, for the annual Feast of Saint Anthony (June 1760, 1761, 1762, and 1764). In Venice he was engaged for the autumn 1760 season and for Carnival 1761 at the Teatro di Sant'Angelo, and in 1764 at the Teatro San Giovanni Grisostomo for the Feast of the Ascension.

It will be useful to stop briefly to consider the professional colleagues and other personalities with whom Magri came into contact, who can help shed light on the quality and versatility of his artistic experience.

In Padua, one of the most internationally noted *prime ballerine* at this time was Elisabetta Morelli, held to be one of the best female grotesque

---

4. Massaro, "Balli e ballerini fra Padova e Venezia," *La danza italiana* 5/6 (Autumn 1987): 77–88 (80).

5. Winter, "Venice," 86 and 81.

dancers of her time. She became one of Magri's most frequent partners; they danced as a couple in Padua in 1760 and 1761; in Reggio Emilia in 1762; in Vienna in 1763–64; in Naples in 1765–66, 1766–67, and 1768–69; and in Turin in 1768.

In his first Venetian engagement Magri appeared not only as *primo ballerino,* but also as "director and composer [i.e., choreographer] of the ballets" (direttore e compositore dei balli). His company included another *primo ballerino,* Pierre Bernard Michel. Called by Magri himself "the best *Ballerino grottesco* that France has produced,"[6] Michel too was a recurring presence in Magri's career. In addition to their Venetian collaborations in 1760 and 1761, the two artists also worked together in Rome in 1762.

The librettos for the Venetian performances of these years make no direct reference to the content of Magri's ballets, though they name all the members of the ensemble. Only in a few cases is it possible to infer the settings and subjects of the ballets, from the descriptions of the scenery. Thus, for the ballets between the acts of Vincenzo Ciampi's opera *Amore in caricatura* (Love in Caricature), performed at the Teatro di Sant'Angelo during Carnival of 1761, we know that the first took place in a "forest where charcoal is made" (foresta dove si fa il Carbone) and hence that it is a ballet of charcoal merchants (carbonai); for the second ballet, on the other hand, the setting is a "delightful apartment for a Mascarade dedicated to Bacchus" (appartamento delizioso per una Mascherata dedicata a Bacco).

In 1764, by contrast, Magri danced in the troupe of Gaetano Cesari, at the Teatro Grimani, in the performances for the Feast of the Ascension.[7] The ballets produced for this occasion were on mythological and pastoral subjects; we know only their titles: *Il giudizio di Paride* (The Judgment of Paris) and *Li amori di Tirsi ed Eurilla interrotti dalla Maga Falsirena* (The Loves of Tyrcis and Eurilla Interrupted by the Sorceress Falsirena). Despite subject matter not typical for Magri's works, one should not assume that he suddenly took up *la danse noble;* mythological and otherwise "serious" ballets commonly included episodes of virtuosic dance that would have been entrusted to the *grotteschi* who specialized in that sort of technique.

6. Magri/Skeaping, 160; Magri, *Trattato,* 1:126 (chap. 60, sec. 9): "il miglior Ballerino grottesco, che abbia dato la Francia."

7. He danced presumably as *primo grottesco,* though the libretto does not specify dancers' functions.

For Magri's Paduan ballets, in which he also danced as *primo ballerino*, we know the titles only of those performed with Baldassare Galuppi's *Muzio Scevola* in 1762. These too are in a pastoral vein: *Zefiro e Flora* (Zephyr and Flora), and a character dance, *Le pescatrici romane* (The Roman Fisherwomen). The first may well have owed something to Angiolini and Gluck's treatment of the same subject (Schönbrunn, 1759), which Magri almost certainly would have witnessed, even if it was performed by the French ballet troupe, rather than the German one of which he was a member.

Sources from the period document the fame Magri enjoyed during this time. Among them is a document that Benedetto Croce found among the administrative papers of the Teatro San Carlo in the Neapolitan State Archives. It is a letter dated 11 October 1761, in which a certain Florentine prior, Viviani, furnishes the theater's impresarios with information and news about artists under consideration for engagement in the next season; Viviani notes in particular the best dancers on the market: "M. Pietro Alnardi [i.e., Pierre Alouard] for serious characters, Gennaro Magri and Giuseppe d'Ercolani, Bolognese, for grotesque. For women the famous Mimì [Favier] . . . and Elena Buttini, who is said to be a great leaper."[8] Another document, dated July 1764, specifically singles out Magri as "insuperable for the grace of his dancing, and his force and agility in leaping, of which he has given clear evidence since his first appearance in the Royal Theater."[9]

During this period Magri's activities were intense and tireless. Fortunately, they are also well documented. In the Veneto and Vienna (where he would return in 1764), two seasons at the Teatro Pubblico in Reggio Emilia stand out, as well as one in Rome, at the Teatro Argentina, in 1762.[10] Roman theatrical practices at that time were unique, differing not

---

8. Archivio di Stato, Naples, political office, secretariat of the royal house, papers of the administration of the theaters (1734–92), fasc. 13, cited in Croce, *I teatri di Napoli*, 750: "In carattere serio M. Pietro Alnardi, per il grottesco Gennaro Magri e Giuseppe d'Ercolani, bolognese. Per le donne la celebre Mimì . . . ed Elena Buttini, che si suppone grande saltatora." Croce (1866–1952), a prominent Italian philosopher, historian, and critic, methodically examined thirty-one thick fascicles of documents of the administration of the Neapolitan theaters for this period, at that time on deposit in the Archivio di Stato. Since many of these documents were destroyed in a fire at the archives in 1944, Croce's extracts constitute the sole source of much information in question.

9. Ibid., fasc. 14, cited in Croce, *I teatri di Napoli*, 508: "insuperabile per la grazia del ballare, e forza, e agilità nel saltare, prerogative delle quali fin dalla sua prima uscita nel Real Teatro ha dato chiari segni."

10. Regarding spectacles at the Teatro Argentina, see Mario Rinaldi, *Due secoli di musica al Teatro Argentina* (Florence: Olschki, 1978).

only from those of other Italian and European theaters but even from those of the Papal States. First of all, the season took place only during Carnival, the one time of the year in which, according to ancient and pagan Roman tradition, every conceivable liberty or folly was allowed. But the stance of the local authorities concerning public spectacles was ambiguous: periods of extreme tolerance passed easily into periods of bitter repression. It is to one of these sudden changes in position that we owe the most curious and most remarked-upon feature of the Roman theaters, namely, the presence on stage of men dressed as women. "Female dancers are not permitted on the stages of Rome," reported the Abbé Jérôme Richard, who visited in the winter of 1762. "They substitute for them boys dressed as women and there was also a police ordinance that decreed that they wear black bloomers."[11] The reactions of foreign travelers to these disquieting figures ranged from amused astonishment at the efficacy of the disguise to disgusted disapproval: "What impression can one have," Joseph Thomas d'Espinchal asked himself, "of ballet in which the *prima ballerina* is a young man in disguise with artificial feminine curves?"[12] In the four ballets produced for the 1762 season at the Teatro Argentina, in which Magri danced male roles as *primo ballerino grottesco*, alongside Pierre Bernard Michel, female roles were filled by Giuseppe Banti and Giuseppe Ercolani, as *primi ballerini*, while the choreography was entrusted to Pierre Alouard. These works were mostly character dances: a *Carnevale dei Turchi o sia la festa e cerimonia del Ramadan* (Carnival of the Turks, or The Feast and Ceremony of Ramadan), a *Pantomima di maschere* (Pantomime of Masked Characters), and *L'accampamento di Tiridate* (The Encampment of Tiridates) set in the same scenery as the opera (Metastasio's *Zenobia*, set by Traetta).

Still in the capacity of *primo ballerino grottesco*, Magri was hired for the 1762–63 season at Turin's Teatro Regio.[13] There, too, the opera season

11. (Abbé) Jérôme Richard, *Description historique et critique de l'Italie* (Dijon and Paris, 1769), cited in Rinaldi, *Due secoli di musica*, 1:143: "Non sono permesse le ballerine sulle scene di Roma; le sostituiscono ragazzi vestiti da donna e vi fu anche una ordinanza di polizia che ordinò loro di portare dei pantaloncini neri."

12. Rinaldi, *Due secoli di musica*, 1:297: "Che impressione può aversi da un ballo nel quale la prima ballerina è un giovanotto mascherato con posticce rotondità di femmina?" D'Espinchal, Rinaldi's source, was a French traveler and author of the manuscript "*Journal d'émigration*," later published as *Journal d'émigration du comte d'Espinchal publié d'après les manuscrits originaux*, ed. Ernest d'Hauterive (Paris: Perrin, 1912).

13. The information in what follows concerning Magri and the Teatro Regio is drawn from Marie-Thérèse Bouquet, *Il teatro di corte, dalle origini al 1788*, vol. 1, *Storia del Teatro Regio di Torino*, ed. Alberto Basso (Turin: Cassa di Risparmio, 1976–88), 308–17.

was very short, being limited to the period between November and the end of Carnival, during which two operas were presented. The ballets were considered no less important than the operas; every performance included at least three ballets. During these years, as earlier, Turin was inclined toward French dance (a reflection of Piedmont's long-standing political and dynastic ties with France), as is clear from the names of the many dancers and choreographers active at the Teatro Regio;[14] Italians, too, were often present, especially as *grotteschi*, but those Italian artists who had worked elsewhere as choreographers were engaged in Turin only as dancers.[15]

In 1762–63 the "Inventor and Director of the Ballets" was the Frenchman Auguste Hus, a dancer and choreographer active above all in Lyon, and later also *Maître de ballet* at the Comédie Italienne in Paris.[16] During this engagement Hus composed ballets primarily on allegorical or mythological subjects—*La morte di Orfeo* (The Death of Orpheus), *Amore, i piaceri, e i giuochi* (Cupid, the Pleasures, and the Games), *Amore vinto dall'amicizia* (Love Defeated by Friendship), *Il rapimento di Proserpina* (The Abduction of Proserpine)—but also some with exotic settings—*I selvatici* (The Hermits)—or with historical plots—*Di guerrieri romani* (The Roman Warriors). All of them, however, were supported by a substantial narrative plot, amply described in the opera librettos, with extended pantomimic episodes alternating with sequences of pure dance. These descriptions delineate a precise formal structure that is confirmed and made still clearer by the musical sources preserved from the period 1748–62.[17] The structure provides for an *Introduzione*, with a setting of the scene

---

14. Gloria Giordano notes, "In Turin, as in the other theatres of the peninsula, a pair of the so-called *danzatori di rango francese*, French dancers by birth or by style, was considered indispensable to the success of the *balletti*." Giordano, "Gaetano Grossatesta, an Eighteenth-Century Italian Choreographer and Impresario, Part One: The Dancer-Choreographer in Northern Italy," *Dance Chronicle* 23, no. 1 (2000): 1–28 (19).

15. See Kathleen Kuzmick Hansell, "Theatrical Ballet and Italian Opera," in *Opera on Stage*, vol. 5, The History of Italian Opera (Chicago: University of Chicago Press, 2002), 177–308 (195).

16. Charles-Auguste Hus (Lyon, ca. 1735– ?) belonged to a large dynasty of ballet dancers, active across all of Europe, for which it is impossible to establish an exact chronology. Active at the Académie Royale de Musique in Paris from 1756, Auguste Hus was engaged numerous times as a soloist from 1761 onward, above all at Lyon. Contracted for the 1762–63 season at the Teatro Regio in Turin, he worked there as choreographer and dancer also during the 1763–64 season, in 1769, and (as choreographer only) in the 1769–70 season. Expelled from the Lyon theater in 1782 because of a choreography judged too risqué (*La Rose et le bouton*), he presumably withdrew from all theatrical activity.

17. The music in question consists of three manuscript volumes entitled *Raccolta de' balli fatti nelle opere del Real Teatro di Torino con la spiegazione dei medesimi e gli nomi dei compositori* (Collection of Ballets

and presentation of the characters or the plot, and in which pantomime is prevalent; a *pas de deux* for the *mezzo carattere* couple (or second grotesque couple); a *pas de deux* for the (main) grotesque couple; an ensemble dance by the *corpo di ballo;* a *pas de deux* by the serious couple; and a *ballo generale* (general dance). For an example of a Turinese ballet of this type (though not by Hus), see appendix 2, part 1.

Magri was hired for Turin on 13 February 1762 with a salary of 200 *zecchini;* his partner was Maddalena Formigli, who substituted at the last minute for the above-mentioned Elisabetta Morelli. At the request of the *Cavalieri* — the impresarios and intermediaries in the administration of the Teatro Regio — Magri also performed in one further character ballet, beyond those for which he had originally been engaged.[18]

This period seems to have been the apex of Magri's career, and his engagements came fast and thick. During the 1763–64 season, as noted earlier, Magri was hired again in Vienna, where he met a decisive personality for the fate of pantomime ballet in the second half of the eighteenth century, Gasparo Angiolini. It was Angiolini who created the ballets, during this same season, for Traetta's reform opera *Ifigenia in Tauride*. Magri himself danced with two other illustrious personalities this season: Onorato Viganò and the omnipresent Elisabetta Morelli. The Viganòs were one of the most prominent families of ballet dancers. The most famous of their number was Salvatore Viganò (1769–1821), choreographer for many years at La Scala and creator of many celebrated masterworks (among which was the ballet *The Creatures of Prometheus*, to music by Beethoven), but his father, Onorato Viganò (1739–1811), was another of the major figures on the theatrical scene in the second half of the eighteenth century.[19] Even before the arrival in Italy of the *ballet d'action*, he pioneered an original form of pantomime ballet notable for its liveliness and variety of subject matter, and in which (in accord with long-term practice in the Italian school) pantomime was integrally linked to dance. Magri was to collaborate again with Onorato Viganò in Naples during the 1768–69 season (see below). In Vienna Magri also met another figure fundamental to eighteenth-century ballet: Giuseppe Salomoni (Venice,

---

Given in the Operas of the Royal Theater of Turin with the Explanation of the Same and the Names of the Composers), preserved in the musical archive of the Biblioteca di Santa Cecilia in Rome. The volumes include the music of approximately ninety ballets from the Teatro Regio from 1748 to 1762. A preliminary analysis of the *Raccolta* is found in Lorenzo Tozzi, "Musica e balli al Regio di Torino (1748–1762)," *La danza italiana* 2 (Spring 1985): 5–22.

18. See Bouquet, *Il teatro di corte,* 1:308–9.

19. For further information on Onorato Viganò, see Hansell, "Theatrical Ballet," 221–23.

ca. 1710–Vienna, 1777), one of the most famous members of a large family of dancers (dynasties of dancers were typical in this period, the lack of dance schools making a family apprenticeship indispensable).[20] Mentioned by Arteaga as one of the choreographers who contributed to bringing "representational dancing to a level of maturity that it had never before attained on the Italian stage,"[21] Salomoni pursued an international career for more than thirty years; he is known to have worked in London, Vienna, Milan, Rome, Venice, and Stuttgart.[22]

Later in 1764 Magri also danced in Florence, at the Teatro della Pergola,[23] where he met another famous French choreographer, Vincent Saunier.[24] In these years influences were arriving from France even more conspicuously than before, and the work of Saunier, together with that of the aforementioned Alouard, represented one of the main contributions to Italian ballet. Saunier, who had danced under Noverre in the

20. Salomoni's two sons were also famous dancers and choreographers: Giuseppe, born in Venice around the beginning of the 1730s and called "di Portogallo" (recalling his work as a choreographer in Lisbon), to distinguish him from his father; and Francesco, called "di Vienna," where he had been born at the end of the 1730s. For a reconstruction of the careers of these three dancers and choreographers, often confused with each other, see Hansell, "Theatrical Ballet," 200–201.

21. Stefano Arteaga, *Le rivoluzioni del teatro musicale italiano* (Bologna: Trenti, 1783–88; repr., Bologna: Forni, 1969), 3:25: "ballo rappresentativo ad un grado di maggioranza, quale non ebbe mai per l'addietro sulla scena italiana."

22. See also Giovenale Sacchi, *Della divisione del tempo nella musica, nel ballo e nella poesia* (Milan: Mazzucchelli, 1770; repr., Bologna: Forni, 1969), 35–36: "Credesi ancora, che l'arte del ballo pervenuta sia nel presente secolo al maggior colmo della sua perfezione possibile; né altro pare, che generalmente esser possa il giudizio di quelli, che veduto hanno i balli composti dal Sig. Giuseppe Salomone Veneziano detto da Vienna per la sua lunga dimora in quella imperial Città, e del Sig. Francesco suo figlio, e degli altri maestri loro simili. Io ebbi già occasione di trattare il Sig. Giuseppe in un nobile convitto, dove egli insegnava, e non senza ammirazione conobbi il suo alto ingegno, che in qualsivoglia arte più nobile l'avria potuto rendere eccellente; ed osservai che studiandosi egli di dare alle invenzioni sue unità, verità, maraviglia, ed incremento continuo, usava nelle sue composizioni quante buone regole, ed avvertenze sono mai state prescritte a' Poeti, ed agli Oratori per le loro." (It is still believed that the art of dancing has reached its greatest heights of perfection in the present century; nor could opinion be otherwise, for those who have seen the ballets composed by the Venetian Sig. Giuseppe Salomone, called "da Vienna" on account of his long residence in that imperial city, and by his son Sig. Francesco, and of other similar masters. I once had occasion to converse with Sig. Giuseppe in a noble boarding school where he was teaching, and not without admiration did I become acquainted with his high intellect, which would have rendered him excellent in any more noble art whatsoever; and I observed that he, in taking care to give his compositions unity, truth, wonder, and continual growth, used as many good rules and as much care as ever have been prescribed for poets and orators for their creations.)

23. For information on and a chronology of the works performed in the Florentine theaters in the second half of the eighteenth century, see Marcello De Angelis, *Melodramma, spettacolo e musica nella Firenze dei Lorena (1750–1800)* (Milan: Bibliografica, 1991).

24. For an account of Saunier's career, see Hansell, "Theatrical Ballet," 202–3.

early 1750s, strove to make his erstwhile master's ballets known in Italy. And in fact during this season he produced one of those ballets (*Admeto e Alceste* [Admetus and Alcestis]), in addition to a "noble" pantomime ballet (*Le furberie d'amore* [The Tricks of Love]). Magri danced in both ballets in the capacity of *terzo ballerino*. (For slightly earlier examples of Saunier's manner, see app. 2, libretto 1.)

Thereafter Magri was again in Turin, for the 1764–65 season, during which he ran into difficulties with the theater's impresarios when he asked to have the ballerina Antonia Heimin dance as his partner.[25] The impresarios judged the ballerina "mediocre" and rejected the contract. As a result, Magri at first asked the administration to release him, too, from his contract, and sent back the sum of money he had already received. But Heimin obstinately refused to cancel her contract, and the impresarios then decided to offer Magri a new agreement with the condition that he convince his partner to renounce hers. This time Magri accepted. As for Heimin, only the threat to make her dance as a simple *figurante* induced her to give up the idea of performing at Turin's Teatro Regio.

Magri was therefore paired with Anna Pallerini and received a salary of 275 *zecchini* for dancing in the troupe whose *primo ballerino* and choreographer was Francesco Salomoni, son of Giuseppe.[26] To follow the three acts of the first opera, *L'Olimpiade* (set by Hasse), Salomoni created character ballets in traditional style — *Festino e mascherata chinese* (Banquet and Chinese Masquerade), *I cacciatori burlati* (The Tricked Hunters), and a *ballo analogo*, *Di atleti vincitori* (Of Victorious Athletes); for the season's second opera, Giovanni Francesco de Majo's *Motezuma*, the three ballets used the same Spanish-Mexican setting as for the opera: *Forieri dell'armata spagnola con Messicani* (Heralds of the Spanish Army with Mexicans), *Europei che conducono fiere al serraglio di Motezuma* (Europeans Leading Beasts to Montezuma's Menagerie), and *Combatto di Don Chisciotte con il gigante*

25. This is almost certainly the same Antonia Heimin with whom Magri had danced during his second stay in Vienna, during the 1763–64 season; there she had originally performed as an actress in the German troupe, and only from the 1762–63 season as a *figurante* in the German theater (see Franz Hadamowsky, "Leitung, Verwaltung und ausübende Künstler des deutschen und französischen Schauspiels, der italienischen ernsten und heiteren Oper, des Balletts und der musikalischen Akademien am Burgtheater [Französischen Theater] und am Kärntnerthortheater [Deutschen Theater] in Wien 1754–1764," *Jahrbuch der Gesellschaft für Wiener Theaterforschung* 12 [1960]: 113–33 [124]). The modern form of her surname would be "Heim"; in earlier centuries the feminine suffix "-in" was commonly appended to German surnames of women.

26. See n. 20.

(Combat of Don Quixote with the Giant). The payment records of Turin's Teatro Regio also show that the impresarios paid "for sedan-chair porters to carry the dancer Magri home after he fell on the stage"[27] —evidence of the risks involved in being a *ballerino grottesco* who was expected to execute truly acrobatic movements. Magri may be referring to this season when he recounts the following episode in his *Trattato:* "To render this jump [the *salto ribaltato*] more difficult, I took it from both feet on the ground . . . Thus such great elevation was reached in this jump that the heads of the tallest men could pass under the [bend] of my knee; furthermore, the second time that I danced in Turin, H.R.H. the Duke of Savoy . . . made a Grenadier much taller than the supernumeraries come onto the Stage attired as he was in Theatrical dress, and with my said jump even he could pass under the [bend] of my knees."[28]

His salary of 275 *zecchini* was the same as that of his 1767–68 season at Turin but more than the 75 *zecchini* of his 1762 engagement. For comparison, we might take Salomoni, who in the same 1764–65 season received 330 *zecchini,* including payment for choreographing the ballets; the *prima ballerina seria,* Lucia Fabbri, was paid 300, while Magri's partner, the *prima grottesca* Anna Pallerini, received 200, and the *mezzo carattere* couple, Innocenzo Gambuzzi and Ippolita Prin, got 70. Only the extraordinarily famous French dancer Antoine Pitrot would earn significantly higher figures—500 *zecchini* in 1767—while the most prestigious singers received 800.[29]

After this Turin engagement, Magri returned to his native city, Naples, where for two seasons (1765–67) he was active at the Teatro San Carlo as *primo ballerino* and as the single "Director and Choreographer of the ballets" (Direttore e Compositore dei balli).[30] I discuss Magri's Neapolitan activities at greater length in chapter 4; here I will simply note that Benedetto Croce, too, in *I teatri di Napoli* (1891), records the

27. See Bouquet, *Il teatro di corte,* 1:314: "a portantini per portare a casa il ballerino Magri in occasione che è caduto sul palco."

28. Magri/Skeaping, 160; Magri, *Trattato,* 1:126–27 (chap. 60, sec. 9): "Io questo salto, per renderlo più difficile, lo solevo prendere con tutti due i piedi a terra. . . . Faceva un'alzata così grande in questo salto, che passava la testa degli uomini più alti per sotto la piegatura del ginocchio: anzi la seconda volta, che ballai a Torino, S.A.R. il Duca di Savoia . . . faceva uscire su'l Teatro il Granatiere più alto tra quei, che facevano le Comparse, in abito di Teatro, com'era, ed io con il detto mio salto il passava pur per sotto la piegatura del ginocchio."

29. On Pitrot, see n36 below.

30. The most up-to-date repertory of the Teatro San Carlo is contained in the volume *Il Teatro di S. Carlo, I: La cronologia (1737–1987),* ed. Carlo Marinelli Roscioni (Naples: Guida, 1987).

activity at the San Carlo of Gennaro Magri, "our Neapolitan, called Jennariello" (nostro napoletano detto Jennariello).[31] Croce also speaks of the woman who was *prima ballerina* and Magri's partner in these two years, Elisabetta Morelli, who likewise recently returned from a prestigious engagement in the Viennese theaters.

In autumn 1767 Magri reached another of the principal centers of European dance, the Regio Ducal Teatro in Milan. There he appeared (paired with Angiola Lazzari) in four ballets directed by Innocenzo Gambuzzi, as a dancer *fuori de' concerti*.[32] These 1767 Milanese productions provide some of the first examples of autonomous ballet scenarios, that is, texts printed separately from the opera libretto. Indeed, the libretto for Pietro Guglielmi's opera *Il ratto della sposa* (The Abduction of the Bride) announces, "The explanation of the ballets will be in a separate booklet, which will be distributed in the booth next to the theater";[33] no trace remains of this booklet, however, so we do not know the content of these ballets.

Teresa Stefani, *prima ballerina* at the Milanese theater that season, deserves special mention. She is relevant here not only as an artist but also as a figure in Magri's biography, for she was destined to become his wife. It is not known precisely when their marriage took place, but from 1776 onward opera librettos list her as Teresa Stefani Magri. Other documents, too, provide evidence of the marriage, in referring to Stefani Magri by the stage name Gennariella, analogous to her husband.[34]

Teresa Stefani was a ballerina of sufficient success to provoke demonstrations of enthusiasm on the part of the audience, not to mention the occasional anecdote. As Antonio Paglicci Brozzi wittily reported in 1767:

> Not only singers moved the Milanese to enthusiasm; ballerinas excited their passions so as sometimes to provoke grave disturbances, on flimsy pretexts. . . . The dancer De Stefani demanded from the impresario a satin costume, while they only wanted to give her one of plain taffeta.

---

31. Croce, *I teatri di Napoli*, 508.

32. See Kathleen Hansell's discussion of this term in chap. 1, 35. In "Theatrical Ballet," 216, Hansell explains, "Among the principal dancers, usually six or eight in number, two or three began from the later 1760s to be singled out under the heading *fuori de' concerti*. Surviving contracts disclose that this distinction meant that they were hired to perform exclusively in pas seuls, pas de deux, and similar soloistic movements; they were exempted from dancing in the movements for the full ensembles, the *concerti*."

33. "La spiegazione dei Balli sarà in un Libretto a parte, che si distribuirà nel Camerino annesso al Teatro."

34. See De Angelis, *Melodramma*, 235.

The beautiful dancer, piqued at such a refusal, claimed to be sick with
desolation, and all her admirers and partisans clamored over the wrong
done to the fair one, as the Romans in other times had clamored for the
destruction of Carthage. It became an affair of state, and snared in even
senators, ministers and the government, nor did the agitation cease until
the night in which the fair De Stefani was able to appear on stage in her
silk costume.[35]

Teresa Stefani danced often as a *prima ballerina di mezzo carattere* and sometimes as *prima ballerina seria,* but she seems never to have danced together
with Magri. She appeared at the Teatro del Cocomero in Florence in
1760 and in 1763, in ballets by Giovanni Guidetti and Vincenzo Galeotti;
in Venice at the Teatro San Samuele in 1761, under the direction of
Pierre Granget (or Granger, a dancer just arrived from Vienna's court
theater); and in Turin in 1763–64, where the choreographer was Auguste
Hus. Thereafter, under the surname Stefani Magri, she was again in Florence in 1776–77, performing as *prima ballerina,* whether in *balli di carattere*
by Francesco Martini or in serious ballets choreographed and danced in
by the great French dancer Antoine Pitrot—ballets that obtained such
success as to merit sonnets in honor of both leading dancers. Finally, she
performed in Livorno in 1777–78 and, again as *prima ballerina seria,* in
Venice in 1778–79, in ballets by Domenico Ricciardi.

For Carnival 1768 Magri again danced in Turin as *primo grottesco,*
paired as before with Elisabetta Morelli, in the troupe led by Antoine
Pitrot, whom Magri mentions several times in his *Trattato.*[36] Though considered by dance historians to be one of the pioneers of the *ballet d'action,*
at the time Pitrot was admired above all for his excellent execution of
*pirouettes.* In his *Trattato* Magri is lavish in his praise for his manner of performing an à *plomb:* "He does not remain in equilibrium on the ball of
one foot as others do but he raises the whole body on the tip of his big
toe."[37] (See also Sandra Noll Hammond's discussion in chap. 5, 121–22.)
The feat he describes is noteworthy: Magri seems to attribute to Pitrot
the beginning of *pointe* technique; and this and other of Pitrot's feats were

---

35. Antonio Paglicci Brozzi, *Il Regio Ducal Teatro di Milano nel secolo XVIII* (Milan: Ricordi,
1894), 89.

36. Antoine-Bonaventure Pitrot, born in Marseille sometime after 1720, was hired as a soloist
at the Opéra in Paris in 1744 and was later (1759) *premier danseur* at the Parisian Comédie Italienne.
Admired in Vienna, in Poland, Saxony, Russia, and at the King's Theatre in London, he spent the
last years of his life at the court of Parma and died after 1792.

37. Magri/Skeaping, 128; Magri, *Trattato,* 1:91 (chap. 45): "Lui non istà in equilibrio come gli
altri su mezza pianta di un piede: ma inalbera la vita tutta su la punta del maggior dito del piede."

(he says) wondrous to behold—"Things apparently supernatural yet borne out by the testimony of eye-witnesses all over Europe."[38] The ballets of this season treated various subjects, though all fell into the usual types: one in a pastoral setting, *Egle e Dafni,* another on a historical subject, *Trionfo romano* (Roman Triumph), and two character ballets, *Mulinari fiamminghi* (Flemish Millers), and *Carovana africana insultata dagli Arabi* (African Caravan Insulted by Arabs).

The 1768–69 season found Magri again in Naples, but only as a dancer. At the Teatro San Carlo, Onorato Viganò had in fact already been engaged as choreographer; he would remain there for the following four seasons, until 1773. For the 1768 marriage of King Ferdinand IV with Archduchess Maria Carolina of Austria, Magri danced alongside another son of Giuseppe Salomoni (he too called Giuseppe, but "di Portogallo").[39]

Following this season in Naples, for the next three years there is no trace of Magri in Italian theaters. One can speculate that he was active outside Italy, yet no such documentation has been found. It is certain, however, that these years did nothing to diminish his fame or the high caliber of his artistic credentials. His return to Naples in 1773 seems in fact to prove his celebrity: it occurred in the very year marking the stylistic revolution of the ballets at the San Carlo, occasioned by the arrival of Charles Le Picq and his introduction of the *ballet d'action* and Noverre's theories on heroic-tragic dance.[40] Magri's role in this context seems to have been that of upholding the tradition of character and grotesque ballets, or in any case, of less demanding works. It was a way of containing and balancing the impact of Le Picq's innovations, which not all Neapolitan audience members were prepared to accept. In fact, Magri had duties not only as *primo ballerino grottesco* but also as "Inventor and Director" (Inventore e Direttore) of the second ballets for every opera production, a role that is discussed in greater length in chapter 4. Here I wish only to emphasize how this sojourn in Naples in 1773–74 represents a return to his home port and seems to mark the end of his performing career. Afterward, he turned toward activities that were less public, such as *Maestro di Sala,* or director of balls that took place in connection with celebrations and receptions at the royal court, or the didactic vocation that

---

38. Magri/Skeaping, 128; Magri, *Trattato,* 1:91: "Cose, che pajono sopranaturali [e]ppure n'è testimonio di vista tutta l'Europa."

39. See n20.

40. For more information on Charles Le Picq, see chap. 4 in this volume, n16.

would have as its crowning achievement the publication of the *Trattato teorico-prattico di ballo*.

A home port, then, after an itinerant life that had led him to tread the most varied stages, to embrace a wide range of roles, and to rub shoulders with artistic partners of differing training and stylistic origins. This itinerant dimension, and the aplomb with which Magri coped with it, allow us rightfully to claim him as an exemplary figure in the historical panorama we are examining.

## Chronology of Magri's Career

Compiled by Patricia W. Rader, with assistance from Salvatore Bongiovanni, Bruce Alan Brown, and Kathleen K. Hansell

The information below does not necessarily represent the sum total of Magri's professional activity in the theater. Coverage is limited by the spotty survival of opera librettos and ballet descriptions or programs, as well as by differing degrees of completeness of the listings within them (and in secondary sources). Thus the listing of Magri merely as a "dancer" does not preclude the possibility of his having had a role as soloist for a given ballet. No references to Magri as a performer or choreographer are known for the period 1770–72, whether because of loss of records, injury to him, or for other reasons.

Information in this table is from original librettos or programs consulted personally by one of the compilers whenever possible but supplemented in many instances by catalogues and other secondary sources. Librettos for cities other than Naples rarely mention the exact dates of premieres, for instance, and some dates below were taken instead from articles in *The New Grove Dictionary of Opera*. Specific dates (where known) are for premieres; we have not attempted to account for further performances.

Entries under "Magri's function" begin with "dancer" and/or "choreog[rapher]," and continue with specific language from the source(s) (where available). Entries for choreographers in the fourth column sometimes include two names; titles of works are listed underneath the name of the choreographer responsible. "Ballet comp[oser]" refers to the composer of the *music* of the ballets. A question mark is given for Gluck during 1759, as attributions of the music of these ballets are based on payment records, rather than on specifically attributed musical sources;

similarly, there is ambiguity in payment records as to which ballet scores from 1763–64 were composed by Gluck and which by Gassmann. Entries in parentheses in the "ballet" column are based on predictable norms of performance of Viennese repertory.

The fifth column lists operas to which ballets that Magri danced in and/or choreographed were linked. But even where no opera is listed, one or more other stage pieces (e.g., spoken plays, or even operas, in rotating repertory) can be assumed to have been performed along with the ballet(s). The composer of an opera can *not* always be assumed to have been the composer of the music for the ballets (who was more often an orchestra member).

Abbreviations for seasons, theaters, and sources are explained at the end of the chronology. For further information, the reader is referred to the relevant chapters.

Table 2.1: *Chronology of Magri's Career*

| Date, season premiere (p) | City, theater | Magri's function, p. ref. in libretto | Choreog. / ballet comp., ballet title(s) | Librettist / opera comp., opera title | Sources, remarks |
|---|---|---|---|---|---|
| **1758** Aut. | Verona, Ac. fil. | dancer: Primo ballerino grottesco (p. [2]) | Pierre Alouard | Metastasio/*Traetta, Olimpiade* | RISM (scene and ballet descriptions on pp. 5–7) |
| **1759** | Vienna, Kth. | dancer | (Hilverding/*Starzer,* previous year's works still in repertoire) | | Gumpenhuber, Brown (Magri's participation presumed for all 1759–60 Vienna listings) |
| | Vienna, Kth. | dancer | Gumpenhuber/*Gluck?* various petits ballets: *Les Turcs en serail, La Mascarade, Les Jardiniers, Les Paisans de[s] montagnes, Les Moissonneurs, L'Hôpital des foux, Les Vendanges, Les Mineurs* | | Gumpenhuber, Brown |
| 16 April (p) | Vienna, Kth. | dancer | Vincenzo Turchi/*Gluck? La Foire* | | Gumpenhuber, Brown |
| 16 April (p) | Vienna, Kth. | dancer | [V. Turchi]/*Gluck? Le Port dans une isle de l'Archipel* | | Gumpenhuber, Brown |

Table 2.1: *continued*

| Date, season premiere (p) | City, theater | Magri's function, p. ref. in libretto | Choreog./ ballet comp., ballet title(s) | Librettist/ opera comp., opera title | Sources, remarks |
|---|---|---|---|---|---|
| 30 May (p) | Vienna, Kth. | dancer | C. Bernardi/ *Gluck?*, *Les Turcs* | | Gumpenhuber, Brown |
| 30 May (p) | Vienna, Kth. | dancer | C. Bernardi/ *Gluck?* *Les Savoiards* | | Gumpenhuber, Brown |
| 26 July (p) | Vienna, Kth. | dancer | C. Bernardi/ *Gluck?* *La Guinguette* | | Gumpenhuber, Brown |
| 26 July (p) | Vienna, Kth. | dancer | C. Bernardi/ *Gluck?* *Le Port de Marseille* | | Gumpenhuber, Brown |
| 26 Sept. (p) | Vienna, Kth. | dancer | C. Bernardi/ *Gluck?* *Les Jardiniers* | | Gumpenhuber, Brown |
| 3 Oct. (p) | Vienna, Kth. | dancer | C. Bernardi/ *Gluck?* *Les Perruquiers* | | Gumpenhuber, Brown |
| 3 Oct. (p) | Vienna, Kth. | dancer | C. Bernardi/ *Gluck?* *Le Marché aux poissons* | | Gumpenhuber, Brown |
| 21 Oct. (p) | Vienna, Kth. | dancer | C. Bernardi/ *Gluck?* *La Reccolte des fruits* | | Gumpenhuber, Brown |
| 17 Nov. (p) | Vienna, Kth. | dancer | C. Bernardi/ *Gluck?*, *Le Suisse* | | Gumpenhuber, Brown |
| 26 Dec. (p) | Vienna, Kth. | dancer | C. Bernardi/ *Gluck?* *Les Corsaires* | | Gumpenhuber, Brown |
| 26 Dec. (p) | Vienna, Kth. | dancer | C. Bernardi/ *Gluck?* *Le Prix de la danse* | | Gumpenhuber, Brown |
| **1760** Jan.– April | Vienna, Kth. | dancer | (C. Bernardi/ *Gluck?*, further repertory ballets) | | HZAB, Brown |

| | | | | | |
|---|---|---|---|---|---|
| 11 June (p; Fiera) | Padua, Nuovo | dancer | François Dupré | Migliavacca/ *B. Galuppi, Il Solimano* | Massaro, *Grove Opera* |
| 12 Nov. (p; Aut.) | Venice, S. Angelo | dancer/chor.: Ballerini . . . il Sig. Gennaro Magri . . . Li balli saranno di direzione, e composizione del Sig. Gennaro Magri di Napoli (p. 6) | Magri | Goldoni/ *Lampugnani, Amor contadino* | Alm 1168, RISM, *Grove Opera* |
| **1761** 18 Jan. (p; Carn.) | Venice, S. Angelo | dancer/chor.: Ballerini . . . il Sig. Gennaro Magri . . . Li balli saranno di direzione, e composizione del Sig. Gennaro Magri di Napoli (p. 4) | Magri, [*Ballo di carbona*], *Mascherata dedicata a Bacco* | Goldoni/ *Ciampi, Amore in caricatura* | Alm 1174, RISM, *Grove Opera* |
| Carn. | Venice, S. Angelo | dancer/chor.: Ballerini . . . il Sig. Gennaro Magri . . . Li balli saranno di direzione, e composizione del Sig. Gennaro Magri di Napoli (p. 6) | Magri | Goldoni/ *Latilla, Amore artigiano* | Alm 1172, RISM, *Grove Opera* |
| 10 May (p; Fiera) | Reggio Emilia, Pubblico | dancer | Giuseppe Salomoni, detto di Portogallo | Metastasio/ *Galuppi, Demofoonte* | Fabbri & Verti |

Table 2.1: continued

| Date, season premiere (p) | City, theater | Magri's function, p. ref. in libretto | Choreog./ ballet comp., ballet title(s) | Librettist/ opera comp., opera title | Sources, remarks |
|---|---|---|---|---|---|
| June (Fiera) | Padua, Nuovo | dancer: Primo ballerino | Marc Antonio Missoli | Metastasio/Galuppi, Demetrio | Massaro |
| 31 Dec. (p; Carn.) | Rome, Arg. | dancer: Ballarini uomini... Il Sig. Gennaro Magri (p. 10) | Pierre Alouard, L'accampamento di Tiridate Re Ruggiero e la maga Alcina | Metastasio/Traetta, Zenobia | RISM (ballet descriptions on pp. 10–11), Rinaldi |
| 1762 3 Feb (p; Carn.) | Rome, Arg. | dancer: primo ballerino grottesco | Pierre Alouard, Carnevale dei turchi o sia la festa e cerimonia del Ramadan Pantomima di maschere | Metastasio/Piccinni, Artaserse | Bongiovanni I-Rsc XVIII.17, Grove Opera, Rinaldi |
| 10 May (p; Fiera) | Reggio Emilia, Pubblico | dancer: Ballano a vicenda ...Sig. Gennaro Magri... (p. 8) | Pierre Alouard | Metastasio/Traetta, Alessandro nell'Indie | Fabbri & Verti, US-NYp |
| June ("solita Fiera") | Padua, Nuovo | dancer: signor Gennaro Magri (p. 12) | Pierre Alouard, Zefiro e Flora Le pescatrici romane | Lanfranchi Rossi/ B. Galuppi, Muzio Scevola | RISM (dance mvts. mentioned, p. 12), Bongiovanni |
| 26 Dec. (p; Carn.) | Turin, Regio | dancer: signor Gennaro Magri (p. VIII) | Auguste Hus, L'amore vinto dall'amicizia Il rapimento di Proserpina Di guerrieri romani | Metastasio/ G. F. de Majo, Catone in Utica | RISM (ballet descriptions on pp. 73–78), Bouquet/ Basso |

| | | | Auguste Hus/*Giuseppe Antonio Le Messier*, | Roccaforte/ *G. Scarlatti*, *Pelopida* | RISM (ballet descriptions on pp. 53–56), *Grove Opera*, Bouquet/Basso |
|---|---|---|---|---|---|
| **1763** 15 Jan. (p.; Carn.) | Turin, Regio | dancer (p. VIII) | *I selvatici* *La morte di Orfeo* *Amore, i piaceri, i giuochi e diversi caratteri* | | |
| 4 April (p) | Vienna, Bth. | dancer | Giuseppe Salomoni (senior)/*Gluck* or *Gassmann*, *La Nôce de village* | | Gumpenhuber, HZAB, Brown (Magri's participation presumed for all 1763–64 Vienna listings; German ballet troupe performed in Burgtheater until 9 July due to reconstruction of Kärntnertortheater) |
| 4 April (p) | Vienna, Bth. | dancer | G. Salomoni/*Gluck* or *Gassmann*, *La Pêche* | | Gumpenhuber, Brown |
| 7 June (p) | Vienna, Bth. | dancer | G. Salomoni/*Gluck* or *Gassmann*, *La Promenade* | | Gumpenhuber, Brown |
| 9 July (p) | Vienna, Kth. | dancer | G. Salomoni/*Gluck* or *Gassmann*, *L'Ecole de peinture* | | Gumpenhuber, Brown |
| 9 July (p) | Vienna, Kth. | dancer | G. Salomoni/*Gluck* or *Gassmann*, *Les Jardiniers* | | Gumpenhuber, Brown |
| 16 Aug. (p) | Vienna, Kth. | dancer | G. Salomoni/*Gluck* or *Gassmann*, *Le Campagnard visite à l'occasion de son jour de nom, ou L'Amante statue* | | Gumpenhuber, Brown |

Table 2.1: *continued*

| Date, season première (p) | City, theater | Magri's function, p. ref. in libretto | Choreog./ ballet comp., ballet title(s) | Librettist/ opera comp., opera title | Sources, remarks |
|---|---|---|---|---|---|
| 16 Aug. (p) | Vienna, Kth. | dancer | G. Salomoni/*Gluck* or *Gassmann*, *Un Port de mer dans la Provence* | | Gumpenhuber, Brown |
| 4 Oct. (p) | Vienna, Bth. | dancer, 4th ballet: le Sʳ genariello [in] pas de trois [with Onorato] Viganò [, Elisabetta] Morelli | Angiolini/*Traetta*, (4th:) di Sacerdoti e de' Grandi, che si dispongono alla partenza | Migliavacca/*Traetta*, *Ifigenia in Tauride* | RISM, Gumpenhuber, Brown |
| 8 Oct. (p) | Vienna, Kth. | dancer | G. Salomoni/*Gluck* or *Gassmann*, *Le Monde renversé* | | Gumpenhuber, Brown |
| 8 Oct. (p) | Vienna, Kth. | dancer | G. Salomoni/*Gluck* or *Gassmann*, *La Conversation angloise, ou Le François à Douvres* | | Gumpenhuber, Brown |
| 5 Nov. (p) | Vienna, Kth. | dancer | G. Salomoni/*Gluck* or *Gassmann*, *Les Vendages* | | Gumpenhuber, Brown |
| 8 Dec. (p) | Vienna, Kth. | dancer | G. Salomoni/*Gluck* or *Gassmann*, *Les Paveurs, ou L'Etudiant méchant* | | Gumpenhuber, Brown |
| 31 Dec. (p) | Vienna, Kth. | dancer | G. Salomoni/*Gluck* or *Gassmann*, *Les Indiens* | | Gumpenhuber, Brown |

| Date | Place | Dancer/role | Ballet | Opera | Sources |
|---|---|---|---|---|---|
| **1764** Jan.–April | Vienna, Kth. | dancer: "III Truppa" (*Indice*) | (G. Salomoni/Gluck or Gassmann, further repertory ballets) | | HZAB, Brown, *Indice* |
| 31 May ( p; Ascen.) | Venice, S. Giov. Grisostomo | dancer: il Sig. Gennaro Magri (p. 6) | chor. not named, but possibly Lépy; *Il giudizio di Paride*; *Li amori di Tirsi ed Eurilla interrotti dalla maga Falsirena* | Roccaforte/B. Galuppi, *Cajo Mario* | RISM, Alm 1221, *Grove Opera* |
| 16 June (p; Fiera) | Padua, Nuovo | dancer: Primo ballerino . . . il Sig. Gennaro Magri (p. 5) | Michele Dall'Agata | Metastasio/Traetta, *Antigono* | RISM, *Grove Opera*, Massaro |
| 5 Sept. (p) | Florence, Pergola | dancer: Primo ballerino grottesco | Vincent Saunier, *Admeto e Alceste*; *Le furberie d'amore* | Metastasio/Guglielmi, *Siroe* | Weaver & Weaver, *Grove Opera* |
| 26 Dec. (p; Carn.) | Turin, Regio | dancer: il Sig. Gennaro Magri (p. VIII) | Francesco Salomoni, detto di Vienna, *Festino, e mascherata chinese*; *I cacciatori burlati*; *Ballo di atleti vincitori* | Metastasio/Hasse, *L'Olimpiade* | RISM, *Grove Opera*, Bouquet/Basso |
| **1765** 19 Jan. (p; Carn.) | Turin, Regio | dancer: signor Gennaro Magri (p. VIII) | Francesco Salomoni, detto di Vienna, *Di forieri dell'armata spagnuolo con messicani Europei, che conducono fiere al serraglio di Motezuma*; *Combatto di D. Chisciotte con il gigante* | Cigna-Santi, after de Solis / G. F. de Majo, *Motezuma* [*Montezuma*] | RISM (ballet descriptions on pp. 59–60), Bouquet/ Basso, Sartori, *Grove Opera* |

Table 2.1: continued

| Date, season premiere (p) | City, theater | Magri's function, p. ref. in libretto | Choreog./ ballet comp., ballet title(s) | Librettist/ opera comp., opera title | Sources, remarks |
| --- | --- | --- | --- | --- | --- |
| 30 May (p) | Naples, S. Carlo | dancer/chor.: ballerino . . . Inventore e direttore de' balli Gennaro Magri napolitano | Magri, *Mercato del pesce in Amsterdam*; *Ritorno di soldati piemontesi alle loro case* | Metastasio/*Piccinni*, *Il re pastore* | Bongiovanni, I-Bl, L. 4149, Sartori |
| 4 Nov. (p) | Naples, S. Carlo | dancer/chor.: ballerino . . . Inventore e direttore de' balli Gennaro Magri napolitano | Magri, *Arrivo di viaggiatori nella posta di Vienna*; *Assalto di corsari lapponesi*; *Di diversi caratteri* | Pizzi/*Sacchini*, *Creso* | Bongiovanni, I-Rsc XVII.46, Sartori, *Grove Opera* |
| **1766** 30 May (p) | Naples, S. Carlo | chor. of secondo ballo Gennaro Magri napolitano | Magri | Metastasio/*Scolari*, *Antigono* | Sartori |
| 4 Nov. (p) | Naples, S. Carlo | dancer/chor.: ballerino . . . Inventore e direttore de' balli Gennaro Magri napolitano | Magri, *Di spagnoli e mori*; *Di zingari e scozzesi*; *Dagli amici di Rodrigo* | Pizzi/*Piccinni*, *Il gran Cid* | Bongiovanni, I-Rsc XVII.70, Sartori, *Grove Opera* |
| 27 Dec. | Naples, S. Carlo | dancer/chor.: ballerino . . . Inventore e direttore de' balli Gennaro Magri napolitano | Magri, *Ballo di mestieri*; *Festa di silvano* | Zeno/*Sacchini*, *Lucio Vero* | Bongiovanni, I-Nc, Rari 9.29/7, Sartori, Marinelli Roscioni, *Grove Opera* |

| | | | | | |
|---|---|---|---|---|---|
| **1767** 20 Jan. (p) | Naples, S. Carlo | dancer/chor.: ballerino.... Inventore e direttore de' balli | Magri, *Festa da ballo* [ballo analogo] *Un bassà turco Pantomimo tra Pulcinella, Arlecchino e Coviello* | Bonechi/*Mysliveček, Bellerofonte* | Bongiovanni, I-Rsc XVII.24, *Grove Opera* |
| 1 Aug. (p; Aut.) | Milan, Regio Ducal | dancer: ballerino, "fuori dei concerti" | Innocenzo Gambuzzi | Martinelli/*Guglielmi, Il ratto della sposa* | Bongiovanni, I-Rsc Fondo Carvalhaes v. 11.3, *Gazzetta di Milano, Grove Opera*. Primi ballerini: I. Gambuzzi, T. Steffani. "Spiegazione dei balli in un libretto a parte" (now lost) |
| 7 Sept. (p; Aut.) | Milan, Regio Ducal | dancer: ballerino, "fuori dei concerti" | Innocenzo Gambuzzi, *Amore trionfante della magia Vindemia alla napoletana* | Goldoni/*Fischietti, La ritornata di Londra* | Bongiovanni, I-Rsc Fondo Carvalhaes v. 11.4, *Gazzetta di Milano, Grove Opera*. Primi ballerini: I Gambuzzi, T. Steffani |
| 26 Dec. (p; Carn.) | Turin, Regio | dancer: Nomi de' ballerini, e ballerine: ... Sig. Gennaro Magri (p. VII) | Antoine Pitrot, *Egle e Dafni Trionfo romano Popolo festeggiante* | Metastasio/*Mysliveček, Il trionfo di Clelia* | RISM (ballet descriptions on pp. 59–61), *Indice, Grove Opera* |
| **1768** 23 Jan. (p; Carn.) | Turin, Regio | dancer: Nomi de' ballerini, e ballerine: ... Sig. Gennaro Magri (p. VII) | Antoine Pitrot/*Le Messier, Di mulinari fiamminghi Carovana africana insultata dagli arabi Mascherata* | Pizzi/*Cafaro, Creso* | RISM, *Indice, Grove Opera*, Sartori |

Table 2.1: *continued*

| Date, season premiere (p) | City, theater | Magri's function, p. ref. in libretto | Choreog./ ballet comp., ballet title(s) | Librettist/ opera comp., opera title | Sources, remarks |
|---|---|---|---|---|---|
| 30 May (p) | Naples, S. Carlo | dancer: primo grottesco fuori concerti | Onorato Viganò, *Gefalo, ed Aurora*; *Pantomimo di contadini e lavandare* | Metastasio/Sacchini, *Alessandro nell'Indie* | Giordano, Marinelli Roscioni |
| 4 June (p) | Naples, S. Carlo | dancer | Giuseppe Salamoni, detto di Portogallo | Basso Bassi/Paisiello, *Peleo e Teti* | Giordano, Marinelli Roscioni |
| 13 Aug. (p) | Naples, S. Carlo | dancer: primo grottesco | Onorato Viganò, *Ballo de' popoli tributarj del re Argo*; *Ballo di scultori*; *Il safi tradito* | Metastasio/de Majo, *Ipemnestra* | Giordano, *Grove Opera* |
| 4 Nov. (p) | Naples, S. Carlo | dancer: primo grottesco | Onorato Viganò, *Passaggio di alcune truppe moscovite*; *Vecchi delusi ne' loro sponsali, per virtù d'un libro maggico*; *Popoli sudditi di Artaserse* | Metastasio/Piccinni, *Artaserse* | Giordano, Marinelli Roscioni |
| **1769** 12 Jan. (p) | Naples, S. Carlo | dancer: primo grottesco | Onorato Viganò, *Ballo di montagnari*; *Il convitato di pietra, o sia D. Giovanni tenorio*; *Ballo di pastori e pastorelle* | Metastasio/Cafaro, *L'Olimpiade* | Giordano, *Grove Opera* |
| **1773** 30 May (p) | Naples, S. Carlo | choreographer: Inventore e Direttore del Secondo Ballo | Charles Le Picq, *Rinaldo e Armida*; Gennaro Magri, *Alla ricerca d'un tesoro* | Metastasio/Borghi, *Il trionfo di Clelia* | Bongiovanni, I-Rsc 15377, Sartori, Marinelli Roscioni |

| 13 Aug. (p) | Naples, S. Carlo | choreographer: Inventore e Direttore del Secondo Ballo Gennaro Magri napolitano | Charles Le Picq, *Ercole e Dejanira* Ballo degli sposi romani con le donzelle sabine, "da eseguirsi al principio del drama" Gennaro Magri, *La festa della lanterna* | Metastasio/ Mysliveček, *Romolo ed Ersilia* | Bongiovanni, I-Nc, Rari 10.7.17 (6), I-Fm, Mel. 2032.2, Sartori, Marinelli Roscioni |
| 4 Nov. (p) | Naples, S. Carlo | dancer/chor.: Primo Ballerino Grottesco . . . , Inventore e Direttore del Secondo Ballo | Le Picq, *Il sagrifizio d'Ifigenia* Magri, second ballet | Metastasio/ Insanguine, *Adriano in Siria* | Sartori, Marinelli Roscioni |
| **1774** 12 Jan. (p; Carn.) | Naples, S. Carlo | dancer/chor.: Primo Ballerino Grottesco . . . , Inventore e Direttore del Secondo Ballo Gennaro Magri napolitano | Le Picq, *Aminta e Clori* Magri, Pantomimo con maschere: Pantalone e sua figlia, Truffaldino, Pulcinella, Flaminia [Le Picq?], *Da' Seguaci di Alessandro* | Metastasio/Piccinni, *Alessandro nell'Indie* | I-Fm, Mel. 2292.5 (ballet descriptions on pp. 8–13); Marinelli Roscioni |

*Notes:*

Italian librettos rendered French choreographers' names in a variety of ways, usually attempting to approximate the French pronunciation, e.g.:

Alouard = Alovar, Alouvar, Alloar, Alloardi, etc. (the first name usually given in Italian as Pietro)

Pitrot = Antoine Pitrot (the first name is often given in Italian as Antonio)

Saunier = Soniè (the first name is often given in Italian as Vincenzo)

*Season abbreviations:*

Ascen.    Feast of the Ascension: in Venice, a secondary opera season; the Feast itself is celebrated 40 days after Easter

Fiera    Fair; in Padua, "la solita fiera di giugno" (the usual June fair)

Aut.    Autumn opera season

Carn.    Carnevale (Carnival): variable from place to place, but generally from St. Stephen's Day (26 Dec.) to the beginning of Lent

*Theater abbreviations:*

Florence, Pergola    Florence, Teatro della Pergola

Milan, Regio Ducal    Milan, Regio Ducal Teatro

Naples, S. Carlo    Naples, Teatro San Carlo

Padua, Nuovo    Padua, Teatro Nuovo

Reggio Emilia, Pubblico    Reggio Emilia, Teatro dell'illustrissimo Pubblico

Rome, Arg.    Rome, Teatro di Torre Argentina

Turin, Regio    Turin, Teatro Regio (or Regio Teatro)

Venice, S. Angelo    Venice, Teatro di Sant'Angelo

Venice, S. Giov. Grisostomo    Teatro Grimani in San Giovanni Grisostomo

Verona, Ac. fil.    Verona, Teatro Nuovo dell'Accademia filarmonica

Vienna, Bth.    Vienna, Burgtheater (French, or court theater)

Vienna, Kth.    Vienna, Kärntnertortheater (German theater)

*Source abbreviations:*

Alm    Irene Alm, *Catalog of Venetian Librettos at the University of California, Los Angeles* (Berkeley: University of California Press, 1993)

Bongiovanni    Salvatore Bongiovanni, "Gennaro Magri e il *Trattato teorico-prattico di ballo*" (unpublished *tesi di laurea*, Università degli Studi "La Sapienza," Rome, 1991)

Bouquet/Basso    Bouquet, Marie-Thérèse, *Il teatro di corte, dalle origini al 1788, Storia del Teatro Regio di Torino*, 5 vols., ed. Alberto Basso. (Turin: Cassa di Risparmio, 1976–1988); vol. 5 = *Cronologie,* ed. Alberto Basso

Brown    Bruce Alan Brown, chapter 3: "Magri in Vienna: The Apprenticeship of a Choreographer," this volume

Fabbri & Verti    Paolo Fabbri and Roberto Verti, *Due secoli di teatro per musica a Reggio Emilia: Repertorio cronologico delle opere e dei balli, 1645–1857* (Reggio Emilia: Edizioni del Teatro Municipale Valli, 1987)

Giordano    Gloria Giordano, "Gaetano Grossatesta, an Eighteenth-Century Italian Choreographer and Impresario, Part Two: The Choreographer-impresario in Naples," *Dance Chronicle* 23:2 (2000): 133–91

*Grove Opera*    Relevant composer articles, *New Grove Dictionary of Opera*, ed. Stanley Sadie (London: Macmillan, 1992)

Gumpenhuber  Philipp Gumpenhuber, Manuscript chronicles: 1758 Kärntnertortheater and Burgtheater (Harvard Theatre Coll.); 1759, 1761, 1763 Kärntnertortheater (Harvard Theatre Collection); 1761–63 Burgtheater (Musiksammlung, Austrian National Library, Vienna)

HZAB  Vienna, Hofkammerarchiv, Hofzahlamtsbücher

*Indice*  *Indice de' teatrali spettacoli* (title varies; published annually in Milan, 1764–1800, thereafter irregularly; modern facsimile edition as *Un almanacco drammatico: L'indice de' teatrali spettacoli 1764–1823*, ed. Roberto Verti, 2 vols. [Pesaro: Fondazione Rossini, 1996])

I-Bl  Bologna, Conservatorio di Musica G. B. Martini

I-Fm  Florence, Biblioteca Marucelliana

I-Nc  Naples, Conservatorio di Musica S. Pietro a Majella

I-Rsc  Rome, Biblioteca del Conservatorio di Santa Cecilia (+ catalog no.)

Marinelli Roscioni  Carlo Marinelli Roscioni, *La cronologia 1737–1987*, in *Il Teatro di San Carlo*, vol. 2, ed. Rafaele Ajello, et al. (Naples: Guida, 1987)

Massaro  Maria Nevilla Massaro, "Il ballo pantomimo al Teatro Nuovo di Padova (1751–1830)," *Acta Musicologica* 57:2 (1985): 215–75. [240–75 = "Elenco cronologico dei balli rappresentati al Teatro Nuovo di Padova 1751–1830"]

Rinaldi  Mario Rinaldi, *Due secoli di musica al Teatro Argentina*, 3 vols. (Florence: Olschki, 1978)

RISM  US RISM libretto project; most librettos in Alfred Schatz Collection, Library of Congress, some also in other locations

I=Rsc  Rome, Biblioteca del Conservatorio di Santa Cecilia (+ catalog no.)

Sartori  Claudio Sartori, *I libretti italiani a stampa dalle origini al 1800: catalogo analitico con 16 indici* (Cuneo: Bertola & Locatelli, 1990–95)

US-NYp  Dance Division, New York Public Library for the Performing Arts (original librettos)

Weaver & Weaver  Robert Lamar Weaver and Norma Wright Weaver, *A Chronology of Music in the Florentine Theater*, vol. 2: *Operas, Prologues, Farces, Intermezzos, Concerts, and Plays with Incidental Music, 1751–1800* (Detroit: Harmonie Park Press, 1993)

# 3

# Magri in Vienna

## *The Apprenticeship of a Choreographer*

### BRUCE ALAN BROWN

Strictly speaking, any portrait one might attempt to sketch of Gennaro Magri during his time in Vienna—two theatrical seasons, four years apart (1759–60 and 1763–64)—will seem strangely lacking of a center. The diaries, librettos, and programs on which we largely depend for information on the city's spectacles are almost entirely silent on this dancer—as indeed they are concerning most of his colleagues; nor is he mentioned in the few contemporary published accounts of Viennese ballet. But in a way, Magri and Vienna can be seen as illuminating each other reciprocally: an examination of the setting in which he worked as a dancer (though not yet as a choreographer), including the impressive group of his professional colleagues, can help us understand the directions in which his talents later developed; and the information contained in his *Trattato teorico-prattico di ballo* of 1779 is rightly considered by dance historians to be one of the most relevant sources on the dance techniques employed not just in Italian ballet but also in the epochal pantomime ballets created in Vienna during these years. Magri's second Viennese sojourn, in 1763–64, came in the midst of Gasparo Angiolini's series of complete danced dramas with programs—though Magri missed the premieres of all three of them.[1] But certain clues in his *Trattato* suggest that he was indeed attentive to the activities of his Viennese colleagues, who, besides Angiolini, included such historically resonant names as Viganò,[2] Boccherini, and Bournonville.

A fundamental feature of Magri's situation in Vienna, which distinguished it from several of his later places of employment, was the city's cosmopolitanism. As the capital of a multinational, multilingual empire, the city required spectacles worthy of a broadly European audience (or so Empress Maria Theresia thought), composed largely of foreign ambassadors, government officials, and the high nobility from throughout the empire (the latter groups overlapping significantly, and including numerous Bohemians, Hungarians, Tuscans, Lombards, and so forth). The ballet troupes of the city's two theaters, the Burgtheater (the court, or French theater) and Kärntnertortheater (the German theater, near the Carinthian Gate), both administered by the court, reflected this cosmopolitanism, drawing not only on local talent but also on dancers and choreographers from France, Germany, and various parts of Italy. A second basic fact about Viennese theatrical life was the relatively long history already (by the late 1750s) of independent pantomime ballets. Starting in 1742 (according to Angiolini's later account), the dancer and choreographer Franz Hilverding had banished masks from the dancers' faces and substituted more "natural characters" in national dances (each with its own well-structured plot) for the indecent antics "of Harlequins, of Pulcinellas, of Giangurgolos, etc."[3] These ballets could serve as *intermezzi* for operas, but more frequently functioned as independent works, given between performances of spoken plays and/or (in the French theater) *opéras-comiques*. While such developments were not unique to Vienna, no other European capital at this time could boast of equivalently steady progress toward a rational model of expressive theatrical dance. The recovery in recent years of a copious manuscript chronicle of performances and rehearsals in both Viennese theaters (with full rosters of

---

1. These were *Don Juan* (1761), *Citera assediata* (1762), and *Sémiramis* (1765). Magri likely witnessed the revival of the first of these works, beginning on 5 April 1763.

2. Magri twice mentions his Viennese colleague Onorato Viganò in his *Trattato*, in describing various sorts of caprioles; see pt. 1, chap. 60, secs. 3 and 12.

3. Gasparo Angiolini, *Lettere di Gasparo Angiolini a Monsieur Noverre sopra i balli pantomimi* (Milan: G. B. Bianchi, 1773), 12–14. On Hilverding's early career, see also Bruce Alan Brown, "Hilverding, [Hilferding] van Wewen, Franz (Anton Christoph)," *New Grove* (rev. ed.), 11:519–20, and Brown, *Gluck and the French Theatre in Vienna* (Oxford: Clarendon, 1991), chap. 5.

performers and synopses of a number of the ballets), prepared for Count
Giacomo Durazzo by Philipp Gumpenhuber, assistant director of the
Burgtheater's ballet troupe, allows one to follow this progress literally
day by day.[4]

Magri's arrival in the Habsburg capital in 1759 came shortly after the departure of Hilverding for the Russian court in St. Petersburg, and Viennese ballet was consequently in some disarray — all the more, since Hilverding had served as choreographer for both theaters. The court's chief
of protocol, Count (later Prince) Johann Joseph Khevenhüller-Metsch,
noted in his diary that the ballets had "suffered a great loss" through the
choreographer's departure, and also that "one of our best ballerinas,
Santini [i.e., Santina Zanuzzi], has been sent away from here on account
of bad conduct, by special order of the empress."[5] (The moral laxity of
certain Italian dancers is a recurring theme also in contemporary polemical literature on ballet.) Angiolini, Hilverding's successor in the Burgtheater, initially felt quite inadequate for the task he had inherited, as he
later recounted.[6] In the German theater no successor to Hilverding was
appointed at first, ballets being composed by a variety of choreographers. In both theaters the ballet music, too, was in new hands, Hilverding's longtime collaborator Joseph Starzer having followed him to Russia. Starzer's replacement, Christoph Gluck (unofficial music director in
the Burgtheater since about 1754), possessed a European reputation as
a composer of Italian operas, but as yet had little experience in writing
music for the dance. One important element of continuity was the court-
appointed director of the two theaters, Count Giacomo Durazzo. Concerning ballet in Vienna, a correspondent for the *Journal encyclopédique*
wrote that "Count Durazzo . . . shares the merit of invention with the
composers [i.e., choreographers], without contending with them for the
glory."[7] This had been the case even before Hilverding left for Russia.

4. Philipp Gumpenhuber, "Repertoire de Tous les Spectacles, qui ont été donné au Theatre pres
de la Cour [. . . de la Ville]": Österreichische Nationalbibliothek, Vienna, Musiksammlung, Mus. Hs.
34580a-c (Burgtheater volumes for 1761–63); Harvard University, Theatre Collection, MS Thr. 248–
48.3 (volumes for both theaters for 1758, and for the German theater only for 1759, 1761, and 1763).
5. Rudolf Graf Khevenhüller-Metsch and Dr. Hanns Schlitter, eds., *Aus der Zeit Maria Theresias.
Tagebuch des Fürsten Johann Joseph Khevenhüller-Metsch, kaiserlichen Obersthofmeisters 1742–1776*, 7 vols. (Vienna: Adolf Holzhausen; Leipzig and Berlin: Wilhelm Engelmann, 1907–25), entry of Tuesday,
15 May 1759.
6. Angiolini, *Lettere*, 16.
7. *Journal encyclopédique*, 15 December 1759, 132: "M. le Comte de Durazzo . . . partage le mérite
de l'invention avec les compositeurs, sans leur en disputer la gloire."

Though Marian Hannah Winter states, "It is certain that there was a 'Hilverding' or 'Vienna' style which characterized the group which had worked under him,"[8] after 1758 the two theaters' ballet troupes became increasingly distinct in composition and character. Describing Charles Bernardi's ballet *Les Perruquiers* (The Wigmakers; synopsis and stage design reproduced in Winter, *Pre-Romantic Ballet,* 105), given in the Kärntnertortheater during 1759, a writer for the *Journal étranger* enthused, "You will be able to imagine the vivacity of this pantomime when you learn that it is made up exclusively of Italian dancers."[9] The German theater's ballet troupe as a whole that year included only eight Italians out of a total of eighteen dancers, but during the next year fully thirteen members of the company to which Magri now belonged were Italians.

Count Durazzo—who was in a position to dictate as well as judge—told his Parisian theatrical agent Charles-Simon Favart that in the German theater "one dances a strong and elevated genre."[10] It is conceivable that Durazzo meant "elevated" in the aesthetic sense, but a more technical interpretation, having to do with elevation and leaps (defining characteristics of "balli . . . in aria," as Lambranzi called them),[11] is more likely. In view of Magri's Neapolitan origins, we might imagine that his style of dance was also strongly gestural—more so even than that of some of his fellow Italians, as the inhabitants of Naples were renowned since ancient times for their propensity to express themselves through gestures.[12]

In the Burgtheater, French dancers predominated numerically, though they were presided over by the Florentine Angiolini. The choreographer later recalled modestly that the success of his early ballets was

8. Winter, *Pre-Romantic Ballet,* 93. Indeed, Hilverding's ballets were copied or imitated across Europe in much the same way that Noverre's were in later years (as that choreographer complained). Hilverding's ballet *Psyché et l'Amour* (Psyche and Cupid) of 1752, for instance (a ballet that was reported on in the international press), was likely the source of Vincenzo Galeotti's ballet *La favola di Psiche* (The Fable of Psyche) for Milan (Carnival 1768–69), particularly as Galeotti had danced in Vienna in 1760; see the description in app. 2.

9. *Journal étranger,* May 1760, 108: "Vous imaginerez la vivacité de cette Pantomime quand vous sçaurez qu'il étoit uniquement composé de Danseurs Italiens."

10. "on danse un genre fort, et Elevé"; letter of 26 October 1763 (Paris, Bibliothèque de l'Opéra, Fonds Favart , Carton I, A, II ), quoted in Brown, *Gluck and the French Theatre,* 158.

11. Gregorio Lambranzi, *Neue und curieuse theatralische Tantz-Schul* (Nuremberg: Johann Jacob Wolraub, 1716), trans. Friderica Derra de Moroda as *New and Curious School of Theatrical Dancing,* ed. Cyril W. Beaumont (New York: Dance Horizons, 1966), title page. On the Italian aerial style, see also Hansell, chap. 1.

12. On this subject see Andrea de Jorio, *La mimica degli antichi investigata nel gestire napoletano* (Naples: Fibreno, 1832), trans. and ed. with an introduction and notes by Adam Kendon, as *Gesture in Naples and Gesture in Classical Antiquity* (Bloomington: Indiana University Press, 2000).

owed "to the ability—which was great in those times—of the dancers who performed them."[13] Durazzo's recruitment efforts with respect to this company were concerned mainly with performers schooled in "la danse noble," or "le genre sérieux," even though (as he told Favart) the public "does not generally enjoy their genre of dance."[14] For this theater directly adjacent to the imperial palace, and serving its pleasures, dance in the serious style was self-evidently necessary. But the "aerial" style of dancing was by no means unknown in the French theater. One spectator reported of Angiolini and Gluck's exotic ballet *La Halte des Calmouckes* (presented there in March of 1761) that "both male and female dancers leapt prodigiously high."[15]

The relative strength of Italian, French, and native talent was an issue that was hardly confined to ballet, or even to the theater, during this period. As a natural consequence of the Habsburg empire's extensive territorial possessions and political entanglements in Italy, the Italian language, and likewise Italian poetry, music, and the other arts, were dominant at the Viennese court during the seventeenth and early eighteenth centuries. The court's official poets were Italians—notably, Apostolo Zeno (from 1718 to 1729) and Pietro Metastasio (from 1730 until 1782)—as were a great many imperial musicians, composers, and dancers. But by the 1750s Italian cultural influences were waning, and the French language and letters gaining in currency and prestige, abetted by the influx of francophones in the entourage of the empress's consort, Francis Stephen of Lorraine (Holy Roman Emperor from 1745 until his death), and by the 1756 *renversement des alliances*, whereby Austria became a political ally of her long-time adversary France. In Viennese dance, too, French influence was on the rise. Already in the 1730s Hilverding had been sent to Paris for training, and by the 1750s even the Italian dancers in the court's theaters would have had extensive prior contacts with the legions of French dancers and choreographers active on the peninsula.[16]

13. "all' abilità, che era grande in que' tempi, de' ballerini esecutori"; Angiolini, *Lettere*, 16.

14. "ne goute pas en général le genre de leur danse"; letter of 13 June 1760, quoted in Brown, *Gluck and the French Theatre*, 158.

15. "Danseurs et danseuses sauterent prodigieusement haut"; Vienna, Staatsarchiv, diary of Carl von Zinzendorf, entry for 23 March 1761.

16. For an exploration of cultural exchange between Italy and the Viennese court, see Don Neville, "Metastasio and the Image of Majesty in the Austro-Italian Baroque," in *Italian Culture in Northern Europe in the Eighteenth Century*, ed. Shearer West (Cambridge: Cambridge University Press, 1999), 140–58.

Gennaro Magri was hired for the theatrical year 1759–60 (the season beginning at Easter) jointly with Bettina Buggiani — apparently his partner, the two of them receiving the considerable sum of 3,093 florins and 45 kreuzer per year, an amount equal to 750 "ordinary" ducats.[17] (By way of comparison: no orchestral player during this period earned more than 300 florins; a virtuoso singer, on the other hand, could earn in excess of 2,000 florins in a single quarter of the theatrical year.) Court payment records provide almost the only means of ascertaining pairings in the German theater's ballet troupe, first, because no programs were printed for ballets given there and, second, because even Gumpenhuber's inhouse chronicle of theatrical activities distinguishes only between soloists ("danseurs seuls" or "premiers danseurs") and "figurants" (those who simply "dance in the ballets"). Designations such as "grottesco," "di mezzo carattere," and so forth generally do not appear in printed Viennese sources, though such distinctions were recognized informally (as one sees from Durazzo's correspondence), sometimes also in relation to the style of entire works.[18]

According to the *Journal étranger,* Buggiani had danced at the Comédie Française in Paris for three years prior to coming to Vienna.[19] But Winter reports that her Parisian engagement was actually at the Opéra Comique,[20] and this is confirmed by garbled but still recognizable listings of "Botina Beviani, *Italienne,*" and "Mlle Bucany" respectively in the almanac *Les Spectacles de Paris* for 1752 and 1753 (see also chap. 7 in this volume).[21] Buggiani stayed on in Vienna after Magri's departure, receiving 1,546 florins, 52½ kreuzer (equivalent to 375 ordinary ducats) for each of the next two seasons (1760–61 and 1761–62). This amount, precisely half of the pair's original 750 ducats, suggests that she and Magri were

17. Vienna, Hofkammerarchiv, Hofzahlamtsbücher, No. 354, 30 June to 28 September 1759: "Pugiani und Magri zusammen [. . . . .] 3093 [fl.] 45 [xr.]" (The volume for the first quarter of the theatrical year 1759–60 is missing, but would presumably have shown the same information.) The often quite irregular amounts in florins in the payment books in many cases convert to round numbers in either "ordinary" ducats or Cremnitz ducats (the latter so-called after their place of minting, in what was then a part of Hungary). These were evidently the monetary units specified in the contracts of most better-paid artists. At this time there were 4 1/8 florins per ordinary ducat, and 4 1/5 per Cremnitz ducat.

18. Bernardi's *Le Suisse* of 1759, for instance, is described as being "arrangé . . . d'une maniere grotesque."

19. *Journal étranger,* May 1760, 108–9.

20. Winter, *Pre-Romantic* Ballet, 144.

21. *Nouveau Calendrier historique des théatres de l'Opera, et des Comedies Françoise et Italienne et des Foires* (known in later years as *Les Spectacles de Paris* ) (Paris: Duchesne, 1753), 150; (Paris: Duchesne, 1754), 82. The year covered by each volume in this series is actually the year before that of publication.

considered of equal worth to the troupe during the year in which they performed together. (How the salary for a pair of dancers was divided is otherwise impossible to ascertain; perhaps this was a matter left to the discretion of the dancers themselves.) During 1761 her regular partner seems to have been Onorato Viganò.[22]

The company that Magri joined in 1759 was a distinguished one, as much for its members' future accomplishments and family connections as for their reputations at that date (see table 3.1).[23] Hannah Winter has called attention to the prior choreographic experience of several members of the company, including Giovanni Guidetti, and Onorato Viganò (who only joined the troupe in January of 1760). However, Winter is mistaken in claiming that the Kärntnertortheater ballet troupe for 1759 included Pierre Bernard Michel, a grotesque dancer mentioned admiringly by Magri in his *Trattato*, and who following this season performed in several of Magri's ballets at the Teatro di Sant'Angelo in Venice (where Magri functioned as dancer and choreographer).[24] There is no question, though, that two members of the numerous Boccherini family were dancing in Vienna at this time: Giovanni Gastone in the German company and Maria Ester in the French. Their father and brother had been members of the Kärntnertortheater orchestra the year before and would return again; Giovanni Gastone would later attain prominence as a librettist for Haydn, Gassmann, and Salieri. In 1761, and perhaps already in 1759, he seems to have partnered with Camilla Paganini, supporting her in high leaps, according to the theater-going diarist Count Carl von Zinzendorf.[25]

In terms of salary, Magri was nearly if not quite the best paid performer in his own company, though far behind the stars of the French ballet troupe. The brothers Vincenzo and Francesco Turchi, both long-time members of the German company, received 750 "Cremnitz"

22. According to the 1761 "État" of the troupe in Gumpenhuber's chronicle.

23. The roster in table 3.1 is taken from Gumpenhuber's 1759 chronicle for the German theater, supplemented by information from theater payment records.

24. Winter, *Pre-Romantic Ballet*, 94; see also the librettos (all by Goldoni) to *Amor contadino*, *Amore in caricatura*, and *L'amore artigiano* in the Schatz Collection, Library of Congress. Magri's praise for Michel comes in chap. 60, on caprioles (sec. 9). Though Gumpenhuber's chronicle for 1759 indeed mentions a "Michel" (no other name being given), no such dancer appears in the payment records for that year. Entries in Gumpenhuber's volumes for later years make clear that the dancer in question is Michael Pösinger, whose stage name was "le Sieur Michel."

25. Entry for Saturday, 9 May 1761 (Kärntnertortheater): "Les Ballets étoient bons, le premier [*La Foire*] representoient [*sic*] une foire, des Marechaux qui battoient le fer, on voyoit des Etincelles, La Paganini en habit couleur de Caffé sauta bien haut, étant soutenüe par Boccarini." (The ballets were good, the first showed a fairground, blacksmiths beating iron, you could see sparks, Paganini in a coffee-colored costume jumped quite high, being supported by Boccherini.)

Table 3.1: *The Kärntnertortheater ballet company in 1759, with salaries*

| Men | fl./xr.* | remarks | equivalent in ducats |
|---|---|---|---|
| Guidetti [Giovanni] | 1856.15 | | 450 ordinary ducats |
| Turchi *ainé* [Vincenzo] | (½? of) 3,150.00 | w/brother Francesco | 750 Cremnitz ducats |
| Magri *detto* Genariello | (½? of) 3,093.45 | w/Buggiani | 750 ordinary ducats |
| Viganò [Onorato] | 364.30 | Jan.–Feb. only | |
| Constantini [Cortolo] | 300.00 | | |
| Boccherini [Giovanni Gastone] | 250.00 | | |
| Hornung [Joseph] | 30.00 | per month | |
| Pösinger [Michael ("Michel")] | 22.00 | per month | |
| Seve [Ignaz] | 20.00 | per month | |
| Hopp [Johann] | 12.00 | per month; last quarter only | |
| [Bernardi, Charles] | (part of) 1,344.00 | as choreographer; w/eldest daughter | 320 Cremnitz ducats |

| Women | fl./xr. | remarks | equivalent in ducats |
|---|---|---|---|
| Buggiani [Bettina] | (½? of) 3,093.45 | w/Magri | 750 ordinary ducats |
| Paganini *ainée* [Camilla] | (½? of) 2,142.00 | w/sister | 510 Cremnitz ducats |
| Paganini *cadette* [Elena] | (½? of) 2,142.00 | w/sister | 510 Cremnitz ducats |
| Fusi [Josepha] | 1092.00 | | 260 Cremnitz ducats |
| Scotti [Barbara] | 18.00 | per month | |
| Giropoldi [Andriana] | 14.00 | per month | |
| Gavazzi [Giulia] | 14.00 | per month | |
| Leinhauss | ? | from spoken theatre? | |

*Note:*
*One florin = 60 kreuzer; one "ordinary" ducat = 4 1/8 florins; one "Cremnitz" ducat = 4 1/5 florins

ducats, worth some 50 florins more than Magri and Buggiani's 750 ordinary ducats. Guidetti by himself was paid 1,856 florins, 15 kreuzer per year, or 450 ordinary ducats. But the *premiers danseurs* in the Burgtheater received astronomical salaries in comparison: 5,362 florins, or approximately 1,300 ordinary ducats for Louise Joffroi and her husband, Pierre Bodin, and 5,460 florins, or 1,300 Cremnitz ducats, yearly for Angiolini and his wife, Teresa Fogliazzi; Angiolini earned an additional 1,000 florins annually for composing ballets for the French theater.

Table 3.2: *The Kärntnertortheater ballet company in 1763, with salaries*

| Men | fl./xr. | remarks | equivalent in ducats |
| --- | --- | --- | --- |
| *pas de deux:* | | | |
| Genariello [Magri] | 2062.00 | | ~500 ordinary ducats |
| Turchi *ainé* [Vincenzo] | (½? of) 3,360.00 | w/brother Francesco | 800 Cremnitz ducats |
| Beccari [Filippo] | (½? of) 3,300.00 | w/sister | 800 ordinary ducats |
| Morelli [Domenico] | (½? of) 2,887.00 | w/sister | ~700 ordinary ducats |
| Hornung [Joseph] | 50.00 | per month; probably alternated w/Morelli | |
| *dans les Conçerts:* | | | |
| Felice [= Felice Marchetti] | (½? of) 210.00 | per month; end of 1762/3 only | 50 Cremnitz ducats |
| Constantin[i] [Cortolo] | 400.00 | | |
| Pösinger [Michael ("Michel")] | 28.00 | per month | |
| Vogt [Franz] | 25.00 | per month | |
| Sev[e] [Ignaz] | 20.00 | per month | |
| Him[m]elbauer [Franz] | 14.00 | per month | |
| [Salomoni, Giuseppe] | 1200.00 | as choreographer | |

| Women | fl./xr. | remarks | equivalent in ducats |
| --- | --- | --- | --- |
| *Pas de Deux:* | | | |
| Fabris [Lucia] | 1764.00 | end of 1762/3 only | 420 Cremnitz ducats |
| Beccari [Colomba] | (½? of) 3,300.00 | w/brother | 800 ordinary ducats |
| Morelli [Elisabetta] | (½? of) 2,887.00 | w/brother | ~700 ordinary ducats |
| Falchi [Francesca] | 1237.30 | ~300 ordinary ducats | |
| *dans les Conçerts:** | | | |
| Nicolini [*née* Maddalena Offarelli] | 33.00 | per month | |
| Zochi | 33.00 | per month | |
| Heimin [Antonia] | 30.00 | per month | |
| Heimin *cadette* | 30.00 | per month | |
| Sev[e] *fille* | 14.00 | per month | |
| Grumanin [Francisca] | 14.00 | per month | |

* Women's names ending in -in are now-antiquated feminine forms (e.g., Grumann Gruman[n]in).

Salary figures, while illuminating, tell only a small part of the story; fortunately, several verbal accounts of dance in Viennese theaters also survive from this period. A report from Vienna published in the *Journal encyclopédique* in 1757 (probably at Durazzo's instigation) gives some notion of Hilverding's philosophy and talents; it is all the more valuable since the choreographer himself left no writings on his art. Here we read of Hilverding's ambition, in emulation of the ancients, to create ballets that were "true poems subject to the same rules as tragedy and comedy";[26] the writer also voices his (and presumably also Hilverding's) disdain for those ballet masters who could only enliven their *entrées* by means of "the diversity of their clothing, and of the airs [of music], and at the very most by sequences of steps and movements that are very little related to the subject and the character that one is portraying."[27] Of Hilverding himself, we are told: "No one has succeeded better in varying his dance, and though it seems impossible, he is able to render equally well the *danse noble*, and the dance of even the most comic characters. This was the result of a special study of all the genres of dance and of the steps that are appropriate to them, and that is what gives him that admirable facility in expressing everything in the ballets he presents on the Viennese stages."[28] Though Magri could not have known Hilverding directly,[29] his influence in both theaters would still have been palpable for some time after his departure.

From Magri's first Viennese sojourn we have Gumpenhuber's descriptions of thirteen ballets (see app. 3); there were undoubtedly more, but the 1760 volumes of Gumpenhuber's chronicle (one for each theater) have not survived. The first two ballets of the season were choreographed by Vincenzo Turchi, but the rest (apart from *petits ballets*) are all by Charles Bernardi, Hilverding's successor as head of the German

26. *Journal encyclopédique*, 15 November 1757, 135: "des vrais Poëmes assujetis aux mêmes regles que la Tragedie, & la Comedie."

27. *Journal encyclopédique*, 15 November 1757, 135: "la diversité des habits, & des airs, & tout au plus par des enchainemens de pas & des mouvemens, qui repondent très peu au sujet & au caractere qu'on y traite."

28. *Journal encyclopédique*, 15 November 1757, 135: "Personne n'a mieux reussi que lui à varier sa danse, & il a sçû, ce qui paroit impossible, rendre également bien sa danse noble, & celle des caracteres même les plus comiques. C'étoit l'effet d'une étude particuliere de tous les genres de danses & des pas qui leur sont propres, & c'est ce qui lui donne cette admirable facilité à tout exprimer dans les Balets qu'il fait executer sur les Théâtres de Vienne"; quoted (as also the previous excerpts from this report) in Brown, *Gluck and the French Theatre*, 157.

29. Winter (*Pre-Romantic Ballet*, 94) implies that Magri had been recruited by Hilverding before his departure, but it seems just as likely that Durazzo, with his extensive Italian connections, was responsible.

ballet troupe.[30] His works evidently pleased the discriminating Viennese
public; Zinzendorf recorded in 1761, "In the evening I went to see the
German comedy . . . which as usual was quite bad, but the ballets very
pretty."[31] However, in order for us properly to evaluate Bernardi's ballets of 1759, in most of which Magri would have performed, we must first
consider some normative practices of dance in the Kärntnertortheater,
which differed in certain respects from those in the Burgtheater.

In both Viennese theaters, ballets tended to be introduced into the
repertory in pairs, and held the stage until replaced by a new pair. One
difference lay in the regular distinction that was made in the "German"
company between *grands* and *petits ballets*, the latter mostly not figuring in
the Burgtheater repertory. For 1759, all *petits ballets* were by Gumpenhuber himself, who was apparently never entrusted with more ambitious
choreographic tasks. Large or small, most ballets in the Kärntnertortheater served to separate the spoken plays that constituted the main fare.

Although Angiolini's three Viennese "reform" ballets and ballets for
Italian operas were documented in printed programs or descriptions, the
public seems to have witnessed the dozens of repertory ballets given in
both theaters each year without benefit of programs. This is not to say
that descriptions do not exist; but these were either after-the-fact newspaper accounts or plans apparently submitted by choreographers to Durazzo for his approval. This requirement seems to have applied only to
the German theater, whose offerings had in the past often offended by
their bawdiness. Hilverding had never written programs, according to
Angiolini,[32] and the use of future tense in Gumpenhuber's descriptions
strongly suggests that these were not meant for the spectators themselves.
Rather, these descriptions seem to have been used to convince Durazzo

30. Winter (*Pre-Romantic Ballet*, 95) surmises that this Bernardi belonged to the same clan of actors and dancers by this name that was active in the Low Countries and France around mid-century.
There were two Bernardy women, for instance, in the Ghent company from which several members were recruited for the new French theatrical troupe in Vienna in 1752; see Frédéric Faber, *Histoire du théâtre français en Belgique* (Brussels: J. Olivier; Paris, Tresse, 1878–80), 1:214. The choreographer was not, however, identical to the Sieur Bernardi who acted (along with his wife) in the
Viennese French troupe until his death in 1757, though he may have been related.

31. "Le soir j'allois voir la Comédie allemande . . . qui étoit com[m]e a l'ordinaire, bien mau-
vaise, mais les Ballets tres joli[s]"; Zinzendorf, entry for Monday, 3 August 1761.

32. *Riflessioni di G. Angiolini sopra l'uso dei programmi nei balli pantomimi* (London and Milan, 1775),
16: "Il celebre M. Hilverding, primo e vero ristoratore de' Balli Pantomimi, espose sulle scene ogni
suo ballo senza programma. Il Pubblico era allora meno assuefatto all' opere di quest' arte di fresco
rinascente: eppure que' Balli erano intesi da ognuno." (The famous M. Hilverding, first and true re-
storer of pantomime ballets, staged every one of his ballets without program. The public then was
less used to works in this newly reborn art: and yet those ballets were understood by everyone.)

of the works' decency and stageworthiness and that their creators were upholding Hilverding's legacy.

Time after time we are told that a ballet or a *pas de deux* is "bien travaillé" (well worked out) or "fort intriguant" (very intriguing). The account of *Une Suite de plusieurs incidents qui arrivent ordinairement parmi les païsans* (A Series of Several Incidents That Ordinarily Happen among Peasants) compensates for this ballet's inauspicious title with praise for the "agreeable perspective" of the decoration, the peasants' "tricks . . . which are very funny and witty," a "very diverting pantomime," and for "*pas de deux* that are all in the grotesque genre," and in which "variety . . . is always maintained"; one has the impression that various guiding principles, well known to the choreographers, are being invoked.[33] A critic's remark that *Le Port de Marseille* constituted "a complete play in several scenes" (une piéce entiere à plusieurs Scènes) likewise recalls Hilverding's ambition to create ballets subject to the same rules as governed the spoken theater.[34]

The ungainly title quoted above is symptomatic of the formulaic language in many of Gumpenhuber's descriptions, and even in some newspaper accounts of Hilverding's ballets (perhaps because the writers, whom other evidence shows to have been close to Durazzo, had access to Gumpenhuber's scenarios). The description of Hilverding's *La Foire de Zamoysck* (probably performed during the winter of 1757), for instance, is revealing in its use of the characteristic phrase "different ordinary incidents in these sorts of places," which appears, in one form or another, in no fewer than ten of Gumpenhuber's synopses (see table 3.3).[35] The frequently encountered word "accidens" in these synopses is at least superficially reminiscent of the practice in the same theater of paying actors fixed fees for slaps, pratfalls, and other "Accidenzien."

Of particular interest, in terms of the future choreographer Magri, are the many remarks in these summaries on the integration of pantomime and dance. The distinction between the two is often still apparent, as in Bernardi's *Les Turcs* of 1759 (Gumpenhuber's synopsis and anonymous stage design are reproduced in Winter, *Pre-Romantic Ballet*, 104), in which the "commencement du Ballet" (beginning of the ballet, as opposed to

33. "tours . . . qui sont fort comiques et plaisants"; "Pantomime . . . très divertissante"; "pas de Deux qui sont tous d'un genre grotesque"; "la varieté . . . est toujours conservée"; see Brown, *Gluck and the French Theatre* , 175.

34. *Journal étranger*, May 1760, 107.

35. "differents incidens ordinaires dans ces sortes d'endroits"; *Journal encyclopédique*, 15 January 1758, 118–19. The discussion in the following several paragraphs is based on Brown, *Gluck and the French Theatre*, 173–75.

Table 3.3: *Formulaic language in Kärntnertortheater ballet descriptions, 1757–63*

. . . differents incidens ordinaires dans ces sortes d'endroits.
(Hilverding, *La Foire de Zamoysck*, winter 1757)

. . . accidens propres en telles occasions . . .
(Turchi, *Le Port dans une isle de l'archipel*, 16 April 1759)

. . . un pas de Trois et un pas de Deux, qui representent differents accidents, qui
arrivent en ce païs-là . . .
(Bernardi, *Les Turcs*, 30 May 1759)

. . . differens accidents, qui arrivent ordinairement en tels endroits . . .
(Bernardi, *La Guinguette*, 26 July 1759)

. . . accidents qui arrivent ordinairement en tels endroits . . .
(Bernardi, *Le Marché aux poissons*, 3 October 1759)

. . . ce qui arrive ordinairement au lever du Soleil en tels endroits . . .
(Bernardi, *Le Suisse*, 17 November 1759)

*Une Suite de plusieurs incidents qui arrivent parmi les païsans*
(Bernardi, 23 March 1761)

. . . plusieurs accidens qui arrivent ordinairement dans les Places publiques . . .
(Bernardi, *La Foire*, 2 May 1761)

. . . on exprime les Accidens qui sont ordinaires en des pareils endroits . . .
(Bernardi, *Le Divertissement dans le Stadt=Gutt*, 16 June 1761)

. . . Plusieurs incidens qui arrivent ordinairement dans ces sortes d'endroit . . .
(Bernardi, *La Querelle au cabaret, ou La Jalousie appaisée*, 2 December 1761)

. . . plusieurs incidens qui arrivent ordinairement parmi des Paisans . . .
(Salomoni, *Les Noces de village*, 4 April 1763)

pantomime) comes well into the work. (A similar division is evident in several of Magri's later ballets for Naples; see chap. 4 in this volume.) The stage design of *Les Turcs*, which survives only in a photograph from the 1940s,[36] shows one character obviously dancing and the others lounging, working, or otherwise engaged in pantomime. But in many of his synopses Gumpenhuber takes pains to note that the two means of expression were combined. Of Bernardi's *La Reccolte des fruits* (The Fruit Harvest, likewise 1759), for instance, we read of "different pantomimes, which will be expressed by the ballet";[37] of his *Les Faucheurs* (The Reapers, 1761), it is

36. Reproduced in Winter, *Pre-Romantic Ballet*, 104.
37. Gumpenhuber, volume for Kärntnertortheater, 1759: "differentes Pantom[i]mes, les quelles seront exprimées par le Ballet."

said that "almost the entire ballet is filled with actions = love, jealousy, scorn, and despair are naïvely painted by striking strokes. Dance is always maintained."[38] Further examples include Turchi's episodically constructed *La Foire* (1759), with its "various pantomimes, which are done while dancing,"[39] and Salomoni's *L'Heureuse Bergère ou l'Amant Magicien* (1762), wherein "pantomime is always mixed with dance."[40] Such insistence on the alliance of dance and mimetic action must surely reflect the strong preferences of Hilverding, and probably of Durazzo as well, who had guided his choreographer's efforts. (For further discussion of the integration of pantomime and dance, see chap. 8 in this volume.)

The plots to which these dance principles were applied were simple, bordering even on the childlike, often serving as pretexts for *divertissements* or solos. (One suspects that the *petits ballets*, for which no descriptions survive, may have been entirely without plot.) Kärntnertortheater ballets were set in predominantly rustic or exotic locales, often specifically recognizable ones. (Here Magri's mention of a choreographer's need to know geography [part 1, chap. 3] comes to mind.) The setting could even include musical instruments on stage, as with the drums and flutes playing from the galley in *Le Port de Marseille* (1759), even the occasional sung number.[41] Ballets tended to open with an ensemble, often with diverse, simultaneous actions—as in *La Guinguette* (likewise 1759), where "some play skittles, some eat, and some amuse themselves by dancing."[42] They usually closed with an ensemble, too—a "German dance," in this case. Magri would have had many such opportunities to perform in such "Teitsche" (*taice*), such as those appearing among the contredanses of his

38. Gumpenhuber, volume for Kärntnertortheater, 1761: "Presque tout le Ballet est rempli d'actions = L'Amour, la jalousie, le Mépris, et le Desespoir y sont peints naivement par des Coups frappans. La Danse y est toujours conservée."

39. Gumpenhuber, volume for Kärntnertortheater, 1759: "diverses Pantomimes, qu'on fait en dansant."

40. Gumpenhuber, volume for Burgtheater, 1762 (where the French and German troupes performed alternately, following the 1761 fire in the Kärntnertortheater): "la Pantomime en est toujours melée avec la dance."

41. For instance, the "Cansonette" sung by Mlle. Fusi in the ballet *L'inglese*, which was probably identical with *Le Foxhall* [i.e., *Vauxhall*] *de Londres*, viewed by Zinzendorf in the Kärntnertortheater on Monday, 8 August 1761. Popular operatic airs were also sometimes quoted in purely instrumental form in Viennese ballets, in one case (*Les Aventures champêtres*, choreography by Bernardi, music arr. Gluck; Burgtheater, 19 October 1760) making up the entire musical substance of the work). But the practice was by no means as prevalent as it was in Parisian ballets of the late eighteenth and early nineteenth centuries (see Marian Smith, *Ballet and Opera in the Age of Giselle* [Princeton, NJ: Princeton University Press, 2000], 101–21).

42. "d'autres jouent aux quils, d'autres mangent, et d'autres se divertissent en dansant."

*Trattato.* The vast majority of ballet subjects were comic or picturesque, but tragic endings were not unknown; Bernardi's *Les Faucheurs,* for instance, ended with a "fit of despair," the two lovers throwing themselves in the water, according to Zinzendorf.[43]

A fundamental source of information on the works danced by Magri and others in Vienna's German theater — a source only just beginning to be tapped — is the repository of some 180 orchestral partbooks for Viennese ballets in the Schwarzenberg family archive at Český Krumlov in the present-day Czech Republic. These partbooks, from a period spanning more than seventy years, were mostly ordered directly from the court theaters' copyists, as mementos of pieces witnessed in performance. Elsewhere I have discussed the music of the Burgtheater's ballet repertory in these years, emphasizing the composers' increasing attempts at emotional power, gestural suggestiveness, evocative scoring, and dramatic continuity — the last through linking of individual movements and the creation of ambitious, through-composed finales.[44] Ballets for the Kärntnertortheater (insofar as these have been studied) exhibit the first three of these traits but are conspicuously lacking in continuity, except through occasional groupings of dances of the same sort. The differing nature of the music for ballets in the French and German theaters was no doubt due in part to the absence of mythological and tragic ballets in the latter venue. But one also gets the impression that Count Durazzo (or persons he answered to) specifically arranged things so that patrons of one or the other theater could rely on seeing a distinct type of ballet product — one in accord with the sung and spoken offerings there. The count's repeated boasts of his ability to combine at will the resources of both theaters suggest that he could easily have enforced a more uniform ballet practice, had he wanted to.[45] Following a short *sinfonia,* in most "German" ballets there are upwards of twenty, thirty, or even forty mostly binary movements, the majority of them quite short;[46] most ballets for the French the-

43. Entry for Saturday, 9 May 1761.

44. See Brown, *Gluck and the French Theatre,* chaps. 5 and 8.

45. See, for instance, Durazzo's initial letter of instructions to Favart concerning the latter's role as Parisian theatrical agent for Vienna, dated 20 December 1759, in the edition by Favart's grandson (Charles-Simon Favart, *Mémoires et correspondances littéraires, dramatiques et anecdotiques,* ed. A.-P.-C. Favart, 3 vols. [Paris: Léopold Collin, 1808], 1:3–4), but of an indeterminate date during 1760 in the original in the Bibliothèque de l'Opéra, Paris (Fonds Favart, Carton I, A, II).

46. Insofar as one can tell from the few surviving sources, this general plan was common also in Italian ballet music from the 1740s and '50s; see the collection of *Balli teatrali a Venezia (1746–1859):*

ater include around fifteen or twenty rather longer, and less consistently binary movements. Nevertheless, in several of Bernardi and Gluck's ballets there are more extended numbers—a long, multisectional Allegro assai in *Le Suisse,* for instance, possibly music for a banquet, during which "plusieurs accidents fort divertissants" (several very entertaining events) occur (see the description in app. 3).

It is difficult to characterize the musical style of so vast and various a repertory. But one is immediately struck by the abundance of distinctly folklike melodies—a feature traceable in part to Vienna's position as the capital of a multiethnic empire. Some movement types—the chaconne, for example—rarely occur in works for the Kärntnertortheater, but the presence of courtly minuets is an indication that the *genre gracieux* was not entirely unknown there. For a more specific impression of Gluck's music for the 1759–60 season—music to which Magri presumably danced—we turn now to his score for Bernardi's *Les Corsaires,* first given along with *Le Prix de la danse* on 26 December (see synopsis in app. 3 and selected movements from the score below).

This exotic, action-filled ballet takes place on a desert island, where a shipwreck survivor has long languished in solitude. His rescue by his lover, and the English sailors she has guided to the island, is delayed by not one but two battles with passing pirate ships; the English are taken prisoner but buy back their freedom, and each ship departs for its home port. There being no written indications of action or characters in the instrumental partbooks, one can only use the style of the music to determine, speculatively, which number corresponds to what action or actions. Of the thirty short movements, only two (nos. 2 and 20) are linked by a half-cadence to the following numbers. The few pieces with overt tone-painting are mainly clustered near the beginning. The opening Sinfonia seems (through its stormy scale figures) to depict the shipwreck that has stranded the protagonist on his desert isle; he is introduced effectively, and with a minimum of strokes, in the alternately mournful and savage first number. Numbers 2 and 3, with their wavelike melodic motion, and the following number with its triadic horn fanfares, announce the approach of an English ship (see nos. 1–4, mus. ex. 3.1). The several skirmishes of the pirates and Englishmen may correspond to the noisier numbers of the score (nos. 8, 10, 20, and 24)—all but one of them binary numbers with repeats. But their musical material, which features dotted

*Partiture di sei balli pantomimici di Brighenti, Angiolini e Viganò,* with an introduction by José Sasportes and catalogue and chronology by Elena Ruffin and Giovanna Trentin, 2 vols. (Milan: Ricordi, 1994).

1.

Musical example 3.1: Bernardi/Gluck, *Les Corsaires* (1759), nos. 1–4.

rhythms and/or repeated sixteenth-notes, is not very specifically suggestive of battle (see no. 8, mus. ex. 3.2). Much of the score is fairly rudimentary, with much doubling at the unison or octave, and signs of haste
such as the parallel fifths in measure 7 of number 8. And yet this music
successfully conveys the English nationality of the main characters, in
several lively jigs and rigadoons, and in the prevalence of 6/8 meter generally (see no. 14, mus. ex. 3.3).

Musical example 3.1: continued

The vagueness with which the music of *Les Corsaires* seems to correspond to the actions and Gluck's near-total reliance on periodic phrasing and binary airs are in marked contrast to the composer's ballet scores
for the Burgtheater. Much further study would be necessary to determine whether there were in fact fundamentally different manners in

4.

Musical example 3.1: continued

Vienna's two theaters of incorporating pantomime into the dance. But this music strongly suggests that for major sections of *Les Corsaires*, "dance is always maintained" (see n38).

Magri's experiences as a dancer in the German theater surely helped shape his notions of choreography, but as a talented artist he must also have been curious about the ballet offerings in the Burgtheater, where the subject matter included the mythological and the pastoral, as well as

Musical example 3.1: continued

national and occupational dances. The only references in the *Trattato* to dancers from Vienna's French theater are to persons no longer present during Magri's two stays: Franz Anton Philibois, a ballet master from the pre-Hilverding era; and the famed Antoine Pitrot, later a colleague of both Magri (in Turin) and his wife (in Florence; see chap. 2 in this volume). But one "German" ballet performed in 1761 was explicitly parodistic, in a way that probably required specific knowledge of the techniques of *ballet sérieux* as practiced in the Burgtheater.[47] The work in question was a "Pas de Deux, La Parodie d'Armida, et Rinaldo," danced by Magri's former colleague Camilla Paganini and her partner Vincenzo Turchi in a revival of Bernardi and Gluck's *Les Moissonneurs* (originally given in 1760).[48] Pertinent here is Magri's mention in the *Trattato* of using exaggerated or distorted versions of *serio* steps—the *ballonné*, for example—for grotesque purposes (see chap. 1, chap. 37). Even more

47. The date is from a catalogue of now-lost Esterházy music manuscripts; see János Harich, "Inventare der Esterházy-Hofmusikkapelle in Eisenstadt," *Haydn-Jahrbuch* 9 (1975): 5–125 (73).
48. Gumpenhuber, 1761 Kärntnertortheater chronicle, entry for 2 May. The *pas de deux* may have simply parodied the general subject matter of Armida and Rinaldo, but it is perhaps significant that an operatic treatment of the tale by Giannambrogio Migliavacca and Traetta had been performed in the Burgtheater in January of the same year. In an interesting critique of Paganini's acrobatic technique, the above-cited correspondent for the *Journal étranger* wrote (109), "Elle pirouette, elle saute, le Peuple l'applaudit; mais les Spectateurs délicats voudroient qu'elle dansât." (She spins, she leaps, the people applaud; but discriminating spectators wish that she would dance.)

8.

Musical example 3.2: Bernardi/Gluck, *Les Corsaires* (1759), no. 8.

suggestive of Magri's acquaintance with dance in the French theater is his discussion of the coordination of music and dance (chap. 1, chap. 6, "Of Cadence"). Though ostensibly hypothetical, the ballet described here may in fact be based on Magri's recollection of Angiolini's *Zéphire et Flore*, one of the highlights of the 1759–60 season.[49] After noting how musical

49. This ballet, first performed on 13 August 1759 at Schönbrunn palace and then probably repeated in the Burgtheater, is described in the *Journal étranger* for May 1760, 109–10; see also Bruce

Musical example 3.2: continued

repetitions, changes of motion, and rests should all be reflected in the dance, Magri provides a concrete example:

> Let us imagine Boreas in love with Flora, who disdains him because she is in love with Zephyr; she flees and Boreas follows her; this requires Music which is very wild, and the good *Ballerino* will fill it with a multitude of varied steps and actions expressing the character, and which perfectly match the quality of the Music; he catches up with her, and Flora, exhausted, falls to the ground: the Flowers languish, wherever Boreas passes the little Zephyrs placed in various *Tableaux* are stunned; Boreas reaches Flora, stops, and stays in *attitude:* here the Music must *pause* or be *syncopated;* thus the multitude of steps. The chase is again taken up, the *furioso* must be repeated, and so alternately the steps are adapted to the light and shade of the music, and the dance will be done according to the art, full of action, rich in variety, and it cannot fail to obtain the audience's applause.[50]

The actions related here correspond closely to the *Journal étranger* account of Angiolini's ballet; indeed, Magri's talk here of applause may be an

Alan Brown, "*Zéphire et Flore:* A 'Galant' Early Ballet by Angiolini and Gluck," in *Opera and the Enlightenment,* ed. Thomas Bauman and Marita McClymonds (Cambridge: Cambridge University Press, 1995), 189–216.

50. Magri/Skeaping, 61–62; Magri, *Trattato,* 1:24–25: "Fingiamo Borea, che invaghito di Flora, la quale lo sdegna, per amor di Zeffiro, essa fugge, e Borea la siegue, in questo vi deve essere una

Musical example 3.3: Bernardi/Gluck, *Les Corsaires* (1759), no. 14.

echo of the reception of *Zéphire et Flore*. But his suggestions with regard to
the music seem filtered through his experience in the German theater,
where pieces tended to be short and binary—hence the recommendation to "repeat" the *furioso*. Gluck's score to *Zéphire et Flore*, which survives
(among the partbooks at Český Krumlov), is more fluid than this during
Boreas's rage. Nevertheless, Magri's advice on movement is a valuable
supplement to the other surviving information on this important ballet,
which (unusually) includes an impressively rendered stage design of the
central scene (see fig. 3.1).

After several years spent dancing in Italy, Magri was coaxed back to Vienna in 1763, quite possibly by Giuseppe Salomoni,[51] a colleague of his in

Musica assai furiosa, ed il bravo Ballerino la riempie di una variata moltitudine di passi, ed azioni
esprimenti il carattere, e che abbiano perfetta armonia con la qualità della Musica; la raggiunge, e
Flora soprafatta cade a terra; i Fiori languiscono, i Zeffiretti per dove passa Borea tutti tramortiti, in
varj *Tableaux* situati, Borea raggiunge Flora, si ferma, e resta in attitudine, quì la Musica deve esser
*sincopata*, o *pausata*, ecco, che la moltitudine de' passi non ha luogo, ma riempir si deve la cadenza più
dagli atteggi, che da passi. Si ripiglia la fuga, va replicato il furioso, e così alternativamente con
questo chiaro oscuro dell' armonia si adattano i passi, ed il ballo sarà fatto secondo l' arte, pieno di
azione, ricco di varietà, e non potrà non ottenere l' applauso de' spettatori." Note that Magri speaks
as if the soloist responds directly to the music, helping create his own choreography.

51. See Mary Skeaping's introduction to Magri's treatise, in Magri/Skeaping, 10.

Figure 3.1: Anonymous scenic design for Angiolini and Gluck's *Zéphire et Flore* (1759; University of Salzburg, Friderica Derra de Moroda Dance Archives), a work that possibly inspired Magri's vivid description of a dance wherein Boreas chases Flora (Magri, *Trattato*, pt. 1, chap. 6).

Venice during the 1762–63 season, who was returning to the Habsburg capital in order to take up the post of ballet master in the German theater. Citing "Radamovsky" (*recte:* Franz Hadamowsky), Mary Skeaping calls Magri's salary of 2,062 florins per year (roughly 500 ordinary ducats) "unusually high," and indeed he was the best-paid member of the troupe, receiving far more, even, than the choreographer Salomoni. But as in 1759–60, there were several better-paid soloists in the French theater, reflecting the higher premium placed on *la danse noble*.[52] Just how much Durazzo prized this style and even sought to protect it from contamination is shown by his firing of a dancer in the French troupe, Marianne Le Clerc, for having married the grotesque dancer Louis Frossard; as Durazzo explained to Favart, "that could disturb her noble-style dancing."[53]

52. Magri/Skeaping, 10. The work of Hadamowsky's (for which Skeaping cites no title) is "Leitung, Verwaltung und ausübende Künstler des deutschen und französischen Schauspiels, der italienischen ernsten und heiteren Oper, des Ballets und der musikalischen Akademien am Burgtheater (Französischen Theater) und am Kärntnerthortheater (Deutschen Theater) in Wien, 1754–1764," *Jahrbuch der Gesellschaft für Wiener Theaterforschung* 12 (1960): 113–33 (126).

53. Letter of 28 October 1761; quoted in Brown, *Gluck and the French Theatre*, 70: "cela pourroit deranger sa danse noble."

The 1763 ballet company in the German theater was just as Italian as
that of Magri's earlier sojourn (see table 3.2). Viganò, too, had returned
to Vienna and the Kärntnertortheater, but by now was performing with
the French theater's troupe. Gumpenhuber's more detailed roster for
1763 now indicates pairings for *pas de deux:* Vincenzo Turchi with Lucia
Fabris, the Beccari siblings with each other, Magri with Elisabetta
Morelli, and the latter's brother Felice dancing with his "female companion" (*Compagnon*in), as the payment records have it, Francesca Falchi,
in alternation with Joseph Hornung.

Since Magri had last been in Vienna, ballet had experienced a sea-
change — at least in the French theater — with the production of Angiolini
and Gluck's first full danced dramas with printed programs. In the essays
accompanying these works, and in his later polemical writings, Angiolini
is disparaging of the acrobatic technique that characterized Italian ballet,
when it was not allied with expressive pantomime. Magri cannot have
been oblivious of Angiolini's revolution in theatrical dance; the dancers of
the German theater had all the more opportunity to observe their colleagues' innovations following the destruction of their own theater by fire
in November of 1761; for the next year and a half, the two ballet companies were forced temporarily to share the stage of the Burgtheater, even
on the same evening. Nevertheless, the scenarios for Salomoni's ballets
for the German troupe from the 1763–64 season betray no real departures
from the form and style of Bernardi's works (see the titles in table 3.3). We
are less able to assess the music of this season — now being composed by
Gluck and his protégé Florian Gassmann (archival sources do not specify
the French or German theater for either composer) — since relatively little
of it has survived. But it seems likely that the Kärntnertortheater ballet
company's house style survived both the conflagration of November 1761
and the dancers' encounter with Angiolini's reforms.

For one of the first ballets given in the newly rebuilt Kärntnertortheater, *Un Port de mer dans la Provençe* (A Seaport in the Provinces ["Provençe" probably being a misspelling of "Province"], 16 August 1763),
there exists a finely finished painting by the French artist Jean Pillement,
who during this period was decorating various rooms in the Hofburg (see
fig. 3.2).[54] To judge from Gumpenhuber's description, the ballet was
nearly devoid of plot, but a rich feast for the eye:

---

54. I am grateful to Dr. Mark Ledbury of the Clark Art Institute (Williamstown, MA) for bringing this image to my attention.

Figure 3.2: Jean Pillement, *Market Scene in an Imaginary Oriental Port,* ca. 1764, oil on canvas, 50.2 × 74.9 cm (J. Paul Getty Museum, Los Angeles), depicting Salomoni's ballet *Un Port de mer dans la Provençe* (1763), in which Magri likely performed.

In the decoration of this ballet one sees several vessels at the shore, and many people busy unloading a number of bales of merchandise. Several women are in their boutiques situated on the land to one or the other side, in order to buy or sell, which makes for a pretty view. After having worked, the ones and the others [the buyers and sellers] are taken with a desire to divert themselves, and form a general dance which is the start of this completely merry and diverting ballet. As seaports are always abounding with people of every nationality, [in this] ballet one will have the charm of variety of several characters who will appear in it. A sailor of the country, wishing to amuse himself, plays some tricks on an unsuspecting young girl. After a minor quarrel they are soon reconciled, and this ballet ends as merrily as possible, with the accompaniment of instruments appropriate to the country one aims to represent.[55]

55. Gumpenhuber, volume for Kärntnertortheater, 1763: "On voit dans la Decoration de ce Ballet plusieurs voisseaux [*sic*] au Rivage, et beaucoup de monde occupé à débarquer nombre de balots de marchandises. Plusieurs fem[m]es sont à leurs boutiquet [*sic*] situées à terre de l'un, et de l'autre coté pour acheter, oû vendre, çe qui fait un beaucoup d'œil [*recte* : beau coup d'œil]. aprés avoir travaillé les uns et les autres, l'envie de se divertir les prend, et [elles] forment une danse generale qui fait le comencement de çe Ballet tout à fait gai, et divertissant. Comme les Ports de mer

Although the description does not specify the country in which this port is situated, the tropical foliage, exotic costumes, and crescent ornament atop the tent to the rear of the stage suggest that it is somewhere in the Muslim empire. The moment depicted is evidently near the end of the ballet (for which, unfortunately, the music does not survive): the bales have been deposited on land, the merchants and customers are back in their booths, and six Moors with cymbals dance around a Chinese man in a skullcap swinging bells. It is unlikely that Pillement himself was the scenic designer for this ballet (theatrical payment records for this period make no mention of him), but the work's exotic spectacle clearly captivated his interest — the Chinese dancer in particular, of whom there is a separate drawing preserved in the Viennese Albertina. And it is entirely possible that in the painting's central depiction of Moorish and Chinese dancers — grotesque dancers all — we have a portrait in action of the elusive Gennaro Magri himself.

Magri's activity during this season was not confined to repertory ballets. Since his last engagement, Italian serious opera had been reintroduced in Vienna's court theater, and Magri's participation in this spectacle is documented for at least one production: that of Tommaso Traetta's *Ifigenia in Tauride* (first given on the emperor's nameday, 4 October 1763). In the fourth ballet of "priests and Scythians" (all the dances were linked to the opera) we find Magri dancing in a *pas de trois* of Scythians — a grotesque assignment, assuredly — along with his partner Morelli, and Viganò. With this production Magri was participating directly, for the first and only time, in a Viennese "reform" opera, working directly with Angiolini. Though an Italian almanac gives Magri's name as one of the dancers for the premiere of Gluck's *Ezio*, during Carnival a few months later — for which the ballets were again by Angiolini (see Patricia Rader's chronological table, in this volume) — for reasons unknown his name is not given in the libretto. Still, dancing and choreographing for operas had constituted Magri's principal activities during his four previous seasons in Italy, and would again upon his return.

Assessing the effects on Magri of his time spent in Vienna is a matter largely of conjecture. It seems likely that his exposure to Burgtheater dancers of the caliber of Louise Joffroi and Jean Dupré contributed to his

---

abo[n]dent toujours de personnes de toutes les nations, on aura l'agrement de Ballet de la variete [*sic*] de plusieurs Caracteures qui y paroitront[.] un matelot du pais voulant s'amuser joue quelques tours à une jeune Personne qui ne s'en doutoit pas. après une legere querelle bientôt ils se raccomodent, et çe Ballet se termine gajement autant que possible, avec l'accompagnement des instrument propres au Pais qu'on veut representer."

admiration of French taste, an admiration that he expressed repeatedly in his *Trattato*,[56] and which was fundamental to the aesthetics of Count Durazzo and of the Parisian-trained Hilverding. But though he had witnessed Angiolini's reforms at close hand, Magri does not once mention the Florentine choreographer in his treatise. Indeed, one wonders whether there was some animosity between the two; Angiolini, in his *Lettere . . . a Monsieur Noverre* of 1773, denigrated in the strongest terms "Saltabuffoni" (by whom he meant grotesque dancers) who degraded the stages of Italy with their dances, and humiliated their homeland by going abroad and giving the impression that Italy's taste in dance consisted "solely of leaps, and improbable buffoonery."[57] In 1779, in his diatribe against Magri's as yet unpublished *Trattato*, Francesco Sgai would describe the productions of Gennariello and his fellow "Cantambanc[hi]" in similarly derogatory language (see chap. 4 in this volume). Whatever his opinion of Angiolini, at the very least Magri must have been inculcated with the Viennese doctrine, established under Hilverding, that dance and pantomime worked most efficaciously in combination. (Though this union of techniques was basic also to Italian dance practice, in Vienna the more acrobatic and licentious elements had been purged.) And while in Vienna Magri forged a number of professional relationships that would serve him well both between his two stays and after his ultimate departure,[58] and acquired a ready store of ballet *scenari* upon which to draw as a choreographer. His ballets portraying a *Mercato del pesce in Amsterdam* (Fish Market in Amsterdam) and the *Ritorno di soldati piemontesi alle loro case* (Return of Piedmontese Soldiers to Their Houses; first performed with Metastasio/Piccinni, *Il re pastore*, 30 May 1765) are particularly close to their models by Bernardi (see the descriptions in apps. 3 and 4); Magri's ballet *Arrivo di viaggiatori nella posta di Vienna* (given along with Pizzi/Sacchini, *Creso*, 4 November 1765) is reminiscent of several Kärntnertortheater ballets, one of which he may well have seen or even performed in.[59]

---

56. E.g., in his introduction to pt. 2; see Magri, *Trattato*, 2:5; Magri/Skeaping, 172.

57. "assicurando essere il gusto dell' Italia solamente portato a' salti, ed alle inverosimili buffonate"; *Lettere*, 111n.

58. In 1764, for instance, we find Magri and his former Vienna colleague Lucia Fabris dancing both in the Teatro Grimani in San Giovanni Grisostomo, Venice (Ascension), and in the Nuovo Teatro, Padua (the June *fiera* ), and additionally with Francesco Salomoni (father of the Kärntnertortheater choreographer Giuseppe) in Turin's Teatro Regio during Carnival 1765.

59. Namely, *L'Arrivée des voituriers à l'auberge* (Hilverding/Starzer, Kärntnertortheater, 1752/53), *Les Courriers au cabaret de poste* (*Das Post=haus*) (Salomoni/Starzer, Kärntnertortheater, 1754/55), and *L'Arrivé des charettiers dans un paisage de la Styrie, ou la Noble Pelerine* (Salomoni/Aspelmayr, Kärntnertortheater, 23 January 1763).

Turning things around, we may also ask what Magri's *Trattato* can tell us about the style and technique of ballets staged in Vienna's theaters during the time of Hilverding and Starzer, Angiolini and Gluck. Some of Magri's recommendations of steps have direct applications to situations in Gumpenhuber's scenarios—the use of the *pas de sissone*, for instance (chap. 1, chap. 30), for wounded characters (as in the battles of *Les Corsaires*, and in various hunting ballets from both theaters), or the specifically "Turkish" caprioles he describes (chap. 1, chap. 60, sec. 18). Certainly his contredanse choreographies can be drawn upon for the many such movements among the surviving scores to Viennese ballets. Magri's essentially technical explanation of theatrical dancing is probably better applied to Kärntnertortheater ballets than to the more experimental, less artisanal works given in the Burgtheater, assuming a correlation between short, binary airs, and traditional dance technique. Still, we cannot help regretting that Magri never found the time to write the second treatise, "devoted entirely to the execution of Theatrical Dancing and the duties of Composers, with a selection of Programmes appended, both by myself and by various Authors," that he proposed at the close of part 1 of his *Trattato*.[60] This would have clarified much that is elusive concerning the manner in which the various steps he describes are used in actual dramatic situations.

60. Magri/Skeaping, 167; Magri, *Trattato*, 1:138–39: "continente unicamente l' esecuzione del Ballo Teatrale, ed obbligo del Compositore, annessavi una scelta di Prog[r]ammi sì miei, come di varj Autori."

# 4

# Magri in Naples

## *Defending the Italian Dance Tradition*

SALVATORE BONGIOVANNI
(TRANSLATED BY BRUCE ALAN BROWN)

Although theatrical activity induced Gennaro Magri to lead an itinerant life, Naples was the city of his birth and of his training, as well as a place where he spent a large portion of his career. On the title page of his *Trattato* he defines himself as "Neapolitan"—as he does also in the opera librettos that contain descriptions of his ballets—in order to emphasize his artistic link with the city.

Magri's Neapolitan activities are particularly interesting for two reasons. First, in Naples Magri was able not only to publish his *Trattato teorico-prattico di ballo* but also to work for at least three seasons as "composer of ballets"—the latter activity documented by numerous librettos. Second, Magri's own artistic experience was closely bound up with the vicissitudes of the Neapolitan artistic and cultural scene, which—by virtue of the central and in some ways unique position that this city had assumed in the second half of the eighteenth century—reflected the entire panorama of Italian dance of the period.

The cultural and artistic life of Naples reached new heights of splendor during the later eighteenth century.[1] The royal court had become

---

1. Reports on life in the city are furnished by many foreign travelers who made Naples one of the principal stops on their trips to Italy. Among these are several in which artistic, cultural, and

one of the most brilliant in Europe; it hosted frequent receptions, balls, concerts, and theatrical performances, and its salons were always open. In addition, during the Carnival season gala balls (feste da ballo) were organized in the Teatro San Carlo. In the palaces of the aristocracy, too, there were frequent receptions, some even more sumptuous than the royal ones. All this created an atmosphere favorable to the diffusion among amateurs of those arts that would allow one to participate effectively in the city's lively social life. First among these arts was dance: social dances were, in fact, at the center of every reception and the occasion for each participant to cut a fine figure in society. For these reasons, dance lessons were one of the main preoccupations of the nobility, and the figure of the dancing master became ever more widespread and indispensable. Magri's *Trattato teorico-prattico di ballo* fulfilled the needs of this amateur dance practice; with its entire second half devoted to a discussion of ballroom dancing, and with an appendix of choreographies and explanations of fully thirty-nine contredanses, it attests to the great importance this fashion had assumed.

Magri's *Trattato* also reveals the growing interest of Neapolitans for theatrical dance. We know that Neapolitans were especially enthusiastic about opera, which became even more popular with the addition of extramusical elements that reflected the taste and social inclinations of the time; opera's attraction as spectacle, pastime, and diversion made the theater a place in which to meet friends and entertain guests. Under these conditions, ballet was sure to encounter success, for it often represented the main attraction of the evening. In this connection Stefano Arteaga stated, "It would suffice to turn one's eyes to any theater whatever in order to see how great a stretch of time is occupied by ballet, how inopportunely it interrupts the action of the opera, and how supremely important it has become nowadays, so that one might say, not that dance is the intermezzo to the drama, but rather that the drama is the intermezzo of the dance."[2] Charles Burney, who visited Naples in 1770, noted

---

musical matters are specifically discussed: Samuel Sharp, *Letters from Italy, Describing the Customs and Manners of That Country in the Years 1765 and 1766* (London: Nicol, 1766); Joseph-Jérôme de La Lande, *Voyage d'un Français en Italie* (Paris: Desaint, 1769); Charles Burney, *The Present State of Music in France and Italy* (London: T. Becket et al., 1773; repr., New York: Broude, 1969); and Charles de Brosses, *Lettres familières sur l'Italie*, ed. Yvonne Bezard (Paris: Firmin-Didot, 1931).

2. Stefano Arteaga, *Le rivoluzioni del teatro musucale italiano* (Bologna: Trenti, 1783–88; repr., Bologna: Forni, 1969), 3:5. These sentiments were likely inspired by similar remarks in letters by the librettist Pietro Metastasio (whose correspondence was exerpted in several posthumous editions of his works), as in his letter of 1 August 1750 to the singer Farinelli, in which he noted ironically that "musicians and composers, who are uniquely concerned with tickling the ears and not at all con-

with displeasure the absence of danced entr'actes at the Teatro Nuovo, where an opera of Niccolò Piccinni was being given, affirming that the lack of dance made the opera seem so long "that it is wholly impossible to keep up the attention; so that those who are not talking, or playing at cards, usually fall asleep."[3] Samuel Sharp drew attention to a peculiarity of ballets in Naples: "Notwithstanding the amazing noisiness of the audience, during the whole performance of the Opera, the moment the dance begin, there is a universal dead silence, which continues as long as the dances continue. Witty people, therefore, never fail to tell me, the Neapolitans go to *see*, not to *hear* an Opera."[4]

In regard to content, a predominant though not exclusive genre in ballet was the so-called character dance (*ballo di carattere*),[5] which showed, in caricatured or fantastically embellished form, peoples of far-off or unfamiliar nations (as in operatic *turqueries* and *chinoiseries*), exotic figures, professions of every sort, and archetypal characters (such as masks of the commedia dell'arte). In these ballets the protagonists were played by the *grotteschi*, who were better suited than others to delineate character traits and to indulge in unusual gestures (see also the discussion by Kathleen Hansell, chap. 1). The ballets that Magri produced at the Teatro San Carlo during the 1765–66 and 1766–67 seasons include almost the entire range of types in the grotesque repertory. (See, for example, the scenarios

---

cerned with the spectators' hearts, are for the most part condemned in all the theatres to serve as intermezzi to the dancers, who now claim the greater part of peoples' attention and the majority of the spectacle." (i musici ed i maestri, unicamente occupati a grattar le orecchia e nulla curando il core degli spettatori, sono per lo più condannati in tutti i teatri alla vergognosa condizione di servir d'intermezzi ai ballerini, che occupano ormai la maggiore attenzione del popolo e la maggior parte degli spettacoli.) Metastasio, *Tutte le opere*, ed. Bruno Brunelli, 5 vols. (Milan: Mondadori, 1943–54), 3:555. He repeats these sentiments almost literally in letters of 15 September 1755 to the famous castrato and teacher Antonio Bernacchi, and of 30 May 1771 to Saverio Mattei (*Tutte le opere*, 3:1065, 5:88–89).

3. Burney, *Present State*, 326.

4. Sharp, *Letters from Italy*, 81.

5. This account of ballet in Naples derives primarily from analysis of opera librettos of the time. While librettos from the first decades of the century tell very little about the ballets, at most their titles, from the 1750s onward librettos frequently included a so-called *nota de' balli* containing a brief description of the setting and the name of the choreographer. From 1763 onward they listed all the names of the dancers in the ballet company and began to print a summary of the plots (which became ever more extensive) of the most important ballets. The most up-to-date repertory of the Teatro San Carlo is that compiled by Carlo Marinelli Roscioni, *La cronologia 1737–1987*, vol. 2 of *Il teatro di San Carlo* (Naples: Guida, 1987). On the practice of listing dancers in librettos, see Gloria Giordano, "Gaetano Grossatesta, an Eighteenth-Century Italian Choreographer and Impresario, Part One: The Dancer-Choreographer in Northern Italy," *Dance Chronicle* 23, no. 1 (2000): 1–28 (9–10).

in app. 4, librettos 1 to 4.) In most cases these are entr'acte ballets, ones
not connected to the subject of the opera but dramatically autonomous.
Only in a few cases do the ballets even use the same scenery or setting as
the opera, as did three ballets given between the acts of Piccinni's opera
*Il gran Cid* (first performed on 4 November 1766); all three take place in
the city of Seville—though not without the insertion of certain elements
completely foreign to the setting (such as the Scotsmen of the second ballet)—but the plots are entirely independent of the opera. On the other
hand, the so-called analogous ballets (*balli analoghi*)[6] were also a well-
established tradition in Naples. Inserted as "third ballets," at the conclusion of the performance, these functioned as a collective celebration of
an event tied directly to the happy ending of the opera, as in the "joyous
dance of various characters applauding the peace established between
Cyrus and Croesus," in Antonio Sacchini's opera *Creso* (Croesus) or the
dance "expressing jubilation at the marriage of the Cid Rodrigo with
Climene," in Piccinni's *Il gran Cid*. (In chap. 7, Rebecca Harris-Warrick
and Carol G. Marsh tell about one of the dancers in *Il gran Cid*, Cosimo
Maranesi.) Nor are examples lacking of analogous ballets inserted in
other parts of a production; among the ballets Magri produced for
Joseph Mysliveček's opera *Bellerofonte*, there is one placed at the start of
the opera. The first scene in fact shows "Loggias with a view of the Xantus River, magnificently decorated to receive Bellerofonte," where "a
gala ball [*festa di ballo*] is performed while the chorus sings." This proce-
dure of simultaneously using chorus and dance produced striking theatrical effects, but was employed only infrequently on Italian stages.[7]

In one common type of ballet, dancers represented—at times caricatured—people of far-off or alien lands, often mixed together. For instance, in the first ballet with Piccinni's opera *Il re pastore* (The Shepherd
King), which takes place in the fish market of Amsterdam, we encounter
Scotsmen who dance "with other people who have congregated there."
The second ballet, on the other hand, features "Piedmontese soldiers returning to their homes." It is worth noting the similarities between the

---

6. See the detailed discussion of the *ballo analogo* in chapter 4 of Andrea Chegai, *L'esilio di Metastasio: Forme e riforme dello spettacolo d'opera fra Sette e Ottocento* (Florence: Le lettere, 2000), in particular
165–83.

7. In Naples, as in Milan, it was more usual for a *ballo analogo* to follow the opera's third act, as
a *terzo ballo*; for that reason, the appearance at the very beginning of Mysliveček's *Romolo ed Ersilia* of
a dance of Roman bridegrooms and Sabine women occasioned its strange designation in the libretto
as a *terzo ballo* "which for the sake of the drama is performed at the beginning."

plots of those two ballets and the plots of two ballets given in Vienna in 1759, *Le Marché aux poissons* (The Fish Market) and *Les Savoiards* with choreography by Bernardi, in which Magri participated as a dancer (see chap. 3 by Bruce Alan Brown and the relevant scenarios in app. 3). Evidently Magri sought to put his international experiences to use, even if the results were not always faultless — especially in regard to geography; his placement of Amsterdam "on the banks of the Rhine" presupposes a good amount of approximation, if not outright fantasy![8]

In the ballets with *Creso*, on the other hand, the audience first sees a "post-stage near Vienna with the arrival of various travelers," and then, after the second act of the opera, an attack by Lapp pirates (!) upon a village of other "foreign peoples" (*genti oltremontane*). Both ballets are very close to the style of a *divertissement,* in which the tenuous plot is only a pretext for a series of *entrées.* In other ballets there is a more substantial narrative that presupposes more extensive pantomimic action. In these cases the plot has a two-part structure: the first part sets the stage, presents the characters, and develops the principal plot, in which pantomimic action, entrusted to both the ballet ensemble and the soloists, prevails; the second part has the dénouement, followed by a series of dances by various soloists ( *pas de deux, pas de trois,* quartets, etc.) and then a "joyous group dance" (allegro concerto) performed by the entire troupe. Thus a sort of *divertissement* is juxtaposed with pantomimic action.

In the dances with *Il gran Cid,* the usual sorts of characters are trotted out: Spaniards and Moors in the first ballet, Gypsies and Scots in the second, but they are set in a narrative context requiring scenes in a fully pantomimic style. In the first ballet, for example, as the Spaniards are leading away some Moorish prisoners in order to kill them, "various Moors come running, throwing themselves at the feet of the Spaniards, and with their tears intercede for the lives of the others; to their tears the entreaties

---

8. As noted by Lisa C. Arkin and Marian Smith ("National Dance in the Romantic Ballet," in *Rethinking the Sylph: New Perspectives on the Romantic Ballet,* ed. Lynn Garafola [Hanover, NH: Wesleyan University Press, 1997], 11–68 and 245–52 [app.], ), Magri did require that a ballet master study "'geography in order to know the rites, climates, places, customs, abuses, Islands, seas, Cities of different Nations, especially those of African, Asiatic, and American ones, not known to us, so as to stage properly and express the character in a natural way, if wishing to put one of these Nation's dances into a spectacle.'" (Io vi aggiungo la Geografia, per sapere i riti, i clima, i siti, i costumi, gli abusi, l' Isole, i mari, le Città delle Nazioni, e specialmente di que' Affricani, Asiatici, ed Americani a noi non cogniti, con che si possa ben porre in scena, ed esprimere il carattere al naturale, volendo portare in spettacolo un ballo di tali Nazioni.) Magri/Skeaping, 55; Magri, *Trattato,* 1:18. Arkin and Smith document the persistence of the vogue for national dance far into the nineteenth century.

of some Spanish women are joined, and these finally obtain mercy."[9] At
this point comes the concluding danced section, indicated in the description by a conventional formula, "which occasions a joyful dance,
followed by various other dances of characters appropriate to the aforesaid nations."[10]

In the second ballet, *Of Gypsies and Scots,* Magri inserts, as a narrative
expedient, a Scottish noblewoman who asks the gypsies for a cure for the
convulsions that afflict her. Here too, in order to celebrate the woman's
eventual cure, "a joyous group dance is performed out of happiness at
the [woman's] recovered health, and is followed by various other dances
with pleasing pantomimes."[11]

Also typical during this period were ballets featuring monstrous characters or scenes of combat. Thus in the first ballet with Mysliveček's
opera *Bellerofonte* a Turkish pasha (Bassà turco) condemns various slaves
"to be devoured by certain monsters that he keeps enclosed in a solitary
place."[12] At the climax several other slaves rush on and assault and kill
the monsters just when they are preparing to unleash their ferocity. Then
follows, as usual, the danced section.

The ballet between the second and third acts of *Bellerofonte,* on the
other hand, exemplifies another typical sort of character dance, one
inspired by the masks of the commedia dell'arte.[13] This ballet consists of
a "pantomime between Pulcinella, Harlequin and Coviello," who are
grappling with a magician who brings upon them various "fearful encounters" (spaventosi incontri). Pulcinella, having attained knowledge of
the art of magic, profits from it by playing a prank on Harlequin and
Coviello, thus setting into action a truly comic scene. Here, too, at the
conclusion of the pantomimic section there are various dances "of gracious character."

Though we possess not a trace of their choreography, we can
nonetheless understand how enticing subjects such as these would have
been to the *grotteschi,* whether for their ability to delineate character via

9. "accorrono diverse More, che gittandosi a' piedi de' Spagnoli con lagrime intercedono la
vita di quelli alle quali lagrime si uniscono anche i prieghi [i.e., preghiere] di alcune donne spagnole
che ottengono finalmente grazia."

10. "onde s'intreccia allegra danza, alla quale sieguono [i.e., seguono] diversi altri balli di caratteri."

11. "si forma allegro concerto, al quale sieguono diversi altri balli con piacevoli pantomimi."

12. "ad essere divorate da certi mostri che tiene rinchiusi in un luogo solitario."

13. For a discussion of Harlequin-inspired dances in the eighteenth century, see Meredith
Chilton et al., *Harlequin Unmasked: The Commedia dell'Arte and Porcelain Sculpture* (New Haven: Yale University Press, 2001), esp. 120–28.

pantomime or for their virtuosic abilities, typical of the *danza alta* (high, or aerial, dance) of the Italian school, which this type of ballet required. Let us remember that in order to win over the audience, ballet dancers of the time vied in prowess with castratos and female singers; to the vocal fireworks of the singers, the dancers responded with audacious technical and acrobatic displays.

But opinions about this sort of ballet were not all favorable. Samuel Sharp, who visited Naples in 1765 and witnessed several ballets by Magri (specifically, those accompanying *Creso*), duly noted in his diary the success these works enjoyed with the audience, but he nevertheless commented:

> One would suppose, from the regard shewn to the dances, that a superior excellence was to be expected in this art; but Naples does not, at present, afford any very capital performers, nor do the dances, which have been brought on the stage this season, do much honour to their taste. They are, in general, exceedingly tedious, some lasting thirty-five minutes, and others twenty-five, with incidents and characters too vulgar and buffoonish, but it must be confessed that their scenary is extremely fine, and their dresses are new and rich, the musick is well adapted, but, above all, the stage is so large and noble, as to set off the performance to an inexpressible advantage.[14]

This critical stance, which contrasts with the interest shown by the public, reflects a position fashionable among literati of the time, who were hostile to virtuosic exhibitionism, and called instead for ballet to conform to the theories expounded by Jean-Georges Noverre in his *Lettres sur la danse* (1760) and to the compositional criteria of the *ballet d'action*: namely, a narrative, dramatic ballet that used pantomime to depict a serious action — one not in conflict with the nature of the drama for which it served as an intermezzo.

Starting around 1770 conditions in Naples did in fact favor a stylistic revolution in ballet, in the context of a vast ferment of ideas and initiatives aimed at reforming theatrical spectacles generally. Some signs of the times were performances of reform operas such as Christoph Gluck's *Orfeo ed Euridice* — albeit in altered form — in 1771; Tommaso Traetta's *Ifigenia in Tauride*, a product of Gluckian taste that was presented in 1778; *Paride ed Elena*, also by Gluck, given by the Nobile Accademia di Musica

---

14. Sharp, *Letters from Italy*, 81–82.

in 1779; not to mention the publication of Antonio Planelli's treatise *Dell'opera in musica* in 1772,[15] and of various prefaces to librettos written by intellectuals and poets such as Saverio Mattei, Luigi Serio, the Marquis of Corleto. All of these are indications of Naples having become a center of "reformed" culture, hardly inferior to others north of the Alps.

In this new climate it was also possible for Neapolitans to welcome the sort of reformed ballet being promoted by literati. In 1773, in fact, Charles Le Picq, the most faithful defender and propagator of the ideas of his mentor, Noverre (with whom he had worked in Stuttgart and Vienna), was invited to Naples;[16] for the Teatro San Carlo he produced numerous ballets previously given in Vienna by Noverre, plus a great quantity of original works. For the Neapolitan public this was a veritable revolution, in both aesthetics and in the style of the ballets' performance. One local commentator described it in the following terms:

> In Naples, where heroic ballet has never been tolerated, we owe the revolution in taste to the merit and ability of Mr. La Picque [*sic*]. In order to introduce a new taste into a nation [i.e., city], it is necessary for the person introducing it to be most perfect, mediocrity not being sufficient. If there is anything bad [in this reform], it is that [Le Picq's ballets] now tend to excess in the opposite direction. Everything is the work of the pantomime: the feet dance very little, and every plot is a new [danced] drama three times the length of the principal [sung] drama.[17]

The revolution did not lack opponents, and reactions to Le Picq's ballets were initially mixed; appreciation for the artistic quality of the dancers and the choreographers, and for the grandiosity of the *mise en scène*, was

15. Antonio Planelli, *Dell'opera in musica* (Naples: Donati, 1772; modern ed. by Francesco Degrada, Fiesole: Discanto, 1981).

16. Charles Le Picq (b. Naples, 1744; d. St. Petersburg, 1806) began dancing at the court theater at Stuttgart (1760–64), becoming Noverre's favorite pupil. He later performed in Vienna, Venice, and Milan, restaging ballets by Noverre and composing others of his own. In 1773 he arrived at the Teatro San Carlo in Naples, where he worked assiduously until 1782. He met with notable success also at the Paris Opéra (1776) and at the King's Theatre in London (1782–85); finally, from 1786 until his retirement (1798) he was the director of ballets at the Russian court in St. Petersburg. For further information on Le Picq's artistic career, see Kathleen Hansell's entry on him in *Grove Opera*, 2:1152; Maria Nevilla Massaro, "Balli e ballerini fra Padova e Venezia," in *La danza italiana* 5/6 (Autumn 1987): 77–88 (80–83); and Jeannine Dorvane, "Le Picq, Charles," *International Encyclopedia of Dance* (New York: Oxford University Press, 1998), 4:149–50.

17. "In Napoli, ove non s'è mai tollerato il ballo eroico, dobbiamo la rivoluzione del gusto al merito ed alla abilità di Mr. La Picque. Per introdurre un gusto nuovo in una nazione, bisogna che l'introduttore sia perfettissimo, non bastando il mediocre. Se c'è male, è ora nell'opposto eccesso. Tutto è lavoro di Pantomimo: i piedi ballano poco, e poi ogni argomento è un nuovo Dramma tre

combined with resistance to accepting the new, substantially *terre à terre* (walking) style of dance — a style more dramatic and expressive, but less spectacular than the *danza alta* of the *grotteschi*. Ferdinando Galiani declared in 1773 that "Le Picque . . . is as excellent a dancer as Vestris and Dauberval; nevertheless he has had more trouble than [the actor] d'Aufresne did in Frenchifying the Neapolitans. He thought he was being booed at first. The Neapolitans could not tell that he was dancing, in a theater as enormous and monstrous as ours, because he was not leaping at all. But since he has a very handsome figure, he set out to tame the Neapolitan ladies, and little by little the nation has been converted."[18] On the other hand, even the literati, preoccupied above all with defending the integrity of opera with respect to ballet, had to denounce certain ballets of Le Picq as unsatisfactory — such as his version of Noverre's *Adèle de Ponthieu*, which (they said) was excessively prolix, and on a subject too far removed from that of the opera it accompanied (*Orfeo ed Euridice*). What critics continued to object to was the very idea of ballet's legitimacy as an autonomous spectacle and its resistance to integration into the action of the opera.

Precisely in order to counterbalance those innovations that the Neapolitan public at large was not disposed to accept during the first theatrical season of the "revolution," the Teatro San Carlo called upon Gennaro Magri — as an esteemed and applauded artist and compatriot — to provide continuity by supplying the traditional character and "grotesque" ballets. These were given during the evening's performance as "second ballets," alongside the "principal" ones by Le Picq, normally pantomimic and heroic-tragic, that were performed during the first interval. Thus this season initiated a custom at the San Carlo that would continue in the following decades: two choreographers for the same show, each displaying his own specialty. This model was not exclusive to the Neapolitan theater but came to be used in Italian theaters in

---

volte più lungo del Dramma principale." Editorial commentary in Francesco Algarotti, *Saggio sopra l'opera in musica* (1755), reprinted in Pietro Metastasio, *Opere* (Naples: De Bonis, 1781), 6:L.

18. "Le Picque . . . est aussi excellent danseur que Vestris et Dauberval; cependant il a eu plus de peine que d'Aufresne à franciser les Napolitains. Il a pensé être sifflé au commencement. Les Napolitains ne s'apercevaient pas qu'il dansat dans un aussi énorme et monstrueux théâtre que le nôtre, parce qu'il ne sautait point. Mais comme il est d'une tres jolie taille, il a commencé par apprivoiser les Napolitaines, et la nation peu à peu s'est convertie." "Lettre à madame d'Epinay, 24 Juillet 1773," *Correspondance inédite de l'abbé F. Galiani* (Paris: Calmann Levy, 1881), 2:235. The actor Jean d'Aufresne, formerly of the Comédie Française and (after that) the French theater in Vienna, in January of 1773 brought a company of French actors to Naples, where (according to Galiani) they were enthusiastically received.

proportion to the spread of the grand pantomimic ballets in Noverre's style. Since the Noverrian style of ballet required a staging rich in episodes and grand, complicated, spectacular pantomimic actions, the simpler and more amusing *secondo ballo* often came to be entrusted to a different choreographer.

Magri's ballets for the 1773–74 season follow the traditional *grottesco* typology. In the ballet *Alla ricerca di un tesoro* (In Search of a Treasure), performed between the second and third acts of Giovanni Battista Borghi's opera *Il trionfo di Clelia* (The Triumph of Clelia), the choreographer's intention of exploiting all possible scenic effects in order to impress the public is utterly transparent: hence the presence of monsters, magic spells, and the like as justification for various and repeated changes of setting (much as in the operatic *farsa*). The plot, described in detail in the libretto (something rather unusual for a *secondo ballo*, and clearly a response to the prolixity of Le Picq's descriptions), is extremely dense and includes intrigues of every sort, often rather extravagant and complicated. First come various events and obstacles that interfere with the hunt for the treasure (monsters, destruction of the treasure map, demolition of a wall, chasms that engulf the servants). The scene then changes to a village where the protagonists set about courting two local women, with consequent scenes of jealousy on the part of their husbands and scorn and anger on the part of their father. There follows the repudiation of the wives by their husbands, and then immediately the attempted suicide of the two strangers, who are saved only by the appearance of the "fairy of the treasure." But the surprises are not over yet; there is also the abduction of the women by the two strangers, their flight from the village, which magically disappears and is transformed into a military encampment, the transformation of the four fugitives, and finally the general reconciliation and joyous concluding dance. In any event, notwithstanding the complexity of the plot and the work's purely spectacular purposes, from a stylistic viewpoint one clearly sees that Magri aimed to portray through pantomime a variety of situations, characters, and states of the soul—from the comic to the dramatic, from scenes of anger to those of amorous courtship, from fear to joy. All of this was compatible with the exigencies of pure dance, including virtuosic exhibitionism for soloists as well as ensemble, and with the traditions of "grotesque" dancing.

Magri's ballet for August 1773, *La festa delle lanterne* (The Festival of Lanterns), on the other hand, represents the more usual type of character dance, for which the scenario provides only sparse indications. The setting is Chinese, and within it Magri depicts New Year's festivities.

Magri's final ballet of the season (January 1774) is in a strictly comical vein. The protagonists are the masked characters Pantalone, Truffaldino, and Pulcinella, in a situation typical of the commedia dell'arte: the tricks used by Truffaldino to induce Pantalone to give his daughter as a wife to Flaminio, she already being betrothed to the rich Pulcinella, who will thus be left empty-handed.

Shortly after this compromise season, however, the arrival in Naples of Le Picq was to provoke noteworthy consequences. In fact, through a certain amount of sagacity on Le Picq's part and some concessions to the Neapolitan public, the *ballet d'action* triumphed at the San Carlo, turning the theater into a Noverrian stronghold. Everything that did not fall within the strictures of reformed ballet was forcefully opposed — not so much by the public as by the intellectual elite. Magri himself was probably one of the first casualties, if we are not to attribute to mere coincidence the fact that Le Picq's first season as dancer and choreographer at the San Carlo was also Magri's last in that theater.

But that was not all; when in 1779 Magri's *Trattato teorico-prattico di ballo* was published in Naples, hostile reactions were immediate. Even before the printing had been completed, a certain Francesco Sgai published a libelous pamphlet denigrating the work. Magri, judging that "these fatuous thoughts . . . did not have the strength to bring even the slightest discredit to my treatise,"[19] let his book be printed without any modification of the content, but thought it wise to insert a "Warning to the Courteous Reader" in later printings, in which he countered the attacks in the libel point by point.

The pamphlet in question bears the following title:

To Signor Gennaro Magri / Author of the Theoretical-practical treatise on ballet / REFLECTIONS of FRANCESCO SGAI / Florentine / Under-custodian of the wardrobe of the Royal Theater of San Carlo / and once famous dancer in the service of the / impresarios and itinerant dancers / Macrum pagina nostra nominabit Martial. L.X. Epigr. 78 / In Danzig MDCCLXXIX[20]

19. Magri/Skeaping, 46; Magri, *Trattato*, 1:9: "quelle insipide riflessioni . . . vigor non aveano di recar almen picciolo discredito al mio trattato."

20. "Al Signor Gennaro Magri / Autore del Trattato teorico-pratico di ballo / RIFLESSIONI di FRANCESCO SGAI / Fiorentino / Sottocustode della Guardaroba del Real Teatro di San Carlo / ed una volta celebre ballerino al servizio degli / Impressari [*sic*] e Danzatori ambulanti / Macrum pagina nostra nominabit Martial. L.X. Epigr. 78 / In Danzica MDCCLXXIX." A modern edition of Sgai's treatise can be found in Carmela Lombardi, *Trattati di danza in Italia nel Settecento*

Nothing is known about the author of this volume, whose name might be
a pseudonym for someone among the swarm of and supporters of the
style of dance Le Picq had imposed at the San Carlo from the time of his
arrival in 1773. In his "Warning" Magri in fact confirms that from the
moment he conceived the idea of publishing his *Trattato*, he had sus-
pected that he would "be subjected to the lashes of criticism employed by
my rivals to discredit me," rivals who "brought onto the scene the mis-
erable and obscure *Francesco Sgai* and, having dressed him up as a thinker,
put his name to a most defamatory and infamous libel against me."[21] Examining the contents of this libel, we immediately realize how Sgai's so-
called *Reflections* did not so much aim to refute the material developed in
the *Trattato* as they did to discredit its author and his cultural, artistic, and
even social roots as a *ballerino grottesco*. That is, Sgai wished to attack,
through Magri, the artistic tradition that he represented. In fact, of the
eighty-eight pages comprising Sgai's critique, some twenty are devoted
to a learned reconstruction of the origins of dance and to an enunciation
of the merits and "prerogatives of our art that have been so shamefully
neglected by you, Signor Gennariello" (the dancer's stage name, here
used derogatorily).[22] This Sgai did while interlarding his text with numerous citations of Latin and Greek authors (approximately eighty, all
duly signaled in his footnotes), with the apparent intention of showing,
by contrast, the literary weakness of Magri and his *Trattato*. Another long
section is devoted to demonstrating Magri's cultural deficiencies, merci-
lessly surveying all the "barbarisms," ungrammatical constructions, and
various other offenses against syntax and the Italian language in general.
Sgai reported himself to be Tuscan — a Florentine, to be precise — who
had "by nature" inherited "neatness of language" (la politezza della lingua), and therefore cannot refrain from showing "repugnance" for "the
infinite number of spelling errors" and especially for the "many bar-

---

(Naples: Istituto italiano per gli studi filosofici, 1991). The word "Macrum" (an inflected form of the
name Macer) in the quotation from Martial is a play on Magri's name, appropriate in this context:
"whatever page of mine shall be wafted from thence, . . . it shall speak of Macer's [Magri's] name."
See Martial (Marcus Valerius Martialis), *Epigrams*, Loeb Classical Library 95, trans. and ed. Walter
Ker, rev. ed. (Cambridge, Mass.: Harvard University Press; London: Heinemann, 1968), 2:215.

   21. Magri/Skeaping, 46; Magri, *Trattato*, 1:9: "di dover soggiacere alla sferza de' critici impe-
gnati da' miei emoli i.e., emuli per discreditarmi"; "comparir in iscena il meschino ed oscuro *Francesco
Sgai*, al quale avendo addossata la sopraveste di riflessionista, diedero in suo nome contro a me uno
scostumatissimo famoso libello."

   22. "prerogative dell'Arte nostra da Voi, Signor Gennariello, così indegnamente dimenti-
cate." Sgai, *Riflessioni*, 24–25.

barous words that you have found I know not where."[23] Nor can Magri be excused on the grounds that in a treatise on ballet it suffices simply to give the proper rules of dance. When Sgai moves on to consider technical matters, he quickly reviews a dozen steps (out of the more than 150 described by Magri), mostly limiting himself to pointing out those he considers incorrect—without explaining his objections or proposing his own interpretations—or to complaining about marginal aspects such as the erroneous transcription of names. Some of Sgai's objections are substantive and legitimate; these may pertain to the normal dialectic among styles, schools, and tastes, which accommodate differing interpretations and technical applications. That said, the true intentions of the attack and the source behind it become clear when, in opposition to the scorned art of the "Cantambanco" (or *saltimbanco*, acrobat) represented by Magri, another artistic model is proposed, the only one to have the right to command the field of ballet in Naples: Charles Le Picq. "Observe, if you will," Sgai wrote, "our incomparable and already praised D[on] Carlo Lepicq: see with what art, expression, and diversity of characters he performs stories from antiquity and mythology on the royal stage. What truth, what stagecraft, what geometry, what philosophy there is to admire! . . . This admirable performer could truly (and may Heaven grant it) compose a theoretical-practical treatise on ballet, including in it most useful instructions, and be fully applauded for it."[24]

Sgai's *Reflections* should be seen in the context of the debate occurring in those years that reached its apogee in the polemic concerning pantomime ballet between Noverre and Angiolini. Indeed, in 1773 Naples represented the stronghold of the Noverrian faction, whereas the Angiolini faction prevailed in Milan. But while the Noverre-Angiolini polemic took place on a single front—that of pantomime ballet—the attack on Magri involved another of the main aesthetic themes of the late eighteenth century: the dialectic between a dramatic and expressive conception of theatrical dance and a more virtuosic, spectacular approach. Literary theoreticians, with their treatises, armed also with their

23. "gli infiniti errori d'ortografia," "molte barbare parole, ch'io non so donde mai le abbiate ricavate." Sgai, *Riflessioni*, 25–26.

24. "Osservate di grazia il nostro impareggiabile, e già lodato D. Carlo Lepicq: Mirate con qual'arte, espressione, e diversità di caratteri rappresenta sul Real Teatro l'antiche Storie, e le Favole. Che verità, che sceneggiamento, che geometria, che filosofia vi si ammirano! . . . Quest'egregio Professore potria da vero (ed il ciel lo volesse) comporre un Trattato teorico-pratico di ballo, e porgerne utilissimi insegnamenti, ed esserne pienamente applaudito." Sgai, *Riflessioni*, 41–42.

influence on the management and programming of Italy's public theaters, had furthered the development of an aesthetic favorable to the "expressive" side, and with it the promotion of "serious" pantomime ballet,
tragic in nature.[25] In line with this tendency, then, Sgai's book represents
an attempt to cut short a dissident voice with respect to the Noverrian
monopoly that had become established in Naples—a voice that, in the
*Trattato*, sought to advocate the virtuosic *danza alta,* and to perpetuate the
"grotesque" tradition that some wished to uproot from the Neapolitan
theaters.[26]

It is abundantly clear just how much space and prominence Magri
accorded to the virtuosic dance of the *grotteschi* in his *Trattato,* through his
detailed exposition of a vast repertory of leaps, caprioles, pirouettes, and
aerial spins, adding besides a variety of ways of increasing to the maximum the difficulty of their execution and thus obtaining greater spectacular effects (see the contributions of Linda Tomko and Moira Goff in
chaps. 6 and 8). But he also entered into a resolute defense of the *grotteschi*
in an even more explicit way: "True *Ballerini,* whether *Seri* or *Comici*[,]
must equally be in general possession of everything pertaining to dancing; no real distinction can be made between one Character and another . . . Each one is worthy of applause, each is skillful if he expresses
his Action well, if he portrays his Character well."[27] Such a declaration
of the equality of styles was inconceivable at that time, not only for
dancers and choreographers in the serious style but also for those critics,
literati, and opera librettists who held the serious genre to be the only one
that could raise dance to the level of the other representational arts. The
question goes back to precise aesthetic positions that lay behind the theories of Noverre and to the reasons that made him appreciate the tragic
and heroic genres and disdain the grotesque. This conception of dance
inspired by the eighteenth-century aesthetic of the imitation of nature
and of the direct expression of the feelings could not, in fact, admit the

25. In *Dell'opera in musica* (225), Planelli states that "in theatrical dancing high dance [i.e., the
aerial style] does not figure at all, being incapable of serving the imitation of the affections . . . This
inferior species of dance . . . does not even number among the arts." (Nel ballo teatrale non deve en-
trar mai il ballo alto, come quello ch' è incapace di servire all'imitazion degli affetti . . . Questa in-
feriore spezie di ballo che non va né anche messa nel novero delle arti.)

26. On this subject see José Sasportes, "Due nuove lettere sulla controversia tra Noverre e Angiolini," *La danza italiana* 7 (Spring 1989): 51–78 (57–8).

27. Magri/Skeaping, 153–4; Magri, *Trattato,* 1:116–17: "I veri Ballerini, o sian Serj o Comici devono avere egualmente il possesso generale di tutto quello che si appartiene al ballo; nè distinzione
veruna puol [può] correre da un Carattere all' altro . . . . Ognuno è bravo, se bene esprime la sua
Azione, se bene eseguisce il suo Carattere."

existence of an abstract, "pure" form of dance, as manifested in the virtuosic and spectacular exhibitionism of the *grotteschi*.

But Magri reaches a tone of open polemic when he directly attacks
the denigrators of the grotesque genre, accusing them of fanaticism and
partisanship: "Far be it for me to speak ill of the *Serio*[,] but experience
shows certain people['s] fanaticism, some who declaim against the
*Grottesco* and declare themselves partisans of the *Serio*. These [people] go
to a [theater for] a Tragic [Action] performed by a famous *Ballante Serio*.
These his partisans soon become bored, begin to yawn, to show their
boredom and inertia; and becoming inattentive, and forgetting that they
are on his side, they would rather see something cheerful, something
ridiculous; [for this taste for crying] is a little strange."[28] (This last phrase
is an uncredited quotation from Metastasio's satirical survey of theatrical genres, *Le cinesi* [The Chinese Women; 1735, revised 1749].)[29] Magri's
statements here illuminate certain entrenched habits of Italian spectators, and they cause us to reflect on the actual effect on the audience
(beyond theatrical programming and literary debates) of the innovations
that tended to squeeze out and subdue indigenous traditions.

In any event, starting with Le Picq's arrival, the Teatro San Carlo became known as a prime locus for the propagation of Noverre's doctrines.
As Kathleen Hansell has noted with regard to the Neapolitan situation,
"In the ballet French dominance was so exclusive that developments
elsewhere in Italy long produced only a faint echo there."[30] Le Picq held
the position of choreographer until 1782, but one or another member of
Noverre's faction would be in charge at the San Carlo until nearly the
end of the century, starting with Domenico Rossi and Jean Favier, who
worked alongside Le Picq in presenting ballets by Noverre,[31] and then

---

28. Magri/Skeaping, 154 (translation amended); Magri, *Trattato*, 1:117: "Ben lungi dal dir male
del Serio; con l' esperienza mostro il fanatismo di certuni che declamano contro il Grottesco, e si
dichiarano partitarj del Serio. Portansi questi in Teatro allo spettacolo di un Tragico Avvenimento
rappresentato da un Serio e famoso Ballante. Questi suoi partigiani si stuffano subito, cominciano
a sbadigliare, a mostrar la noja, ad inoziarsi; ed obbliandosi d' esser del di lui partito, già vorrebbero
vedere un allegro, un ridicolo, che quel pianger per gusto è un poco strano."

29. The passage in question comes near the end of this *componimento drammatico*, as Sivene
opines: "Il tragico sarebbe / Senza fallo il miglior. Sempre mantiene / In contrasti d'affetti il core
umano; / Ma quel pianger per gusto è un poco strano." See Metastasio, *Tutte le opere*, 2:352.

30. Kathleen Kuzmick Hansell, "Theatrical Ballet and Italian Opera," in *Opera on Stage*, vol. 5,
The History of Italian Opera (Chicago: University of Chicago Press, 2002), 177–308 (242).

31. Among the Noverre productions restaged by Le Picq in Naples prior to 1782—though
hardly ever with any indication of their original paternity—were: *Armida e Rinaldo* (May 1773), *Adèle
de Ponthieu* (November 1774), *Medea e Giasone* (January 1775), *Gli Orazi e i Curiazi* (January 1776), *Alessandro e Campaspe* (May 1777), *Agamennone vendicato* (May 1778), and *Didone abbandonata* (January 1781).

Paolo Franchi (1783–84), Domenico Lefèvre (1783–86 and 1793–85), and Sébastien Gallet (1787–91). These choreographers "accounted for nearly all the ballets staged there until 1795, when the youthful Gaetano Gioia inaugurated a new artistic era at the San Carlo."[32]

In this climate, then, Magri had to abandon the stage definitively, in all probability already in the 1774–75 season. This hypothesis is indirectly confirmed by Francesco Sgai's pamphlet, in which the author expresses his surprise at Magri's "reappearance" with the publication of his *Trattato teorico-prattico di ballo*, stating explicitly, "Everyone, besides, had thought that you had already rendered your arms to Jupiter (as they say), and that far from thinking any further about dance, you had taken honorable leave of the theater . . . You have been retired, and hidden away for some time, it is true; but . . . you have recently reappeared on the stage, consecrating your already advanced years to the immortality of the pen."[33] From a reading of this libel one can also surmise that Magri's retirement from the stage was due to an accident; referring to Magri, Sgai states, "Before my leg was injured, I too earned the applause of full theaters. . . . The same sort of misfortune as was the case with you took away my pursuit of such a noble career; and I believe that if we wished to dance now, we could play the goatish satyr, or perhaps the bear leaping around in the piazzas."[34]

The last information we have on Magri — deducible from his own *Trattato* — indicates a turn toward didactic activity, starting in 1773, with duties of some sort at the Noble Cavaliers' Academy of Music and Dance (Nobile Accademia di Musica e di Ballo de' Signori Cavalieri), to whose members he dedicated the *Trattato;* and also a position as Maestro di Sala (Master of the Ballroom), i.e., director of the dances that took place in connection with festivities and receptions at the royal court. "To invent these [*Contredanses*]," Magri states, "has been my task in the recurring royal festivals for my most amiable Sovereign Ferdinando IV . . . during six years[,] from the first memorable [sojourn] in Portici, where he gave

32. Hansell, "Theatrical Ballet and Italian Opera," 242.

33. Sgai, *Riflessioni*, 3–4: "Ognun per altro credevasi, che Voi aveste già rese, come suol dirsi, l'armi a Giove, e che ben lungi dal pensar più alle danze, aveste preso, con onesta missione, congedo da' [dal] Teatro . . . Siete stato, è vero, qualche tempo come ritirato, e nascosto; ma . . . siete comparso novellamente in iscena, consacrando gli anni già maturi all'immortalità della penna."

34. Sgai, *Riflessioni*, 4: "Prima che mi restasse offesa la gamba, ho riscosso pur' io de' pieni teatri l'applauso . . . Tal incomodo, come a Voi, tolse a me pure il proseguimento di così nobile carriera; e credo, che se volessimo ballare adesso, potremmo figurare il caprigno Satiro, o l'orso saltante per le piazze."

eight most splendid banquets, with regal entertainment."[35] Other occasions to "direct and invent the *Contredanses*" were provided by the visits of various princes and princesses, and by the "festivities celebrating the most happy births [i.e., parturitions] of our most Clement Sovereign Lady."[36]

A further, specific confirmation of Magri's activities in these years comes in a petition he wrote in February of 1778, described in these terms by Croce: "In a petition of February 1778 he claims to have danced for many years at the San Carlo as *primo ballerino*, and to have been choreographer of the dances on the occasion of the royal wedding. From 1773 onward, dancing master of the royal entertainments for the birthdays of hereditary princes and of royal princesses, and other recurring feasts. Therefore he requested to succeed to the post of Maestro Brighenti, should he predecease him."[37] Finally as another document in the Neapolitan State Archive attests, Magri was among the Maestri di Sala for the twelve banquets given in the Teatro San Carlo starting on 30 December 1781, during the 1782 Carnival. This is the last date for which Magri's presence at a public event is confirmed.[38]

The *Trattato teorico-prattico di ballo* thus represents the crowning achievement of Magri's didactic vocation. With this work he addresses not only "lovers of dance," for whom he has prepared an efficient tool with which to learn ballroom dances (with choreographic and musical notation for thirty-nine contredanses), but also all those who wish to embark upon the dance profession, lavishing on his treatise all his experience, ripened (as we have seen) on the stages of Europe's theaters and through contact with the main protagonists of eighteenth-century dance.

35. Magri/Skeaping, 171; Magri, *Trattato*, 2:3–4: "D' inventar [le Contraddanze] è stata mia la carica nelle ricorrenze delle reali feste del mio amabilissimo Sovrano FERDINANDO IV . . . per la continuazione di anni sei, dal primo memorabile Accampamento fatto in Portici, ove diede otto splendidissimi festini con regio trattamento."

36. Magri/Skeaping, 171; Magri, *Trattato*, 2:4: "similmente nelle venute de' Serenissimi Principi, e Pricipesse . . . , nelle feste de' felicissimi Parti della nostra Clementissima Sovrana, mio è stato l'onore di dirigger, ed inventar le Contraddanze."

37. Benedetto Croce, *I teatri di Napoli* (Naples: Pierro, 1891), 550n2: "In una sua supplica del febbraio 1778 diceva di aver ballato per più anni al San Carlo come primo ballerino, e d'essere stato compositore dei balli nell'occasione delle nozze reali. Dal 1773 in poi, maestro di ballo dei regi divertimenti pei natali del principe ereditario e delle reali principesse, ed altre ricorrenze. Chiedeva dunque di succedere al posto del Maestro Brighenti, se questi premorisse." The "Maestro Brighenti" mentioned by Magri is in all probability Giacomo Brighenti "di Bologna," a famous *ballerino* and choreographer active on Italian stages especially during the 1740s and '50s (Reggio Emilia 1741, Venice 1743, 1747, 1751; Rome 1748, Turin 1748–49, Milan 1749–50, Naples 1753–54).

38. Naples, Archivio di Stato, Casa Reale Antica, fasc. 966.

It seems to have been his intention to continue this work of populariza-
tion; in fact, in the pages of the *Trattato* he announces the publication of
another series of contredanses and of a new treatise specifically devoted
to the composition of theatrical dances.[39] But none of this ever saw the
light of day—perhaps owing to the critical hostility Magri had already
endured.

39. Magri/Skeaping, 173; Magri, *Trattato*, 2:7.

# 5

# International Elements
# of Dance Training in the
# Late Eighteenth Century

## SANDRA NOLL HAMMOND

In his *Avvertimento,* or "Warning to the Courteous Reader," that precedes chapter 1, Magri acknowledges that "the art of dancing did not originate from my hands. Others had already dealt with it, and many will after me." Thus, Magri suggests that his *Trattato* on dance technique should be viewed as part of a continuum — building upon the technical heritage of previous ballet generations but anticipating that succeeding authors, like himself, also will find it "necessary" to make "use of the thoughts of others, having found them judicious and correct."[1] Indeed, all textbooks on ballet technique reach both backward and forward in time, for ballet technique requires a system of training that, unlike choreography, is not discontinuous. The technique and the teaching methods change, of course, but only very gradually.

This gradual process, handed down from teacher to student, amounts to a tradition that stays alive much longer in the dance studio than on the stage. It also reflects a general universality within the training process

---

1. Magri/Skeaping, 49; Magri, *Trattato,* 1:14: "L'arte del ballo non usciva per la prima volta dalle mie mani. Altri ne trattarono prima, e molti ne tratteranno dopo di me. Era necessità ch' io mi servissi dei pensieri altrui, avendoli ritrovati guidiziosi e giusti."

and the technique espoused. Magri, writing in Naples, tells his readers that "we are obliged to the French for the precision which dancing shows today. They have refined it on the lathe of good taste."[2] Although the *Trattato* can be viewed as a unique view into the theatrical practices of the Italian *grotteschi*, it also reveals even more about the "refined" technique that every kind of *ballerino* throughout the ballet world needed to know. The glory of Magri's *Trattato* is in the information it offers on those two aspects of ballet technique — acrobatic virtuosity and refined elegance.

The organizational structure of the *Trattato* suggests the pedagogical intent of its author; the chapters progress from the most rudimentary material to the most complex, suggesting not only an order in which the material was learned but also an order in which the material could be practiced on a regular basis. Although Magri does not lay out a ballet lesson per se, he writes about exercises and steps that, by his time, were fundamental to a dancer's training, and he describes others that were the foundation for many of the classroom exercises documented in the nineteenth century. A systematic list of the exercises and steps in their order of practice, referred to as "the lesson," was not published until over forty years after Magri's text, but, as Magri shows us, versions of these exercises had been in use long before. Magri begins his book with a brief argument for the benefits that dance training bestows, a theme frequently encountered in other dance texts. And, as in many of those texts, the first technical requirement discussed is how to stand properly so that the body is balanced, or in equilibrium, whether on both feet or one foot, with either the soles of the feet or the balls of the feet on the floor. The stance must be in one of the five positions of the feet or a derivation of those positions, which Magri describes in great detail and with variations rarely encountered in other texts. Beginning with chapter 10, Magri gets into the heart of things: descriptions of the movements and steps that make up the lexicon of ballet technique.

The technical terms used by Magri are, as he acknowledges, the "names by which they are ordinarily known, most of them being in French."[3] French had become the language of ballet following the establishment in 1661 of the Académie Royale de Danse in Paris and the subsequent international propagation of the influence of French teach-

---

2. Magri/Skeaping, Preface, 44; Magri, *Trattato, Prefazione*, 1:10: "Alli Francesi siam tenuti della lindura, in cui è posto il ballo al presente. Essi lo hanno ripulito al tornio del buon gusto."

3. Magri/Skeaping, 66; Magri, *Trattato*, 1:31: "per ordinario nominare, essendo di maggior numero in Francese."

ers, dancers, and choreographers. Although Magri relies on French terminology, he often respells the words, presumably to enhance correct
pronunciation by his Italian readers. Usually he precedes the French
term with an Italian equivalent, as in "passo gettato, pas jettè."

The format Magri uses for discussing each step is fairly consistent: he
gives a brief and general definition, such as, "The *pirouette* is a step which
is always done turning on the same place."[4] Then, he lists, but does not
yet describe, all the variations that the step may have, usually leaving the
modifying words in Italian rather than French. Thus, for example, he indicates that the *pirouette* may be "turning to the right, to the left; disfatta,
sur place sustained, forced of indeterminate number, low, in retiré, toe
and heel, heel and toe, extended open, crossed."[5] Next, Magri describes
the most basic form of the step, and then he proceeds to describe, sometimes in great detail, how each variation of the step is done. Occasionally
Magri mentions how a step is timed to the music or comments on how
one step can connect to another step. And, he gives some examples
of how the performance of a step can differ according to the staging
requirements, the type of character being portrayed, or the particular
qualities of a particular dancer. Thus, the same step might be executed
in various ways, such as in a restrained manner by a dancer in a *serio* role
or with great exaggeration by a dancer in the part of a *grottesco*.

As other essays in this volume point out, by Magri's time dancers
were very mobile, going from country to country and from job to job.
Company rosters included dancers from a wide geographical area. This
reflected the very real existence of a prevalent agreement on theatrical
dance technique, otherwise a dancer would not have been able to leave
a French troupe and immediately join an Italian one, or vice versa. Note
that I am speaking here of the technical training and capacity of dancers,
not of the choreographic styles shown on various stages. The latter could
and did vary from country to country, from city to city, even from theater to theater within a city, as documented by Bruce Brown in this volume (chap. 3). And, a good dancer, as Magri frequently reminds us, was
expected to cultivate a certain individuality. But, a professional dancer,
no matter where he or she was located, also was expected to have

---

4. Magri/Skeaping, 126; Magri, *Trattato*, 1:88: "La Pirola è un passo, che si fa sempre girando
su l'istesso terreno."

5. Magri/Skeaping, 126; Magri, *Trattato*, 1:88: "si gira a dritta, a sinistra, si fa disfatta,
sotto al corpo sostenuta, forzata incerta, bassa, ritirata, ponta e tacco, tacco e ponta, distesa aperta,
incrocciata."

achieved a certain level of competence in universally agreed upon basics of ballet: equilibrium or balance, positions and poses, and the steps, which were, as Magri asserted, "the soul of this fine art."[6]

When Magri's *Trattato* is examined in the context of other instructional ballet texts, many points in common emerge. This commonality is not obscured by Magri's documentation of some stylistic particulars of his time and of the sites of his professional career. A comparison of the *Trattato* with other texts also has the value of helping us interpret some of Magri's more ambiguous step descriptions.

The sources used in this comparison study of ballet exercises range in time of publication and/or date of manuscript from the beginning of the eighteenth century to the middle of the nineteenth century. They originated in many locations, including London, Paris, Turin, Württemberg, Lausanne, and Philadelphia. Their authors also worked in various other locations, including Milan, Amsterdam, Lyons, Stuttgart, and St. Petersburg. Like Magri, these authors were dancing masters although, unlike Magri, not all had had outstanding professional careers as performers (see table 5.1).

Indeed, the majority of available sources describing eighteenth-century dance technique are books about ballroom dancing or the "Common-Dancing usually taught in Schools." It is important to understand that in the eighteenth century, the dance of the ballroom and the dance of the theater were related but distinctly different. They did share a similar dance vocabulary of technical terms, many of the same steps, and certain fundamental movement principles. Thus, the ballroom dance manuals provide valuable information about those shared characteristics. Many of the ballroom dance texts allude to, but seldom describe, the bolder gestures, more vigorous movements embellished with beats and turns, and, particularly, the steps of high elevation—all of which were aspects of "stage dancing." Magri is unique among eighteenth-century dance writers for his primary emphasis on theatrical dance technique, even as he, as in part 2 of the *Trattato*, reached toward a broader audience of amateurs and dancing masters who might be preparing minuets and contredances for an assembly.[7]

Most importantly, with Magri's text we get a greater understanding and appreciation of how ballet differed from ballroom dancing both by

---

6. Magri/Skeaping, 66; Magri, *Trattato*, 1:30: "l'anima di questa bell'arte."
7. Magri/Skeaping, 172–73 and following.

Table 5.1: *Primary sources for comparative study*

| R. A. Feuillet | *Chorégraphie ou l'art de décrire la danse* | Paris | 1700 |
|---|---|---|---|
| Pierre Rameau | *Le Maître à danser* | Paris | 1725 |
| C. Sol | *Méthode très facile et fort nécessaire* | The Hague | 1725 |
| Pierre Rameau | *Abbrégé de la nouvelle méthode* | Paris | 1725 |
| John Essex | *The Dancing-Master* | London | 1728 |
| Giovanni Battista Dufort | *Trattato del ballo nobile* | Naples | 1728 |
| Kellom Tomlinson | *The Art of Dancing* | London | 1735 |
| Jean-Georges Noverre | *Lettres sur la danse et sur les ballets* | Stuttgart & Lyon | 1760 |
| Magny | *Principes de chorégraphie* | Paris | 1765 |
| Malpied | *Traité sur l'art de la danse* | Paris | ca. 1780 |
| J. J. Martinet | *Essai ou principes élémentaires de l'art de la danse* | Lausanne | 1797 |
| V. G. | *Elements and Principles of the Art of Dancing* | Philadelphia | 1817 |
| Carlo Blasis | *Traité élémentaire, théorique et pratique de l'art de la danse* | Milan | 1820 |
| Charles Mason | *A Short Essay on the French Danse de Société* | London | 1827 |
| Carlo Blasis | *The Code of Terpsichore* | London | 1828 |
| Michel St. Léon | "Cahier Exercices de 1829" | MS Paris | 1829 |
| Michel St. Léon | "Cahier d'Exercices pour les Princesses" | MS Paris | 1830 |
| E. A. Théleur | *Letters on Dancing* | London | 1831 |
| Giacomo Costa | *Saggio analitico-pratico intorno all'arte della danza* | Turin | 1831 |
| Michel St. Léon | untitled ms. | MS Paris | 1833, 1834, 1836 |
| A. Saint-Léon | *La Sténochorégraphie ou art d'écrire promptement la danse* | Paris | 1852 |
| G. Léopold Adice | *Théorie de gymnastique de la danse théâtrale* | Paris | 1859 |

*Note:*
See footnotes for full citations.

the selection of steps and gestures and by the way those movements were performed. Because his descriptions suggest so many correspondences to ballet technique as it was documented in the nineteenth century, it is useful to compare the *Trattato* with the works of later dance authors. The comparative sources used in this discussion are by no means exhaustive of the texts from the period, roughly 150 years, but rather they are a sampling of the materials available for appreciating the consistencies as well as the changes in ballet's technical history.[8] Nor is this discussion a complete inventory of all of Magri's material, which would call for a much more extensive treatment. However, from this brief overview, the overwhelming impression is of a truly international art form with remarkable continuity, especially in the training of its practitioners. Therefore, it seems useful for the present purposes to read Magri's *Trattato* as a training manual and to present its components in the format of a ballet lesson.

It is interesting to realize that by 1779, the basic nature of almost all of the exercises and steps for the ballet lesson of the nineteenth century was already established, even though the exact outline of the lesson apparently was not published until 1820 with the appearance of Carlo Blasis's first text, *Traité élémentaire, théorique et pratique de l'art de la danse*.[9] Blasis was a young dancer who went on to become an influential ballet teacher in Milan at the ballet school at La Scala and the author of many books on ballet. In the first of his publications, Blasis almost seems to echo Magri as he reminds his readers that the instructions he offers have emanated "from the schools of leading masters who have contributed immensely to the progress and beauty of modern dancing," and thus they were not new or unique to him. In this context, Blasis mentions Jean Dauberval (with whom he had studied), Pierre Gardel (in whose choreography he made his Paris Opéra debut), and Auguste Vestris (innovative dancer and teacher at the Paris Opéra).[10] Blasis had inherited from the previous century the elements that became "the combination of elementary exercises and the principal steps of dancing" that by the early nineteenth century were "usually termed the *lesson*."[11]

The following discussion is divided according to the outline of the ballet lesson as it was recorded in the early nineteenth century. The subheadings within those categories refer to the chapter numbers, titles, and page numbers of the chapters in Skeaping's translation of Magri (fol-

8. Two volumes by Edmund Fairfax, *The Styles of Eighteenth-Century Ballet* (Lanham, MD: Scarecrow, 2003), and "The Technique of Eighteenth-Century Ballet" (in preparation), offer detailed and sweeping accounts of theatrical dance practices.

9. *Elementary Treatise*, trans. and ed. Mary Stewart Evans (New York: Dover, 1968), 62. A more detailed account of the lesson appears in a later work by Blasis, *The Code of Terpsichore*, trans. R. Barton (London: James Bulcock, 1828), available also in a reprint edition (New York: Dance Horizons, 1976), 99–103.

10. Blasis, *Treatise*, 5.

11. Blasis, *Code*, 102.

lowed by those in the original *Trattato*) that correspond to, or that seem to be related to, classroom material. Rather than try to address every example of these correspondences that occurs in the *Trattato*, I have chosen to treat fewer chapters but in more depth than would otherwise be possible. And, it is important to keep in mind that even when we find clear relationships between a step described in the *Trattato* and a step described by earlier and/or by later authors, the actual performance of the step might be given different stylistic and technical nuances by dancers trained in different eras and different locales.

## The Lesson: First Principles

Before discussing particular exercises and steps, Magri addresses the correct stance that a dancer must acquire in order to practice any of those movements. He declares, "The Equilibrium is one of the fundamental principles of the Dance. It keeps the body straight and upright."[12] He defines this as though, when the body is balanced evenly on the soles, toes, or heels of both feet, a straight line could divide the body in half, falling as a plumb line ("un filo con un piombo") from the sternum to a point exactly between the feet. He mentions the slight incline that the body must have in order to maintain equilibrium when it is balanced on only one foot. Writing fifty years later, Blasis begins his *Code de Terpsichore* with a chapter on "General Instructions to Pupils," in which he also advises one to "take especial care to acquire perpendicularity and an exact equilibrium."[13]

Fundamental to the proper way in which movements were performed in this balanced verticality were the five turned-out positions of the feet. In 1725, dancing master and writer Pierre Rameau credited Pierre Beauchamps with the codification of those five positions.[14] A French dancer, dancing master, choreographer, and composer of dance music, Beauchamps was instrumental in the production of ballets at the

---

12. Magri/Skeaping, 56; Magri, *Trattato*, 1:19: "L'Equilibrio è uno de' fondamenti principali della Danza. Egli mantiene il corpo ben dritto, e fermo in piedi."

13. Blasis, *Code*, 52.

14. Pierre Rameau, *Le Maître à danser. Qui enseigne la maniere de faire tous les differens pas de danse dans toute la régularité de l'art, & de conduire les bras à chaque pas* (Paris: Jean Villette, 1725), 9. Hereafter, translated material from Rameau is quoted from John Essex ("Done from the French of Monsieur Rameau"), *The Dancing-Master: or, The Art of Dancing Explained, Wherein the Manner of Performing All Steps in Ball Dancing Is Made Easy by a New and Familiar Method* (London: Essex, 1728).

court of Louis XIV, the Paris Opéra, and the Jesuit Collège Louis-le-Grand. The codification of the positions of the feet that are attributed to Beauchamps became, in Magri's words, the "five positions accepted by all" (le cinque positure da tutti ammesse),[15] and they continue to be the foundation of ballet technique today.

In his discussion of the positions, Magri states that first position is with "the toes well turned out opposite each other, and the heels together, forming an obtuse angle,"[16] but we don't know from his description how much that angle exceeded 90 degrees. Dance writers prior to Magri also often simply state that the legs are "well" turned out, but sometimes they say "entirely turned out" (tout à fait tournez en dehors).[17] Both admonitions probably imply that the degree of turnout should be as much as an individual's anatomy allowed. Many illustrations of dancers in those earlier texts show their feet turned out to an angle that is indeed obtuse, but nearer to 180 degrees than to 90.[18] Magri's other mention of degree of turnout is in his discussion of the fifth position, which is formed "by placing the heel of one foot touching the toe of the other in such a way that a right angle is formed between the toe of one and the heel of the other."[19] This would seem to correspond to the fifth position as described and notated in a 1728 publication, *Trattato del ballo nobile*, in which the feet form "quasi un angolo retto." The author, Giambatista Dufort, was a fellow Neapolitan dance writer, whom Magri often denigrates for his simplistic or narrow interpretations of dance technique.[20]

The turned-out positions of the feet were considered the true positions as opposed to the corresponding false positions, also described by Magri, in which the feet were turned inward. It was necessary to know the false positions, Magri says, because the *ballanti grotteschi* make such use

15. Magri/Skeaping, 63; Magri, *Trattato*, 1:26.

16. Magri/Skeaping, 63; Magri, *Trattato*, 1:26: "le punte ben rivolte oppostamente al di fuori, ed i talloni faranno congiunti, formando angolo ottuso."

17. C. Sol, *Méthode très facile et fort nécessaire, pour montrer à la jeunesse de l'un & l'autre sexe la maniere de bien dancer* (The Hague: l'Auteur, 1725), 52.

18. See, for example, illustrations in the Rameau and Essex volumes (see n14). Edmund Fairfax kindly shared with me information on turnout from his forthcoming volume on eighteenth-century theatrical dance technique.

19. Magri/Skeaping, 64; Magri, *Trattato*, 1:27: "La quinta si forma con mettere il tallone di un piede toccante la punta dell'altro, talmente che si facci angolo retto tra la punta di uno, ed il tallone dell'altro."

20. Giovanni Battista Dufort, *Trattato del ballo nobile di Giambatista Dufort, indirizzato all'eccelenza delle signore dame, e de' signori cavalieri napoletani* (Naples: F. Mosca, 1728), 8. For Magri's objections to Dufort, see Magri/Skeaping, 57, 66, 89.

of them for almost all their characterizations.[21] The importance of these turned-in positions for theatrical dance is implied by their appearance in 1700 in the first published book of dance notation, *Chorégraphie*, a volume that deals not only with steps appropriate for the ballroom but also with many that would be performed only in a theatrical context. The author and notator, Raoul-Auger Feuillet, a Parisian dancing master and choreographer, placed the notated table of *fausses positions* directly following that of the *bonnes positions*.[22]

Magri helpfully includes other positions of the feet rarely described and, to my knowledge, not treated systematically by authors prior to Magri. These include: five positions "in the air" (*in aria*), which correspond to the five true positions but with one foot raised from the ground; three forced (*forzate*) positions, which correspond to the second, fourth, and fifth true positions but with a greater distance between the feet; and the five Spanish positions in which the feet are parallel to each other, rather than turned outward or inward.[23] Earlier examples of the use of the feet either turned inward or parallel can be found in the notated choreographies (ca. 1725) that employ "waving" steps or positions, such as the "Chacone of Amadis Perform'd by Mr Dupré" (LMC 1840) and the "Spanish Entrée Performed by Mr Desnoyer" (LMC 8100).[24] Both

21. Magri/Skeaping, 64; Magri, *Trattato*, 1:27–28.

22. Raoul-Auger Feuillet, *Chorégraphie ou l'art de décrire la danse* (Paris: Chez l'Auteur, 1700), 7–8. It should be mentioned here that the degree of turnout depicted in *Chorégraphie* is no more than ninety degrees. This possibly reflects an earlier style that later, certainly by the third decade of the eighteenth century, developed into the more turned-out stance depicted in the illustrations of other texts. Or, as Edmund Fairfax has pointed out, Feuillet's notation was, in effect, more like a skeletal abstraction that must be interpreted by a knowledgeable reader rather than a literal depiction of how a step was performed (correspondence with the author). For example, the notation symbols can indicate that a leg is raised but not how high. The issue is complicated somewhat by the fact that two later notator-authors show quite different degrees of turnout. In Magny's *Principes de chorégraphie suivis d'un traité de la cadence* (Paris: Duchesne et La Chevardière, 1765; repr., Geneva: Minkoff, 1980) foot symbols show more turnout than in the Feuillet volume. For example, Magny clearly shows first position as an obtuse angle. However, notation in *Traité sur l'art de la danse* (Paris: M. Boüin, ca. 1780) by Malpied shows a ninety-degree turnout in the foot symbols. Another argument is that notators, like dancers, had their own individual styles, and thus they simply shaped the symbols differently on the page.

23. Magri/Skeaping, 64–65; Magri, *Trattato*, 1:28–30. Presumably, the forced fifth position is an overcrossing, in which the heel of the front foot crosses beyond the toe of the back foot. In the second Spanish position, the feet are not laterally apart as one might expect, but rather they are in a straight line, one behind the other at a distance of one foot-length apart.

24. Both dances appear in *A New Collection of Dances, Containing a Great Number of the Best Ball and Stage Dances: Composed by Monsieur l'Abbé, Dancing-Master to Their Royal Highnesses, the Three Young*

dances were choreographed by Anthony l'Abbé, a Parisian dancer of some renown who in 1698 was brought to London, where he enjoyed great success as dancer, dancing master, and choreographer. It seems that by 1800, ideal turnout was 180 degrees, and soon most dance texts, even ballroom texts, had instructions to that effect. Thus, in the first position of the feet "the toes of the right foot [should be] turned towards the right shoulder, and those of the left foot towards the left shoulder, in such a way as to bring both feet in one straight line,"[25] and the fourth position usually was more crossed than Magri had advocated. Early nineteenth-century dance texts simply used the term "positions of the feet," and by that was meant the five turned-out positions. One early nineteenth-century author who did acknowledge and number additional positions of the feet was E. A. Théleur, an English dancing master who had studied in Paris. His idiosyncratic but very explicit system included numbered positions (which he called stations) where the body was balanced on only one foot and some where the feet were either more open or more crossed than in the standard five positions.

Like Magri, Théleur justified naming and numbering so many positions or stations because they were already in use.[26] Many ballets of the nineteenth century also contained significant elements derived from national or folk dances.[27] These could include steps such as the *tortillé*, in which one foot and then the other turns inward and outward, making use of the false as well as the true positions. A description of a *tortillé* appears in a *Kosaque composée pour la princess Auguste*, which is contained in a notebook compiled from 1833 to 1836 by Michel St. Léon, a retired dancer from the Paris Opéra, who took up the post of dancing master at the Court of Württemberg.[28] The *tortillé* he describes closely resembles the

---

*Princesses*, notated and published by "Monsieur Roussau" ca. 1725. Examples of the waving steps and positions occur on p. 63, m. 5 ("Chacone"); p. 73, m. 1; and p. 74, m. 7 ("Spanish Entrée").

25. V. G., *Elements and Principles of the Art of Dancing from the French of J. H. G. Professor of Dancing in Paris* (Philadelphia: J. F. Hurtel, 1817), 15. This is a translation of J. H. Gourdoux-Daux, *Principes et notions élémentaires sur l'art de la danse pour la ville* (Paris: Chez l'auteur, 1811).

26. E. A. Théleur, *Letters on Dancing, Reducing This Elegant and Healthful Exercise to Easy Scientific Principles* (London: Sherwood, 1831); republication in *Studies in Dance History* (Pennington, NJ: Princeton Periodicals, 1990).

27. For an enlightening account of the importance and prevalence of national dances in nineteenth-century ballets, see Lisa C. Arkin and Marian Smith, "National Dance in the Romantic Ballet," in *Rethinking the Sylph: New Perspectives on the Romantic Ballet*, ed. Lynn Garafola (Hanover, NH: Wesleyan University Press, 1997), 11–68.

28. In all, St. Léon compiled four notebooks during his tenure at the Court of Württemberg: "Cahier Exercices de 1829"; "Cahier d'Exercices pour L.L. A.A. Royalles les Princesses de Wurtemberg 1830; 2me Cahier Exercices de 1830" (containing material also dated 1831); and an un-

*tortigliè* in the *Trattato,* a step that Magri says is used only by the *ballerini grotteschi*,[29] whose repertory, as described in other chapters in this volume, also included national dances.

In this brief introduction to the lesson, we can see some of the threads of ballet's technical tradition from the beginning of the eighteenth century through the early decades of the nineteenth century. The vertical, balanced posture and the five turned-out positions of the feet continued to be the norm, with the required degree of turnout increasing to 180 degrees. We also can begin to see how Magri's effort to document all the variations of the positions of the feet was an important comment on the variety of dance choreographies and the technical range needed to perform them. This continued to be true in the next century, when even a young princess might be taught a step once reserved for the *grotteschi*.

## The Lesson: Elementary Exercises

The ballet lesson proper began with what were called the elementary or preparatory exercises. The first of those exercises was the bending and straightening of the knees in the five positions of the feet, followed by rises onto the balls of the feet.

Chapter 10, Of the *plié,* and the rise, 68 / Del *piegare, e rilevare,* 32–33

Magri states that the bending and straightening of the knees can be done "in any position and on any equilibrium" ("in qualunque posizione, e sopra qualunque equilibrio"). His general rule for bending is that the "feet must always be turned out and the knees also face outwards, not forward."[30] So, it is clear that here he is referring to bending only in the five turned-out positions, balanced either on both feet or on one foot. The importance of these fundamental movements of bending and rising was noted succinctly by Pierre Rameau in 1725, in his text on ballroom dancing: "Dancing is no more than to know how to sink and rise

---

titled manuscript volume containing *exercices, enchaînements,* and theatrical dances dated 1833, 1834, and 1836 (F-Po Rés. 1137 and 1140). The description of the *tortillé* is in the last notebook on p. 5 in a section containing other national dances composed for the royal children: a "Tirolième," a "Bolero," and a "Guarachia danse Espagnole ou nouvelle Kachucha."

29. Magri/Skeaping, 85; Magri, *Trattato,* 1:50.

30. Magri/Skeaping, 68; Magri, *Trattato,* 1:33: "che nel piegare le punte de' piedi devono star sempre rivolte al di fuori, ed i ginocchi, che escano pur fuori, e non avanti."

properly."[31] Magri, too, seems to be speaking in this chapter of the bend
and rise as an essential element for dancing rather than as a training
exercise. However, in part 2 of the *Trattato*, in discussing the duties of a
dancing master, Magri is quite clearly advising the correct practice of
bends and rises as the first exercises that a dancer should learn. Moreover, he says the dancer should first practice these movements while
holding on to the master's hands for support, then later he should "lightly
lean against a chair" (leggermente appoggiarlo ad una sedia), and finally
perform them without support.[32] Here Magri is referring to the instruction and practice for ballroom dancing, but the use of a chair or rail has
a long history in theatrical dance practice as well. It is probably impossible to know the first use of a support during the practice of leg movements, but illustrations in a 1602 dance treatise show a dancer standing
between a table and an armchair, using them for support.[33]

Magri says that bending and rising should be done softly or gently
(*soavemente*), but he does not mention the depth of the *piegare*. Carlo Blasis,
in his 1828 description of "the First Exercises" of the lesson, requires that
the knees be bent "without raising the heels in the least from the
ground,"[34] and one can imagine that Magri meant to imply that as well
(see fig. 5.1). In 1831, E. A. Théleur, in a chapter entitled "Observations
on Practice," concurs with this precept, because "when a dancer bends
so low as to cause the heels to quit the ground, he loses in a considerable
degree his steadiness."[35] Note, however, that the authors are referring to
the practice of exercises, not the performance of certain steps, which occasionally were done from or with a lower or "forced" bend of the knees
as, for example, Magri's *pirola bassa*.[36]

The rise, as described by Magri, referred not only to the straightening of the knees after the bend but also to a rising onto the balls of the feet
("su le punte de' piedi").[37] C. Sol, writing in 1725, states that the rise "sur
la pointe des pieds" must be done with the knees quite tight and straight,
and he recommends that both the bend and the rise be done several
times as the "premiers Exercices."[38] As an exercise, the rise *sur les pointes*,

---

31. Rameau/Essex, *Dancing-Master*, 11.
32. Magri/Skeaping, 175–76; Magri, *Trattato*, 2:10–11.
33. Cesare Negri, *Le gratie d'amore* (Milan: Pacifico Pontio & Gio. Battista Piccaglia, 1602), 80.
34. Blasis, *Code*, 100.
35. Théleur, *Letters*, 54.
36. Magri/Skeaping, 127; Magri, *Trattato*, 1:89.
37. Magri/Skeaping, 58; Magri, *Trattato*, 1:21.
38. Sol, *Méthode*, 18.

Figure 5.1: Bending in the first position (Blasis, *Code* [1830], plate 2, fig. 4)

or on the toes, was practiced in order to "give flexibility and strength to the instep."[39]

Before 1831, illustrations in dance technique manuals showed the rise as either onto the balls of the feet or onto a high three-quarter point position. But Théleur's descriptions and illustrations distinguish between positions on the balls of the feet and those on the "points of the toes," the latter being practiced with a gradual rise and descent, "keeping the joints of the toes perfectly straight from the commencement of the movement."[40] Even earlier, and in manuals written primarily for ballroom dancing, advice was given for practicing rises onto the tips of the toes.[41] Magri, however, makes only a passing reference to raising the whole body on the tip of the big toe, "su la punta del maggior dito del piede," and this is in the context of his description of "the incomparable M. Pitrot," the French dancer and director Antoine-Bonaventure Pitrot.

39. Blasis, *Code*, 100.

40. Théleur, *Letters*, 95, 55. For another description of how to rise onto full point, or "sur les orteils," see also Michel St. Léon, "Cahier Exercices de 1829," 3.

41. V. G., *Elements and Principles*, 54–55, 57.

Pitrot's aplomb in this and other actions was "apparently supernatural yet borne out by the testimony of eyewitnesses all over Europe."[42] Magri's description of Pitrot's balance, with his joints perfectly extended so that "the whole thigh, leg and foot itself fall into one perpendicular line," is graphic testimony of the trend toward the eventual dancing on the tips of the toes that became identified with female dancers in the romantic ballet. As an added technical requirement, it eventually would acquire a place in a dancer's daily training, but this was not yet the case in Magri's time.[43]

Chapter 13, Of the Beating of the Foot, the *Battements*, 73–75 / Del *Battimento del piede, de Battimente*, 37–41

To practice the *battements*, Magri would have the beginner "supported by a chair."[44] His descriptions find close counterparts in those of Giacomo Costa in his dance treatise published in Turin in 1831.[45] Costa helpfully includes illustrations showing a dancer practicing his *battemens* or *battimenti* while holding onto the back of a chair.

As the lesson became systematized and the order of exercises written down, the *battement* exercises typically were practiced from large to small, that is, the *battements* requiring the highest leg movements came immediately after the bending and rising exercises, and then the lower, quicker *battements* were practiced, usually interspersed with various exercises of *ronds de jambe*. However, Magri and Costa reserve their discussion of the high *battements* until the end of their section on *battement* exercises.

Magri and Costa refer to *battimento disteso* as an action in which the straight gesture leg beats in fifth position in front of the straight supporting leg, then opens to the side, and then beats in fifth position in back.

---

42. Magri/Skeaping, 128; Magri, *Trattato*, 1:91: "Cose, che pajono sopranaturali, [e]ppure, n'è testimonio di vista tutta l'Europa."

43. Magri/Skeaping, 128; Magri, *Trattato*, 1:91: "che tutta la coscia, gamba, e piede istesso cadono in linea perpendicolare." Pitrot (b. Marseille ca. 1720; *fl*. 1744–70) had an international career, including Paris (the Opéra and the Comédie Italienne), Milan (La Scala), and London (King's Theatre). For more on early exercises for *pointe* technique, see Sandra Noll Hammond, "Searching for the Sylph: Documentation of Early Developments in Pointe Technique," *Dance Research Journal* 19 no. 2 (1987–88): 27–31.

44. Magri/Skeaping, 73; Magri, *Trattato*, 1:38: "un principiante fa d'uopo, che si appoggi a qualche sedia."

45. Giacomo Costa, *Saggio analitico-pratico intorno all'arte della danza per uso di civile conversazione* (Turin: Mancio, Speirani e Campagnia, 1831), 13–25. All terms and quotations taken from Costa use his original spelling.

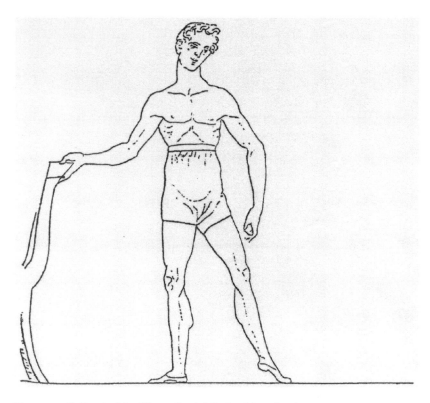

Figure 5.2: *Battimento disteso* (Costa, *Saggio* [1831], table 3, fig. 1)

For both Magri and Costa, the ball of the working foot skims along the floor during the many repetitions of this exercise (see fig. 5.2). A more fully pointed foot was also in use for this exercise in Costa's time, 1831, as Théleur illustrates for the "little *battemens*" in his text of the same year.[46]

Again, there is much similarity between the *battimento basso piegato* of Magri and the *battimenti piegati* or *battemens pliés* of Costa. The knee of the gesture leg bends as the foot comes behind the straight supporting leg, then the knee extends as the leg opens again to the side. The movement is quickly repeated with the foot crossing in front. The illustration of a *battimento piegati* by Costa shows the legs forming the "obtuse angle" described by Magri for his similar exercise (see fig. 5.3). These beats seem to echo one of the types of *battements* described in 1725 by Rameau, wherein the gesture leg bends as it crosses in front or in back of the

46. Théleur, *Letters*, plates 11 and 15.

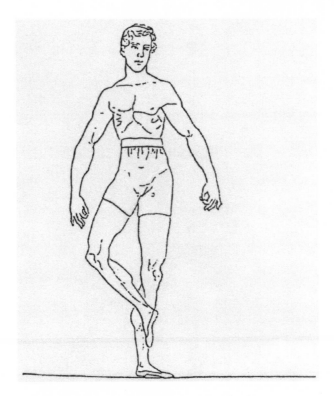

Figure 5.3: *Battimento piegato* (Costa, *Saggio* [1831], table 4, fig. 1)

supporting leg and extends as it opens to the side. Rameau advises the
dancer to practice the beats with one leg and then with the other and to
be "observing at each beat to extend the Knee after you have bent it."
He also advises making several beats in succession "till by practice you'll
come to make them quick."[47] Magri also urges the dancer to repeat the
beating action as many times as possible and with the greatest possible
speed so that the movements may be used freely when dancing.[48]

In these and the related *battimenti sul collo del piede*, or *battements* on the
instep, Magri, along with all the other authors, also encourages speed,
"for the quicker it is, the more beautiful."[49] Blasis would seem to heartily

47. Rameau/Essex, *Dancing-Master*, 110.
48. Magri/Skeaping, 74; Magri, *Trattato*, 1:38.
49. Magri/Skeaping, 74; Magri, *Trattato*, 39: "che sia possibile, che quanto è più sollecito, tanto
è più bello."

agree, urging the pupil to perform the "*petits battements* on the instep" by gradually increasing in quickness, "till you can perform them so rapidly, that the eye cannot count them."[50] Magri describes how these *battimenti* on the instep are used in performance when "jumped, by taking a little spring accompanied by two beats but with the rule that the first is done with a little spring and the second when the foot is on the ground, whereas if it is desired to do more of them, this is left to the *Ballerino's* judgement."[51] Rameau, in 1725, also describes how *battements* can occur while "hopping on one leg, afterwards the Leg which is off the Ground makes two Beats, one before and the other behind."[52]

The *battimento alto staccato*, as described by Magri, is detached "at least as high as the shoulder."[53] Early nineteenth-century authors seem to be more cautious, advising that in the large or *grands battements* the leg be raised only to a horizontal or hip level (see fig. 5.4).[54] This height would correspond to the many "h. de la h." or "hauteur de la hanche" references for leg movements described by Michel St. Léon in his various notebooks dated 1829–36. Magri urges the dancer not to perform these high *battements* too furiously and to take care "to keep the supporting leg very steady," giving vivid examples of injuries resulting in careless practice.[55] Théleur would seem to agree, when he says, "I assuredly do not admire the system of throwing up the leg in the act of making the *battement*," and he also cautions the dancer to keep the "inactive leg, hip, and loins, perfectly steady." Théleur goes on to advocate "forcing" the leg "more and more every *battement*, until it is raised as high as it is required,"[56] perhaps at least to shoulder height, as required by Magri fifty years before. Obviously referring to practice rather than to performance, Magri wants the lifting and the lowering of the leg to be done as fast as possible, and repeated as many times as possible. An account of the number of repetitions of the exercises that became the norm in the lesson of Blasis appears in a

---

50. Blasis, *Code*, 101.

51. Magri/Skeaping, 74–75; Magri, *Trattato*, 1:40: "Questo battuto su'l collo del piede si puol far saltato, il quale si fa spiccando un piccolo salticello, accompagnato con due battimenti; ma con regola, che il primo si facci co'l salticello, ed il secondo quando il piede sta a terra; ove se ne vuol far degli altri, resta l'arbitrio al Ballerino."

52. Rameau/Essex, *Dancing-Master*, 111.

53. Magri/Skeaping, 75; Magri, *Trattato*, 1:40: "eguagliare la spalla in altezzi."

54. See, for example, the discussion "*Dei Distcacchi*" in Costa, *Saggio*, 19–21; "Battements" in Blasis, *Code*, 100.

55. Magri/Skeaping, 75; Magri, *Trattato*, 1:41: "tener bene appoggiato il piede a terra."

56. Théleur, *Letters*, 55.

Figure 5.4: Manner in which a dancer should hold himself in practicing; leg in the second position (Blasis, *Code* [1830], plate 2, fig. 5)

book published in 1859 by one of Blasis's disciples, G. Léopold Adice, a dancer and ballet instructor at the Paris Opéra. Adice recalls that the practice at the *barre* included 128 *grands battements*, 96 *petits battements*, 64 slow *petits battements sur le cou de pied*, and 120 rapid ones.[57]

Chapter 15, Of the *Tordichamp*, 76 / Del *tordichamp*, 41–42

Immediately following his discussion of the various *battimenti*, Magri offers a brief and rather vague description of the circling leg movement he calls *tordichamp*.[58] Writing fifty years later, Costa also follows his dis-

57. G. Léopold Adice, *Théorie de la gymnastique de la danse théâtrale* (Paris: Chais, 1859), 74–75.
58. Magri/Skeaping, 76; Magri, *Trattato*, 1:41–42.

cussion of *battimenti* with a section entitled "Giri di gamba/Ronds de jambe," in which he describes in more detail several types of circling leg movements.[59] An antecedent of these exercises was surely the *ouverture de jambe* or opening of the leg, described by Rameau in 1725 in the chapter just preceding his discussion of *battements*.[60]

For the Magri version of *tordichamp*, the gesture foot glides from first position in the air into fifth position as the knees bend. It is then "detached" into the air, both legs straightening, where "the foot itself forms a circle in the air, with a well stretched instep."[61] The first type of *giro* described and illustrated by Costa also involves a bend of the knees (in first position or *prima posizione piegata*), but the point of the circling foot always stays on the floor.[62] An interpretation of Magri's example would seem to be that, once the leg is carried into the air "either to the front, or to the back," the leg is brought to the side, then the thigh is kept motionless so that the circling movement is made by the leg below the knee. Thus, it is the foot which traces the outline of the circle.

In discussing the *tordichamps*, Magri also mentions those made entirely to the side, that is, without ever lowering through fifth position. Later in his text, Magri discusses various jumps — types of capriole — and turns — *pirole* — which incorporate this type of *tordichamp*, in which case the circling movement can be "repeated two and three times" within the same step. These *tordichamps* would be analogous to the *petits ronds de jambe* described by many authors. Théleur gives a succinct description of these little *ronds de jambe* "in the air": "a circle should be described as large as possible, taking care at the same time, as soon as the thigh is placed in its proper position [to the side], never to move the hip joint, the action being only at the knee."[63] Magri tried to explain this action fifty years prior, by saying that it is only "the foot itself" which traces a circle in the air.

According to Magri, all three categories of *ballerini* needed to know how to perform all the variants of the *tordichamp*, and he recommends that "in studying it, start slowly and, having become accustomed to making the exact circling and movement of the leg, gradually increase the speed

59. Costa, *Saggio*, 26–33.
60. Rameau, *Le Maître*, 187–89.
61. Magri/Skeaping, 76; Magri, *Trattato*, 1:41: "poscia staccandolo, con il piede istesso formerassi un cerchio in aria, con tenere il collo del piede ben disteso."
62. Costa, *Saggio*, 26.
63. Théleur, *Letters*, 58.

until it is exercised with the utmost velocity."[64] Théleur agrees: the dancer "should do the little *ronds de jambes,* commencing slowly, and gradually encreasing their velocity, as in doing the little *battemens.*"[65] All variants of the *tordichamp, giro di gamba,* or *rond de jambe* could be performed both outward (*en dehors* — the leg circling away from the body) and inward (*en dedans* — the leg circling in toward the body), and they were practiced equally with each leg. Adice recalls that in Blasis's time the series of exercises at the *barre* included a total of 256 *ronds de jambe.*[66]

Such emphasis on practicing *battements* and *ronds de jambe* was clearly known even before Magri. For example, in 1760 Jean-Georges Noverre, in his *Lettres sur la danse,* urged "moderate and regular exercise," especially the practice of "ronds ou tours de jambe en dedans ou en dehors et grands battements tendus" in order to facilitate turnout of the legs.[67]

## The Lesson: Center Work

Accounts of early-nineteenth-century ballet training state that, after practicing these first exercises at a chair, rail, or *barre,* some variant of the exercises was repeated in center floor before going on with the rest of the lesson.[68] The lesson then continued with a series of exercises that emphasized balance and control in center floor, away from the support of a *barre* or rail. These exercises, ranging from simple to complex, were derived from steps used in ballroom and/or in theatrical dances of the previous century. Magri's text offers helpful insights into the continuity of much of this material, including the exercise that began the series, the *temps de courante.*

Chapter 25, Of the *Pas Grave* or *Courante,* 92–93 / Del *passo grave, ou courante,* 55–57

Magri states that this "serious and majestic" step is "used in the Theatre and the ballroom" in all kinds of dances, and is especially found in the *se-*

---

64. Magri/Skeaping, 76; Magri, *Trattato,* 1:42: "Nello studiarsi si comincia a far gravamente, ed avendo fatto l'uso al guisto giro, e moto della gamba, va crescendo gradatamente di celerità, finchè s'esercita di farlo velocissimo."

65. Théleur, *Letters,* 96.

66. Adice, *Théorie,* 74.

67. Noverre/Beaumont, 119.

68. See, for example, Adice, *Théorie,* 76.

*rio* or noble style of dancing.[69] He attributes the invention of the *courante* steps to the "celebrated Dancing Master Monsieur de Beauchamp, who had the honour of giving lessons to Louis le Grand."[70] Other forms of *courante* steps are documented prior to the era of Louis XIV, but they bear little resemblance to the later versions referred to by Magri.[71]

Examples of the *tems de courante* were at the beginning of the tables of notated steps published in 1700 by Raoul-Auger Feuillet in his volume of *Chorégraphie*.[72] *Courante* steps continued to head the list of notation tables published later in the century by Magny (1765) and Malpied (ca. 1780). By the nineteenth century the step seems no longer to have been used in choreographies, but it continued as a classroom exercise. A sequence of sixteen *tems de courante*, derived from the earlier tradition, served "as a prelude to the lesson in the center."[73]

The *passo grave sotto al corpo* described by Magri shows connections to earlier eighteenth-century accounts of the step and also to the nineteenth-century classroom versions. His example begins "with the right [foot] in fourth behind the left; bend, and stretch sliding the toe of the same, hardly touching the ground, carrying to second position, and, after skimming and bringing it almost into first, place the same in the natural fourth."[74] In his 1728 translation of Rameau's text, Essex describes a similar "Courant Step or March": "having therefore the left Leg foremost, and the Body upon it, with the right Foot in the fourth Position, the Heel up ready to move; from thence you sink, opening the right Foot [sideward]; and when you rise rise again with the Knees extended, you slide the right Foot forwards to the fourth Position, and the body goes intirely upon it."[75]

---

69. Magri/Skeaping, 92: Magri, *Trattato,* 1:55: "la qualità del Passo Grave esser seria, e maestosa. Serve per Teatro, e per Sala: entra in tutte le sorti di ballo, e specialmente nel ballar serio."

70. Magri/Skeaping, 92; Magri, *Trattato,* 1:55: "Monsieur de Beauchamp, celebre Maestro di ballo, qui ebbe l'onore di dar lezione a Luigi il Grande, fu l'inventore di esso."

71. See, for example, François de Lauze, *Apologie de la danse et la parfaicte méthode de l'enseigner tant aux cavaliers qu'aux dames* (1623), republished as *Apologie de la danse by F. De Lauze 1623. A Treatise of Instruction in Dancing and Deportment,* given in the original French with a translation, introduction, and notes by Joan Wildeblood (London: Frederick Muller, 1952), 87–99.

72. Feuillet, *Chorégraphie,* 47–48.

73. Adice, *Théorie,* 76: "qui servaient de prélude à la leçon du milieu." For related material, see also Sandra Noll Hammond, "Clues to Ballet's Technical History From the Early Nineteenth-Century Ballet Lesson," *Dance Research* 3 (1984): 53–66 (55–6), and "Steps through Time: Selected Dance Vocabulary of the Eighteenth and Nineteenth Centuries," *Dance Research* 10 (1992): 93–108 (94–96).

74. Magri/Skeaping, 93; Magri, *Trattato,* 1:56–57: "il destro in quarta dietro al sinistro: Si pieghi poi, e si rialzi, e glissando la punta dell'istesso, che appena tocchi la terra, si porti in seconda posizione, e dopo strisciando, ed accostandolo quasi alla prima, si metta il medesimo alla quarta naturale."

75. Rameau/Essex, *Dancing-Master,* 66–67.

Comprehensive descriptions of *tems de courante*, including explanations of the accompanying arm movements, are given by Michel St.
Léon in 1829, a hundred years after Essex. In St. Léon's "simple" version, the initial bend of the legs in fifth position is made with the body
very straight as the heels raise slightly. This is followed by the straightening of the knees. The back foot then glides to second position and continues forward to fourth position.[76]

Magri describes another version of the step in which, after the bend,
the leg is carried to second position in the air and then to the fourth, the
"movement entirely done from the hip joint."[77] Another *passo grave* described by Magri has four movements, that is, the legs bend and stretch
twice: after the first bend of the knees, they straighten as the gesture leg
is carried to the side, and then there is another bend of the knees in second position before the leg is carried forward as the other leg straightens.
This version closely corresponds to the *tems de courante à deux mouvements*
(St. Léon, 1829), as well as the *temps courant double* (Théleur, 1831), and the
*temps de courant composés* (Adice, 1859). Music for the exercise is included by
St. Léon; it is a tune by Jean-Philippe Rameau from his opéra-ballet *Les
Fêtes d'Hébé ou Les Talens lyriques* (1739).

According to Adice, the various versions of the exercise, with the appropriate arm and head movements, were practiced traveling both forward and backward, for a total of sixteen repetitions. He laments that at
mid-nineteenth century the exercise is practiced only by the children because the artists see no use in it.[78]

Chapter 17, Of the *Coupé* or *Passo Tronco*, 79 / Del *coupè, o sia
passo Tronco*, 44–45

In the lesson of the early nineteenth century, the *temps de courant* usually
were followed by the *coupé* exercises, attributes of which can be linked to
their eighteenth-century *coupé* "cousins." In brief, the eighteenth-century
*coupé* consisted of a preparatory bend of the knees, the weight being on

76. St. Léon, "Exercices de 1829," 2–3: "Tems de courante simple, placez vous à la 5me position les deux bras bas: pliez bien droit enlevant un peu les talons, relevez sur les deux pieds les genoux
bien tendus, développez les deux bras à la h. des épaules en même tems que vous glissez le pied de
derrière à la 2de position, en glissant le même pied en avant à la 4me vous opposez le bras contraire
en attitude, il faut qu'il soit bien arrondi et qui dépasse un peu la h. de la tête, que l'autre forme une
ligne droite avec l'épaule."

77. Magri/Skeaping, 93; Magri, *Trattato*, 1:57: "che si fa tutto dall'articolazione dell'Anca."

78. Adice, *Théorie*, 96.

only one foot, and then a step onto the other foot (actions termed *demi-coupé*), followed by another step or leg gesture.[79]

Magri's description agrees in the main with the basic *coupé* of his predecessors. It begins with a *mezzo coupè* or *demi-coupé*, "one of the principal steps in the Dance," which he describes: "bend the knees evenly . . . supporting the body on the left, the right is slowly brought to fourth position in front where, stretching the knees, the left foot is brought to second position, touching the ground only with the ball of the foot and the heel slightly raised."[80] Magri explains that in reality the foot extends only halfway between first and second position. Then, to complete the full *coupé*, the left leg "is carried in a half circle to fourth position in front" (if performing a *coupé* forward), and the left foot then placed on the ground.[81]

Half a century earlier, Essex, in translating Rameau, says that the "common Coupee" is "composed of two steps, a half Coupee and a slide." To perform the sequence forward, beginning with the right foot, "the Body must rest on the Left, and the Right be brought in the first position; then bend both the Knees equally, and, being bent, move the right Foot forward in the fourth Position and rise on the Toes, extending the Knees." The *pas glissé* or slide can then be performed by lowering the right heel, bending the knee, and sliding the left foot forward to fourth position "with the Weight of the Body resting on it, which finishes the Coupee." Alternatively, the right foot can remain "on the Toes" as the left foot slides forward.[82]

The Magri and Rameau examples differ in the way the second step is performed. For Magri, the leg makes a half-circle as it moves to fourth position, whereas for Rameau the leg moves directly forward as the foot slides to fourth position. Rameau acknowledges that the second step can be made in various ways, and he also discusses more elaborate versions of the full *coupé*. Magri offers only one other variant, the *coupé a tre movimenti*. After the *demi-coupé*, a second bend and rise is made and the gesture leg is lifted to second position in the air, then it is lowered as it is carried forward for the step into fourth position.

79. See, for example, the *Table des Coupés* in Feuillet, *Chorégraphie*, 54–62.

80. Magri/Skeaping, 77; Magri, *Trattato*, 1:42: "piegansi egualmente le ginocchia . . . , ed appoggiando il corpo, su'l manco, il dritto si porta gravamente in quarta positura avanti, ove distendendosi le ginocchia, il sinistro piè si porta alla posizione seconda, toccando la terra con la sola punta, ed il calcagno alquanto rilevato."

81. Magri/Skeaping, 79; Magri, *Trattato*, 1:45: "si porta a mezzo cerchio in quarta posizione avanti."

82. Rameau/Essex, *Dancing-Master*, 76–77.

As Feuillet's notation tables attest, even by 1700 there were many varieties of *coupé*, so it is not surprising that by the nineteenth century there also were many forms, including the *coupé* sequences or *enchaînements* incorporated into the center practice of the lesson. A typical example is the *coupé en avant et en arrière* documented in 1852 by Michel St. Léon's son, the dancer/choreographer Arthur Saint-Léon.[83] In his system of notation, *Sténochorégraphie*, Saint-Léon shows that after an initial bend of the knees in first position, a forward step is made onto the ball of the foot; the other foot is brought quickly behind the supporting ankle, and then that leg is extended to the side at hip level.[84] This notated example and other accounts of nineteenth-century *coupé* exercises indicate that, following the initial *plié*, the first step (forward, sideward, or backward) is made directly onto a straight leg and usually onto *demi-pointe* (half toe). This differs from early eighteenth-century versions, and apparently from Magri's version as well, in which the leg straightens as the weight is being transferred. The nineteenth-century *coupé* sequences were elaborated to include one or more slow turns, both *en dehors* and *en dedans*, with the extended leg remaining at hip level. No doubt such elaborations also were practiced before the nineteenth century. According to Adice a total of thirty-two of these *coupés* were included in the lesson.[85]

Chapter 58, Of the *Attitude*, 148–50 / Dell'*Attitudine*, 109–12

Following the *coupés*, the early nineteenth-century lesson usually continued with "the *attitudes*," a series of exercises that emphasized slow, integrated transitions from one pose to another. By then, the term *attitude* referred both to the exercise sequence and to certain poses sustained while balanced on one leg. Among those poses were ones analogous to the ballet *attitude* as practiced even today.

In the early eighteenth century, the term *attitude* was used in a more general sense, including the notion of any figure or form of the dancer at

83. Michel St. Léon was the name (and spelling) used by Léon Michel in his writings, correspondence, and contracts following his retirement from the Paris Opéra. His son, Charles Victor Arthur Michel, used as his professional name (and spelling) Arthur Saint-Léon (and sometimes, as in his publication *La Sténochorégraphie*, A. Michel Saint-Léon). For more information, see Sandra Noll Hammond, "A Nineteenth-Century Dancing Master at the Court of Württemberg: The Dance Notebooks of Michel St. Léon," *Dance Chronicle* 15 (1992): 291–315.

84. Arthur Saint-Léon, *La Sténochorégraphie ou art d'écrire promptement la danse* (Paris: Chez l'Auteur et chez Brandus, 1852), ex. 11. See also Théleur, *Letters*, 64; St. Léon, "Article des coupés," in "Exercices de 1829," 3–4; Adice, *Théorie*, 77–78.

85. Adice, *Théorie*, 78

a given moment. For example, Rameau uses *attitude* and *figure* interchangeably in the captions under his illustrations of how movements are to be performed, such as "Premiere Figure des saillies ou pas échappée" (which shows the dancer in a fourth position *plié*, right foot front) followed by "Deuxieme attitude des saillies" (the dancer in the same position, but with the left foot front). The same examples in the translation of Rameau's text by Essex read "The first attitude of the Sallies or Starting Steps" followed by "The second Attitude of the Sallies." The final illustration of the series shows the dancer in first position, knees straight. Rameau captions this "Troisieme Figure des saillies," which Essex translates as "The third Attitude of Sallies or Starting Steps."[86]

Magri also uses the term *attitude* in several ways. At the beginning of his discussion, he emphasizes the integrating factors of the theatrical *attitudine:* the arms, legs, head, and eyes must be in harmony. He refers to Noverre's comments on the importance of a knowledge of drawing in order to achieve these poses with ease and correct proportion. Later, Magri discusses various *attitudini sforzate*, or exaggerated and expressive poses, used by different theatrical characters. One wishes that he had included illustrations.[87]

From nineteenth-century sources, we know that the *attitude* exercise sequences usually began with a bend of the knees and/or a rise — the rise being made either as a simple straightening of the knees or as a rise onto half or full point. The sequence also could begin with a *demi-coupé*, or a rise in fourth position, or a *pas marché en avant*.[88] Then, with the body balanced on a straight supporting leg, the other leg would be raised to the front, side, or back and either bent at the knee (*plié en l'air*) or straight (*tendue*). The body then could turn in this pose or change to another pose while turning.

Several important aspects of these *attitude* exercises can be found in Magri's description of the theatrical *attitude sur place:* the initial bend and stretch of the knees, the lifting of one leg, which is curved at the knee, with accompanying arm movement in which the arm on the same side as the lifted leg is raised in a curved position, with the palm of the hand facing the chest. Magri goes on to discuss the turn of the body and head in this pose, as well as the expression of the eyes.[89] In that example, Magri

---

86. Rameau, *Le Maître*, 186; Rameau/Essex, *Dancing-Master*, 108.

87. Magri/Skeaping, 148–50; Magri, *Trattato*, 1:109–12; Noverre/Beaumont, 36.

88. Adice, *Théorie*, 78; St. Léon, "Exercices de 1829," 4–6, and his untitled manuscript ca. 1833–ca. 1836, 59–61; Saint-Léon, *Sténochorégraphie*, ex. 11, 43.

89. Magri/Skeaping, 148–49; Magri, *Trattato*, 1:110.

does not specify whether the leg is raised to the front or to the back, but we know that it would be the back leg, because later he succinctly cites the accepted practice for the accompanying arm movement: if the leg is lifted to the front, the opposite arm will be curved in front; if the leg is lifted to the back, the arm on the same side as the raised leg will be curved in front.[90] This rule continued to be observed, thus leading to the accepted notion of *bras en attitude*, with the forward arm often being raised at least to the height of the head.[91]

In describing the attitude *in fianco* or to the side, Magri states that the lifted leg is stretched, rather than curved or bent, to second position in the air, and the arms can be "egualmente alzate" (equally raised), which would seem to mean they also are lifted to the side. From there, he says, the arms can be carried to other poses. In the next sentence he specifies that in turning, "only a quarter turn and nothing more is added,"[92] presumably describing an example of a possible elaboration or continuation of the exercise into another pose. In St. Léon's notebook of 1829, in an *Article des Attitudes*, there is a description of a similar exercise in which, after the *pliez et relevez*, the right leg is raised to the side at hip level and the arms raised to the height of the shoulders. From there the body makes a quarter turn to the left.[93] In all, thirty-two *attitude enchaînements* were included in the lesson, according to Adice.[94]

Chapter 43, Of the *Fouetté*, 124 / Del *Fuetè*, 86–87

The basic elements of the *fuetè* described by Magri are intrinsic to the center exercise that became known as the *grands fouettés* and a regular part of the lesson. After an initial bend of the knees, the legs straighten as the gesture leg is lifted into the air for a circling movement from fourth front to second position in the air; from there the knees bend again as the foot is brought sharply behind the supporting leg. The knees straighten once more as the gesture leg extends again to second position in the air.[95]

90. Magri/Skeaping, 149; Magri, *Trattato*, 1:110.

91. See, for example, St. Léon, "Exercices de 1829," 4–6.

92. Magri/Skeaping, 149; Magri, *Trattato*, 1:111: "In giro niente più vi si aggiungerà, che un solo quarto del giro."

93. St. Léon, "Exercices de 1829," 6: "Etant à la 5me les bras bas, pliez et relevez en développant la jambe à la 2de h. de la hanche et les bras à la h. des épaules. Si vous avez développé la jambe D. faites un attitude en tournant le corps d'un quart de tour à gauche, le genou tendu."

94. Adice, *Théorie*, 78.

95. Magri/Skeaping, 124; Magri, *Trattato*, 1:86–87: "si piegano appena i ginocchi, e nel distendersi si leva il piede dritto alla quarta in aria, da dove circolando giunge alla seconda similmente in

This version is Magri's *fuetè sotto al corpo,* or in place, but he also briefly mentions a *fuetè girando,* or turning, with a full turn made before the final extension of the leg to second position. The *grands fouettés* in Blasis's list of center exercises also were to be done "facing and revolving."[96] Notations by Théleur of *fouetté* finishing in an *attitude* and by Arthur Saint-Léon for *grand fouetté lent, posé attitude* show that the circling leg is carried in the air from the front through second position to the back, where the knee remains extended (Théleur) or bends in an attitude (Saint-Léon).[97] In these examples, the final extension of the leg is made to the front, rather than to second position as Magri describes, and from there it can simply be lowered into fifth position as in Théleur's version, or a step forward can be made onto that leg as in the version documented by Saint-Léon. In all cases, the distinguishing features are the circling of the leg in the air, coordinated with the bending, then the straightening and another bending movement of the supporting leg. These movements were enhanced by the accompanying movements of the arms and incline of the torso.

Although not named as such, the basic movements of this type of *fouetté* can be found in notations of early eighteenth-century dances. A good example is in the "Entrée de deux hommes dancée par M[rs] Blondy et Marcel au feste venitienne" (LMC 2920), a virtuoso theatrical duet performed at the Paris Opéra. The dance notation, published in 1713, shows the gesture leg circling in the air from fourth position front to fourth position back, accompanied by a bend and a rise on the supporting leg as a quarter turn is made. Then the gesture leg passes forward, accompanied by another bend and rise on the supporting leg as the dancer returns to the original direction for the final transfer of weight.[98] As demonstrated in this example, the movements of the *fouetté* were established well before Magri, but his *Trattato* seems to be the earliest source for the technical term. However, the term most likely was already in use elsewhere. For example, the term *foitte batue* appears in the 1782 collection of dances notated by Auguste Frédéric Joseph Ferrère.[99]

---

aria, e quivi arrivato, si piegano ad un tempo tutti due i ginocchi, quanto il dritto piede mandisi in dietro alla quinta in aria, da dove, tornandosi a distendere, si cava l'istesso alla seconda in aria."

96. Blasis, *Code,* 102.

97. Théleur, *Letters,* 70: "*fouetté* finishing in an *attitude*"; Saint-Léon, *Sténochorégraphie,* ex. 13: "grand fouetté lent, posé attitude."

98. Michel Gaudrau, *Nouveau Recüeil de dance de bal et celle de ballet* (Paris: Gaudrau, 1713), notation mm. 42–43 on p. 91.

99. A sequence of "foitte battue temps levée assemble lache le pied chasse a 3. pas" appears on the second page of the Ferrère manuscript in *Le Peintre amoureux de son modèle.* The Ferrère manuscript

Adice recalls a long series of *grands fouettés* performed both *en face* and *en tournant* with one, two, and three turns.[100] As documented by Michel St. Léon, the series might conclude with *grands foités en sautant*, which were performed in the same manner but *plus vite*, or quicker, without actually leaving the ground in the *tems levés*.[101] Magri also mentions a livelier version in which the movements of the *fuetè* can be made with "two little springs, either on the instep or scarcely lifted from the ground."[102]

## Chapter 38, Of the *Développé*, 115–16 / Del *Deviluppè*, 79–80

Nineteenth-century center floor practice included a series of *développés*, an unfolding of the gesture leg to the height of the hip or shoulder. From there the leg could be slowly either lowered or carried in a quarter or a half circle before lowering. Thus, the *développé* exercise was closely related to another exercise, the *grands ronds de jambe*. The fundamental movements of the latter exercise were the unfolding of the gesture leg to fourth position front at hip level, a circling of that leg at the same level through second position in the air to fourth position back in the air, another unfolding of the leg to the front (thus completing the full circle of the leg), and finishing either by carrying the leg once again to the side or by continuing with a second circling of the leg.[103]

Magri's discussion of the "group of thigh movements" ("groppo di tempi di coscia"), which he says the French call *deviluppè*,[104] shows the connection between the two exercises, as other authors also do. For example, St. Léon immediately follows his descriptions of *développé* exercises with descriptions of *grands ronds de jambe* exercises. Costa also follows his discussion of *développé* with a discussion of the *grand rond*.[105] Indeed, in his discussion of *développé*, Costa says that he uses the term *incavare* (to carve) when the leg moves in the *foggia* or manner of the *rond de jambe*, but that the French say *développé*. This was undoubtedly the understanding that Magri had.

---

is discussed in detail in chaps. 7 and 9 of this volume. I gratefully acknowledge the information on *fouetté* that Edmund Fairfax shared with me.

100. Adice, *Théorie*, 78.

101. St. Léon, "Exercices de 1829," 13.

102. Magri/Skeaping, 124; Magri, *Trattato*, 1:87: "e puol far due salticelli, o su 'l collo del piede, o levati appena da terra."

103. See, for example, St. Léon, "Exercices de 1829," 11.

104. Magri/Skeaping, 115–16; Magri, *Trattato*, 1:79–80.

105. Costa, *Saggio*, 29–33.

A distinctive feature of both the *développé* and the *grand rond de jambe* was the graceful unfolding of the leg: the gesture leg bends slightly as the foot is raised at the ankle of the supporting leg, and from there it gradually unfolds as it rises through the position of *attitude* (rather than being brought up to the knee) before straightening.[106] As center floor exercises, the movements were made slowly with sustained balance, sometimes with the supporting heel raised. Blasis includes the *grands rond de jambes* in his list of center floor exercises as does Théleur, who refers to the great *ronds de jambe* as one of the exercises "to be practiced in the middle of the room without any support."[107]

## Chapter 41, Of the *Ballotté*, 121 / Del *Balottè*, 84

Magri gives a succinct description of this step: "It consists of three *jetés* done on one, then the other leg, and ends with an *assemblé*."[108] As he explains earlier in his text, there were many ways to perform *jetés* and *assemblés*. Briefly, the essential nature of the *jeté* was a rise or slight spring from one foot to the other, and, for the *assemblé*, a slight spring or rise from one foot to both feet.[109] Upon these basic movements of three *jetés* and an *assemblé* were built the classroom exercises eventually known as the *grands ballottés*.

The sequence of *G[rand] balotté* described in the 1830s by St. Léon begins with "Jettez dessus, jettez dessous, jettez dessus," or a spring over, under, over on alternating feet.[110] The sequence continues, with *tems levés* and *développés*, a rather lengthy *enchaînement* that he attributes to "Vest.," no doubt a reference to the famous dancer Auguste Vestris, who had become a solo dancer at the Paris Opéra in 1776 and, by St. Léon's time, was a leading instructor in the Opéra's ballet school. Immediately following the Vestris sequence, St. Léon has another *Grand balotté* exercise, which he attributes to "Alb.," a reference to Albert, the professional

---

106. A clear depiction of this movement is seen in the notation by Saint-Léon, *Sténochorégraphie*, ex. 7, *grand rond de jambe lent*.

107. Blasis, *Code*, 102; Théleur, *Letters*, 97. Adice describes the "grand rond de jambe" in his manuscripts "Grammaire et Théorie chorégraphique/Composition de la gymnastique de la danse théatrale," dated 17 May 1868–17 July 1871, now located in Paris, Bibliothèque de l'Opéra, B.61 (1–3). For an analysis of the manuscripts, see Sandra Noll Hammond, "Ballet's Technical Heritage: The Grammaire of Léopold Adice," *Dance Research* 13 (1995): 33–58.

108. Magri/Skeaping, 121; Magri, *Trattato*, 1:84: "Egli costa di tre *Jettè* fatti con l'uno, e con l'altro piede, e finisce con un' *Assemblè*."

109. Magri/Skeaping, 80–82 and 119–20; Magri, *Trattato*, 1:45–48 and 82–84.

110. St. Léon, untitled manuscript, ca. 1833–ca. 1836, (F-Po Rés. 1140), 47.

name adopted by François Decombe, a dancer acclaimed for his noble
style, who also became an influential ballet teacher and a choreographer
of some note. The Albert version of the exercise ends with an *assemblé
soutenu*. Elsewhere, St. Léon devotes an entire page of a notebook to an
explanation of the *assemblé soutenu*, in which one foot describes a semi-
circle along the floor and then closes into fifth position *plié*. This is coordinated with arm movements and the option of a rise *sur les orteils* (onto
the tips of the toes, full pointes) at the finish.[111]

St. Léon's son Arthur notated a version of the *ballotté* sequence, which
he called *grand ballotté, assemblé soutenu, double port de bras*.[112] It is a sequence
with many similarities to one described by Costa entitled *Grande Ballotté*.[113] In these examples, the three changes of weight are performed not
with springs, but with a rise and then a bend of the supporting leg as the
gesture leg unfolds to a horizontal level. These extensions are made only
to the front and to the back, never to the side. Costa's sequence concludes the three *ballottés* with a *jeté* forward and an *assemblé*. The *assemblé
soutenu* at the end of Saint-Léon's sequence finishes with a rise onto full
*pointes* in fifth position. During the rise, the *double port de bras* is made.

The connection of these nineteenth-century sequences of the *grands
ballottés* with early eighteenth-century material is seen through Magri's
description of *balottè*: his three *jetés* on alternating feet relate to the *jeté-
chassé*, a sequence described by Rameau as three changes of weight performed one after the other without a pause, like the swinging of a pen-
dulum.[114] Rameau refers the reader to a passage in which the sequence
occurs in the popular ballroom dance "L'Aimable Vainqueur" (LMC
1180), a *loure* composed by Guillaume Louis Pécour, an esteemed dancer
who had studied under Pierre Beauchamps and eventually succeeded
him as choreographer for the court and the Opéra. Originally notated
and published by Feuillet in 1701, this *loure* is one of several dances that
Rameau notated in his second book, *Abbrégé de la nouvelle méthode* (1725).[115]

In part 2 of his *Trattato*, where he deals with ballroom dancing, Ma-

111. St. Léon, "Exercices de 1829," 13. See also the notation example of "*Assemblée Soutenue*" in
Théleur, *Letters*, 66.

112. Saint-Léon, *Sténochorégraphie*, ex. 12.

113. Costa, *Saggio*, 130–31.

114. Rameau, *Le Maître*, 178–79.

115. Pierre Rameau, *Abbrégé de la nouvelle méthode, dans l'art d'écrire ou de tracer toutes sortes, de danses
de ville* (Paris: L'Auteur, 1725). The notated passage is the first measure on page 43. Another example
of "l'Aimable Vainqueur" is notated by Magny, *Principes*, in which the *jeté-chassé* passage appears on
the first measure of p. 187.

gri includes a detailed description of his version of this dance, entitled "l'Amabile," including drawings of the tracks or patterns of the dance figures. Although the music is different from the earlier version and, as Magri discloses, he has tried to improve upon the original, including the addition of new steps, he does retain the two sets of *tre mezzi Jettè* or three *demi-jetés*, as in the original version of the dance.[116]

This sequence of movements, with the addition of the *assemblé*, can be found in other early eighteenth-century choreographies, such as the "Chacone of Amadis Performed by Mr Dupré" (LMC 1840), composed by Anthony L'Abbé, whose career in London from 1698 to the mid-1730s included dancing, dance composition, and eventually dance instruction for members of the royal family.[117] The sequence lived on into the next century and no doubt was the basis of the *grand ballotté* exercise for daily classroom practice.

## The Lesson: Steps, Turns, and *Temps de Vigueur*

Following the *grands fouettés* and *grands ballottés* came practice of the *pas de bourrées* and many types of *pirouettes*. *Enchaînements* or combinations of these and other steps followed, and finally the class ended with various *temps de vigueur*. Magri offers many examples of steps in these categories, a sampling of which will be discussed here.

### Chapter 29, *Pas de Bourrée*, 98–103 / *Pas de Bourèè*, 60–68

Eighteenth-century choreographies for both the stage and the ballroom abound in *pas de bourrées*, the basic movements being three steps, each with a change of weight, which allowed for various changes of level, direction, timing, and embellishments, such as beats and turns. In 1700, Feuillet notated ninety-three examples of *Pas de bourrée, ou Fleurets.*[118] In 1725, Rameau declared that the true *pas de bourrée* consisted of "un demi-coupé, un pas marché sur la pointe du pied & d'un demi-jetté," but he asserted that it had largely been replaced by the simpler *fleuret*, which was "un demi-coupé & deux pas marchés sur la pointe des pieds."[119]

---

116. Magri/Skeaping, 232–36 (233); Magri, *Trattato*, 1:93–100 (95).
117. Le Rousseau, *New Collection of Dances*, 58, 64.
118. Feuillet, *Chorégraphie*, 63–70.
119. Rameau, *Le Maître*, 122–23.

Magri discusses many versions of *pas de bourrée*, a step which he says has more diversity than any other, and he goes on to cite twelve ways to perform the *semplice* or simple version: forward, backward, sideways, over and under sideways, under and over sideways, all over sideways, all under sideways, over and under turning, under and over turning, all over turning, all under turning, and turning *disfatto* (making half a turn by stepping under, then to the side, and finishing to the fourth position in front).[120]

For Magri, the simple *pas de bourrée* begins with a movement that sounds similar to his description of *mezzo coupè* or *demi-coupé*, and continues with two natural steps (*due passi naturali*). This seems to resemble Rameau's earlier description of the *fleuret*, except that in Magri's examples the final two steps are not "Walks on the Toes."[121] In addition to the examples of the simple *pas de bourrée*, Magri discusses eight more types of *pas de bourrées*, all of which have many versions, which he describes in some detail. For example, his *passo di bourèè fatto in gittato*, or *pas de bourrée* done with a *jeté*, begins with a circling of the front foot forward and then a *jeté* to the side; the second foot then passes through first position to fourth position front, and the initial foot closes behind in third or fifth position.[122] Magri says that this type of *pas de bourrée* is often used in the theater when one needs to progress across the floor. These movements are the essence of the step called *pas de basque* in nineteenth-century sources. The similarity can been seen in the detailed description of *pas de basque* in a book about French social dances published in 1827 by an Englishman, Charles Mason: "Spring, and throw the right foot to a second, thence to the half-position, between the third and fourth, *en épaulant;* that is, gracefully slipping back the right shoulder, and turning the head slowly to the left: when in that position, point the left, pass it to a first, thence to a fourth position before; rest upon it, and make a *coupé dessous* with the right foot."[123] This step appears in a well-known late-eighteenth-century choreography, the "Gavotte de Vestris," a dance attributed to Gaetano Vestris, the "renowned Florentine Sig. Vestris" mentioned by Magri.[124]

120. Magri/Skeaping, 98–9; Magri, *Trattato*, 1:60–63.

121. Rameau/Essex, *Dancing-Master*, 70.

122. Magri/Skeaping, 101–02; Magri, *Trattato*, 1:66: "portasi alla quarta in aria il piè, che sta innanzi, esempigrazia il destro, da dove si getti l'istesso piede alla seconda, ed il manco passando per la prima si porta alla quarta avanti, ed il dritto appresserassi alla vera terzi sotto; sebbene error non farebbe portarlo alla quinta indietro."

123. Charles Mason, *A Short Essay on the French Danse de Société* (London: R. Ackermann, 1827), 26.

124. Magri/Skeaping, 128; Magri, *Trattato*, 1:90.

The "Gavotte de Vestris" was later notated by Théleur and described in detail by Michel St. Léon.[125]

## Chapter 28, Of the *Fioretto, Fleuret,* 135–37 / Del *Fioretto, Fleuret,* 97–100

Magri does not seem to relate his *pas de bourrée* with his *fioretto* or *fleuret,* since the latter step appears in the *Trattato* thirty-two pages after his discussion of *pas de bourrée.* The basic movements for Magri's *fioretto* are a step into a bend or *plié* in an open position, a close to third position with a rise on "le punte de' piedi," and a plain walking step into another open position. Magri asserts that the *fioretto* is found in almost every *danza.* As described by Magri, the *fioretto* seems to be similar to one of the basic *allemande* steps used at the time in the popular couple dance the allemande, and in contredanses.[126]

By the nineteenth century the term *fleuret* or *fioretto* largely disappears and is not mentioned as part of the ballet lesson. Costa is one nineteenth-century author who continues to use the term *pas fleuré,* but, like Magri, he does not link his discussion of *pas fleuré* with his discussion of *passi di borè.* Indeed, the *fleuré* described by Costa seems to be the same as Magri's *fioretto saltato,* that is, it begins with a little hop before the first step. Costa says that three sets of these *fleuré* can finish with a *jeté* and an *assemblé* and that this sequence is used to *traversé* in the *contradanze.*[127] The sequence was a familiar one for patterns in quadrilles and cotillons, the successors of the contredanse in the nineteenth century.[128]

## Chapter 45, Of the *Pirola, Pirouettes,* 126–28 / Della *Pirola, de Piroùettes,* 88–91

Magri begins this discussion with his definition: "The *pirouette* is a step which is always done turning on the same place. The body may be

125. For information on the "Gavotte de Vestris," see Sandra Noll Hammond, "The *Gavotte de Vestris:* A Dance of Three Centuries," *Proceedings* (Society of Dance History Scholars, 1984), 202–8, and "Dances Related to Theatrical Dance Traditions," in *The Extraordinary Dance Book T B. 1826,* commentaries and analyses by Elizabeth Aldrich, Sandra Noll Hammond, and Armand Russell (Stuyvesant, NY: Pendragon, 2000), 40–46.

126. For a description of basic *allemande* steps, see Simon Guillaume, *Almanach dansant, ou Positions & attitudes de l'allemande* (Paris: Chez l'auteur, 1770), 13.

127. Costa, *Saggio,* 196–98.

128. See, for example, V. G., *Elements,* and Aldrich, Hammond, and Russell, *Extraordinary Dance Book,* 26–28.

turned one quarter, one half, three-quarters or a full turn."[129] This seems to echo Rameau, who, in 1725, begins his discussion of *pirouettes* with a similar definition: "The Pirouette is a step which is made in one Place, that is to say, it neither moves backwards or forwards, but its Property consists in the body's turning about either on one Foot or both as on a Pivot."[130] The first examples described by Magri are the turns which are made on "le due punte de' piedi." They correspond both to Rameau's description of turns *sur les deux-pointes* and also to the *tours de pirouette sur les deux pointes* of Michel St. Léon in his various notebooks of 1829–36.

Other *pirouettes* described by Magri include those of multiple spins on the ball of one foot (*le Pirole forzate incerte* or forced indeterminate *pirouettes*) while at the same time the other leg makes various *tordichamps* or some *battimenti.* He says that the *serio* dancer is permitted to do these turns, but in a sustained manner ("sostenuta"), that is, slowly with control. Magri describes another *pirouette, la Pirola distesa aperta,* that is appropriate for "tutti i caratteri." It is a spin on the ball of the foot with the other leg extended to second position in the air. These types of *pirouettes* were documented prior to Magri, and they continued to be among the most common forms of turns in the next century. For example, in 1735 in his text *The Art of Dancing Explained by Reading and Figures,* Kellon Tomlinson described a *pirouette* begun in second position, in which the leg is "extended in the Air, the Toe pointed, and Knee stiff." He says that this turn, performed with the leg raised about "half a Foot from the Floor," may be done "twice *round,* three Times *round.*" Tomlinson refers to other "Ways of performing this Step" that include "beating before and behind during the Turning, and many more," which, alas, he did not go on to describe.[131] In 1765, Magny's notations of *pirouettes* end with an example of a turn taken from second position in which the raised leg makes *battues* "dessus & dessous deux fois," and finishes with a *rond* or *tour* of the leg, that is a *rond de jambe* in the air.[132]

One of the *pirole* appropriate to the *grottesco* that Magri describes is the *pirola incrocciata* performed with the raised foot placed on the instep of the

129. Magri/Skeaping, 126; Magri, *Trattato,* 1:88: "La Pirola e un passo, che si fa sempre girando su l'istesso terreno. Si puol girare la vita, o per un quarto, o per mezzo, o per tre quarti, o per giro intiero."

130. Rameau/Essex, *Dancing-Master,* 86.

131. Kellom Tomlinson, *The Art of Dancing Explained by Reading and Figures Whereby the Manner of Performing the Steps Is Made Easy by a New and Familiar Method* (London: author, 1735), 97–98.

132. Magny, *Principes,* 106.

foot on which the turn is made. By 1820, according to Blasis, this position of the raised foot on the instep is one of the three "best known and most generally used in *pirouettes*" by all dancers, the other two being with the leg raised in second position and *en attitude*, that is, with the leg raised in back with the knee bent.[133] Magri does not describe a *pirola* in the latter position, although he alludes to the fact that there are other turns which he is leaving aside.

Magri gives little information on the preparation for a *pirouette*, other than mentioning that "usually it is begun from the fourth position,"[134] the initial position he prefers for all steps. But in his chapter on caprioles Magri does explain how to prepare for a *salto tondo sotto al corpo* or *tour* in the air in place, which "is taken from second position."[135] This preparation corresponds closely to one of the positions that Blasis suggests as "best suited" for the preparations for *pirouettes* "from the outside," or *en dehors* (see fig. 5.5).

Following the practice of *pirouettes*, the typical ballet lesson, as recorded in the early nineteenth century, concluded with the *temps terre-à-terre*, or steps in which the feet scarcely leave the ground, and the *temps de vigueur*, or vigorous steps performed with jumps and quick, intricate leg movements.[136] It is not possible in this chapter to discuss all of the many *temps* or steps that would fall into these categories and that Magri includes in the *Trattato*, but the following brief survey will give an idea of some of the material that dancing masters continued to use in the decades following Magri.

Chapter 24, Of the *Contratempo, Contretemps*, 129–31 / Del *Contratempo, Contratems*, 91–95

The essential movements of the *contretemps*, a hop and two steps, can be found in dance treatises throughout the eighteenth century, from Feuillet to Magri to the 1797 description by J. J. Martinet in his *Essai, ou principes élémentaires de l'art de la danse*,[137] and on into the following century.

133. Blasis/Evans, *Elementary Treatise*, 50.

134. Magri/Skeaping, 126; Magri, *Trattato*, 1:88: "e si suol principiare dalla quarta posizione."

135. Magri/Skeaping, 161; Magri, *Trattato*, 1:128: "Quello sotto al corpo va preso dalla seconda posizione."

136. Blasis, *Code*, 102.

137. J. J. Martinet, *Essai, ou principes élémentaires de l'art de la danse, utiles aux personnes destinées à l'education de la jeunesse* (Lausanne, 1797), 50–52.

Figure 5.5: Position of the dancer in beginning his pirouette from the outside (Blasis, *Code* [1830], plate 7, fig. 3)

Embellished versions of the step, such as Magri's *contratempi battuti*, or beaten *contretemps*, find a counterpart in Michel St. Léon's *contretemps ou balonné sur le cou de pied* of 1830.[138]

Chapter 35, Of the *Passo Scacciato, Pas Chassé*, 110–12 / Del *Passo Scacciato, Pas Chassè*, 73–76

The basic *chassé* began in an open position (second or fourth) and was a traveling step in which one foot was chased out of position by the other foot. For Magri, this was a *mezzo scacciato* or *demì-chassè*, because it did not conclude with "another natural step . . . with that leg which hit the other," as in his description of the simple version of *passo scacciato, pas chassè*.[139] This latter description by Magri would resemble the *chassé à trois*

138. St. Léon, "Exercices pour les Princesses," 29; Magri/Skeaping, 131; Magri, *Trattato*, 1:91.
139. Magri/Skeaping, 113 and 110–12 (110); Magri, *Trattato*, 1:77 and 73–76 (74): "e facendo poi un altro passo naturale . . . con quel piede, che l'altro percosse, sarà fatto."

*pas* or *chassé* of three steps in the terminology of other authors, as described, for example, by Charles Mason in 1827 in his *Short Essay*.[140]

## Chapter 32, Of the *Galliard* Step, *Pas de Gaillarde*, 107 / Del *Passo di Gagliarda, Pas de Gagliarde*, 71–72

It is fascinating to follow a step such as the *pas de gaillarde* over a hundred-year period. In his text on his new method of notation, Rameau explains that the step consists of an *assemblé* (performed either with a rise or a spring) and a *pas marché*, followed by a *pas tombé*, or falling step under the supporting foot, and a *demi-jeté*. This sequence is shown traveling forward or sideward.[141]

The *passo di gagliarda, pas de gagliarde* described by Magri begins with a movement certainly akin to the *passo unito, assemblè* discussed later in the *Trattato:* a bend of the knees is followed by a "rise stretching with the return to first" (straighten the knees and rise or spring on the left foot as the right opens to second position in the air, then lower the left foot as the right returns to first position). Then the right foot walks to second position and immediately the left foot slides to fifth position behind the right. Instead of finishing with a *demi-jeté*, as in the Rameau version of *pas de gaillarde*, Magri's version ends by raising the right leg to fourth position in the air and then quickly closing it to fifth position front.[142]

In 1829, Michel St. Léon describes a *temps de gaillarde* as an *assemblé devant*, followed by a glide or slide to second position ("glissez à la seconde") and a raising of the body "sur la pointe" (onto the ball of the foot that glided to second). This is followed by a *pas marché* to fifth position behind, and a *grand développé en avant* to fourth position at the height of the hip, from where the leg is taken *à la seconde* before closing to fifth position front.[143]

The connection of these three examples of the *gaillarde* step is unmistakable. Magri says that it is one of the steps—along with *jeté*, *chassé*, and *glissade*—used "by all three kinds of *Ballerini: Seri, mezzo Carattere* and *Grottesco*" when two dancers dance in a *Carè* or square formation.[144] St.

---

140. Mason, *Short Essay*, 23–24.

141. Rameau, *Abbrégé*, 59–60.

142. Magri/Skeaping, 107; Magri, *Trattato*, 1:71–72: After explaining the *passo di gagliarda*, Magri summarizes its five parts as follows: "I suoi movimenti sono cinque. Il primo è il piegato, il disteso rilevato il secondo con la tornata in prima, il terzo l'andante, lo sdrucciolato il quarto, ed quinto lo staccato."

143. St. Léon, "Exercices de 1829," 15.

144. Magri/Skeaping, 146; Magri, *Trattato*, 1:107–8.

Léon's only account of *temps de gaillarde* is in his first *Cahier*, where it is in the series of center-floor classroom exercises: *temps de courante, coupés, attitudes, pirouettes, développés, grands ronds de jambes, foités, assemblés soutenus, pas de bourrée, temps de gaillarde.* In the course of time, the step seemed to disappear from theatrical use and remained only as a classroom exercise, in the same way that the *temps de courante* left the stage but endured in the ballet lesson.

## Chapter 54, Of the *Flinc Flanc*, 144 / Del *Flinc, Flanc*, 105–56

Some of Magri's uses of terminology can be confusing at first glance, as in the *flinc, flanc*. As described by Magri, it was a traveling step that also was useful as a preparation for a *capriola*. His *flinc, flanc* consisted of a *jeté* and step to second position, a *chassé*, and an *assemblé*,[145] which indeed would serve as a wonderful impetus for a jump with beats or turns. It is related to the *flinc e flanc/flic-flac* as described by Costa,[146] but it is very different from the meaning of *flic-flac* today, which is done in place, or turning in place, with a whipping movement of the foot in front and in back (or back and front) of the supporting leg, usually just above the ankle. In the nineteenth century, this latter version usually was called *petit fouetté* (or *foité*) *en dedans* or *en dehors*.

## Chapter 60, Of the *Caprioles*, 155–67 / Delle *Capriole*, 118–38

The more vigorous steps, or *temps de vigueur*, which concluded the lesson would, according to Adice, include "les séries d'entrechats sous le corps, de ronds de jambe, de brisés, d'entrechats à cinq, de fouettés sautés, de sisonnes."[147] In his lengthy chapter 60, "Delle Capriole," Magri discusses numerous vigorous jumps that required interweaving of the feet, beats of the legs, and circling leg movements corresponding to the categories of *temps de vigueur* listed by Adice. Because Magri's caprioles are discussed in greater detail elsewhere in this volume (see Linda Tomko, chap. 6, and Moira Goff, chap. 8), only a few observations about them are offered here.

Although Magri does not use the French term *entrechat*, he describes how the interweaving *tagli* or cuts are made and how the number of cuts are counted. In 1700, Feuillet, in his "Table des Entre-chats et demy entre-chats," uses the same counting system, that is, each opening and

145. Magri/Skeaping, 144; Magri, *Trattato*, 1:105–6.
146. Costa, *Saggio*, 242–24.
147. Adice, *Théorie*, 80.

closing of the legs is counted. Magri explains the difference between the interwoven caprioles done *alla Francese* (which begin and end in closed positions, third or fifth) and those done *all'Italiana* (which begin and end in an open position, second). Costa makes the same distinctions, such as in his discussion of *Quarta capriolata. Entrechats quarte.*[148]

Magri discusses the differences between these interwoven caprioles and the *capriole battute* or beaten caprioles. In the latter, only one leg opens and then beats one or more times against the other either in front or behind. The landing from these caprioles can be on one foot or on both feet.[149] These distinctions follow the similar differences between the *cabrioles* and the *entre-chats* shown in the notation by Feuillet. Magri notes that the interwoven and the beaten caprioles can be done with legs extended (*distese*) or drawn up (*ritirate*). Such distinctions could not be shown in the Feuillet notation but they appear in illustrations, such as in Gregorio Lambranzi's *Neue und curieuse theatralische Tantz-Schul* (1716).[150]

One of the caprioles described by Magri is the *tordichamp in aria saltata*. In its simplest form, it corresponds to "the little *rond de jambe* in jumping" of Théleur and the *petit rond de jambe sauté* of Arthur Saint-Léon.[151] Magri credits himself as the inventor of some of the more difficult versions of *tordichamp in aria*, various *gorgugliè*, but he acknowledges that the French "in their *Serie* dances" have another type of *gorgugliè* performed close to the ground: "in the same jump two *tordichamp* are done, the first, for example, with the right foot outward, and the other with the left foot inward."[152] An example of this type of *gorgugliè* is found in a dance by Anthony L'Abbé, in "Loure or Faune," published in 1725.[153]

Magri was justified in devoting such a large discussion to the *capriole*, for they were, and had been throughout the eighteenth century, essential technical tools for theatrical dancers. Audiences admired the aerial

148. Costa, *Saggio*, 276–77.

149. Magri, *Trattato*, 123. It would seem that Skeaping's note 78, p. 243, is misleading in describing these steps as having a "supporting leg" under the body.

150. *New and Curious School of Theatrical Dancing*, trans. Friderica Derra de Moroda, ed. Cyril W. Beaumont (New York: Dance Horizons, 1966). For examples of a knee drawn up, see Lambranzi's illustrations on 14 and 36.

151. Théleur, *Letters*, 74, 97; Saint-Léon, *Sténochorégraphie*, 36.

152. Magri/Skeaping, 159; Magri, *Trattato*, 1:124–25: "V'è un'altra sorte di Gorgugliè, nella quale si fanno nel salto medisimo due Tordichamp, il primo verbigrazia co'l destro piè fuori, e l'altro co'l sinistro per dentro."

153. The step appears in measure six of the first figure of the first dance in the collection, the "Loure or Faune performd before his Majesty King William by Monsr. Balon and Mr L'abbé" (LMC 5260). I am grateful to Edmund Fairfax for alerting me to this example of the step.

qualities of the dancers, who understood that it was "with *entrechats* that they attract the staring eyes of the crowd." The quotation is from Noverre, who, as an advocate for dramatic pantomime ballet, felt that ballet at mid-century was in dire need of reform from such acrobatic excesses. One of his suggestions for reform was for dancers to "renounce *cabrioles, entrechats* and over-complicated steps" in order to bring more expressive movement to the service of the dramatic plot of the ballet.[154] But as Noverre acknowledged toward the end of his life, his efforts had done little to bring dancers back down to earth. The popularity of ballets featuring acrobatic virtuosity could not be denied. Noverre once again derided the dancers "who run, who jump, who lunge and who no longer dance."[155] By 1830 Blasis could declare that a "serious dancer" was required to perform "*entrechats*, and all other *tems d'èlèvation*," as well as "the most beautiful developments, all the *grands temps*, and the noblest steps," and the "finest pirouettes in the second position, in attitude, or on the instep."[156] His long list of *entrechats* and *cabrioles* (including "la cabriole Italienne") rivals the lengthy list by Magri. According to Magri, ten cuts were the maximum one could perform with precise interweavings.[157] Fifty years later, Blasis asserted that in the *entrechats* one "may cut . . . even twelve times, if you have the requisite strength."[158] Clearly, Noverre had lost the battle for the renunciation of *cabrioles, entrechats*, and all the other complicated *temps de vigueur*.

In his summation of the lesson, Adice recalls that individuality was expected of dancers, even with classroom material. A dancer could choose certain movement sequences or *enchaînements* to practice, not only to perfect them but also to render an interpretation of the movements that was uniquely his. Such practice would be important if individuality, even invention, was required of soloists in performance, as Magri implies when he discusses, for example, the *chaconne*, in which "for the most part, all the solos are danced impromptu."[159] Individuality continued to be valued as a mark of the good dancer in the following century, as Blasis's "general instructions to pupils" reflect: "Form, therefore, a style of your own, as originality is the chief means to procure yourself distinction."[160]

154. Noverre/Beaumont, 27–29.

155. As quoted in Kathleen Kuzmick Hansell, "Jean-Georges Noverre," in *International Encyclopedia of Dance* (New York: Oxford University Press, 1998), 4:694–700 (700).

156. Blasis, *Code*, 90.

157. Magri/Skeaping, 156; Magri, *Trattato*, 1:119.

158. Blasis, *Code*, 78.

159. Magri/Skeaping, 143; Magri, *Trattato*, 1:104: "e per lo puì si ballano all'impronto tutti gli a soli."

160. Blasis, *Code*, 53.

In the ballet lesson, one could strive to acquire "novelty" as well as to practice a technical tradition.

As this brief survey shows, much of the material in the *Trattato* relates directly to the training of dancers in a tradition of ballet technique that began well before Magri and continued long after his era. Magri does not provide an outline for a ballet class, but he deals with most of the components that were in "the lesson" as it was documented by later authors — the elementary exercises to be practiced with the support of a chair (later a rail or *barre*); the exercises to be practiced in center floor without support; and the turns, steps, and vigorous jumps that made up the rest of the lesson. His book helps us appreciate the fundamental principles as well as the lexicon of steps that all dancers, regardless of specialization, were expected to master in their training. By comparing his descriptions of that material with those in other dance texts from a period of 150 years, 1700–1850, we come closer to an understanding of what Magri is trying to tell us, as well as a better appreciation of how ballet technique changed during that period — for example, the ideal turnout increased to a 180-degree angle; balancing on toe tip ceased to be a stunt and became part of a dancer's training; certain steps that at one time were assigned primarily to the *grotteschi* were absorbed into the vocabulary required of all dancers and thus became a part of the training regimen.

Despite these and other differences over time, the impression one gets of ballet technique during this period is of a technical tradition that shows more steady continuity than radical change. One can follow that continuity into our own time, through the three methods of training or "schools" that were most influential in twentieth-century ballet, and thus passed on to ballet dancers today. Those methods, usually referred to by the names of the pedagogues associated with their development, were August Bournonville and the Danish School, Enrico Cecchetti and the Italian School, and Agrippina Vaganova and the Russian School. Bournonville, who had begun his training with his father, Antoine (a pupil of Noverre's), continued his studies with Auguste Vestris at the Paris Opéra, where he also was influenced by the works of Pierre Gardel and Albert. Cecchetti's teacher, Giovanni Lepri, was a pupil of Blasis, who had studied with Jean Dauberval in Bordeaux and performed in works by Gardel and Salvatore Viganò. Vaganova's training at the Imperial Theatre School in St. Petersburg benefited from influences from both the French and the Italian traditions (the former including Christian Johannson and Nikolai Legat and the latter Cecchetti) as well as a

developing Russian national style. These examples of the ballet tradition, these variants of an international art form, illustrate that dancers,
through their systematic training, are closely connected to both their ballet ancestors and to their ballet progeny.

Magri's advice to the would-be dancer rings true through the ages:
success in dancing requires "a long patient study of the first rudiments
and then, little by little, bringing them together, adjusting them with precise symmetry and, in order to make great headway, taking them
slowly."[161] His *Trattato* contributes to the understanding of those rudiments, the fundamentals of ballet practice. Magri acknowledges that
some things cannot be explained or demonstrated in a book but can be
learned only through practice, that is, in systematic repetition, and in the
theater, that is, in performance.[162] His *Trattato* has been singled out by
historians as offering a rare view of the grotesque style of theatrical dance
performance, which it most certainly does, but at the same time the *Trattato* is thoroughly grounded in the principles of an international ballet
technique. Dance historian and writer Marian Hannah Winter rightly
asserted that the *Trattato* "is a key to understanding the development of
ballet technique, for Magri knew and discussed all the genres."[163] But
even by Magri's time the distinctions among those genres were disap-
pearing in performance. The acrobatic virtuosity favored by Italian
dancers was influenced by the restraint and elegance of form favored by
French, or French-trained, ballet masters who worked throughout the
international ballet scene. They in turn began to incorporate more technical virtuosity in their choreography and in their classes.[164] It was this
blending of ballet's traditional elegance of form with its ever-present acrobatic capability that led to new technical and artistic achievements in
the nineteenth century and that has informed the ballet of our own time.

161. Magri/Skeaping, 53; Magri, *Trattato*, 1:16: "una lunga sofferenza d'imparare i primi rudi-
menti, e quindi tratto tratto unirli tra loro, andarli disponendo con giusta simmetria, e caminare a
lento passo per far gran strada."

162. Magri/Skeaping, 91; Magri, *Trattato*, 1:54.

163. Winter, *Pre-Romantic Ballet*, 151–52.

164. Dance historian Gloria Giordano, in discussing the career of the dancer, choreographer,
and impresario Gaetano Grossatesta (fl. 1720–69), asserts that by the 1720s "the French technical-
stylistic model was already widely used in Italy, as in the rest of Europe." She goes on to say that
manuscripts of the balletti and the data provided by the opera librettos convince her that in his choreography Grossatesta "joined the French style with typically Italian virtuosic and pantomimic elements." "Gaetano Grossatesta, an Eighteenth-Century Italian Choreographer and Impresario,
Part One: The Dancer-Choreographer in Northern Italy," *Dance Chronicle* 23, no. 1 (2000): 1–28 (18).

# 6

# Magri's *Grotteschi*

## LINDA J. TOMKO

*Ballerini grotteschi* figure significantly in Gennaro Magri's treatise, right alongside the two other principal categories of dancers in the eighteenth-century European scheme of theatrical dancers' differences. Whereas the *ballerini seri* perform with gravity and "composure," and the *mezzo carattere* dance "with great velocity," the *grotteschi* render dance steps "on a grand scale," he explains in a discussion of the *tordichamp*.[1] One achievement of Magri's treatise is indeed the argument for equal appreciation of the *grotteschi* that he advances through the literary structure of the *Trattato teorico-prattico di ballo*. Readers looking for specifics are certainly rewarded for turning quickly to the chapter on capriole steps, the sprung, inter-laced, and beaten steps of many kinds that typify the *grotteschi*'s assign-ments. The sheer variety of capriole steps and the level of detail Magri accords them occupy twenty-three pages, far greater in number than the typical one to two pages comprising earlier chapters devoted to indi-vidual steps, or the four pages specifying the use of the arms. Thus the

---

1. Magri/Skeaping, 76; Magri, *Trattato*, 1:42: "Si adopera da tutte le tre specie de' Ballerini, con tal differenza, che per ordinario nel ballo grave si fa con ogni posatezza, nel mezzo carattere si fa ve-locissimo, nel Grottesco si fa in grande."

physical power and dynamic vibrancy of the *grotteschi* shine in several ways in this culminating chapter of part 1; part 2 turns to ballroom dance and contredance choreographies in particular. But citations of the *grotteschi* also surface early and then in numerous succeeding chapters of part 1. Step by step, as it were, as Magri moves from discussion of one step to the next, the grotesque dancer's range and characterizations are written into the 1779 record that the author creates for theatrical and ballroom dancing in Italy during preceding decades.

If the *grotteschi* can be fingered at no single point in the text, what notions or conceptions of the *grotteschi* emerge across Magri's chapters? At an immediate, biographical level, readers soon realize that Magri himself was a skilled *grottesco* and inventor of steps. Moreover, the references Magri makes at various points in the *Trattato* to names of exemplary dancers such as Le Picq and Pitrot further signal his own investment, and also that of his peers not confined to Italy, in the particular skills and repertoire of character types for grotesque dancers.[2] Magri articulates analytical and theoretical senses of the grotesque dancer as well. First the analytical. These discussions clearly draw on texts from much earlier periods. Magri himself indicates awareness of historical manuals by Fabritio Caroso, Rinaldo Rigoni, and Giambattista Dufort.[3] Aimed at noble amateur readers, the texts by Caroso and Dufort had much in common with treatises such as Pierre Rameau's *Le Maître à danser* (1725) and Kellom Tomlinson's *The Art of Dancing* (1735).[4] These pedagogical works parsed period movement lexicons in a series of rhetorical steps. They addressed the recommended carriage of the body and articulated an organization of the body's potential for motion via codified "positions" of the feet and fundamental locomotor steps. They tutored readers in making additions to basic steps of sliding, springing, and turning actions. *Le Maître à danser* modeled the principles for coupling arm positions and

---

2. Magri/Skeaping, 123, 128; Magri, *Trattato*, 1:86, 91.

3. Magri/Skeaping, 44; Magri, *Trattato*, "Prefazione," 9. (It should be noted that the pagination of Magri's "Prefazione," "Avvertimento," and the main body of the treatise is not entirely continuous.) Magri cites Rigoni's *Il ballerino perfetto* (Milan 1468); Caroso's *Raccolta di vari balli* (Rome 1630); and Dufort's *Trattato di ballo nobile* (Naples, 1728). While it is not known whether Magri possessed copies capable of inspection, his ability to cite publication dates suggests the possibility that he had the books at his elbow. In a 1989 review of the Magri/Skeaping translation, A. William Smith notes that "no one has been able to locate Rinaldo Rigoni's treatise printed in 1468." See Smith, "Theoretical and Practical Treatise on Dancing," *Dance Research Journal* 21, no. 2 (Fall 1989): 34–37 (36).

4. Pierre Rameau, *Le Maître à danser* (1725; repr. New York: Broude Brothers, 1967); Kellom Tomlinson, *The Art of Dancing* (1735; repr. Farnborough, UK: Gregg, 1970).

motions with step vocabulary. Both Rameau and Tomlinson detailed the technique of etiquette and the ballroom dance *de rigueur* for their day, the minuet. As Sandra Hammond also has pointed out in chapter 5, Magri uses much the same approach, and the grotesque dancer enters in early in the rhetorical sequence, during discussion of the equilibrium of the body.[5] Here the author spells out the faltering that results when *grotteschi* fail to maintain *à plomb.*[6] Describing positions of the feet, another fundamental principle, Magri again invokes grotesque dancers. He specifies the typical French positions and their normative outward rotation of the legs; the false positions — inwardly rotated — that were much used by the *grotteschi;* and also the Spanish positions — neutral in turnout. He conceptualizes positions in the air to deal with locations for the lifted leg. Forced positions he describes as those which exceed normative distances separating paired feet; the capacity of these positions for accentuation becomes blazingly clear in later discussion of "attitudes" adopted by furies, a grotesque characterization.[7] The method of "horizontal ranking" deployed in this discussion returns in succeeding chapters. That is, Magri sets out several possibilities for foot positions and accords each a similar depth of treatment, without ranking one as superior to another. French, false, Spanish — the options are available as needed across a range of uses.

Magri proceeds to analyze locomotor steps, and here several dimensions of the *grotteschi's* movement emerge. Discussion of the *tordichamp,* for instance, indicates something of what I call the "iterated footwork" focus that the lexicon for *grotteschi* seems to emphasize. The *tordichamp* involves a crescent-shaped wrapping or circling skimming of the working foot in front of (or behind) a supporting foot, and then a return of the free foot to first position (heel touching heel). The wrapping by the free foot can remain at the side of the supporting foot when multiple circlings by the same foot are repeated in a row. The step can be jumped; dancers in all three categories do it, but *grotteschi* do it on a "grand scale."[8] The *pas tortillé,* done only by the *ballerini grotteschi* according to Magri, mobilizes another footed iteration. It calls for locomotion accomplished through alternating transfers of weight across the dancer's heels and toes, in an

5. Smith (n. 3) notes that "much of Magri's second chapter was derived from Dufort's twenty-fourth chapter" (36).

6. Magri/Skeaping, chap. 4 (57); Magri, *Trattato,* 1:20–21.

7. Magri/Skeaping, chap. 7; for furies see chap. 58, 149 ( Magri, *Trattato,* 1:111).

8. Magri/Skeaping, 76; *Trattato,* 1:42.

eighteenth-century variant of what the 1960s called the "mashed potato" step.[9] Italians introduced the step into theatrical dances that represented England, Magri avers, but the English themselves do not use it. He gives no indication that choreographers in other countries employ it.[10] He may not have been aware of the several uses of the *pas tortillé* made by Anthony L'Abbé in dances notated and published in *A New Collection of Dances* (ca. 1725). These included a solo man's "Chacone of Amadis" (LMC 1840; see fig. 6.1); the "Pastoral Performed by a Gentleman" (LMC 6720); and the "Spanish Entrée" (LMC 8100).[11]

Sprung steps for *grotteschi* offer opportunities for accentuation and also for preparations for more vigorous airborne and beating steps. In the *pas échappé*, for example, the dancer's feet and legs spring suddenly apart to second position, and then spring to rejoin.[12] The limbs draw the viewers' attention through the dynamic quality of their action. In a different vein, Magri identifies the *demi-sissonne* and the *pas brisé* as steps favored to precede and launch larger-scale and more complex caprioles.[13] (The *pas dégagé* falls in this category too; the dancer literally detaches a foot from floor and carries it into the air, the better to transition to the next step.)[14] Fashions in preparatory and breath-catching steps do change, Magri reveals, citing the fall into disfavor of the "*contretemps* and *pas de bourée disfatto*" combination of steps. Once used to facilitate traveling across the stage and to enable *ballanti* to draw breath, this combination no longer appeals in Magri's professional circle.[15]

Spinning — pirouettes, or steps done turning on the same place — belong to *dilettanti* as well as theatrical performers. The pirouettes on two feet that Magri details seem destined for the noble amateurs, whereas the spins on one foot, revolving "indeterminately" (for as many turns as possible), are claimed in large part as the province of *grotteschi*. Among these, "low" pirouettes can be turned with both knees bent; in *retiré* the toe of

9. Magri/Skeaping, 85–86; Magri, *Trattato*, 1:50–51.

10. The translation in Magri/Skeaping, 85, is misleading on this point. It credits Magri with saying, "The Italians introduced it into English dancing and in other national dances, although those nations do not use it themselves"; Magri, *Trattato*, 1:50: "Gl'Italiani l'hanno introdotto nel ballo Inglese, ed in altri balli nazionali, ancorchè nella stessa Nazione da loro non è adoperato."

11. For English choreographic practice, see Anthony L'Abbé, *A New Collection of Dances*, Music for London Entertainment 1660–1800, intro. Carol G. Marsh (ca. 1725; repr. London: Stainer & Bell, 1991), 63, 65, 72–74.

12. Magri/Skeaping, chap. 27; Magri, *Trattato*, 1:58–59.

13. Magri/Skeaping, 106; Magri, *Trattato*, 1:71.

14. Magri/Skeaping, 69; Magri, *Trattato*, 1:33–34.

15. Magri/Skeaping, 130; Magri, *Trattato*, 1:94.

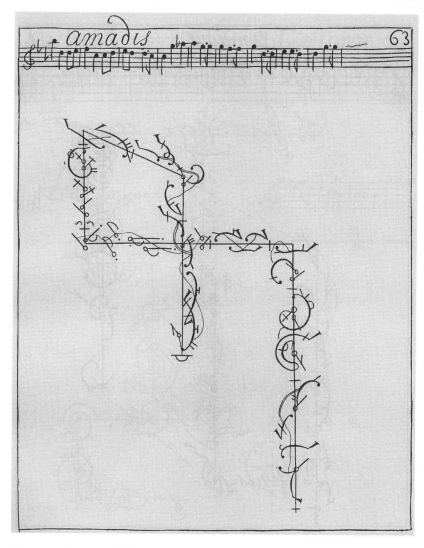

Figure 6.1: Measure 5 of "Chacone of Amadis Perform'd by Mr. Dupré" notates a *pas tor-tillé* resembling that described by Magri in pt. 1, chap. 21 of the *Trattato*. (Anthony L'Abbé, *A New Collection of Dances* [ca. 1725], plate 63)

the free foot touches the knee of the extended, turning leg. In the "toe and heel" variant, the toe of the free foot touches the heel of the spinning leg; for the "heel and toe" option, the heel of the free foot rests at the toe of the spinning leg. In a "crossed" pirouette, the free foot rests on the instep of the turning foot. At issue in the *grotteschi*'s turns is not just the virtuosity required to turn many times, a capacity Magri considerably understates by explaining his own ability to do nine turns as a function of a smooth floor, "a place on the Stage where I could turn without hindrance." Also in play is the focus and direction given to viewers' eyes by the many possible placements of the dancer's "free" foot on the length of turning leg, ankle, and foot.[16]

Iterated footwork focus returns again in the fourth area of the dance lexicon that Magri links with *grotteschi*, the caprioles (see fig. 6.2). For these airborne steps, he first spells out "interweaving" of the dancer's legs in terms of the "cuts" they make in the air in leaving and returning to their ground positions of the feet.[17] In the French manner, dancers leave the ground from fifth position, opening the legs to the sides and closing them in the air a given number of times before the final closure brings the body to earth again. Caprioles in the Italian manner depart the ground from the open second position, closing and opening while airborne before landing in open position. Dancers who launch from a closed position can choose to land in an open position, and vice versa; the Spanish positions also offer points of departure and neutral turnout while in the air. Also comprising caprioles are airborne beaten steps, jumped steps in which one leg passes over the other, and jumps in which the two legs circle in different directions in mid-air.[18] Beats are added to the locomotor steps described earlier in the treatise, including the *sissonnes* and the *contretemps*. Dazzling even in its textual rendition is the capriole called *spazza campagna* in which the airborne dancer's body seems to fold at the waist while the extended legs, pressed together, draw up in front of the chest and head, then open and stretch to the sides and join again in fifth position on the floor.[19] This capacious category of caprioles includes as well the steps used to characterize certain cultural groups and staple types in mid-eighteenth-century productions. Again the disposition of the feet directs attention. Establishing a Turkish identification, for instance, the Turkish capriole requires dancers to draw the legs up underneath the groin and beat the soles of the feet together rather than interweaving the legs or beating one calf upon the other. The *forbice* capriole invokes the commedia character Pulcinella. Here dancers launch into

16. Magri/Skeaping, chapter 45; quotation on 127; Magri, *Trattato*, 1:90.
17. Magri/Skeaping, chap. 60, secs. 1–3; Magri, *Trattato*, 1:119–22.
18. Magri/Skeaping, chap. 60, sec. 4 and ff.; Magri, *Trattato*, 1:122ff.
19. Magri/Skeaping, chap. 60, sec. 10; Magri, *Trattato*, 1:127–28.

Figure 6.2: "A dancer, dressed as an English sailor and hung with wooden spoons, jumps in with a big cabriole, and continues to dance to and fro with curious but correct cabrioles, until the air has been played twice." (Lambranzi, *Neue und curieuse theatralische Tantz-Schul* [1716], pt. 2, plate 22)

the air with knees joined "as if nailed together," then the legs separate simultaneously, one forward and one backward, before the legs join in landing on the ground.[20] The *salto dell'impiccato* codes "the eccentric" as offbeat or off-balance, a social or temperament type rather than a stock character from contemporary productions.[21] This capriole requires great elevations so that the vertical extension of the trunk contrasts greatly first with the fall of the extended arms to the thighs while airborne, and then the one-footed landing with the second leg detached "well into the air as much as possible."[22]

In the course of analyzing the dance vocabulary of his day, then, Magri specifies some key lexical dimensions of *grotteschi* as a category of movers. Wrapping steps, sprung steps (frequently with beats), steps of multiple turns, and myriad airborne steps interweaving and beating the legs particularly characterize the *grotteschi*'s traversal of space. Specific iterations of footwork emerge as key vehicles for drawing viewers' eyes and designating significant movement. Magri does not neglect to discuss the *grotteschi*'s use and configuration of arm gestures, or the composite arrangement of body parts that he embraces with the term *attitude*.[23] These he addresses in two separate chapters that immediately precede the final chapter's discussion of the capriole.[24] This sequencing of chapters and their contents notably departs from the prior example of Rameau's *Le Maître à danser*. Having first completed a step-by-step analysis of the lexicon, Rameau's treatise then returned to and devoted individual chapters to key step-units and their incorporation of appropriate arm gestures. Yet even before Magri conceptually brings the parts together to form a whole, a theoretical notion of the body erupts in the text and casts a different light.

20. Magri/Skeaping, chap. 60, sec. 18 (164; Magri, *Trattato*, 1:133); sec. 22 (166; Magri, *Trattato*, 1:136).

21. Magri/Skeaping, chap. 60, sec. 20 (165); Magri, *Trattato*, 1:134: "Il *Salto dell' Impiccato* detto *Saut Empedù* si fa nel carattere di Pulcinella, di un' Ubbriaco, o d' altro Goffo, e talvota si fa per bizzaria."

22. Magri/Skeaping, chap. 60, sec. 20 (165); Magri, *Trattato*, 1:135: "si distacca bene in aria un piede, quanto più si puole."

23. For a close study of some changes over time in the meaning of "attitude," see Francesca Falcone, "The Arabesque: A Compositional Design," *Dance Chronicle* 19, no. 3 (1996): 231–53, and "The Evolution of the Arabesque in Dance," *Dance Chronicle* 22, no. 1 (1999): 71–117.

24. Magri/Skeaping, chap. 58, "Of the Attitude" and chap. 59, "Of the Use of the Arms."

## Bodies Ever Becoming

Discussion of the body erupts amidst discussion of the *contretemps,* that sprung step practiced by every kind of *ballerino* in Magri's day. These, he explains, can be done with a flying bound, "and involve a force, a greater impetus, that serves either to take any capriole, or to travel any figure." Increased force is essential both to gain height in the preparatory *contretemps* and to enable rebound and launch into the next thing. It also serves to move a figure from one place to another. Further, "A body, speaking of bodies in general, not only of the living one," Magri says, "will have more strength in its resilience when it is more controlled, this resilient force being nothing more than a continuous, violent movement of extension."[25] Here Magri draws a parallel between human bodies and other forms of matter, articulating a kinetic principle. One invests or puts energy into the preparation for a jump in order to get energy out in the form of the jump. The more concentrated or controlled the input of energy, in his view, the more explosive the jump that results.

In a phrase Magri summons up the competing vectors of unceasing extension and countervailing control as the heart and soul of resilience. Rather than steps themselves defining the characteristics of *grotteschi,* it is the body as vortex of force that seems to shape the grotesque dancer in Magri's telling. Reading back to earlier chapters, this emphasis on continuous, violent extension helps explain the place given to "forced positions" that exceed the regular length or spacing of steps, and also the substantive option of "accentuation" proffered by steps like the *pas échappé.* The repeating wrap of an arcing foot, the multiple "indeterminate" spins on a single foot, these can be read as issuings of energy, outflows extending the body in space. Continuous and violent, in Magri's words, such steps configure "grotesque" bodies as what I call "bodies ever becoming." These are bodies that cycle again and again, that focus and forcefully release their energy as a consistent hallmark of their activity.

25. Magri/Skeaping, 130; Magri, *Trattato,* 1:93: "Ogni spiegato passo di Contratempo puol farsi di *sbalzo volato,* e vale una forza, un impeto di più, che si dona al corpo, e serve o per prendere qualche Capriola, o per passare qualche figura un pò discosta. Se sarà di prevenzione alla Capriola, fa di mestiere sforzarlo per far maggiore alzata al salto, che se prenderassi con lentezza, non si potran ben raccogliere le articolazioni, le quali non ben raccolte non potran dare al corpo quell'elaterio necessario al risaltare, perchè un corpo, si parla de' corpi in generale, non solo del vivente, avrà più veemenza nella elasticità, che una continua violenza di distendersi; *Vis elastica est continua vis se dilatandi.*"

At the same time, however, the movement lexicon in Magri's treatise includes devices that endeavor to harmonize and balance dancing bodies. Chapters on the *attitude* and the use of the arms describe actions that literally frame dancers' bodies and seem to have capacity to compose or contain extension. One description Magri offers for an *attitude* sounds quite similar to a step still practiced in late-twentieth-century ballet: balancing on one foot, the dancer extends the other and curves it at the knee, matching the lifted leg with the same arm raised and curved at chest height.[26] Another description recasts the *attitude* as exceeding any single step, comprising instead a "union of several poses, being an accompaniment of the arms, the legs, the head, the eyes, which must express in which emotional state the person is found."[27] Here an *attitude* is a composite configuration that signals affective states, channeling energies to that representational end. This signaling function holds true even for forced attitudes used for characters such as furies. Their poses will be more exaggerated than usual, and they will depart from regularity in their gnashing of teeth and arms "lifted beyond measure." Nonetheless, they more than other character types require "bodily agility, swiftness of legs, with grand and free gestures of the arms"—expertise to focus and vivify the desired image.[28]

The arm gestures allocated to *grotteschi* confirm the never settled alternation between extension and containment as facets of the *grotteschi's* movement profile. Opposition arms—gestures arranged to counter the forward leg with motion of the opposite arm—may be deployed as low, half-height, high, and *les grands bras*, or exaggerated arms; these four manners of moving the arms are available to all the categories of *ballerini*. Magri reports that the *grotteschi* make great use of exaggerated arms for both comic and regional character depictions, deciding at their discretion about the height to which to carry arms and the need to follow principles of opposition. Rounded arms forsake opposition and move together, forward or back, in any of the four manners. Whereas high rounded arms would be used by *ballerini seri* "in a finale, in a solo, in retiring, and such like," or by *ballerini* executing a *brisé* followed by a capriole, Magri specifies that *grotteschi* would "take the *capriole* with low rounded arms, which

26. Magri/Skeaping, 148–49; Magri, *Trattato*, 1:110.

27. Magri/Skeaping, 148; Magri, *Trattato*, 1:109: "una unione di più atteggi, dovendo essere un accompagnamento di braccia, di piedi, di testa, di occhi; che deve esprimere in qual stato di passione si trova la persona."

28. Magri/Skeaping, 149; Magri, *Trattato*, 1:111: "velocità delle gambe, con grande, e spedito atteggio di braccia."

gives greater force and impetus to the jump."[29] Here the erstwhile containing and complementary action of arm gestures is configured to support the surging force of continuous, violent extension.

## Closed Versus Open Bodies

Contending with drives to extension and drives to containment, the grotesque dancing body evoked in Magri's treatise illuminates the challenge of calibrating the dancing body's energy, a concern still present in twenty-first-century ballet. It also intersects with a broad cultural shift that Mikhail Bakhtin has termed the struggle between the grotesque and classical bodies. In *Rabelais and His World* Bakhtin uses the French Renaissance literary characters of Gargantua and Pantagruel to theorize a notion of the grotesque.[30] In Bakhtin's view, grotesque imagery before the modern period (prior to the sixteenth century) was seated in bodies that blurred the boundaries between themselves and their surroundings. Orifices occupied pride of place in this imagery, enabling exchange with the environment of streaming bodily fluids and ingested materials. Appetites and activities of grotesque bodies always seemed excessive — the adjective "gargantuan" has come to signal outsize scale. And in the process of exceeding boundaries between themselves and their surround, grotesque bodies continually renewed themselves. Earthy, gluttonous, ever in process, grotesque bodies were messy and transgressive, but also a site of taking great pleasure in the material world. The grotesque as porous, open body began to be challenged in the sixteenth century, Bakhtin explains, facing a new, so-called classical canon of the smooth, closed body. Orifices are closed in the new canon, body surfaces cannot be penetrated, internal processes remain sealed within it, and now pride of place is given to "the individually characteristic and expressive parts of the body: the head, face, eyes, lips, to the muscular system and to the place of the body in the external world."[31] Moderation restrains

---

29. Magri/Skeaping, chapter 59, quotations on 153; Magri, *Trattato*, 1:115–16: "ne fanno uso i Ballerini Serj in un fine, in uno a solo, in una ritirata, e simili; . . . vogliono per esempio fare una Capriola sotto al corpo, la pigliano con un Brisè avanti, e le braccia alte rotonde. I Grotteschi però prendono la Capriola con le braccia basse rotonde, con quali si prende maggior forza, e si dona impeto maggiore al salto."

30. Mikhail Bakhtin, *Rabelais and His World*, trans. Hélène Iswolsky (Bloomington: Indiana University Press, 1984), 303–67.

31. Bakhtin, *Rabelais*, 321.

transgression; the parallel is clear with the harmonizing and configuring of bodily parts and their expression performed by the union of several poses in Magri's *attitude* chapter. While Bakhtin concentrates almost exclusively on literary imagery, he recognizes the history of dress and fashion as a realm in which the contest between grotesque and classical conceptions of the body plays out. And in the same footnote, he perceptively remarks, "Even more interesting is this struggle in the history of dance."[32] The *lazzi* of Harlequin and other *zanni* among the commedia dell'arte offer ready application of Bakhtin's idea. These stock figures were steadily represented on musical theater and other stages through the mid-eighteenth century, and they parlayed eating and excreting motifs into numerous representations of gluttony and excess. In his explanation of the large-scale caprioles that grotesque dancers used to enact *commedia* figures and cultural types, discussed later in this essay, Magri reveals a connection between one dimension of the *grotteschi*'s repertoire and the grotesque body that Bakhtin sees at issue in a large cultural shift to the closed, classical body.

Bakhtin extends the argument made from French literature to all of Europe, and indeed claims that grotesque imagery has covered all time and space. The classical canon has operated for a short time in comparison, he indicates, as "a tiny island."[33] We may rightly reserve judgment on Bakhtin's claim that the reach of grotesque imagery was universal. Nonetheless, his notion of a struggle between competing conceptions of the body enables us to appraise the grotesque dancers in Magri's treatise as participating in a broader period querying of the body and the way that it signifies. That the contest was very much in progress and far from settled in the 1770s is revealed by the difference that Magri decries between Italian and French expectations about *grotteschi*'s skills and repertoire. Magri complains vigorously in the chapter on the *attitude* that Italian practice forces *ballerini* to dance several types of characterizations, not without poor results. He asks:

> Do you wish to know why in our Italian Theatres characters of this kind [furies] do not succeed? Usually because many times they take a *serio ballerino*, accustomed to gentle and [soft] *attitudes*, versed in the pathos of his languid impassioned gestures, and give him the task of portraying the violent character of a fury. How can this be done, if great vivacity and

32. Bakhtin, *Rabelais*, 323.
33. Bakhtin, *Rabelais*, 319

fire is needed in the Action? If he is accustomed to soft gestures, how can he adapt himself to violent ones? This is trying to make him contradict his character, to take him away from his system and to put him in another where, so to speak, he is out of place.[34]

The French system, in contrast, allows *ballerini* to specialize and to devote themselves to specific instead of wide-ranging skills and characterizations.

Whoever is capable of being a *serio* gives everything of himself to that genre. The *Grottesco* will concentrate on his speciality and does not put on buskins. The *mezzo carattere* puts all his effort there: the *gavottine,* the *tempi brillanti* are always his constant exercise; and thus they are all done to perfection.[35]

Does this passage index Magri's envy of the professional conditions available to his French peers? Or does it ventilate professional jealousy at having lost employment to other dancers he deemed less qualified? In either case, the proposed narrowing of a dancer's responsibilities to only the grotesque range, solely the *serio* or the *mezzo carattere,* would have significantly changed the skill set of Italian dancers in Magri's day that Kathleen Hansell details in chapter 1 of this volume. Analyzing Italian printed libretti between 1750 and 1800, Hansell reports that "at least half of all the dancers named in a libretto, whether ranked or not, have at one time or another performed as *grotteschi.*" Further, "Italian dancers performed in a variety of styles and did not remain confined to a single category."[36] Had the French system been imported to Italy, release from the requirement to dance the *seri's* languid, soft, and sustained qualities would have positioned a *ballerino* to focus exclusively on grotesque characters and skills, on the continuous violent extension of the body. Such

---

34. Magri/Skeaping, 149–50; Magri, *Trattato,* 1:111–12: "Si vuol sapere perchè spesso delle volte ne' nostri Teatri Italiani non riescono simili caratteri? Perchè più delle fiate prendono un serio ballerino alle sue dolci, e molti [recte: molli] Attitudini costumato, versato nel patetico del suo languido appassionato gestire, e gl' incaricano il violento carattere della furia. Come poterlo questi fare, se ha di bisogno di tutta la vivacità, e fuoco nell' Azione? Se usitato a molleggi, come adattarsi alli violenti atteggi? E' un volerlo contrafare dal suo carattere, torlo dal suo sistema, e metterlo in uno, che vi sta, per così dire, a piggione."

35. Magri/Skeaping, 150; Magri, *Trattato,* 1:112: "Chi è capace del serio a quel genere si dona tutto. Il Grottesco si aggira nel suo specificio, e non calza il coturno. Il mezzo carattere lì si lambicca sempre: le gavottine, i tempi brillanti sono tuttora il suo continuo esercizio; e così vengono a far tutto con perfezione."

36. See chap. 1, p. 26.

an opportunity to specialize would seem to favor the prodigious, self-exerting body ever becoming of Bakhtin's grotesque theory, and offset, or delay, the smoothing effects of the classical canon.

Magri returns to the issue of appreciation for the *grotteschi* as a distinct *emploi* in the very next chapter (59), "Of the Use of the Arms." In addition to using rounded arms at low level to empower the thrust of their caprioles, Magri explains, the *grotteschi* use exaggerated rounded arms for the characters of Scaramuccia, masked characters, and Truffaldino — characters danced in chaconne tempo. Here the responsibility to characterize stock and masked personages places expressive demands on *grotteschi* that are not so different from those required of other *ballerini*. "Should the *Grottesco* be less skilled in the art of expressing through gestures the Pantomime and comic Action than the *Serio* to express the same in Tragedy?" he asks rhetorically.[37] Magri is far from collapsing the *grotteschi* back into the *seri* because both face demands for expression. Rather, he seeks to challenge a privileging of the *seri* on the basis of the different "merit" or ranking attached to the characters they enact. That is, the *seri* should not be valued more highly than the *grotteschi* simply because the heroes played by the former enjoy higher social or aesthetic rank than the shepherds or the artisans depicted by the latter.[38] Taking as a matter of fact the distinct category of grotesque dancing that he argued earlier should be still further distinguished, what Magri commends as the matter for evaluation is the excellence of the practitioners in their respective endeavors. He admonishes spectators of *seri* and *grotteschi*, "The prudent man, the wise man, despises neither the former nor the latter and is only interested in whoever performs his duties well."[39] The emphasis Magri here places on merit as the basis for evaluation echoes the rejoinder he makes to criticisms received from Francesco Sgai before the *Trattato* was even published. In the "Warning to the Courteous Reader" Magri writes, "To my expertise in dancing, the public is witness, to whose impartial judgement I willingly submit without heeding the malicious voice of the thinker."[40] Quite a shrewd debater, Magri

37. Magri/Skeaping, 153; Magri, *Trattato*, 1:116–17: "E che forse l'arte di esprimere per mezzo de' gesti la Pantomima, l'Azione comica la deve avere il Grottesco meno di quella del Serio, per esprimer questi la sua Tragica?"

38. Magri/Skeaping, 153; Magri, *Trattato*, 1:117.

39. Magri/Skeaping, 154; Magri, *Trattato*, 1:117: "L' Uomo prudente, l' Uomo savio non vilipende nè questo, nè quello e sol s' interessa di chi bene adempie il dovere."

40. Magri/Skeaping, 46; Magri, *Trattato*, "Avvertimento," 10: "Della mia espertezza nel ballo, . . . n'è testimonio il pubblico, all' imparzial giudizio di cui ben volentieri mi sottometto."

turns the theoretical discussion to account to deftly defend his professional status.

The two kinds of assignments placed on the shoulders of *grotteschi*—to command steps that iterate and surge and extend the body in space, and to mobilize unions of poses to represent certain kinds of cultural figures and stock characters—suggest that the struggle between canons of open and closed, grotesque and classical bodies, was hardly resolved in the 1770s. Certainly, category specialization in the French manner that Magri proposed might well have permitted greater concentration by *grotteschi* on the focusing and forceful releasing of bodily energy flows. In this sense specialization might act to retard the advance of classical, closed bodies. But Hansell's data on *grotteschi* as performers of more than one category type, together with Magri's commentary on the harmonizing *attitudes* required of *grotteschi*, suggest that the actual requirements of the dance workplace impelled the inclusion of closed as well as open, smooth as well as rough embodiments, in Italian dancers' skill sets. These considerations allow us to conceptualize the Bakhtinian shift from grotesque to classical bodies as far from a sudden or total change. They allow us as well to appreciate the (at least) dual capacity of theater dance to instate and buttress cultural norms as well as transgress them.

## Inscribing Gender, Coding Cultural Identities

Creating a better place in the sun for *grotteschi*, Magri's account attempts to reordinate prevailing Italian rankings of theatrical dancers. At the same time, it contributes a linguistically gendered picture of dance performance as man's work that does not comport with other data about actual practitioners. It also illuminates ways in which dance strategies compose vivid codes for regional and cultural identities.

From the opening pages of the dedication citing "gentlemen of the Academy," to the closing chapter of part 1 devoted to caprioles, the subject and audience for Magri's remarks seem to be almost exclusively male. This is due in considerable part to Italian linguistic convention, where the masculine singular and plural nouns are taken to stand for all genders. Then, as today, such usage shores up patriarchy. To be sure, part 2 of the treatise is devoted to ballroom etiquette and contredanses for mixed groups, and thus ladies and gentlemen alike receive repeated references. The commentary of part 1 addresses the *dilettanti* as well as theatrical dancers, all of whom mobilize the lexicon of steps the author so carefully sets out. Some mentions are made of female dancers when discussion turns to noble amateurs, and at least one of these passages is supremely negative. Magri discusses the *pas assemblé* as a step more customary in France than Italy because the French prefer *terre à terre* dancing to caprioles.[41] He links it as well to those *ballanti* who when required to do one capriole forward followed by another turning — not a simple task — substitute the unbeaten *assemblé* for one of the caprioles. His ire truly rises when he assigns the origin of the *assemblé* to the stupidity of Italian ladies who, wishing to avoid fatigue, substituted *assemblés* for caprioles in the course of a figured *pas de deux*. Their selfish desire to shine drives them to use the easier step regardless of the effect on the *ballo* as a whole — to which Magri attaches greater importance. Not all women behave so poorly, he admits; some ladies "who [care for the glory of others no less than for their own], do not do this because all their skill is applied from the beginning to the end."[42] His tone hardly makes it seem possible that the more responsible females could neutralize the damage done by the vainglorious. The weight of his rhetoric about noble amateur dancers specifically identified as female is disparaging.

Use of masculine nouns in part 1 to stand for all dancers seriously occludes the demographic picture of dancing as a profession in Italy, however. Kathleen Hansell has shown not only that substantial numbers of women were employed as theatrical dancers, but that significant numbers of them actively pursued grotesque roles as well (see app. 1). This confirms the sense conveyed by Gregorio Lambranzi in his *Neue und curieuse theatralische Tantz-Schul* (1716), whose illustrations represent women as theatrical performers alongside men, again and again.[43] Some aspects of the step vocabulary assigned to Magri's *grotteschi* were not unknown to female performers in 1720s Britain, as revealed in choreographies by Anthony L'Abbé such as the "Chacone of Galathé" (LMC 1860) or the "Passagalia of Venüs & Adonis" (LMC 6580). Women dancing this repertoire were required to execute a full air turn in the couple dance "Chacone." Nearing the complexity of steps bearing similar names in the *Trattato*, women performed the *demi-entrechat* and *demie-*

41. Magri/Skeaping, 119; Magri, *Trattato*, 1:82.

42. Magri/Skeaping, 119; Magri, *Trattato*, 1:82: "ma questo non fanno quelle Donne, a quali troppo cale l' altrui nommen della propria gloria, che queste impegnano dal principio sino al fine tutto il loro sapere."

43. *New and Curious School of Theatrical Dancing*, trans. Friderica Derra de Moroda, ed. Cyril W. Beaumont (New York: Dance Horizons, 1966).

*cabriole* in the solo "Passagalia," and other beaten steps.[44] Of course, these are some of the most virtuosic dances in the extant notated repertoire from early-eighteenth-century Europe. Closer in time to Magri's era, dances from Auguste Ferrère's 1782 manuscript also made strong demands on female dancers' technique, as discussed by Moira Goff in chapter 8 of this volume. My own reconstruction of Ferrère's "La Sabotière," a wooden shoe dance for a woman from *Les Bûcherons et les sabotiers*, confirms the substantial requirements posed by this grotesque role. The dancer must possess a keen rhythmic sense as well as the capacity to launch suddenly into surging paths through space. The wooden shoes required for this solo are perforce blockier and more cumbersome than softer shoes or slippers, and they increase the difficulty posed by the dance's numerous, quick changes of direction and hopped, beaten-leg steps. The very material of which the shoes are composed adds weight — and an audible, humorous dimension — to the frequent stamped steps specified in the notation. Further, the steps required of the *grottesca* in Ferrère's "La Sabotière" include several that sustain correlation with the *demi-sissonne, tordichamps,* and *contretemps* steps that Magri details and links to *grotteschi* performance. This coincidence impels the hypothesis that the challenging repertoire articulated by Magri's *Trattato* for (linguistically male) *grotteschi* was available to women professionals, to some significant degree at least.

If gender assignments are difficult to parse, the linkages in the treatise between grotesque dancing and constructions of regional and cultural representations are vivid. That is, Magri frequently details the ways in which particular movement skills belonging to the *grotteschi* can be used to produce characterizations. He does not mean this in a Stanislavskian sense. Rather, I take his use of characterization to indicate a physicalization of a type, the registering by corporeal means of an affective bundle or set of qualities associated with an articulated theatrical figure or personage. A long tradition for this kind of characterization exists in European theater dance history, and Magri's instructions in the capriole chapter provide welcome details on how such roles were fashioned. The high jump and off-balance landing that produce "the eccentric" provide a physical code for stage presentation of a temperament. Equally specific are the movement indicators that signal the identification of Scaramuccia and other stock theatrical characters. I readily acknowledge that the

44. L'Abbé, *A New Collection of Dances,* 26, 49, 52, 50.

identifications created by costuming for commedia characters were equally powerful, and mutually reinforcing, in Magri's time. The point here is the power of specified physical signs to telegraph distinctive identities and their associated regional ties, affective tics, even occupations. Movement codes communicated as well some insider/outsider relationships in the fragmented nonstate called Italy in the 1770s, with the example of the *oltramontani*. The term conveys the sense of being a foreigner, someone not Italian, and the stage personages bearing this name are depicted with exaggerated poses. They are frequently shown dancing the *carré* spatial pattern, which Magri describes as two people simultaneously tracing the perimeter of a common rectangle, now facing each other, now moving back to back.[45] The characterization constructed by these physical signals is one of poorly calibrated resources, thus — to my mind, and lacking further elaboration from Magri — clumsiness or lack of sophistication. Greater force than necessary is expended; the method of mapping a spatial form suggests comic indecision, inconsistency, or even naïveté. One plausible reading of this movement code is that the *oltramontani* are "beyond the pale," socially and even geographically. These and other regional and national dances of several kinds were the stock in trade for *grotteschi*, and Magri offers meaningful insight into the nuance as well as the broad strokes that inform them.

The representational work done by grotesque characterizations extends to cultural identifications as well. The English and the French appear frequently in Magri's text as peoples actively practicing stage dancing, in some cases exceeding and in other cases borrowing from Italian models for theatrical dancing. In an important sense, they supply the community of peers and cultural affinity in which Magri situates himself. The author's chapter on the positions of the feet instates some elements of these relationships.[46] Set forth first among the five categories of positions presented, the "true" positions are those attributed historically to French dancing master Pierre Beauchamp, although Magri does not cite this etymology. Next Magri gives the "false" positions. These were published as early as 1700 in Raoul Feuillet's *Chorégraphie*, again a French source that goes uncredited. Magri specifically links the false positions to the *grotteschi*, for use in depicting "almost all the characters," and he adds

---

45. Magri/Skeaping: references to *carré*, 146 (Magri, *Trattato*, 1:107–8); references to *oltramontani* on 146, 149 ( Magri, *Trattato*, 1:108, 111). Contributors to this volume use the term differently from the translation offered in Magri/Skeaping, 242n64.

46. Magri, *Trattato*, chap. 7.

"particularly in dancing the steps in the English manner, but according to Italian usage." In the next breath he lauds the English for using neither the true nor the false positions and for the great freedom that typifies their national dancing.[47] How can these two statements be reconciled? One speculative interpretation is that Magri in this passage reports the use of false positions by Italian performers to signal the "Englishness" of character types that they are assigned to perform, even though the English themselves use neither true nor false positions when dancing their national dance — here arguably the country dance. Discussion follows of positions "in the air" — specifically, the disposition of the working foot when freed from the ground — and the "forced" positions, which exaggerate or increase as much as desired the distance separating feet in the true second, fourth, and fifth positions. Of all the categories given for foot positions, only "those in the Spanish manner" are linked by name directly to a cultural group. Beyond detailing issues of turnout, distance, and relationship, Magri offers no cultural commentary on things Spanish, and readers gain no indication that Spanish Bourbons had reigned in Naples since 1734. Was inclusion of the Spanish positions a matter of aesthetic accuracy or felt political obligation? We do not know. In similar vein, it is true that French forces at various historical points occupied areas that today comprise Italy. The treatise invokes French techniques many more times than it does things Spanish. It positions French techniques as something of an aesthetic *Urtext,* a cultural archive, rather than the movement signature imposed by a current political force.

Beaten jumps associated with grotesque dancers serve both to encode and to render "other" still another cultural group: the Turks. As described above, these jumps bring together and beat the soles of the feet beneath the airborne, bent-kneed dancer. These soles can beat to the side as well, the body held obliquely, with the dancer landing on one foot.[48] Perhaps these bent knees echo the repeated raised-leg hops and switchback *jetés chassés* that recur as motifs in the virtuosic "Turkish Dance" (LMC 8220) choreographed by Anthony L'Abbé in 1720s London.[49] (While this is the only surviving notated choreography for Turkish characters, numerous Turkish personages are included in ballet and opera librettos of the period; see fig. 6.3.) Magri includes no details about

---

47. Magri/Skeaping, 64; Magri, *Trattato,* 1:27: "particolarmente ne[l] ballare i passi all' Inglese, all' uso però Italiano."

48. Magri/Skeaping, 164; Magri, *Trattato,* 1:133.

49. L'Abbé, *A New Collection of Dances,* 85–86, 89, 96.

Figure 6.3: "Four Turks enter, one after the other, and dance with joined hands as shown; backwards, forwards, and to the right and left, with *ballonnés* and other suitable *pas*." (Lambranzi, pt. 2, plate 38)

signature arm gestures or torso inclinations; the movement code is sketched in the barest of terms. The provision of this minimalist index for the Turk is all the more striking given the absence of a specified code for registering things French or English. As had France and Spain with regard to Italy, Turkey had posed a military threat to eastern Europe and the Mediterranean through the 1690s. A key difference may have been the greater religious divide between Christian Italy (and Europe) and Muslim Turkey. The physicalization of Turkish identification that Magri offers continues a long line of references to and Baroque stagings of things Turkish, from Molière and Lully's *Le Bourgeois Gentilhomme* (1670) to "La Turquie" in Campra's *L'Europe galante* (1697) and "Le Turc généreux" in Rameau's *Les Indes galantes* (1735).

Charting differences in corporeal terms, these "grotesque" characterizations positioned cultural groups as distinguishable "others" for theatrical representation. If stagings have long provided ways for Euro-American people to represent themselves to themselves, such "grotesque" characterizations participated in the important social and political tasks of grappling with identities and differences at a time of foreign conquest of Italy, emerging capitalism, and nascent nationalism. The depictions detailed by Magri do not, or do not yet, link language and cultural groups with territories and state structures in exclusive alignments that would characterize nineteenth-century nationalism, and indeed late twentieth-century nationalism. Neither does the connection that Magri feels with French and English theater dance practice, nor the long-standing array and circulation of commedia characters (themselves crystallizations of regional Italian types) comprise the kind of imagined *political* communities, aspiring to sovereignty, that Benedict Anderson recognizes as formative of nations.[50] At the same time, Magri's treatise contributed to and reminds us of the continuing concern among European people to parse the difference and significances of cultural others "close to home"—including the Turks, Savoyards, and *oltramontani*—in a period of vigorous and continuing exploration in the Americas, Africa, and Asia. The methods that Magri's work details for coding "difference" as differences in behaviors buttressed the social rankings in play in *ancien régime* Europe, and it made such coding further available to the burgeoning models of capitalist and nationalist organization. By the end of the century, European thinking about the right structuring of society would

50. Benedict Anderson, *Imagined Communities; Reflections on the Origins and Spread of Nationalism*, rev. ed. (London: Verso, 1991).

demonstrate increasing receptivity to biological explanations of human-kind and social change. As literary scholar Roxane Wheeler explains it, the signs of difference or similarity that mattered most in the early and middle eighteenth century were those of behaviors and subscription to Christianity.[51] As depicted in the mid-eighteenth-century novels that Wheeler analyzes, these characteristics could trump or outweigh differences in appearance such as skin color and complexion that would come to matter greatly in the emerging, modern senses of race and nation. What Magri helps readers see is the movement materials with which the coding of behavior was comprised in the early and middle eighteenth century. If he does not analyze the social or political ends to which this coding capacity was put at the time, we may take that question as an obligation to investigate further. We may absolutely appreciate Magri's clarity in showing the kinesthetic and material means with which dance movement — his own and that of numerous theatrical peers and productions across Europe — signaled period ideas about temperament, regional and national associations, and the divides between insiders and outsiders.

51. Roxane Wheeler, "The Complexion of Desire: Racial Ideology and Mid-Eighteenth-Century British Novels," *Eighteenth-Century Studies* 32, no. 3 (1999): 309–32 (327).

# 7

# The French Connection

## REBECCA HARRIS-WARRICK AND CAROL G. MARSH

Although France and Italy had distinguishable dance traditions during the eighteenth century, there was a good deal of artistic cross-fertilization between the two countries. French dancers were a national export and many worked in Italy; similarly, a considerable number of Italian dancers performed in Paris and left their impact on French ballet. Extensive documentation from librettos, scenarios, payment records, and journalistic accounts is now allowing us to construct a rich picture of the theatrical contexts in which ballet operated across Europe,[1] but the

1. Marian Hannah Winter's *Pre-Romantic Ballet* provides an insightful overview of Europe's theatrical traditions and their interconnections, even if the documentation is not always as complete or accurate as one might wish. Substantial studies of localized theaters include Paul-Marie Masson, "Introduction" and "Les 'symphonies de danse'" in *L'Opéra de Rameau* (Paris: H. Laurens, 1930), 5–38 and 367–422 (an account that covers much of French opera and ballet, not just Rameau); Kathleen Kuzmick Hansell, "Opera and Ballet at the Regio Ducal Teatro of Milan, 1771–1776" (Ph.D. diss., University of California, Berkeley, 1980); the same author's "Theatrical Ballet and Italian Opera," in *Opera on Stage*, vol. 5, of the series The History of Italian Opera (Chicago: University of Chicago Press, 2002); Bruce Alan Brown, *Gluck and the French Theatre in Vienna* (Oxford: Clarendon, 1991); Susan Leigh Foster, *Choreography and Narrative: Ballet's Staging of Story and Desire* (Bloomington: Indiana University Press, 1996); Ivor Guest, *The Ballet of the Enlightenment: The Establishment of the Ballet d'Action in France, 1770–1793* (London: Dance Books, 1996); Moira Goff, "Art and Nature Join'd:

relative paucity of choreographic evidence makes a picture of actual dance practices harder to discern. Of the two most important choreographic documents from the second half of the century — Magri's *Trattato* and a remarkable manuscript of pantomime ballets compiled by Auguste Ferrère — one originated in Italy, the other in France; the question then arises as to whether or not they may be seen as complementary in regard to the dance styles they transmit. Magri's book tells us about dance steps, but not about whole dances and still less about entire works; Ferrère's manuscript, on the other hand, preserves the music and choreography for eight little works, but does not describe how to execute the steps. On that level alone, then, the two documents would seem to make a useful pair. This essay seeks to illuminate the points of contact between the dance worlds in which the two documents originated and to establish the extent to which it may make sense to use the one to help interpret the other.

The Ferrère manuscript, which dates from 1782, three years after the publication of Magri's *Trattato*, contains a remarkable level of detail about several pantomime ballets, entr'acte divertissements, and individual dances.[2] Using a mixture of Feuillet notation, drawings, and verbal descriptions over its fifty pages, it contains sufficient information about these works for reconstructing them with a reasonable degree of confidence. The titles alone of the works suggest reciprocities with the kinds of light-hearted ballets found on the stages of Italy and Vienna: *The Painter in Love with His Model, The Village Celebration, The Woodcutters and the Cloggers.*

Auguste Ferrère worked in Valenciennes, a city with an active theatrical life located in northeastern France near what is now the border with Belgium.[3] His father, who choreographed some of the works pre-

Hester Santlow and the Development of Dancing on the London Stage, 1700–1737" (doctoral thesis, University of Kent, Canterbury, 2000).

2. The full title as it appears on the manuscript is "Partition et Chorographie / Ornée des figures et habillements des Balets donnee Par / Auguste, frederick, Joseph, ferrere. / A Valencienne en 1782" (F-Po Rés. 68 ). The manuscript is discussed briefly in Winter, *Pre-Romantic Ballet*, 164–65, with two of its pages reproduced on 182–83.

3. "Auguste Ferrère was in Valenciennes (in the north of France) in 1782, the year in which he copied the manuscript, although in what capacity is not known. Valenciennes in the late eighteenth century had an active cultural and intellectual life. It boasted a Jesuit school and two important theatres: a municipal theatre that produced operas and other dramatic works, and a well-equipped private theatre at the chateau of the Duc de Croÿ." Carol G. Marsh, "French Theatrical Dance in the Late Eighteenth Century: Gypsies, Cloggers, and Drunken Soldiers," *Proceedings of the Society of Dance History Scholars*, Ryerson Polytechnic University, Toronto, Ontario, 10–14 May 1995, 91–98 (91).

served in the manuscript, was a dancer at the Dresden court of Elector of Saxony Augustus II (also king of Poland as Augustus III), where many French dancers were employed; moreover, Ferrère Senior is known to have performed in Paris and in London.[4] As far as is known, Magri himself never performed in France or had direct contact with Auguste Ferrère; nonetheless, the two had only two degrees of separation from each other. Ferrère's manuscript says that one of the ballets, *Les Bûcherons et les sabotiers* (The Woodcutters and the Cloggers), was performed in Paris in 1751 by the Italian *grottesco* Cosimo Maranesi; Maranesi's presence in Paris can, in fact, be documented for the years from 1751 to 1754, during which time he danced in at least two of the principal theaters. His partner during this sojourn was Bettina Buggiani; she was to become Gennaro Magri's partner during his first season in Vienna, 1759. Because she and Maranesi are almost always mentioned together in French accounts of their performances, it seems reasonable to hypothesize that she performed in the Ferrère ballet as well — all the more since the two of them made a specialty of wooden shoe dances, which they inserted into existing ballets. Yet another Magri connection exists: Maranesi was to dance alongside Magri in Naples in 1766, in the ballets between acts of *Il gran Cid*, which were choreographed by Magri. It would appear that Magri and Maranesi traveled in related theatrical circles and that at least one of the Ferrère works can be seen as belonging to that orbit.

Whereas coverage in the French press shows that Maranesi and Buggiani were clearly a special attraction in Paris when they arrived, they belonged nonetheless to a long tradition of Italian performers in French theaters. In order to see how their performances fit into this larger history, let us now take a look at the Parisian theatrical dance world in the years around 1750. First, it is important to remember that ballet in Paris, as in Italy, was performed not by itself as an evening's entertainment but rather within or alongside other kinds of stage works. The four main venues for ballet were the Académie Royale de Musique (also known simply as the Opéra), the Comédie Française, the Comédie Italienne, and the Opéra Comique, each of which had its own repertoire and its own conventions for how dance operated on its stage. All of them, however, put dance into close proximity to vocal music; works that were danced throughout and set entirely to instrumental music represented only one of the possible ways dance could be used.

---

4. Documentation for the information in this paragraph appears later in this chapter and in the chapters by Bruce Alan Brown and Salvatore Bongiovanni elsewhere in this volume.

Although only one of these four theaters announced its Italian connections in its very name, the others had also received infusions of Italian dance and music at various times and to varying degrees. Italian comedians had performed in France on an irregular basis starting in the sixteenth century, but since 1661 an Italian troupe had become established in Paris under royal protection. During the 1680s the troupe began to move from a purely improvised theater based on schematic scenarios of the commedia dell'arte repertoire toward fully worked-out plays written for the troupe by French authors. In 1697, however, the theater was closed from one day to the next by royal degree and the troupe expelled, due to the licentiousness of some of its performances.[5] Only after Louis XIV died in 1715 was another Italian troupe invited to establish itself in Paris. The new troupe, variously called the Comédie Italienne or the Théâtre Italien, and consisting largely of actors who were Italian by birth (although many were or became naturalized French), was granted occupation of Paris's oldest theater, the Hôtel de Bourgogne, where they performed plays, pantomimes, and ballets. Luigi Riccoboni, nicknamed Lelio and the head of the troupe, generally played a young lover (*innamorato*); his adherence to the traditions of the commedia dell'arte notwithstanding, he sought to raise the tone of his theater and to put on serious as well as comic works.[6] Whereas some of the troupe's repertoire was improvised on the basis of familiar Italian scenarios — its Arlequin, Thomas Antoine (Thomaso Antonio) Vicentini, was particularly adept at physical comedy — more and more of its plays were new works by French playwrights such as Marivaux, who gave the stock characters of the commedia dell'arte greater depth and subtler wit. But regardless of the origins of the works performed, an evening at the Théâtre Italien always included music and dance. Plays generally incorporated little interludes of singing and dancing, and always ended with a *diver-*

---

5. See Virginia Scott, *The Commedia dell'Arte in Paris, 1644–1697* (Charlottesville: University Press of Virginia, 1990). The troupe's leader at the time of its demise, Evaristo Gherardi (the troupe's Arlequin), published a six-volume collection of its plays, mostly from after 1692, by which time the troupe was performing almost entirely in French: see *Le Théâtre italien* (Paris, 1700, and many subsequent editions). For a selection of some of the plays by a French playwright, see Charles Mazouer, ed., *Le Théâtre italien: Les Comédies italiennes de J. F. Regnard*, 2 vols. (Paris: Société des textes français modernes, 1996); this edition includes a useful introduction about the troupe in general and an extensive bibliography.

6. For a history of the new Italian Theater, see Clarence Brenner, *The Theatre Italien: Its Repertory, 1716–1793, with a Historical Introduction* (Berkeley: University of California Press, 1961). Regarding Luigi Riccoboni's aspirations to create a different type of Italian theater, see the article on him in *L'enciclopedia dello spettacolo* (Rome: Sansoni, 1962).

*tissement,* usually consisting of several songs and dances, rounded off by a *contredanse générale,* that is, a dance for the entire cast. Moreover, parody was part of the troupe's stock in trade—both of operas put on at the Académie Royale de Musique and of plays from the Comédie Française. The operatic parodies, which mixed speech, song, and dance, made fun not only of the plots (a standard device was to make Arlequin the hero of the opera, as in *Arlequin Atys,* which parodies Lully's *tragédie en musique*) but also sometimes of operatic dances. In 1735, for instance, the *Mercure de France* reported on a one-act comedy in French called *Les Ennuis du Carnaval,* written by François Riccoboni (Luigi's son) and Romagnesi, another member of the troupe: "This play was followed by a dance for six people, in imitation of the *pas de six* danced at the Opéra following the tragedy *Omphale.* This figured dance is very well characterized and perfectly executed by the actors in the troupe; it is composed of an Arlequin and Arlequine, a Pierrot and Pierette, a Polichinelle and a peasant or wooden shoe dancer. The tunes are parodied from those that were composed for the *pas de six* at the Opéra."[7]

Between the plays and the operatic parodies, the dancing skills of Arlequin and other commedia masks found regular expression on the stage of the Théâtre Italien. It seems reasonable to suppose that the movement vocabulary of such comic characters would have drawn upon both the acting and the dance traditions of the actors' native Italy, although it probably also absorbed at least some features from the French dancing they saw around them. The Italian word "lazzi," meaning the comic routines that were a staple of the commedia dell'arte style of theater, shows up in scenarios both of plays and of ballets—even in the middle of a French text (see below the excerpt from the scenario for Dehesse's pantomime ballet, *Les Bûcherons,* quoted in full in app. 5), as a measure of how this kind of comedy had extended beyond its country of origin (see fig. 7.1). Magri's own discussions of steps not infrequently allude to the commedia characters for whom they are appropriate, as when he says that forced *attitudes* are used by Coviello or Scaramuccia;[8] for him such dances were a normal part of the *ballerino grottesco*'s repertoire. Moreover,

7. "Cette piece fut suivie d'une entrée de six personnes, à l'imitation du pas de six, qu'on a dansé à l'Opéra après la tragédie d'Omphale. Cette danse figurée est fort bien caractérisée, & parfaitement bien exécutée par les Acteurs de la Troupe, & composée d'un Arlequin & d'une Arlequine, d'un Pierrot & d'une Perrette, d'un Polichinelle & d'un Paysan ou Sabotier; les airs sont parodiés sur ceux qui ont été composés pour le pas de six de l'Opéra." *Mercure de France,* February 1735, 364.

8. Magri/Skeaping, 149; Magri, *Trattato,* 1:111 (chap. 58).

Figure 7.1: A "chicona" danced by Arlequin and Scaramouche. "Arlequin enters as shown and begins to dance step by step in his own manner. Then Scaramouche approaches him with a lantern, dances and mimics him, but finally resolves to go away." (Lambranzi, *Neue und curieuse theatralische Tantz-Schul* [1716], pt. 1, plate 29)

Magri's own scenarios include commedia characters; see, for example, the ballet he choreographed in Naples in 1766 following the second act of *Bellerofonte* (app. 4, no. 4), which involves Pulcinella, Arlecchino, and Coviello in a scene of magic and gluttony.

Whereas it is clear that the Théâtre Italien shaped its productions to cater to French tastes, and that as a result the performing traditions of the Comédie Italienne were not identical with those of the commedia dell'arte as practiced in Italy, it is also clear that French audiences had opportunities from time to time to see dancers fresh from Italy performing in the more vigorous style for which Italian dancers were famous. One such was the Sieur Roland, a native of Provence, but formerly the leading dancer for the Duke of Mantua, who "executed a comic and grotesque peasant dance" on the stage of the Théâtre Italien in May of 1732, which was warmly received by the audience. His seventeen-year-old daughter, who had been born in Venice and was reported to be as good an actress in both French and Italian as she was a dancer, appeared at the same time; "caprioles and entrechats cost her no effort," reported the *Mercure de France*, and she later performed "an *entrée* as a sorceress, with surprising vivacity and lightness."[9] In August of 1742, the Venetian Campioni and his sister performed a *pas de deux* at the Théâtre Italien, then moved to the Opéra Comique, with equal success.[10] An anecdote reported in 1760 concerns another visiting virtuoso: "Grimaldi, nicknamed Jambe de Fer [Iron Leg], Italian dancer, the most intrepid *cabrioleur* ever seen, made his debut at the Opéra Comique at the Foire Saint-Germain in 1742, in the divertissement from the *Prix de Cythère*, in an entrée for a Turkish sailor. He had wagered that he could leap to the height of the lamps, which he did, and from the blow he gave to the one in the middle, he sent a stone flying into the face of Méhemet Effendi, the Turkish ambassador, who was in the king's box."[11]

By the mid-1730s the Théâtre Italien had expanded its danced offerings to include substantial pantomime ballets, which were either

9. "les cabrioles & les entrechats ne lui coûtent rien"; "une Entrée en Magicienne, avec une vivacité & une légéreté surprenante." *Mercure de France*, May 1732, 992–93; August 1732, 1845.

10. François and Claude Parfaict, *Dictionnaire des théâtres de Paris* (Paris, 1756; repr. Geneva: Slatkine, 1967), 7:424–25.

11. "Grimaldi, surnommé Jambe de Fer, danseur Italien, le plus intrépide Cabrioleur que l'on ait vu, débuta à l'Opera Comique de la Foire Saint Germain 1742, dans le Divertissement du *Prix de Cythere*, par une Entrée de Matelot Turc. Il avoit parié qu'il s'éleveroit à la hauteur des Lustres; ce qu'il exécuta: & du coup qu'il donna dans celui du milieu, il en fit sauter une pierre au visage de Méhemet Effendi, Ambassadeur de la Porte, qui étoit dans la Loge du Roi." *Les Spectacles de Paris* (1760), 84–86.

interleaved with one-act plays that might also include dancing or performed at the end of multiple-act works. Sometimes the play included a
setup for the ballet, even if the two plots were otherwise separate. For instance, in *Le Réveil de Thalie*, performed there in 1750, the Muse of Comedy, Thalie, has fallen asleep from having watched too many boring
comedies. The *comédiens italiens* try various means of waking her up, the
last of them being a pantomime ballet (*Les Bûcherons, ou Le Médecin de village*), which then ends the performance.[12] The Italian-born, French-
educated François (Francesco) Riccoboni, son of Luigi, was responsible
for choreographing many ballets, including a *Pygmalion* in 1734, in which
he danced with Mlle Roland.[13] He was followed by Jean-Baptiste
François Dehesse, another actor/dancer, who choreographed at least
fifty-eight pantomime ballets at the Théâtre Italien between 1747 and
1757.[14] The titles alone of many of these works show their affinities with
the kinds of ballets also being danced in Italy and Vienna: *L'Opérateur chinois* (The Chinese Medicine Man, 1748), *La Guinguette* (The Cabaret,
1750), *Les Femmes corsaires* (The Women Pirates, 1754), *Les Matelots hollan-
dois* (The Dutch Sailors, 1756), *Les Artisans* (1756). Many of Dehesse's ballets were huge successes, warranting praise such as the following from the
September 1749 issue of the *Mercure de France*, regarding *Les Savoyards*:
"Monsieur Dehesse, who can never be praised with as much spirit and
variety as he puts into his wonderful compositions, has given a ballet that
had a tremendous success and whose characters are animated and
comic." A later article, in July 1751, praised the acting abilities of his
dancers in *Les Meuniers* (The Millers): "Monsieur Dehesse joins to his talent for imagining piquant ballets, the ability to create, so to speak, actors.
He succeeds in getting dancers who have little familiarity with the stage

12. Desboulmiers [Jean Auguste Jullien], *Histoire anecdotique et raisonée du Théâtre Italien* (Paris:
Deladoué, 1769), 5:479.
13. Susan Foster has suggested that this ballet was a derivative of Marie Sallé's famous *Pygmalion* in London earlier the same year; see her *Choreography and Narrative*, 1–2 and 278n2. The *Mercure de France* (July 1734, 1617) pointed out the connection in the story between the two works, but
without further comment. The music for Riccoboni's *Pygmalion*, along with approximately 140 other
*divertissements* for the Théâtre Italien from between 1717 and 1737, was composed by Jean-Joseph
Mouret and published in reduced score in a series of *Recueils;* see the complete list in Renée Viollier,
*Jean-Joseph Mouret: Le Musicien des Grâces* (Paris: Librairie Fleury, 1950), 221–25.
14. Dehesse was born in The Hague in 1705 but by 1729 was living in Valenciennes. He joined
the troupe of the Comédie Italienne in 1734. See Nathalie Lecomte, "Jean-Baptiste François Dehesse: Chorégraphe à la Comédie Italienne et au Théâtre des Petits Appartements de Madame
de Pompadour," *Recherches sur la musique française classique* 24 (1986): 142–91; for a list of his works, see
158–59.

to express the most comic ideas; they owe him their talent."[15] The dance troupe performing both Dehesse's ballets and the dances within the plays numbered around twenty during this period, with approximately an equal number of men and women.[16]

The scenario for *Les Bûcherons, ou Le Médecin de village* (The Woodcutters, or the Village Doctor; see app. 5), one of the few Dehesse ballet scenarios that survives in any degree of detail, contains a mixture of dance and comic pantomime, whose conventions were apparently so well known that they could be indicated by simply calling for *lazzi*. After one of the woodcutters falls from a tree and appears to have broken several bones, the doctors recommend amputation and other drastic measures. The distressed wife rejects any such solution, and "the surgeon lets it be known that he has more effective secrets. He brings out some wine and fills a glass, which produces several *lazzi*. The wine [has] a marvelous effect, the wounded man regains all his strength, the doctors admire him ecstatically, and the woodcutters express their joy. [ This is followed by a] *contredanse générale,* in which the doctors and the surgeon join."[17]

The Opéra Comique, offspring of the various theaters that had operated for decades at the two main seasonal fairs in Paris, the Foire Saint-Germain and the Foire Saint-Laurent, had much in common with the Comédie Italienne, although its financial position was more precarious, since it was not under royal protection.[18] In fact, it had been forced to shut its doors at various times, due to legal actions on the part of the

15. "M. de Hesse, qui ne peut jamais être loué avec autant de génie et de variété qu'il met dans ses aimables compositions, a donné un Ballet . . . qui a un succès des plus éclatans, et dont tous les personnages sont animés et comiques"; "M. de Hesse joint au talent très-rare d'imaginer des Ballets piquans, celui de créer en quelque sorte des Acteurs; il vient à bout de faire exprimer les idées les plus comiques par des Danseurs et des Danseuses qui n'ont la plupart que peu d'usage du Théâtre, et qui lui devront leur talent." *Mercure de France* (Sept. 1749 and July 1751). Both accounts are cited in Lecomte, "Dehesse," 166, 172.

16. The names of the dancers in the various troupes during this period may be traced in the pages of *Les Spectacles de Paris* (published annually). Their numbers fluctuated from season to season; in 1753, for example, the Théâtre Italien employed twelve male and ten female dancers.

17. For the French text, see the transcription of the entire scenario in app. 5. Although the composers for Dehesse's ballets are often known, the only music for a ballet of his to have been located to date is for *Le Mai;* see Lecomte, "Dehesse," 170.

18. Regarding the wide variety of entertainments provided by the fair theaters, see Robert Isherwood, *Farce and Fantasy: Popular Entertainment in Eighteenth-Century Paris* (New York: Oxford University Press, 1986). For many primary documents from these theaters, see the Web site put together by the late Barry Russell, "Le Théâtre de la foire à Paris," http://www.er.uqam.ca/nobel/c2545/foires/. For a succinct telling of the complex history of the Opéra Comique (both the genre and the theater), see Martin Cooper, *Opéra Comique* (London: Chanticleer, 1949).

official theaters, who saw the fair theaters as unwelcome competition; the longest such closure lasted from 1745 to 1752. As with the Théâtre Italien, its repertoire depended largely on parodies of operas and plays, many of them also making using of Arlequin and other commedia characters. The number of new works increased over time, particularly after Charles-Simon Favart, author of the enormously successful *La Chercheuse d'esprit* (1741), became its principal librettist during the 1740s.[19] Although during this period this theater's main bread-and-butter depended on the genre known as the *comédie à vaudevilles,* in which spoken dialogue alternated with well-known songs and operatic borrowings set to new words, it, too, participated in the ever-increasing vogue for pantomime ballets. In 1734, for example, it put on a pantomime ballet entitled *Dom Quichotte chez la Duchesse,* in which the dancers were dressed as the kings, queens, and jacks from a deck of cards who dance around Don Quixote, with a goal "to represent, through figured dances, the different follies that this wandering knight committed during his stay with the duchess. This ballet is ingenious and very well executed."[20] In 1754–55 Jean-Georges Noverre was the choreographer at the Opéra Comique for a single season,[21] mounting, among other works, a production of his own earlier ballet, *Les Fêtes chinoises* (from 1748) or new ones such as *Les Réjouissances flamandes* (see app. 5). In 1762 the Opéra Comique and the Théâtre Italien, whose repertoires and styles of performance had always been similar, merged, under the direction of Favart.

The most prestigious theater, thanks to its status as a royal academy, and the one with the most eminent dance troupe, was the Paris Opéra, known officially as the Académie Royale de Musique.[22] During this period the plots of all of the large works performed on the stage of the Opéra were carried by singing—not only the *tragédies en musique* or the

19. For a list of Favart's works, see Bruce Alan Brown's article on Favart in *Grove Opera,* 2:136–38.

20. *Mercure de France,* July 1734, 1618: "On a voulu représenter par des Danses figurées, les différentes folies que ce Chavalier Errant fit chez la Duchesse pendant le séjour qu'il y fit. Ce Balet est inégnieux et fort bien exécuté." See also Parfaict, *Dictionnaire,* 4:349–51. This work does not appear to have any connection with the three-act ballet (of the type where the plot is carried by singing) by Boismortier performed at the Opéra in 1743.

21. See Kathleen Kuzmick Hansell, "Noverre," *International Encyclopedia of Dance* (New York: Oxford University Press, 1998), 4:694–700.

22. Contrary to what is stated in some dance histories, the name of this institution was never the Académie Royale de Musique et de Danse. The Académie Royale de Danse, founded in 1661 by Louis XIV, was a separate institution, whose functions remain to be fully understood. See Régine Astier, "Académie Royale de Danse," *International Encyclopedia of Dance,* 1:3–5.

*pastorales héroïques*, but even the works classified as ballets or *actes de ballet*. But no matter what the genre, all of these works accorded a large place to dance, which was integrated into the story line as a bearer of dramatic meaning, not performed between the acts, as in Italy.[23] Contrary to received notions about the stuffiness of this institution, the works performed on its stage included comedies, such as the much revived *Fêtes de Thalie* (1714) or *Les Amours de Ragonde* (1742), both composed by Jean-Joseph Mouret, who made his primary living at the Théâtre Italien. In mid-century the leading composer at the Opéra was Jean-Philippe Rameau, whose works spanned the full range of genres from the mythologically based tragedy on the Lullian model (e.g., *Castor et Pollux*), to lighter ballets with a separate plot in each act, a genre today called opera-ballet (e.g., *Les Indes galantes*), to the pastoral (e.g., *Acante et Céphise*), to the overtly grotesque *ballet bouffon* (*Platée*).[24] Rameau's expressive and dramatic dance music was admired all over Europe and was often excerpted for use in other Parisian theaters or even outside of France.[25] Whereas in all the French operatic genres the place accorded to dance within the works had been growing as the century progressed — and had begun including stretches of narrative pantomime, as in the "Ballet des fleurs" within the Persian entrée of *Les Indes galantes* — so had the public's taste for the lighter genres; by the mid-1770s the proportion of tragedies to the

23. Regarding the integration of ballet into French opera, see Rebecca Harris-Warrick, "'Toute danse doit exprimer, peindre . . .': Finding the Drama in the Operatic Divertissement," *Basler Jahrbuch für historische Musikpraxis*, 23 (1999), ed. Peter Reidemeister (Winterthur, Switzerland: Amadeus Verlag, 2000), 187–210.

24. Some dance historians, out of an understandable desire to give the role dance played at the Opéra its due, have sometimes called all of the works performed there "opera-ballets," regardless of what they were called at the time. Such usage, however, masks important distinctions in structure and content. It thus seems more useful to restrict the term "opera-ballet" to the meaning it has in musicology (and which was used intermittently already in the eighteenth century) of a work that has an independent plot in each *entrée* (the term used to indicate an act in such works).

25. Within only the repertoire under discussion in this book, several Rameau borrowings have been identified. At least two dances by Rameau appear in the Ferrère manuscript: the contredanse from "La Danse," the last entrée in the opera-ballet *Les Fêtes d'Hébé*, which Ferrère used to conclude *Le Peintre amoureux de son modèle*, and a tambourin from *Castor et Pollux*, used by Ferrère for the *tambourin sérieux* danced by a *Paysan galant* in *L'Embarras des richesses*. Bruce Alan Brown has identified several pieces by Rameau among the ballet music Starzer provided for Hilverding in Vienna (see his *Gluck and the French Theatre in Vienna*, 164–65). And the Italian opera composer Niccolò Jommelli is reported to have said that "without Rameau, Terpsichore [the Muse of the dance] would have been obliged to abandon Italy." (Le fameux *Jomelli* avouoit que sans *Rameau*, Terpsichore eût été obligée de déserter l'Italie.) Anonymous, "Lettre au rédacteur du Journal des Théâtres," in *Journal des théâtres ou Le Nouveau Spectateur* 3 (1777): 85, as cited by Mary Cyr in "Rameau e Traetta," *Nuova rivista musicale italiana* 12 (1978): 166–82 (168).

other, still more dance-oriented genres, which had stood at about three-to-one in 1700, had been completely reversed. This change was mirrored in the size of the dance troupe, which grew from twenty-two members in 1714 to ninety-one in 1770.[26]

Notwithstanding the size and quality of its own dance troupe, the Opéra brought in outsiders — especially Italian virtuosi — from time to time. In 1739, for example, the Italian dancer Antonio Rinaldi, called Fossano (or the Frenchified "Fossan" in some press accounts), appeared in Paris with his star pupil Barbara Campanini, known to the French as Mlle Barbarinne or Mlle Barbarini, who was only sixteen at the time. Both created such a sensation that they were soon performing dances added to various operas in settings designed to feature their particular abilities. Rameau's opera-ballet *Les Fêtes d'Hébé* had premiered in May 1739, but in July of the same year Rameau composed four new dances for Mlle Barbarinne that were added to Entrée II, "La Musique."[27] Works that temporarily acquired Italian dance music as vehicles for the couple included Royer's *Zaïde*, where they danced as court buffoons in an appended ballet entitled "Momus amoureux," and Campra's *Fêtes vénitiennes*, in which Fossano performed a wooden shoe dance.[28] The dance for two gardeners the couple performed at the Opéra was imitated by child dancers at the Théâtre Italien in 1741.[29] Taken together, the accounts of these performances suggest that the Parisian audience was watching dances imported directly from Italy, even if these had to be given a dramatic context in order to make them performable on the stage of the Opéra. Thus even the Académie Royale de Musique afforded the French public the chance to see Italian dancing fresh from Italy, at least some of it in the grotesque style, and not filtered through long-time residents such as the regular performers at the Comédie Italienne.

The remaining official theater in Paris, the Comédie Française, had always incorporated music and dance into its performances, despite continuous efforts on the part of the Opéra ever since the time of Lully to limit the numbers of singers, instrumentalists, and dancers it was allowed to employ. Although the repertoire of the theater consisted of spoken plays,

26. Rebecca Harris-Warrick, "Paris" (secs. 1–3), *Grove Opera*, 3:855–65.

27. See the score in the appendix to Jean-Philippe Rameau, *Oeuvres complètes*, vol. 9, *Les Fêtes d'Hébé* (Paris: Durand, 1904; repr. New York: Broude Brothers, 1968), 427–30; see also lxvi and lxxix for historical information.

28. The anonymous music for at least some of their dances was published in Paris by Boivin, probably shortly after these performances; see one of the extant copies in F-Po 𝄞 1404 (2–6).

29. Parfaict, *Dictionnaire*, 7:481.

both tragedies and comedies, some of them, such as the comedy-ballets of
Molière, which remained on the boards decades after their creation, incorporated sung and danced scenes throughout, whereas others, such as
the plays of Florent Dancourt, set up musical interludes between the acts
and ended with a vaudeville or *contredanse générale*. In fact, one of the ballets in the Ferrère manuscript presents *divertissements* to follow the acts of
Dancourt's much-performed play *Les Trois Cousines*. Even though Ferrère's choreography almost certainly originated in performances of the
play at the municipal theater in Valenciennes in 1782,[30] it uses much of the
music Claude Gilliers composed for the play at its premiere in Paris in
1700 and adapts the play's sequence of songs and dances. In 1753 the
Comédie Française received permission from the crown to establish a
troupe of approximately fifteen dancers, after which time the amount of
dance, including pantomime ballets, increased, although this theater still
did not feature dance to the same extent as the other three. This innova-
tion on the part of such a venerable institution did not pass unnoticed by
the other theaters: in July of that year the Opéra Comique performed a
satiric prologue in which "Melpomene [the Muse of Tragedy], shocked
that the Comédiens Français were giving comedy-ballets more often than
tragedies, takes refuge at the Opéra Comique and wants to establish her
residence there; since her children [i.e., the actors of the Comédie Fran-
çaise] are now only performing *divertissements* worthy of the fairs, she wants
the fairs to put on works appropriate to her theater."[31]

It was within this active and competitive theatrical context that still
more Italian dancers appeared in Paris, moving among the various theaters as the opportunities presented themselves. The one who appears to
have had the most extensive career in Paris was the Roman Pietro Sodi,
who, according to the Parfaict brothers, was "born with a singular talent
for the composition and performance of pantomime dances."[32] He

---

30. Ferrère's title reads (complete with grammatical and spelling errors), "Agrement de danse
Des Trois Cousine opera en trois Acte tel qu'il ont ete donne a Valencienne en 1782."

31. "Melpomene choquée de ce que les Comédiens François donnent des Comédies-Ballets
plus souvent que des Tragédies, vient se réfugier à l'Opéra-Comique, & veut désormais y fixer son
séjour; & puisque ses enfans ne donnent plus que des Divertissemens propres de la Foire, elle veut
qu'à la Foire on joue les Pieces qui appartiennent à son Théatre." Synopsis in *Les Spectacles de Paris*
(1754), 191ff.

32. "SODI (Pierre) Romain, né avec un talent singulier pour la composition & l'éxécution des
danses Pantomimes"; Parfaict, *Dictionnaire*, 5:179–86. This dictionary devotes considerably more column inches to Sodi than to any other dancer; the Parfaict brothers apparently drew at least some of
their information from Sodi himself. The information about Sodi presented here relies primarily on
their account.

joined the dance troupe of the Académie Royale de Musique in 1744, where he choreographed and performed in such comic pantomime dances as a *pas de trois* for Polichinelle, Dame Gigogne, and Arlequin in *Les Fêtes vénitiennes*, or a dance of crazy people for *Le Carnaval et la Folie*. During the period he was working at the Opéra (which ended in 1751), Sodi also choreographed a number of ballets or entr'acte dances for the Théâtre Italien and the Opéra Comique, on a variety of topics ranging across the Italian grotesque style, from peasant dances to pantomimes for drunks, hunters, or artisans of various types. One of his pantomime dances, however, "L'Allemande" for the Théâtre Italien, is described as being "dans le genre gracieux," and he also choreographed *Les Nouveaux Caractères de la danse* for Camilla Veronese, a dancer/actress at the same theater. In 1753 he was hired as the choreographer for the newly established dance troupe at the Comédie Française, where he worked for three years; after spending the 1756–58 seasons in Vienna and Venice, he returned to Paris and served as choreographer at the Théâtre Italien from 1758 to 1760.[33]

It may be thanks to Sodi that Cosimo Maranesi, the dancer named as performing in Ferrère's *Les Bûcherons et les sabotiers*, came to Paris; at least the Parfaict brothers make a point of saying that Sodi was doing compatriots a favor when in 1752 he choreographed a ballet called *Le Jardin des fées* for the Opéra Comique, into which Maranesi and his partner, Bettina Buggiani, inserted a wooden shoe dance. With them he also danced a *pas de trois* for hay threshers in the same work.[34] Maranesi and Buggiani, who can be documented as performing to great acclaim in Paris from 1751 to 1754 and who are even listed as members of the dance troupe at the Opéra Comique in 1752 and 1753,[35] were very young at the

33. The information about Sodi's career after 1756 comes from *L'enciclopedia dello spettacolo* (Rome: Sansoni, 1962), 9:78, which also reports that after leaving Paris in 1761 he went to London for several years and from there to the United States. He died in Charleston, South Carolina, in 1774.

34. Information regarding the Parisian performances of Maranesi and Buggiani may be found in the Parfaict brothers' *Dictionnaire*, 5:180–81, 6:229–31, 7:392, 7:411, 7:555, 7:574, 7:586, 7:617, 7:639–40, 7:707, and 7:721. The articles about them under their own names (7:574–75) say that they "shared the applause of the public at the Opéra Comique and the Comédie Française during the summers" of those years, which may mean that they performed elsewhere during the other seasons. ("MARANESI, (Cosimo) en François *Cosme;* ce jeune Danseur, Italien de nation, a partagé les applaudissemens du Public au Théatre de l' *Opéra Comique,* & depuis à celui de la Comédie Françoise, pendant l'été de 1752, 1753, & 1754, avec la Dlle *Bugiani,* Danseuse de la même nation.") The article about Buggiani gives the same information.

35. *Almanach des spectacles de Paris* (1753), 149–50, where their names are misspelled as Cosimo Paranesi and Botina Beviani; they, along with Sodi, are identified as Italian. In the 1754 issue of *Les*

time, estimated in 1752 by a critic in London, where they also performed during this period, as sixteen and fifteen years old respectively. They clearly had wooden shoe dances as a specialty item, one that must have particularly pleased the public, since after dancing "Les Sabotiers" at the Opéra Comique, they took the same dance to the Comédie Française the following year,[36] where they performed several other pantomime ballets as well. The Parfaict brothers do not document them as performing at the Théâtre Italien, which is where Ferrère's manuscript claims that *Les Bûcherons et les sabotiers* was performed by Maranesi in 1751 ("Dansé à la Comédie Italienne à Paris en 1751 par Maranesi" [*sic*]), but given the fluidity with which works moved among the various theaters, it could well have been done there. In any case, Ferrère Senior was undoubtedly the means of transmitting Maranesi's dancing to his son, as he, too, was performing in Paris during the same period—in fact, at the Théâtre Italien.[37] Moreover, the three dancers were also in London during the fall of 1752, when Signor Maranesi and Signora Buggiani performed yet more wooden shoe dances at Covent Garden (*Les Sabotiers tyrolese*) and Monsieur Ferrère danced at Drury Lane. Their previous

---

*Spectacles de Paris*, 82, their names appear as M. Cosimo and Mlle Bucany. Their dancing at the Comédie Française was critiqued by Grimm, who was surprised by their athleticism, but found them less graceful than French dancers; see Grimm, *Correspondance littéraire*, July 1753, as quoted in Foster, *Choreography and Narrative*, 290n5.

36. Wooden shoe dances already had a long history on the Parisian stage. In 1714, for example, a Tuscan dancer performed a peasant dance in wooden shoes at one of the Fair Theaters; see Jacques Bonnet, *Histoire générale de la danse* (Paris, 1723), 172–73 ("son Entrée de Paysan avec des sabots, étoit d'une légereté & d'une naïveté sans pareille"). The Parfaict brothers mention a wooden shoe dance for a peasant performed by the younger Nivelon at the Foire St. Laurent in 1728, "with admirable skill, all the lightness and accuracy possible, and using the most burlesque contortions" (une Entrée de Paysan en sabots, avec une adresse admirable, toute la legereté et la justesse possible, & dans les attitudes les plus burlesques et les plus contortionnées); see Parfaict, *Dictionnaire*, 3:504–5. Moira Goff (personal communication) has pointed out many such dances in London from 1710 onward, including a description of one by William Hogarth in his *Analysis of Beauty* (1753); Hogarth's description is quoted by Winter, *Pre-Romantic Ballet*, 183.

37. Parfaict, *Dictionnaire*, 7:516, has the following information about the senior Ferrère: "Danseur au service du Roi de Pologne, Electeur de Saxe, a paru au Théatre Italien de Paris, dans l'année 1753. La Pantomime intitulée *le Rempailleur de chaises*, faisant partie du Ballet *des Arlequins & Arlequines*, lui fit beaucoup d'honneur, aussi bien qu'à Mlle Riviere, qui l'exécuta avec lui. Il avoit profité d'un congé pour venir établir sa réputation à Paris, & il est retourné où ses engagemens l'appelloient." (Dancer in the service of the king of Poland, Elector of Saxony, who appeared at the Théâtre Italien in Paris in 1753. The pantomime entitled *Le Rempailleur de chaises* [a person who weaves the straw seats for chairs] . . . did him much honor, as it did Mlle Riviere, who performed with him. He had taken advantage of a leave in order to make his reputation in Paris, and has returned home to honor his commitments.) The Parfaict article about Mlle Riviere (7:700), says that she was employed at the same court, and that all Paris was sorry to see her leave when she returned to Germany. Her style of dancing was characterized as "le genre gracieux."

performances in France were used as selling points: Ferrère was adver-
tised as "a Comic Dancer, lately arriv'd from Paris," Maranesi and Buggiani as "two celebrated Italian Comic Dancers from the Opera at
Paris."[38] Perhaps Auguste Ferrère, notating *Les Bûcherons et les sabotiers*
much later, conflated the Parisian theater in which his father had danced
with the ones in which Maranesi performed—not surprising, given that
the Opéra Comique and the Théâtre Italien had merged by that time.
But whatever its original venue, a ballet that features wooden shoe
dances seems like a natural for the team of Maranesi and Buggiani and
might even have been a vehicle for them.

The careers of Maranesi and Buggiani recall that of Gennaro Magri,
who also traveled extensively in order to make his living. It is thus not surprising that their professional lives were to intersect later: Bettina Buggiani was Magri's partner in Vienna during 1759, his first season there,
and Maranesi danced under Magri's direction in Naples in 1766, in the
ballets between acts of the opera *Il gran Cid* (see apps. 3 and 4). Moreover,
it appears that virtuosos such as Maranesi and Buggiani, or Fossano and
Barbara Campanini before them, traveled with what might be called
"suitcase dances," ones that they had ready to plug in to any appropriate
work.[39] They sometimes even brought the music for such dances with
them, as the account of Maranesi and Buggiani's 1754 performance in *La
Fête villageoise* at the Comédie Française shows.[40] Such visiting performers
injected exciting new elements into the already rich range of dancing
available in the theaters of Paris.

Given this web of connections, the Ferrère manuscript seems like a document that should be studied for not only for what it says about certain

---

38. In October of 1752 Maranesi and Buggiani were performing at Covent Garden, Ferrère at
Drury Lane. See G. W. Stone, ed., *The London Stage, 1660–1800*, pt. 4, *1747–1776* (Carbondale: Southern Illinois University Press, 1960–68). The playbills and newspaper accounts included in this com-
pilation are also the source for the two dancers' ages. The Parfaict *Dictionnaire* (7:392) also mentions
that Maranesi and Buggiani had been in London that year, where they danced *Les Batteurs en Grange*,
later performed in Paris. For a summary of the London careers of these dancers, see Philip H. High-
fill Jr., Kalman A. Burnim, and Edward A. Langhans, *A Biographical Dictionary of Actors, Actresses, Musicians, Dancers, Managers and Other Stage Personnel in London, 1660–1800* (Carbondale: Southern Illinois
University Press, [1973]–93), 5:231–33 (Ferrère, father and son), 10:87–88 (Maranesi).

39. This term is used by analogy with "suitcase arias," which singers of *opera seria* carried with
them from city to city and inserted into operas by other composers, because the music suited their
particular vocal talents.

40. For the scenario of this ballet, see appendix 5. The account in the Parfaict *Dictionnaire*, 6:
229–31, says that the music was composed by d'Avennes, excepting the *pas de deux* by Maranesi and
Buggiani, whose music "is by an English composer and was brought by them."

kinds of French dancing but also for what may well apply in other parts of Europe where similar practices were in place. There are, of course, caveats. We do not know, for instance, whether the ballet in which Maranesi danced in 1751 was notated at that time, or remembered by one or the other Ferrère thirty years later, or notated by Auguste Ferrère from a version current in 1782. Moreover, it is important to remember that no matter what their origins, these works come to us filtered through the sensibilities of a French dancer. Still, Ferrère's ballets seem largely consonant both with what Magri has to say and with what scenarios suggest he did in his own works. The following overview of the Ferrère manuscript will clarify these connections, and subsequent chapters will mine its ballets in greater detail.

Even though at least two of the manuscript's pages have been lost, the fifty large pages that remain are remarkably thorough in what they communicate about the ballets: music; choreography for soloists, small ensembles, and larger groups; pantomimic gestures; the use of props such as sticks or tambourines; the timing of entrances and exits; other elements of staging, such as where the dancers go when they are not dancing; the timing for raising the curtain, and so forth. The music alone is more complete than in other dance sources, usually being notated in score, ranging from a simple treble-bass texture to four- and five-part scorings that include strings and winds. The dancers' movements are communicated in a variety of ways: Feuillet notation alone; Feuillet notation interspersed with verbal instructions; drawings supplemented by verbal explanations; and a pared-down version of Feuillet notation for the group dances. (See figs. 8.3, 8.5, and 9.1–2.) These notations, too, thus offer a richness unseen in any other choreographic source, even if some ambiguities remain. It appears that the manuscript was actually used for performances; the worn corners, occasional stains, and the addition of numbers indicating a revised order of dances all suggest that the manuscript was more than a choreographic commonplace book. The entire contents — music, text, and choreographic notation — appear to be in one hand, presumably that of Auguste Ferrère himself.

The manuscript contains eight separate works, ranging in length and complexity from a single *entrée* to pantomime ballets that contain a number of individual dances; they are listed in table 7.1. Four of them (nos. I, II, IV, and V) are complete works that could be performed in a variety of theatrical contexts; these Ferrère called "ballets." He called three others (nos. III, VI, and VIII) "agréments," by which he meant that they were for use within specific plays. The remaining work (no. VII) is a

Table 7.1: *Outline of the Ferrère manuscript*

| Pages | No. and Title | Subtitle | Performers | Comments |
|---|---|---|---|---|
| 1–10 | I. *Le Peintre amoureux de son modèle* | Ballet pantomime avec sa musique | 4 soloists: painter, wife, *model, *servant; 12 *figurants* (6 couples) | Musically unrelated to Duni's *opéra-comique* of the same title. Final dance comes from Rameau, *Les Fêtes d'Hébé* (1739). |
| 11–17 | II. *Les Galants villageois* | Ballet demi-caractère | 2 soloists: shepherd, wife; 8 *figurants* (4 couples) | |
| 17–24 | III. *Les Trois Cousines* | Agrément de danse; opéra en trois actes tel qu'il a été donné à Valenciennes en 1782 | at least 3 soloists who take various roles; 8 *figurants* (augmented by by 6 singers) | Play by Dancourt (1700); some music by Gillier (1700); 3 *intermèdes.* |
| 25–36 | IV. *La Réjouissance villageoise; ou, le sabotier* | Ballet pantomime de composition du Sr Ferrère père; dansé par lui, et ensuite par son fils | 6 soloists: 2 Savoyards (M/F), 2 soldiers, a village woman, *sabotier*; 8 *figurants* (4 couples); *6 peasant men, *servant, *cook | |
| 36–42 | V. *Les Bûcherons et les sabotiers* | Dansé à la Comédie Italienne à Paris en 1751 par Maranesi [Ballet pantomime] | 3 soloists: *sabotière*, 2 woodcutters; 12 *figurants* (6 couples) | Musically unrelated to Philidor's *opéra-comique Le Bûcheron* (1763). |
| 42–46 | VI. *L'Embarras des richesses* | Agrément | 2 male soloists: Plutus, *paysan galant*; 12 *figurants* (6 couples) | Play by d'Allainval (1725); one piece ("tambourin sérieux") from Rameau's *Castor et Pollux* (1737); 2 *intermèdes.* |
| 46–8 | VII. *Entrée d'un esclave turc* | Dans Crispin brulle | 1 soloist: Turkish slave | |
| 48–[52] | VIII. *Myrtil et Lycoris* | Agrément de danse | 2 unidentified soloists (M/F); 6 *figurants* (3 couples) | Some musical concordances with Desormery's pastorale *Myrtil et Lycoris* (1777). |

*Note:*
*non-dancing role

single dance for a Turkish slave, the only item in the manuscript to involve only one dancer and only one piece of music. The manuscript does not contain written-out scenarios per se; the synopses given below have been extrapolated from the notations and the verbal explanations that accompany them. They follow Ferrère's practice of indicating what characters "say," even though the conversations are carried on entirely through gestures.

## I. *Le Peintre amoureux de son modèle* (The Painter in Love with His Model)

Of the eight works in the manuscript, this one has the most narrative content; Ferrère called it a "ballet pantomime." (The ballet has no connection to Duni's *opéra-comique* by the same title.)

The curtain rises at the end of the overture to reveal the painter's studio. Six couples, presumably friends of the painter's, arrive and perform a group dance, following which they exit to the sides. The painter and his wife enter and dance together, at first performing steps in mirror-image symmetry, and then mixing dance steps with pantomime. The wife indicates she must leave, the two say farewell, and the wife exits.

At this point there is an extended scene set entirely in pantomime; neither the servant nor the model dances, nor does the painter when he interacts with them. The painter signals to his servant to bring in his easel and paints. The model arrives; the painter kisses her hand and tells her he is going to paint her. As the painter sketches his apparently nude model, the wife appears and stares unbelievingly at what she sees. The model beats a hasty retreat, at which point the painter notices his wife's presence. He covers the painting of the model with a landscape, and invites his wife to look at it; she seems satisfied, and they dance a tender minuet. Growing suspicious, the wife abandons her husband during the last sixteen bars of this duet and goes to the easel, where she discovers the portrait hidden behind the landscape. Furious, she smashes the portrait over her husband's head; confused, he spins into the wings while his wife expresses her desire for vengeance. The painter returns meekly and begs his wife for forgiveness, which she finally grants. The two dance a formal *pas de deux*, following which four couples perform a short group choreography to celebrate the reconciliation. They remain on the sides of the stage to watch a second *pas de deux* by the reconciled couple, one which begins with lengthy solos for each partner before becoming a duet. The concluding *contredanse générale* involves six couples, as at the opening of the ballet; after the mid-point of the dance they are joined by the painter and his wife.

## II. *Les Galants villageois* (The Village Swains)

Ferrère characterized this work as a "ballet demi-caractère," a term which, in the context of the manuscript, seems intended to distinguish it from the ones that have entire scenes in pantomime and more of a story line. The designation may alternatively (or in addition) refer to the style of the dancing.

The curtain rises at the end of the overture to reveal a verdant countryside. Four village men enter from the wings and dance, joined after eight bars by four village women. They greet each other; each man gives his partner a bouquet, which she puts in her bodice. They continue dancing, ending along the sides of the stage. A shepherd enters and dances a solo; a shepherdess arrives, first dancing a solo of her own, to which he responds in kind, in a pattern of alternation that continues even as the danced phrases grow shorter. They end their dance upstage, from where they watch another group dance performed by the eight villagers, who in their own turn remain onstage for the second *pas de deux* by the shepherd and shepherdess. At the end of their duet the man exits; the woman dances alone, looking for her partner. The shepherd returns without letting the shepherdess see him, his finger to his nose. At first she is sad, but after she spots her partner they dance happily together, exiting upstage left. The eight villagers then dance a *contredanse générale*, after ninety-six bars of which they are joined by the two soloists, who perform first with each other and then with the villagers. All exit to the sides.

## III. *Les Trois Cousines* (The Three Cousins)

The title is actually that of a comedy by Florent Dancourt, written for the Comédie Française in 1700 and frequently revived;[41] the Ferrère manuscript records choreography for the *divertissements* performed at the end of

---

41. It was performed in Vienna during the 1750s, for example, as well as in various theaters throughout France.

each act, some portions of which use the music composed by Gillier for the premiere.

The play is set in the village of Créteil and concerns the romantic intrigues of a miller's widow, her two daughters, her niece, and their suitors. The *divertissements* do not have plots within themselves, but grow out of the situations at the end of their respective acts. At the end of act 1, one of the suitors arrives with several millers and peasants in order to entertain the widow. Following act 2 several gypsies are brought in to tell fortunes; they predict that everyone will get married and their dancing features a man doing fancy tricks with a tambourine. At the end of the play, after a supposed pilgrimage has served as a ruse to allow all the couples— young and old—to unite, the *divertissement* prolongs the idea by revealing that the true pilgrimage is a metaphoric one to the Temple of Love. All three of the *divertissements* mix songs and dances, and each ends with a *contredanse générale*.

## IV. *La Réjouissance villageoise, ou Le Sabotier* (The Village Celebration, or The Clogger)

The manuscript calls this a "pantomime ballet by Ferrère Senior, danced by him and later by his son." It is the longest work in the manuscript.

After a comic introductory scene entirely in pantomime in which six village men enjoy a meal at the local inn (even after the waiter drops the roast), eight more villagers arrive dancing. A Savoyard couple appears next; she carries a hurdy-gurdy, he a triangle, which they play intermittently as they dance. The villagers ask if the couple will play for their own dancing and the Savoyards oblige. Two soldiers then enter, each carrying a bottle of wine; they take glasses out of the front corners of their hats and have a drink. They then make the mistake of putting down their bottles and glasses as they continue to dance, whereupon a village woman steals them. After the soldiers hunt in vain, the woman returns with the bottles, but tries to keep the soldiers from getting at them. Finally, she promises to return them if the two men will dance with her; the soldiers comply, and following their *pas de trois* six of the eight villagers also dance. A man in wooden shoes enters, carrying a basket on the end of a stick. He distributes his wares—a rabbit and fruit—to the villagers, after which they prevail upon him to dance for them. Still in his wooden shoes, he performs a fancy solo that includes tricks with his stick. The ballet concludes with a *contredanse générale* for the eight villagers, who are joined by five of the soloists toward its end.[42]

## V. *Les Bûcherons et les sabotiers* (The Woodcutters and the Cloggers)

This is the work that, according to Ferrère, was performed by Cosimo Maranesi at the Comédie Italienne in Paris in 1751. If so, then he and his partner, Bettina Buggiani, would have been the ones who performed the wooden shoe duet.

The curtain rises to reveal a mountain scene, in front of which six woodcutters are chopping wood and tossing the pieces to be stacked. A woman arrives on the mountain, sees the men working, and calls to five other women, who enter carrying baskets covered by napkins. They descend from the mountain, and tell the men that they are bringing food. The men suggest a dance, so the women put down their baskets. After they dance and leave, a woman in wooden shoes enters, collecting wood chips and putting them in her basket. In a *pas de trois* that mixes dance steps with pantomime, two men greet her and suggest that she dance. At first she refuses, pointing to her wooden shoes, but after some cajoling accepts the challenge. Her virtuosic solo notwithstanding, one of the men makes fun of her, claiming he can do better. In a competitive choreography during which both of them now wear wooden shoes, the man and the women dance together and separately, even resorting to pushing each other. After peace is restored, the woodcutters and their wives return to perform a *contredanse générale,* in which the two cloggers join.

## VI. *L'Embarras des richesses* (The Embarrassment of Riches)

The title refers to a play by Léonor-Jean-Christine Soulas d'Allainval, first performed at the Théâtre Italien in 1725.[43] Ferrère calls this work an

---

42. Since only five soloists participate in the *contredanse générale* it is possible that two of the male roles — the Savoyard and the *sabotier,* for example — were danced by the same person.

43. The music for the original production was composed by Mouret; see Viollier, *Mouret,* 127–28.

*agrément;* the manuscript includes two *intermèdes* for performance follow-ing the acts of the play, the second one labeled "Acte 3ième." The first *intermède* contains a song and two male solo dances; the second has a long and virtuosic solo dance for a *paysan galant* (a genteel peasant) set to a tambourin by Rameau, plus a *contredanse générale* for twelve dancers.

## VII. *Entrée d'[un] esclave turc* (Entrée for a Turkish Slave)

Ferrère's subtitle for this single-character dance, "dans Crispin brulle," indicates that it was performed in one of the many plays about the ser-vant Crispin, a stock character in French comedy (e.g., Hauteroche, *Crispin médecin* [1673], and Marivaux, *Le Père prudant et équitable, ou Crispin l'heureux fourbe* [1706], *inter alia*). The likeliest source is La Font's one-act play *Le Naufrage, ou La Pompe funèbre de Crispin*, which premiered at the Comédie Française in 1710. Here Crispin finds himself about to be burned at the stake, as part of an elaborate hoax designed to scare him. There is a sung and danced ceremony in preparation for the burning, to which a dance such as this could easily belong. As does the slave in the dance, Crispin ultimately regains his freedom.

The slave enters with chains on his hands and feet. During the first part of the dance he explores the limits of his movements while chained; the difficult choreography is made even more so by the chains. The movement quality changes after the chains are removed and the dancer revels in his freedom, holding out his arms, leaping to second position, and performing *entrechats*. This specialty dance, of a type very popular across Europe, is unique among surviving dance notations.

## VIII. *Myrtil et Lycoris*

*Myrtil et Lycoris* was a very successful one-act pastorale by Leopold-Bastien Desormery performed at the Paris Opéra in 1777. Ferrère de-scribed his choreographies, set to Desormery's music, as "agréments de danses"; they were presumably inserted into the stage work at a perfor-mance in Valenciennes. Unfortunately, one or more folios of the manu-script are missing at this point; all that remain are the last thirty-seven bars of a male solo, a short group dance for four men and two women, and a duet for two unidentified characters. Ferrère did not notate the *contredanse générale,* indicating instead that the final ballet uses approximately the same figures as the preceding group dance ("le ballet sur cette finale fait à peu près la même figures et s'en vont avec les premiers danseurs" [*sic*]).

Synopses cannot do justice to these light-hearted works, whose pleasures derive from the seeing, and where telling a compelling story is decidedly *not* the point. Rather, the scenario supplies a frame on which to hang gracious or virtuosic dances, as well as amusing scenes of pantomime. In this regard, the Ferrère works clearly resemble ballets performed elsewhere in Europe. Take, for instance, one of the ballets in which Magri probably danced in Vienna in 1759, *Les Savoyards:*

> This ballet represents the return of the Savoyards to their homeland. The stage shows the mountain Mont-Cenis in Savoy, where the women are occupied with the preparations for a feast for the return of their husbands: their arrival occasions a large entertainment, which is accompanied by song and dance. After that the whole company gets ready to eat a meal in the manner of that country, but it is interrupted by a Savoyard who, in order to mock them, makes them think that the village is burning, whereupon there follows a *pas de deux,* and a *pas de trois,* which perfectly show the manner and the vivacity of these people, and since everyone participates in the joy that reigns among them, this ballet will be most entertaining to the eyes of the spectators [see app. 3].

Savoyards were stock characters; Dehesse at the Théâtre Italien in Paris composed a ballet by the same title, and in Naples Magri produced a ballet very similar to the one described here (see app. 4). But thanks to Ferrère, we can fill out this skimpy scenario—all that remains of this ballet—by envisaging what might lie behind some of its key words. It seems reasonable to imagine that this ballet initiated with a scene predominantly in pantomime that imitated day-to-day actions, and perhaps also included a group dance for the women; the arrival of the husbands could well give rise to a sequence of dances for all the couples. The eating of the meal might prompt pantomimes on the order of the horseplay near the start of Ferrère's *Réjouissance villageoise,* or the jokes with the wine bottles from later in the same work. The interruption by the mocking Savoyard probably gave him a chance for a solo dance, in addition to mimed action, and the duet and trio that followed probably featured the best dancers in the company, showing off movements that were deemed on

the stages of Europe to be typical of Savoyards. The work then undoubtedly drew to a close with a *contredanse générale*.[44]

Another ballet, *Mercato del pesce in Amsterdam* (The Fish Market in Amsterdam), this one of Magri's own making in Naples and still skimpier in
its description, also becomes easier to envisage when seen through the
lens of Ferrère.

> In the fish market of Amsterdam, situated on the banks of the Rhine,
> some Scotsmen disembark, who, along with other people who have con-
> gregated in that place, will form a lively concerted number, which will
> be followed by various dances, which will finally be terminated by a gra-
> cious finale [see app. 4].

This ballet, performed between acts 1 and 2 of Piccinni's opera *Il re
pastore* in 1765, apparently had no plot at all. Instead, it sounds as if there
were three groups set up for different kinds of character dances: fishermen and their wives, Scottish sailors, and Dutch locals. There was probably pantomime as the fishermen unloaded and sold their wares, some
kind of Scottish character dance, a big group dance in the middle (the
concerted number), followed by solo dances, *pas de deux* and/or *pas de trois*
for the various characters—possibly including wooden shoe dances,
given the Dutch location—and, as usual, a *contredanse générale* to end (the
gracious finale).

In scenario after scenario, from around Europe, certain conventional types and activities recur with regularity: artisans engaged in
humble outdoor occupations; women bringing food in baskets; national
dances; character dances for types such as drunks or commedia masks;
specialty dances using props such as chains, sticks, or wooden shoes, and
so forth. It happens that French pantomime ballet scenarios tend to be
lengthier and more detailed than the surviving ones for similar comic
works from elsewhere; see, by way of comparison with the examples
from Vienna and Naples in appendices 3 and 4, three ballets from different Parisian theaters in appendix 5, by the choreographers Dehesse,
Noverre, and Dourdé. Their fuller descriptions can be used, cautiously,
to flesh out the bare-bones descriptions choreographers such as Magri
left behind, just as the Ferrère manuscript can be studied for possible

---

44. It is useful in this context to remember that part 2 of Magri's *Trattato* ends with choreographies for thirty-nine *contraddanze*—the last for thirty-two dancers—although these were all composed for balls at the court of Naples.

ways of getting from Magri's step descriptions to the choreography of an entire ballet.

The Ferrère manuscript does not cover the full range of dancing seen in this kind of ballet scenario: mostly notably, it lacks any commedia dances, even though there were many such characters on the French stage, and the dancing roles are mostly village types, a propensity noticeable in French ballets in general. Magri's ballets, with their pirates, gypsies, and Turkish pashas, had a wider range of characters. Moreover, the dancing style was not identical; the fact that Italian dancers repeatedly created sensations on Parisian stages shows that they had something different to offer French audiences. Nonetheless, Ferrère preserves enormous amounts of precious information about practices that were common currency around Europe: steps identifiable in Magri's *Trattato* but not found in earlier notations; notations of extensive *pas de deux* and *pas de trois;* long and intricate group dances; gestures that express actions and emotions; concrete instances of how pantomime and dance were integrated; and examples of how all these various movements fit with the music. Whereas it would be an error to construct a vision of Italian grotesque dancing solely on the basis of the Ferrère manuscript, it would be just as serious an error to ignore what can be learned from it.

# 8

# Steps, Gestures, and Expressive Dancing

*Magri, Ferrère, and John Weaver*

MOIRA GOFF

Gennaro Magri's career coincided with significant developments in dancing as a theater art, and his dance works are potentially valuable sources of information about theatrical dancing in the late eighteenth century. However, Magri wrote his *Trattato teorico-prattico di ballo* as a teacher and a dancer rather than as a choreographer, concentrating on the vocabulary of steps used in the theater and saying little about dances and ballets, so we must look elsewhere for information which will help us to get an idea of the actual dancing in his works. Bruce Alan Brown, in his essay about Magri in Vienna (chap. 3), discusses what the dancer could have learned in a city where Hilverding and Angiolini were leading choreographers. Ingrid Brainard, in an essay about Angiolini and expressive dancing published in 1996, referred to Magri within a wider context of theory and practice which included Hilverding, Dehesse, and John Weaver, as well as de Pure, Ménestrier, Dubos, and Cahusac, all of whom contributed to the development of expressive dancing.[1] Magri's

---

1. Ingrid Brainard, "The Speaking Body: Gaspero Angiolini's *Rhétorique Muette* and the *Ballet d'Action* in the Eighteenth Century," in *Critica Musica: Essays in Honor of Paul Brainard*, ed. John Knowles (Amsterdam: Gordon and Breach, 1996), 15–55. Brainard also referred to the relationship

participation in these developments is shown in his own dance works, as well as in the references to gestures and expressive steps which are scattered throughout his treatise.

The ballets in which Magri performed in Vienna brought together dance and gesture, following practices established by Hilverding. Although Hilverding never set down his precepts, his follower Angiolini wrote about expressive dancing in relation to his own ballets *Le Festin de pierre* and *Sémiramis,* produced in Vienna in 1761 and 1765, respectively.[2] Angiolini looked to classical antiquity for inspiration as he strove to create "la danse pantomime," much as John Weaver had done nearly fifty years before for his "Scenical Dancing"; both were following the path taken by dance theorists from the seventeenth century onward.[3] Angiolini referred to "speaking gestures" and "expressive signs" as "a type of declamation made to be seen," but he did not describe them.[4] It is necessary to go back as far as the scenario for John Weaver's *Loves of Mars and Venus,* published in 1717, to find the only detailed explanation of such gestures and their use by dancers.[5]

Weaver's gestures turn up in what might seem an unlikely source — the manuscript compiled in 1782 by the French dancer and choreographer August Ferrère, in which he recorded several pantomime ballets and balletic interludes (see chap. 7). It not only records in their entirety short comic ballets which are similar to those created by Magri but also shows the complete structure of individual dances and, even more important, the integration of dance steps and gestures within those dances. Unlike Weaver, who described gestures but said nothing about the accompanying steps, and the many dances surviving in Feuillet notation, which give steps but rarely the accompanying arm movements, Ferrère recorded both.

---

between rhetoric and acting, drawing on the work of Dene Barnett and his *Art of Gesture: The Practices and Principles of 18th-century Acting* (Heidelberg: C. Winter Universitätsverlag, 1987).

2. Gasparo Angiolini, with Ranieri Calzabigi, preface to *Le Festin de pierre,* and *Dissertation sur les ballets pantomimes des anciens, pour servir de programme au ballet pantomime tragique de Sémiramis,* reprinted in Calzabigi, *Scritti teatrali e letterari,* ed. Anna Laura Bellina, 2 vols. (Rome: Salerno Editrice, 1994), 1:147–76. The *Don Juan* preface is given in facsimile, and the scenario of *Sémiramis* is quoted in both French and German, in Richard Engländer, ed., Christoph Willibald Gluck, *Sämtliche Werke,* ser. 2, vol. 1 (Kassel: Bärenreiter, 1966); there are also facsimiles of both scenarios, and of Angiolini and Calzabigi's *Dissertation sur les ballets pantomimes* (Vienna, 1765), in *Sämtliche Werke,* ser. 7, supp., vol. 1 (Kassel: Bärenreiter, 1995).

3. John Weaver, *An Essay towards an History of Dancing* (London: J. Tonson, 1712), 168–69.

4. Angiolini, *Festin de pierre,* "gestes parlans," "signes expressifs," "une espèce de déclamation faite pour les yeux," in Calzabigi, *Scritti teatrali,* 1:148.

5. John Weaver, *The Loves of Mars and Venus* (London: W. Mears, J. Browne, 1717), 21–23, 28.

This essay looks at Magri's treatise, Ferrère's manuscript, and Weaver's works for evidence about expressive dancing, particularly the integration of gestures with the step vocabulary available to theatrical dancers. It draws on my experiences of reconstructing and performing dances from Ferrère's manuscript;[6] these show how dance steps and gestures could be interwoven in different ways and for different purposes, rather than being separated as if they were unrelated modes of expression. All are representative of dances from works belonging to the comic genre of pantomime dance which was popular in theaters throughout Europe during the eighteenth century, and thus provide valuable insights into the choreographic style of Ferrère's near contemporary Gennaro Magri.

# Magri

Gennaro Magri worked within concepts and practices shared with both his contemporaries and his predecessors. In the final chapter of part 1 of his *Trattato*, he declared that "no properly equipped theater should lack the *Ballante serio* or that of *mezzo Carattere* or the *Grottesco* for the Heroic, the Comic and the Burlesque characters which ordinarily enter into the dances."[7] He did not describe the three types of dancer, although throughout the treatise he made references to them, but his categorization can be compared with definitions by other writers on dancing. It was much simpler than that of Angiolini, who had distinguished between *danses grotesques*, with dancers who specialized in acrobatic stunts; the *genre comique*, with dancers who used a virtuoso technique but avoided the *tours de force* of the grotesque dancers; *danses de demi-caractère*, with dancers whose technique was close to that of *belle danse* (which Angiolini usually called "haute danse") and who might use gestures to express the lighter affections; and *danse pantomime*, which he regarded as "the most sublime"

---

6. The duet from *Le Peintre amoureux de son modèle* was reconstructed and performed with Jennifer Thorp to illustrate a paper given by Carol Marsh at the twenty-fifth anniversary meeting of the American Society for Eighteenth Century Studies, Charleston, SC, 11 March 1994. The trio from *Les Bûcherons et les sabotiers* was reconstructed and performed, with Jennifer Thorp and Madeleine Inglehearn, to illustrate Carol Marsh's paper at "La memòria de la dansa," the fifth international conference of the European Association of Dance Historians, Barcelona, 28 October 1994.

7. Magri/Skeaping, 167; Magri, *Trattato*, 1:138: "in ogni fornito Teatro non deve mancarvi nè il Ballante serio, nè quel di mezzo Carattere, nè il Grottesco, per l'Eroico, il Comico, ed il Bernesco carattere, che per ordinario entrano ne' balli."

and whose dancers were able to express through *belle danse* and gestures "all the passions and all the agitations of the soul" belonging to tragedy.[8] The *serio* and *grottesco* dancers referred to by Magri were much closer to Weaver's division of *"Stage-Dancing . . .* into three Parts, *viz. Serious, Grotesque,* and *Scenical.*"[9] All three dancing-masters distinguished between the step vocabulary and technique as well as the characters appropriate to each genre, but Angiolini claimed *danse pantomime* based on serious dancing as the most expressive (defining grotesque dancing as mere acrobatics), whereas Magri and Weaver saw grotesque dancing as particularly expressive (associating it with Angiolini's *genre comique* and *danses de demi-caractère*).[10]

Magri said relatively little about the *mezzo carattere*, concerning himself chiefly with the *ballerino serio* and the *ballerino grottesco*. He described the *ballerino serio* as "accustomed to gentle and [tender] *attitudes,* versed in the pathos of his languid impassioned gestures," as unable to portray such violent characters as Furies, and as a dancer for whom such steps as the *pas grave* (*passo grave*) "done with grandeur," the *ballonné* (*balonnè*) danced "with the utmost gravity," and forced indeterminate pirouettes (*pirole forzate incerte*) with an added *tordichamp* (*tordichamb* — i.e., *tour de jambe*) or beats (*battimenti*) performed "in a sustained manner" were most suitable.[11] His remarks have similarities to Weaver's 1712 description of serious dancing, to which he assigned *"Capers,* and *Cross-Capers* of all kinds: *Pirouttes, Batteries,* and indeed almost all Steps from the Ground," adding that "the most *Artful* Qualification is a *nice Address* in the Management of those *Motions.*" Weaver further divided serious dancing into "the *Brisk,* and the *Grave"*;[12] Magri's emphasis in the *Trattato* is on the latter, with its slow and flowing steps performed with grace and amplitude.

Magri's emphasis on grotesque dancing is particularly welcome, since other writers (including Weaver) said little about it and grotesque dances were rarely if ever notated.[13] He provided much valuable infor-

8. Angiolini, *Sémiramis,* in Calzabigi, *Scritti teatrali,* 1:170–74; 173, "la plus sublime," "toutes les passions et tous les mouvemens de l'âme." See also Brainard, "The Speaking Body," 21, 39–40.

9. Weaver, *Essay,* 158–59.

10. Weaver later revised his views in favor of serious dancing; see *The History of the Mimes and Pantomimes* (London: J. Roberts and A. Dod, 1728), 55–56.

11. Magri/Skeaping, 150, 92, 114, 127; Magri, *Trattato,* 1:112: "alle sue dolci, e molli Attitudini costumato, versato nel patetico del suo languido appassionato gestire" (translation amended); 1:55:"maestosa"; 1:77: "ne' maggior gravi"; 1:89: "farla sostenuta."

12. Weaver, *Essay,* 162–63.

13. A handful of notated dances could claim to belong to the grotesque genre: the 1688 mascarade *Le Mariage de la grosse Cathos* includes an "Air des Ivrognes," which is a duet for two drunken

mation about the step vocabulary available to the *ballerino grottesco*, for whom a well-established technical armory included the five false positions (*positure false*), steps which turn in and out (*tortigliè*), a great variety of forced indeterminate pirouettes, exaggerated arms (*braccia forzate* or *grands bras*), and a wide range of virtuosic caprioles. Magri also made claims for the *ballerino grottesco* as an expressive dancer, asking pointedly, "Should the *Grottesco* be less skilled in the art of expressing through gestures the Pantomime and comic Action than the *Serio* to express the same in Tragedy?"—a remark that reflects an impatience with the traditional hegemony of tragedy rather than a criticism of *serio* dancers.[14] His claim that "pastoral dancing, like that of the Artisans, has always been the *Grottesco*'s speciality" is perhaps less surprising given Weaver's much earlier statement that "*Grotesque Dancing* is wholly calculated for the Stage, and takes in the greatest Part of *Opera-Dancing*."[15] Indeed, Magri explained that the three types of dancer also shared certain steps, for example, the *tordichamp*, the *pistoletta*, the *ballonné*, and even a *gargugliè* listed among the *capriole* in his final chapter, although he also made clear that some of these steps would be performed in different ways according to who was dancing.

Most of the sixty chapters in part 1 of the *Trattato* were devoted to descriptions of individual steps, many of which are recognizable from the much earlier treatises of Feuillet and Rameau.[16] Magri included all the basic steps from the early eighteenth century, for example, *demi-coupé* (*passo mezzo tronco*), *coupé* (*passo tronco*), *pas de bourrée*, *temps de courante* (*passo*

---

men; see Rebecca Harris-Warrick and Carol G. Marsh, *Musical Theatre at the Court of Louis XIV* (Cambridge: Cambridge University Press, 1994), 149–53, 269–73; there are also three notated chaconnes for a Harlequin, the latest of which has been assigned a publication date of 1729, and one "Turkish" dance published in 1725; see LMC 1880, 1980, 2760, and 8220; Francine Lancelot, *La Belle Dance: Catalogue raisonné* (Paris: Van Dieren, 1996), FL/Ms05.1/07, FL/1728.3s, FL/Ma17.1/2, FL/1725.1/13.

14. Magri/Skeaping, 153; Magri, *Trattato*, 1:116–17: "E che forse l'arte di esprimere per mezzo de' gesti la Pantomima, l'Azione comica la deve avere il Grottesco meno di quella del Serio, per esprimer questi la sua Tragica?" For Magri's championship of comedy against tragedy, see Magri/Skeaping, 154; Magri, *Trattato*, 1:117–18.

15. Magri/Skeaping, 153, Magri, *Trattato*, 1:117: "Il ballar Pastorale, come quello dell'Artigiano è stato sempre specifico del Grottesco." Magri presumably did not mean the heroic pastoral of the Paris Opéra, but his earlier references to Mirtillo and shepherds, and his juxtaposition of pastoral dancing with that of artisans, indicate that he did not see the *grottesco* as limited to dancing peasants. Weaver, *Essay*, 164.

16. Raoul-Auger Feuillet, *Chorégraphie ou l'art de décrire la dance*, 2nd ed. (Paris: l'Auteur, Michel Brunet, 1701); Pierre Rameau, *Le Maître à danser* (Paris: Jean Villette, 1725). For a complete list of the steps in Magri's *Trattato* see appendix 7.

*grave), jeté (passo gettato), pas de sissonne ( passo di sissone)*, and *contretemps (contratempo)*. Some, for example, the *pas de bourrée* (equivalent to Rameau's
*fleuret)*, had hardly changed at all, while others, such as the *temps de courante*
which had acquired a second step (but not a second transfer of weight),
had changed a little. Steps familiar from the notated dances (but ex-
cluded from Rameau because they were not used in the ballroom) were
described and even specifically named, like the *brisé* which was Feuillet's
*jeté battu* with an added step.[17] Other steps, like pirouettes, had developed
many new versions alongside the already extensive range to be found in
Feuillet's treatise and the notated dances. The *Trattato* demonstrates
much continuity of vocabulary and technique from the early eighteenth
century, but Magri also indicated important changes, particularly in the
height of leg extensions and the force and height of jumped steps, which
were steadily moving theatrical dancing toward the ballet technique of
the nineteenth century. In chapter 5 Sandra Hammond explores some
of these changes.

Magri associated certain steps with particular characters, providing
glimpses of the meaning and expressive content attached to a vocabulary
too often seen as wholly abstract by modern writers on dance. He several
times referred to the Furies, for whom the *soubresaut* (a step "done in
contratempo"), exaggerated arms, and a forced *attitude (attitudine sforzata)*
which ignored the opposition of arm and leg and lifted the arm "high
beyond measure" were suitable to express their violent and vengeful
characters.[18] Magri's remark that Furies and Winds were similarly
danced puts into a different perspective Weaver's complaint that on the
London stage the same entry was used to represent Furies one week and
Winds the next.[19] The commedia dell'arte character Scaramuccia also
used a forced *attitude*, a pose which was illustrated in the early-eighteenth-
century engraving by Bonnart of "Monsieur Dubreil dansant le Scaramouche"[20] as well as in Lambranzi's *Neue und curieuse theatralische Tantz-
Schul* of 1716 (see fig. 8.1). The characters called *oltramontani* (foreigners) by
Magri shared the same forced *attitudes* and also made use of the *gorguglie*

---

17. Feuillet, *Chorégraphie*, 84. The *jeté battu* (usually notated with a *sauté* rather than a *cabriolé* sign)
with an extra step appears in many of the notated theatrical dances.

18. Magri/Skeaping, 145, 152, 149, in the translation of the passage describing the *attitude* (149)
the words "to the front" ("avanti") are omitted so that it is not evident that the pose is out of opposition; Magri, *Trattato*, 1:106: "fatto a Contratempo"; 1:114, 111: "alto fuor di misura."

19. Weaver, *Essay*, 167. Weaver's criticism was aimed at French dancers appearing in London.

20. Magri/Skeaping, 149; Magri, *Trattato*, 1:111. The engraving of Dubreil is reproduced in
Winter, *Pre-Romantic Ballet*, 27.

Figure 8.1: Scaramouche in his characteristic attitude. (Lambranzi, *Neue und curieuse theatralische Tantz-Schul* [1716], pt. 1, plate 24)

with a bound (*gorgugliè di sbalzo*) "which, with awkward and clumsy dress, made a good impression" when Magri performed it.[21]

If steps could be expressive through their association with particular characters, Magri made clear that they could also be expressive in themselves, because their particular qualities made them appropriate to a specific dramatic context. He established the general principle in his description of a scene with Boreas and Flora which should have "a multitude of varied steps and actions expressing the character" as Boreas chases Flora and she flees from him.[22] Magri went so far as to describe how individual steps could be expressive. He referred to the *pas marché* (*passo marciato*) as "useful in the Theatre, either to walk across the stage with majesty, or for acts of surprise and admiration, or to impose some order"; in the last case the step was to be accompanied by a suitable gesture.[23] The *attitude* was "a union of several poses, being an accompaniment of the arms, the legs, the head, the eyes, which must express in which emotional state the person is found"; Magri's view was very similar to that of Weaver, who in 1721 had written of the dancing-master, "Let his *Attitudes* be suitable to his Subject, so as to express the Thoughts and Conceptions of the Mind, by the Motions of the Hands, Eyes, and whole Body."[24]

Magri described the performance of the *bourrée tombé* (a *pas de bourrée* which began with a *demi-tombé* instead of a *demi-coupé*) in such detail that it seems possible that he himself might have used it for expressive purposes: "This step is used in the Theatre in precise gestures, in emphatic actions: as of a personage afflicted by extreme pain, or mortally wounded, gradually falling with the movement of the *demi-tombé*, and to raise himself, driven to the end of natural forces, he uses the two simple movements, with accompanying expressiveness of the arms. It can also

---

21. Magri/Skeaping, 159; Magri, *Trattato*, 1:124: "che con abito caricato, e goffo faceva un bel vedere." The term "oltramontani" means literally "foreign" or "from beyond the Alps"; it thus refers to non-Italian "northerners" who, as Magri's description indicates, might be characterized as unsophisticated or boorish.

22. Magri/Skeaping, 61; Magri, *Trattato*, 1:24–5: "una variata moltitudine di passi, ed azioni esprimenti il carattere." The whole passage is given in Bruce Brown's essay, chapter 3.

23. Magri/Skeaping, 71; Magri, *Trattato*, 1:36: "Serve egli per Teatro: o per passeggiarlo con maestà, o per atti sorprendenti, ed ammirativi, o per imporre qualche ordine."

24. Magri/Skeaping, 148; Magri, *Trattato*, 1:109: "una unione di più atteggi, dovendo essere un accompagnamento di braccia, di piedi, di testa, di occhi; che deve esprimere in qual stato di passione si trova la persona." John Weaver, *Anatomical and Mechanical Lectures upon Dancing* (London: J. Brotherton, 1721), 146.

serve for one in a fury, wanting to wound another but, prevented by inner remorse, or restrained by circumstances, he stops with the arm raised, in the act of striking the body."[25] Although Magri referred to accompanying gestures, it was plainly the step itself which he regarded as expressive. He implied that the *demi-tombé* was performed differently in each case, and that the timing of the step could be changed (in the second example perhaps by the addition of a pause before the two final steps). Such variations in dynamic and timing appear in earlier notated dances, and Magri's description suggests that these were not merely notational variants but indicated deliberate changes for expressive purposes. Magri's account of the *bourrée tombé* shows clearly how such small changes could affect the meaning and expression of a step.

Magri did not discuss choreographic structure directly, but he did hint at some of the conventions used by late-eighteenth-century dancing-masters. He occasionally mentioned steps which were used with a specific relationship to the musical structure, for example, "The *fouetté* is a very brilliant step which, like the *ballotté*, serves to end a cadence."[26] He was particularly concerned with the use of repetition, and he several times referred to steps being repeated according to the wish of the performer. The beaten *jeté* ( *jetè battuto*) can be repeated "as many times as is wished," with the *pas de sissonne* ( *passo di sissone*) "two or three of them are repeated with one foot, and then changing it another two or three more are done with the other," and the *brisé* "you can repeat with the same foot doing as many as you wish."[27] Since these were all small jumping steps, the dancer presumably wished to show audiences his or her strength and stamina through the number of repetitions that could be performed with ease. Referring to the repetition of steps with musical repeats, Magri said that "if in a *grave*, the pace of the Music is *sostenuto*, and if from time to time certain repeated bars of notes were to appear, the *Ballerino* would also

25. Magri/Skeaping, 102; Magri, *Trattato*, 1:67: "Questo passo si adopero in Teatro in atteggi precisi, in azioni segnate; come in un Personaggio assalito da un estremo dolore, o colpito da ferita mortale, va tratto tratto cadendo, co 'l movimento del mezzo Tombè, e per sollevarsi, spinto dagli ultimi sforzi naturali, si serve de' due semplici movimenti, accompagnando l'espressione con le braccia. Serve pure per uno furibondo, che voglia un'altro ferire, e vietato da rimorsi interni, o trattenuto da circonstanti, si arresta co 'l braccio sollevato, nell'atto di violare il corpo."

26. Magri/Skeaping, 124; Magri, *Trattato*, 1:86: "Il *Fuetè* è un passo assai brillante, che suol servire per fine di cadenza, come il *Balottè.*"

27. Magri/Skeaping, 81, 105, 138; Magri, *Trattato*, 1:47: "si possono pur raddoppiare per quanto se ne vorrà"; 1:70: "se ne raddoppiano due, o tre con un piè, e poi cambiandolo se ne fanno altri due, o più con l'altro"; 1:102: "Si replica con l'istesso piede facendosene quanti se ne vogliono."

repeat."[28] These remarks point to changes since the early eighteenth century in the conventions governing choreographic structure. The repetition of individual steps is not found in the notated dances of the early 1700s, where steps are rarely repeated more than twice (except in dances like the menuet or the passepied), and the repetition of sequences of steps with musical repeats is uncommon.[29] Magri's references to repetition may reflect a greater emphasis on technical display as a result of more recent developments in virtuoso technique. It is noteworthy that he does not refer to expressivity in this context; perhaps for him, as well as for Angiolini (and by implication Hilverding), virtuosity and expressivity were diametrically opposed.

Since in his *Trattato* Magri was not concerned with dances, he rarely described sequences of steps, usually limiting his remarks to the preparations necessary for virtuoso steps, and sequences that formed well-known compound steps. The capriole required preparatory steps to give them impetus, and he identified the *demi-échappé (mezzo sfuggito)*, *demi-sissonne (mezzo sissone)*, and *contretemps* with a flying bound *(contratempo di sbalze volato)* as suitable for this purpose.[30] Elsewhere Magri explained that *brisé, demi-sissonne* was a sequence used by *ballerini seri* before cutting "an attractive caprioletta," but the sequence *contretemps, bourrée disfatto,* and "some other unnamed steps" once used to travel across the stage had been discarded as taste had changed. Other sequences which Magri mentioned had no other function than to form compound steps, for example, the *pas trusé*.[31]

Such snippets of information are of limited help in understanding late-eighteenth-century choreographic structures, but Magri does provide a very interesting analysis of those for the chaconne, a dance in triple meter with music in a continuous variation form:

> It is not given to all the *Ballerini seri* to dance the *Chaconne* because they
> dance on their own and, for the most part, all the solos are danced im-

---

28. Magri/Skeaping, 61; Magri, *Trattato*, 1:24: "Se in un *grave* l'andamento della Musica sarà *sostenuto*, e di tanto in tanto uscisse con qualche battuta di note raddoppiate, il Ballerino raddoppj anche lui."

29. For the repetition of steps with musical repeats, see Ken Pierce, "Repeated Step-Sequences in Early Eighteenth Century Choreographies," in *Structures and Metaphors in Baroque Dance, Proceedings of the Conference at the University of Surrey Roehampton, March 21 2001*, comp. Kimiko Okamoto (London: University of Surrey Roehampton, 2001), 52–59.

30. Magri/Skeaping, 97, 106, 130, 157, 158; Magri, *Trattato*, 1:59, 1:71, 1:93, 1:121, 1:123.

31. Magri/Skeaping, 141; Magri, *Trattato*, 1:103.

promptu, and if the *ballerino* is not accustomed to dancing in a group, he cannot do this because of the groups of steps, now free, now linked, now held, now violent, now languid, which are in it.

The airs of these are to be compared to the furies, to the role of Boreas, to the *Grande Vitesse,* which is now violent, now interspersed with so many moderations, rendering this style the most difficult of all, and its execution becomes as difficult for the *Ballerino* as for the composers of the dance [i.e., choreographers], because of the great diversity of the varia-tions in the tunes; this [diversity] applies to the [*tutti* sections of the cha-conne] as well as to the [character].[32]

They [chaconnes] require a group of *figuranti,* for the equal balance of the figures is a very necessary thing, since it is from these that the [*tutti* sections] of the *Chaconne* will begin. After the said *figuranti* have danced twenty-four bars, more or less, the *Ballerino* comes out with a *Solo,* or with a *Duet,* and dances as many bars again, at most thirty-two. A *Ballerino* or *Ballerina* cannot dance any more than this and if some are to be found who dance any more, they are those who do not specialise in a similar kind of Dance; they keep doing the *aplomb,* the *attitudes,* things which use much music but no dance: in this form one might freely dance more than twenty-four or thirty-two bars, but if the *aplombs* were adapted to the amount of Music, it would be certain that one would not be able to dance more than the already stated bars.[33]

32. The sense of this passage is obscure, and is not much aided by Skeaping's overly literal translation. We have taken the meaning to be that the diversity ("gran moti di variazione") just men-tioned—the only masculine plural object to which "vanno . . . adattati" could plausibly refer—is found not just in the music but also in the character (affect) of the dance, and of the *tutti* or en-semble sections (from one to the next?).

33. Magri/Skeaping, 143; Magri, *Trattato,* 1:104–5: "Il Ballar delle Ciaccone non è da tutti i Bal-lerini serj; motivo del suo ballar di distacco, e per lo più si ballano all'impronto tutti gli *a soli,* e se il ballerino non è assuefatto al ballare aggruppato, non può far questo per i groppetti de' passi o sciol-ti, o ligati, o pausati, o furiosi, o languidi, che per mezzo si vanno.

"L'arie di queste si paragonano alle furie, ad un parte di Borea, alla *Grand Vitesse,* che or furiosa, or tramezzata con tante, e tante moderazioni [s]a render questo genere il più difficile all ballerino di esecuzione, quanto a compositori di ballo per li gran moti di variazione dell'arie; oltre al carat-tere vanno similmente adattati ne' corpi de' balli.

"Hanno esse bisogno di una truppa numerosa di figuranti, e l'uguaglianza delle figure è cosa molto necessaria; poichè da essi va cominciato il corpo del Ballo della Ciaccona. Dopo di aver bal-lato detti figuranti ventiquattro battute, o più, o meno, il Ballerino vien fuori con un *a Solo,* o con un *Duetto,* e si ballano altre tante battute, al più 32. che più di tanto non può ballare un Ballerino, una Ballerina, e se sen trovano chi ne balla di più, sono que', che non essendo sua spezione simil sorte di Danza, van facendo le *a-plomb,* le *attitudini,* cose, che occupano molta musica, e niente ballo: in tal guisa vi si puo con franchezza ballar più di ventiquattro o 32. battute; ma se le *a-plomb* fossero adat-tate alla quantità della Musica, certa cosa sarebbe, che riuscir non potrebbe ballar più delle già dette battute" (translation amended).

No choreographies for chaconnes requiring a large number of dancers were ever recorded, so there are no sources for direct comparison with Magri's description.[34] He dealt only with the opening sections of a dance which would have had 150 to 200 bars of music, or more, but he did indicate that the dancing alternated between groups of dancers (the *figuranti*) and soloists who performed solos or duets, and that the soloists participated in at least some of the ensemble dancing. Magri declared that, notwithstanding the use of a choreographer to arrange the dancing in a chaconne, the leading *ballerini* improvised their solos, hinting also that their improvisation made use of the choreography created for the *figuranti*. This suggests that there were choreographic conventions which dancers could draw on, and this is supported by Magri's rather dismissive reference to the *à plomb* and the *attitudes* as ways to fill out the music with very little dancing. The repetition of other kinds of steps, which Magri mentions elsewhere without disapproval, would also be helpful in such improvisation. The *figuranti*, whose dances were probably based as much on floor patterns as on steps, would have needed prior rehearsal, providing opportunities for the soloists to see their choreographic material before the performance.

Of greatest interest, however, is Magri's emphasis on the expressive aspects of the chaconne, which was not merely a display of steps and figures. Significantly, he referred to grotesque dancing to make his point, taking Furies and Winds as models appropriate for both soloists and *figuranti*. He also referred to the varied expressions, from violent to languid, which the music demanded from the dancers. The deployment of dancers in groups, solos, and duets enhanced the range of affects they could express and allowed marked contrasts between sections. The chaconne described by Magri contained no narrative, but it was intended to be expressive.

# John Weaver

The English choreographer John Weaver, who pursued a career in the London theaters between the 1690s and 1733, was much concerned with

---

34. Feuillet notation was not suited to recording choreographies with large numbers of dancers; there is only one notated theatrical dance for more than two dancers, Feuillet's "Balet de neuf danseurs" published in 1700; see LMC 1320; *Belle Dance*, FL/1700.1/15. The Favier notation for *Le Mariage de la grosse Cathos* includes several group dances; see Harris-Warrick and Marsh, *Musical Theatre*.

dancing as an independent, expressive theater art.[35] Weaver was a theorist as well as a practitioner, and his written works are important sources of information about the development of dancing on the London stage in the early eighteenth century. In his 1712 *Essay towards an History of Dancing*, he (like other theorists from de Pure to Angiolini) traced the history of dancing in classical antiquity and drew parallels between it and the dancing of his own day. Weaver's theoretical works ranged over many aspects of dancing, but this essay will focus on his ideas about the use of gesture as well as steps for expressive purposes. Of particular interest is Weaver's 1717 *Loves of Mars and Venus*, a "Dramatic Entertainment of Dancing" in which he tried to put into practice the theories he had advanced in his *Essay*. This work has been much discussed by dance historians, but has rarely been considered in the context of contemporary dance treatises and notated dances.[36] There have been few attempts to recreate it, not least because none of the music survives.[37]

In his *Essay*, Weaver devoted chapter 6 to the "*Mimes* and *Pantomimes*" who "tho' *Dancers*, had their *Names* from *acting*, that is from *Imitation*, *copying* all the *Force* of the *Passions* meerly by the *Motions* of the *Body*" and "perform'd all by *Gesture*, and the *Action* of Hands, Legs, and Feet."[38] In the seventh and last chapter of the *Essay*, entitled "*Of the Modern Dancing*," Weaver made a case for expressive dancing: "Stage-Dancing was at first design'd for *Imitation*; to explain Things conceiv'd in the Mind, by the *Gestures* and *Motions* of the Body, and plainly and intelligibly representing *Actions*, *Manners*, and *Passions*; so that the Spectator might perfectly understand the *Performer* by these his *Motions*, tho' he say not a Word."[39]

35. For information about Weaver's life and career see Richard Ralph, *The Life and Works of John Weaver* (London: Dance Books, 1985). Ralph includes facsimile reprints of all Weaver's published works.

36. Several of these accounts are referred to by Ralph, *John Weaver*, 49–50, and he adds his own, 53–64. For a discussion of *The Loves of Mars and Venus* in the context of dancing on the London stage, see Moira Goff, "Art and Nature Join'd: Hester Santlow and the Development of Dancing on the London Stage, 1700–1737" (doctoral thesis, University of Kent, Canterbury, 2000), 212–20.

37. Mary Skeaping recreated parts of the work for the company Ballet for All, and her version was broadcast by Thames Television in London in 1970. A copy of the program is available for viewing at the New York Public Library Dance Collection (*MGZHB 12–2165, reel 1). Skeaping created her version before the surviving early eighteenth-century theatrical dance notations became widely known and available. Without access to these sources, she was unable to draw on contemporary floor patterns, step vocabulary, and choreographic conventions for her work. Similarly, she could not have had access to the later work of Dene Barnett to help with her reconstructions of Weaver's gestures. Thus, her choreography for *The Loves of Mars and Venus* unavoidably reflects a limited knowledge of the style and technique of dance and gesture in Weaver's time.

38. Weaver, *Essay*, 120–21.

39. Weaver, *Essay*, 158–59, 160.

Weaver's use of the words "imitating," "representing," and "expressing" throughout this chapter, together with his identification of *"Actions, Manners,* and *Passions"* as key elements of expressive dancing, provide clues to the nature of pantomime in eighteenth-century ballets.

Weaver's description of grotesque dancing shows that he considered it to be, first and foremost, expressive: "A Master or Performer in *Grotesque Dancing* ought to be a Person bred up to the Profession, and thoroughly skill'd in his Business. . . . He must be perfectly acquainted with all Steps used in *Dancing,* and able to apply 'em properly to each *Character:* . . . The Master must take peculiar Care to contrive his Steps, and adapt his *Actions,* and *Humour,* to the *Characters* or *Sentiments* he would represent or express."[40] Writing of the grotesque dancer, Weaver added, "His Perfection is to become what he performs; to be capable of representing all manner of *Passions,* which *Passions* have all their peculiar *Gestures;* and that those *Gestures* be just, distinguishing and agreeable in all Parts, Body, Head, Arms and Legs."[41] From grotesque dancing, Weaver derived scenical dancing, which he described as "a faint Imitation of the *Roman Pantomimes,* and differs from the *Grotesque,* in that the last only represents *Persons, Passions,* and *Manners;* and the former explains whole *Stories* by *Action,"* thus adding a narrative to expressive dancing.[42]

Weaver's definition of grotesque dancing was much wider in scope than Magri's. It was perhaps too broad, for in *The History of the Mimes and Pantomimes* (his revision of the *Essay)* published in 1728, Weaver limited grotesque dancing to performances by commedia dell'arte characters, referring to the general use of the term for "all *comic* Dancing whatever."[43] He did not relinquish his earlier concept of expressive dancing; he simply relabeled it as serious dancing. Weaver may have been bowing to pressure from his fellow dancers and dancing-masters. He may have thought that the word "grotesque" had gained unwelcome associations with the huge success of pantomimes on the London stage in the 1720s. He may have revised his views following his productions of *The Loves of Mars and Venus* and *Orpheus and Eurydice,* and wished to identify expressive dancing with *belle danse* and with tragedy rather than comedy, thus enhancing its status. Although his successive descriptions and the reasons for his changes are difficult to interpret satisfactorily, Weaver

40. Weaver, *Essay,* 165.
41. Weaver, *Essay,* 166.
42. Weaver, *Essay,* 168.
43. Weaver, *Mimes,* 56.

does make plain that he saw expressive dancing as the integration of dance steps with gestures.

## The Loves of Mars and Venus

*The Loves of Mars and Venus* tells the story of the love affair between Mars and Venus, and the revenge exacted by Venus's husband, Vulcan, who catches them together and exposes them to the derision of their fellow deities. The work was first performed on 2 March 1717 (old style) at the Drury Lane Theatre, with Louis Dupré (who, although probably French, was not "le grand" Dupré) as Mars, Hester Santlow as Venus, and Weaver himself as Vulcan.[44] The scenario was published to coincide with the opening performance, and, to help audiences to follow not only the story but also the passions expressed by the principal characters, it included explanations of their gestures. Weaver's first "Dramatic Entertainment of Dancing" was a pastoral with mythological characters; the Cyclops introduced comedy into the work, but Weaver's version (which he had adapted from a masque of the same title by Peter Motteux) was closer to the comedy of manners than to farce.[45]

*The Loves of Mars and Venus* is a mixture of the new with the well tried. The action is divided into six scenes. Scene 1 opens with a "Pyrrhic Dance" for Mars and his followers, which includes what was probably a virtuoso solo for Mars much like those recorded in several surviving notations.[46] Scene 2 introduces Venus, who dances a passacaille with the Graces and one of the Hours; this dance probably also used figures and steps associated with theatrical solos.[47] Venus's passacaille is followed by a pantomime dance with Vulcan. After a scene change, Vulcan is joined

44. Hester Santlow was the leading English dancer-actress. Louis Dupré danced in the London theaters between 1714 and 1734. See Moira Goff, "The 'London' Dupré," *Historical Dance* 3 no. 6 (1999): 23–26.

45. For the third performance on 12 March 1717, the Cyclops were billed as "by the Comedians"; see Emmett L. Avery, ed., *The London Stage, 1660–1800*, pt. 2, *1700–1729* (Carbondale: Southern Illinois University Press, 1960). Motteux's masque *The Loves of Mars and Venus* was first performed at Lincoln's Inn Fields Theatre on 14 November 1696, with music by John Eccles and Gottfried (Godfrey) Finger.

46. The solo "Chacone of Amadis" created by Anthony L'Abbé for Dupré gives a good idea of the genre and Dupré's technical skills; see Anthony L'Abbé, *A New Collection of Dances: Originally Published by F. Le Roussau c. 1725*, introduction by Carol G. Marsh (London: Stainer & Bell, 1991), 57–64.

47. A solo passacaille, the "Passagalia of Venüs & Adonis," created by L'Abbé for Hester Santlow, was recorded in notation; see L'Abbé, *New Collection*, 46–56.

by the Cyclops for scene 3, and they perform a dance which unites steps
and gestures. Scene 4 provides a contrast, as Mars and Venus meet (with
a sequence of expressive gestures) and a *divertissement* ensues with a series
of dances by their followers which they join. Vulcan and the Cyclops return for scene 5, in which Vulcan performs a solo in the grotesque style
between pantomime exchanges with the Cyclops. The final scene, like
the fourth, begins with gesture, first between Mars and Venus, pleased
with their amorous encounter, and then, with a complete change of
mood, by Vulcan and the Cyclops as they catch the lovers unawares and
expose them to the ridicule of their fellow gods and goddesses. The work
ends with a "Grand Dance" for all the onstage characters, following a
long-established convention. In *The Loves of Mars and Venus*, Weaver skill-
fully integrated conventional dances with expressive gestures in order to
convey a complete narrative without the help of sung or spoken words.

In his preface to the scenario, Weaver referred back to the *Essay* by
writing of the Roman pantomimes who "perform'd all by Gesture and
the Action of the Hands, Fingers, Legs and Feet," adding that the "Face
or Countenance had a large Share in this Performance."[48] The gestures
that he specified and explained were those intended to express passions,
but *The Loves of Mars and Venus* also contained examples of other narrative
gestures. Some imitated real actions; the most striking were those in
scene 3 "*where the* Cyclops *are discover'd at Work; some at the Forge; some at the
Anvil; some Hammering; and some Fileing; while* Cupid *is pointing his Arrows at
the Grindstone.*"[49] Others represented speech, for example, in scene 5
when Vulcan "*approves*" of the net which the Cyclops have made, or in
scene 6 when Neptune "*intercedes*" with Vulcan on behalf of Mars and
Venus.[50] Others used bodily attitudes and facial expressions to imitate
manners, as in scene 4 when Venus responds with "*affected Bashfulness*"
and "*wishing Looks*" to the "*Gallantry*" of Mars; Weaver described the gestures in this scene as "so obvious, relating only to Gallantry, and Love;
that they need no Explanation."[51]

---

48. Weaver, *Loves*, x–xi. Weaver had not referred to the use of the face in his 1712 *Essay*, and it
is uncertain whether or not he was familiar with the *Conférence sur l'expression* of Charles Le Brun,
which had been published in an English translation in 1701. For a recent account of Le Brun's
theory, with a reconstruction of the text of his original lecture, see Jennifer Montagu, *The Expression
of the Passions* (New Haven, CT: Yale University. Press, 1994).

49. Weaver, *Loves*, 24.

50. Weaver, *Loves*, 26, 27.

51. Weaver, *Loves*, 25, 26.

The most important pantomime sequence came in scene 2, when Venus and Vulcan performed a duet "*in which* Vulcan *expresses his* Admiration; Jealousie; Anger; and Despite: *And* Venus *shews* Neglect; Coquetry; Contempt; and Disdain"; the dance was defined by Weaver as "being altogether of the *Pantomimic* kind."[52] This dance used gestures to express passions, and those described in the following pages of the scenario outline the mute argument between the ill-matched couple. Vulcan moved from Admiration, through Astonishment, Jealousy, Upbraiding, Anger, Threats, Power, and Impatience, to Indignation, and Venus responded with Coquetry, Neglect, and Contempt, rising to Distaste, and ending with Detestation, as she left the stage to meet Mars. Reconstruction of the gestures shows that some can be performed with steps, for example Venus's distaste, "The left Hand thrust forth with the Palm turn'd backward; the left Shoulder rais'd, and the Head bearing towards the Right," while others require stillness to make their full effect, for example Vulcan's Power, "The Arm, with impetuous Agitation, directed forwards to the Person, with an awful Look."[53] Unfortunately, Weaver did not make clear whether this "Dance" consisted entirely of gestures, or incorporated them into a *danse à deux*, and the loss of the music has removed crucial evidence for the interpretation of his design.

Weaver's description of the performances of the Roman pantomimes in the scenario and his *Essay*, his description of the exchange between Venus and Vulcan as a "Dance," and his admission that he had "too much inclin'd to the Modern Dancing" in order to accommodate his dancers and meet the expectations of the public, all indicate that the duet integrated dance and gesture.[54] Weaver may well have used some of the choreographic conventions and devices which can be found in the notated *danses à deux*, for example, the opening passage downstage toward the audience, mirror and coaxial symmetry (see fig. 8.2), asymmetric figures (in which one dancer might circle the other, who remains on the spot), and question-and-answer or echo effects. He would probably have avoided virtuoso steps, and paid particular attention to the spatial relationships between the couple and between them and their audience. It is likely

52. Weaver, *Loves*, 20.
53. Weaver, *Loves*, 23, 22.
54. Weaver, *Loves*, xiii.

Figure 8.2: Circular figure from "Chacone of Galathee," danced by Hester Santlow and Delagarde; an example of co-axial symmetry from a dance in the serious style. (Anthony L'Abbé, *A New Collection of Dances* [ca. 1725], plate 28)

that Vulcan remained still at several points during the dance, in order to make his gestures with full effect, while Venus continued to dance around him or away from him, or stopped to respond to his gesture with one of her own. Weaver replaced words with dance steps and gestures, to create a highly developed example of "danse pantomime."[55] *The Loves of Mars and Venus* brings dance and gesture together in several different ways: they are used successively in scenes 4 and 6, alternately in scenes 3 and 5, and integrated in the duet in scene 2. As early as 1717, therefore, Weaver had created an expressive dance work which had many features in common with those of Angiolini, Magri, and Ferrère.

## Ferrère

In his manuscript, Ferrère included dances in which dance steps and gestures were brought together into "danse pantomime" for comic works very like those created by Magri. Ferrère's dances deal with this integration in several ways, and use a variety of types of gesture, which he recorded through notation and verbal description and occasionally both. The manuscript also shows how dances that included gestures could be structured, and that there was no single model for them. Dances from only two of the eight pieces in the manuscript, *Le Peintre amoureux de son modèle* and *Les Bûcherons et les sabotiers*, are examined here, chosen because of the insights gained in the course of reconstructing and performing them.

### Le Peintre amoureux de son modèle

Ferrère's *Le Peintre amoureux de son modèle* tells the story of a painter whose wife is furious when she discovers that he is painting a nude portrait of his model; they quarrel, but are finally reconciled (see the synopsis in chap. 7). Central to this little drama is an extended *pas de deux* in which steps and gestures are intertwined to tell the story and express the passions of the two central characters. This analysis concentrates on the three linked dances that form the *pas de deux*, from the wife's discovery of the portrait to the reconciliation between her and the painter; I reconstructed and danced the role of the painter in the second and third of these dances.[56] The whole *pas de deux* is written in a mixture of Feuillet

---

55. Brainard showed how Weaver's gestures might be applied to the action of Angiolini's *Le Festin de pierre* and *Sémiramis;* see "The Speaking Body," 30–34.

56. The role of the wife was reconstructed and danced by Jennifer Thorp. My account of the role draws on her performance, our work together reconstructing the duet, and my own analysis of

notation, quasi-notational representations of gestures (partly based on Feuillet conventions for notating arm movements), and verbal explanations. Ferrère did not notate every step, but occasionally wrote "le même" where steps (or sequences of steps) are repeated by one or both dancers, or "contrepas" where he notated only one side of the duet and the painter and his wife perform the same steps but on opposite feet. His version of Feuillet notation appears to be orthodox, with bar lines marked on the track (gestures as well as steps are notated in specific bars) and liaison lines used to indicate the timing of steps within the bar, although in these three dances he made sparing use of rest signs and there are many instances where the signs for sinking, rising, or springing appear to have been omitted.[57]

The first of the three dances in this *pas de deux* has sixty-four bars of music in 3/8 marked "tempo di Minuetto," with an AABACABA musical structure (each section has eight bars of music). It begins with the painter and his wife facing crossing diagonals, so that each is turned partly to the other and partly to the audience, on their "proper" sides.[58] Most of the dance (the opening AABACA sections) is a formal *danse à deux*, with the symmetrical floor patterns familiar from the early 1700s. Although the music is a minuet, the dance contains very few *pas de menuet* and bears almost no relation to the steps and figures of the ballroom minuet as recorded in the late eighteenth century.[59] The painter and his wife have the same steps throughout, based around the *demi-contretemps battu*, Magri's *brisé*, and the *assemblé battu*. A number of steps begin with a *pas tombé*, perhaps to provide impetus (from an open position and a deeper *plié*) for the *pas sauté battu* which usually follows, thus linking the technique to that described by Magri in his *Trattato*. There is also some repetition of steps, for example in the C section, where a sequence of two steps is repeated four times. Of the three dances, this has the most varied and complex vocabulary, as the painter and his wife dance happily together— much as they had done in their *pas de deux* before the painter began work.

---

the notation. The reconstruction was significantly helped by a transcription of the notation from the original manuscript by Carol Marsh, which has also been used to assist the analysis in this essay. We did not reconstruct the first of the three dances that comprise this *pas de deux*.

57. These omissions and inconsistencies posed no serious problems during the reconstruction process; in fact, they provided opportunities to explore a range of solutions.

58. The man is on the woman's left, as he would have been in the *danses à deux* of the early eighteenth century. Ferrère notates only the man's side for most of this dance.

59. Magri described the minuet in pt. 2 of his treatise; see Magri/Skeaping, 179–91; Magri, *Trattato*, 2:14–34.

The last part of the dance, the closing BA sections, is quite different. In the B section, the painter performs an eight-bar solo while his wife, with her finger to her nose ("le doigt au nez," a gesture which perhaps denotes suspicion; see fig. 7.1), takes off in the direction of her husband's easel, first with slow and then with fast steps.[60] Ferrère notates only her first three bars, giving no instructions for the remaining five (for which he merely marks the bar lines on the track), and this may indicate either improvisation by the performer or repetition of the previous steps. The painter continues to dance as she circles around the easel, discovers the portrait, and seizes it ("decouvre le portrait et le prend"), then hides it behind her back with her finger again to her nose ("Elle cache le portrait derriere son dos, le doigt au nez"). Thus, during the B section, the onstage action is divided simultaneously between dancing by the painter and pantomime by his wife. The concluding A section is mainly gesture. The painter and his wife turn to face each other and smile ("Ils se sourient"); she then calls him to her ("Elle l'appelle"), but has to call him again before he steps toward her.

The next duet (the second dance) follows with hardly a pause, in order to maintain the momentum in this *pas d'action*. (See fig. 8.3.) It has music in 2/4, with an AB musical structure (A = four bars marked Largo, B = twenty bars marked Allegro), and begins with the painter and his wife in positions similar to those of the start of the previous dance, but he is now to her right (the "improper" side, perhaps to signal the impending quarrel). During the brief A section, she takes the portrait from behind her back and shows it to him ("Elle lui montre le portrait"). The painter bows and takes a step back as if to leave ("Il s'excuse"). In the first bar of the B section she smashes the portrait over his head so that it ends hanging round his neck ("Elle lui casse sur la tête," "La tête au travers du portrait"). The two then begin a sequence of dance steps (with no gestures) in which the painter is pursued by his wife, only briefly fighting back as they stamp at each other. Their steps are very similar, and closely related to those in the previous dance— open *chassé* (*chassè aperto*), beaten *chassé* (*chassè battuto*) with added turns, and beaten *contretemps*—most are steps recognizable from Magri's treatise.[61] The painter whirls off the stage, leaving his wife to perform a short but furious solo, set to the last eleven bars of the B section, before she too exits. Throughout this section, the

---

60. Quotations in this and the following paragraphs are from the choreographer's own notes on the original manuscript. Question marks indicate words which are illegible.

61. Magri/Skeaping, 111; Magri, *Trattato*, 1:75.

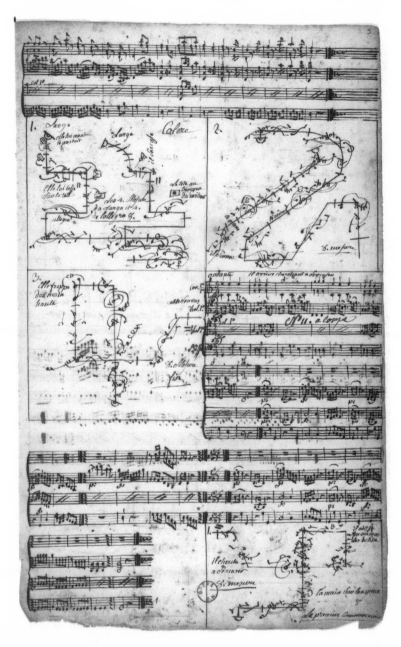

Figure 8.3: In this sequence from *Le Peintre amoureux de son modèle*, the painter's wife smashes the portrait over her husband's head (box 1); they dance diagonally upstage, the wife chasing the painter into the wings (box 2); and the wife dances a triumphant solo (box 3). (Auguste Ferrère, *Partition et chorographie*, F-Po Rés. 68, p. 5; photo, Bibliothèque Nationale de France, Paris)

floor patterns have more to do with dramatic effect than the conventions of the early-eighteenth-century *danse à deux*, and the steps with their turns, stamps, and beats are obviously intended to be expressive of the argument between the couple.

In the context of our knowledge of dancing in the early eighteenth century (the only other period for which theatrical dances survive in notation), the technique expected of the wife in her first solo is surprising. Not only are her steps similar to those that had been reserved for men in the early 1700s, but she has a more difficult vocabulary of steps than the painter. One of her steps is very like Magri's *gorguglié* "just off the ground," although no rise or spring is notated.[62] This is immediately followed by a double pirouette on the ball of the foot, presumably Magri's open extended pirouette (*pirola distesa aperta*).[63] This latter is familiar from the earlier repertoire of dances for men. The difficulty of the steps and the range of technique expected clearly indicate the development of female dancing during the eighteenth century toward greater virtuosity, and even a degree of competition with male dancers. This development has often been noted in general histories of dancing, but without reference to the specific evidence provided by a comparison between the notated dances of the early 1700s and the choreographies recorded by Ferrère.

The wife's gestures in this first solo are familiar from a different early source. In one gesture she claps her hands together ("Elle frappe des mains haute," the notation shows a handclap), a gesture very much like Weaver's anger: "The left Hand struck suddenly with the right; and sometimes against the breast; denotes *Anger*."[64] Jacques Bonnet, in his *Histoire générale de la danse* of 1724, also described the expression of anger through dancing: "Anger, which is a fiery passion, flares up impetuously; there is nothing regular about it; all its motions are violent; and to express it through dance, the steps must be hasty, with irregular falls and cadences; there must be beating steps, darting movements, threatening movements by the head, eyes and hands, wild and furious glances."[65]

62. Magri/Skeaping, 159; Magri, *Trattato*, 1:125: "quasi a fior di terra."

63. Magri/Skeaping, 127; Magri, *Trattato*, 1:90

64. Weaver, *Loves*, 21.

65. Jacques Bonnet, *Histoire générale de la danse, sacrée et prophane* (Paris: D'Houry fils, 1724), 64: "La colere qui est une passion fougueuse, s'emporte avec impétuosité; elle n'a rien de réglé; tous ses mouvemens sont violens; & pour l'exprimer par la danse, les pas doivent être précipitez, avec des chutes & des cadences inégales; il faut battre du pied, aller par élancemens, menacer de la tête, des yeux de la main, jetter des regards farouches & furieux." Bonnet's "il faut battre du pied" would usually be

Ferrère was unable to notate the "wild and furious glances," but he certainly used suitably expressive steps and gestures. The wife's angry hand-clap is followed by another gesture, with her arm as well as her foot movements notated but no verbal annotation, in which she may well be performing a variant on Weaver's indignation, "steping back the right Foot, leaning the Body quite backward, the Arms extended, Palms clos'd, and Hands thrown quite back; the Head cast back, and Eyes fix'd upwards."[66] (See fig. 8.4.) She gives emphasis to this gesture by stamping her foot before she takes a step into second position, as a preparation for the steps with which she rapidly leaves the stage. In this solo, the gestures are seamlessly integrated into the sequence of steps.

The third of these dances is equally expressive. It has music in 3/4, marked Andante, with an ABCABD musical structure (each section of which has eight bars of music), and there may well have been a distinct pause between it and the preceding dance, just long enough to prepare for a complete change of mood as the stage is briefly empty. This dance opens with the painter's return to the stage, seeking to apologize for his folly ("Il cherche a s'excuser"); he is presumably inviting the audience to sympathise with his plight as he faces them following his entrance from the wings. He begins a solo dance (A section), but after just a couple of steps he covers his eyes with his hand ("la main sur les yeux"). His gesture is closely related to Weaver's shame: "The covering the Face with the Hand, is a Sign of *Shame*."[67] The painter's next step is lively, incorporating a *demi-contretemps battu* and finishing with a *brisé*, but when he sees his wife (who is in the wings, "il voit sa femme dans les coulisses") he begins to beat a hasty retreat.[68]

She enters with her hand over her forehead ("sa main sur le front"), for a solo which also mixes gestures and dance steps (set to the first B section of the music). Her opening gesture is difficult to interpret, but the context suggests that it expresses indignation, using Weaver's alternative of "applying the Hand passionately to the Forehead."[69] She begins simply, with two *pas marchés*, but her subsequent steps incorporate many beats, and one appears to be a version of Magri's *capriola* in the Italian

---

translated as an ordinary stamp of the foot; however, since he is writing about dance, Bonnet's words could perhaps be intended to refer to specific dance steps like *pas battus*. I am grateful to Nathalie Lecomte for this clarification.

66. Weaver, *Loves*, 22.
67. Weaver, *Loves*, 28.
68. Magri/Skeaping, 138; Magri, *Trattato*, 1:101.
69. Weaver, *Loves*, 22.

Figure 8.4: A gesture expressing anger. (Johann Jakob Engel, *Ideen zu einer Mimik* [1785-86; Berlin, 1802], fig. 43)

manner, beginning from second position and beating behind and in front before closing behind in fifth position.[70] Her following gesture, which is notated as well as annotated ("Elle menace"), could easily be Weaver's threats—"*Threatning*, is express'd by raising the Hand, and shaking the bended Fist"—although there is no way of knowing whether she added the accompanying "knitting the Brow; biting the Nails; and catching back the Breath."[71] Her steps, with their stamps as well as jumps and beats, show that she is still very angry. As she dances, the painter at first withdraws upstage as inconspicuously as possible ("il recule doucement et avec timidité") and then advances downstage ("il avance") toward his wife who, after her threatening gesture apparently commands him to her side.[72]

After these two solos, the couple are on their "proper" sides to begin the duet (C section) in which the painter begs for forgiveness ("il prie") and his wife rebuffs him with a series of emphatic *chassés* ornamented with beats and turns, as he runs across the stage to get first to one side of

70. Magri/Skeaping, 156; Magri, *Trattato*, 1:119-20: "all'*Italiana*."
71. Weaver, *Loves*, 22.
72. The annotation says "la point sur le côté," while the notation indicates that she has her right hand on her hip while her left gestures toward the floor, perhaps commanding her husband to join her in order to explain himself.

her and then the other. She stands still as he steps forward to make his gesture, but responds with a sharp *tombé* as he does so. The interplay between the couple (and part of the humor for the audience) comes from such touches as the painter's steps following his wife's hostile reactions to his plea for mercy; the first time he scuttles off forward, the second time his steps stagger backward.

She then performs another angry solo without gestures (second A section), while her husband at first stands watching her fearfully ("il regarde avec peur") and then begins to sneak upstage again ("il recule timidement"). Bonnet also wrote about how fear should be danced: "Fear approaches slowly, and retreats hastily, with a halting and trembling walk, a distracted gaze, arms at a loss, and an air of uncertainty."[73] This description perhaps provides clues to the painter's movements (described in general but not notated by Ferrère) during his wife's solo. She shows her continuing anger with a furious series of *battements,* in a step which is a variant of the *coupé* with multiple beats by the right foot—back, front, back, front—similar to Magri's *battement basso piegato* in that Ferrère, like Magri in his description, omits any indication of a sink, rise, or spring.[74] She also has several complex steps incorporating small jumps and sharp beats, as she too moves backward in order to come face to face with her retreating husband.

This *pas d'action* of three successive dances ends quietly with a pantomime sequence in which the painter and his wife are finally reconciled (they are again on their "proper" sides, perhaps a sign of their return to domestic harmony). The closing B and D sections consist entirely of gestures. The painter begins by kneeling and possibly *"suing* for *Mercy"* before holding out his hands in Weaver's "Expression of *Submission.*"[75] After threatening him again, his wife holds out her hand in Weaver's gesture of Forgiveness ("elle lui donne la main").[76] He kisses it ("il baise sa main," the notation shows him taking her hand in both of his), and she bids him rise ("elle lui dit de se lever"), which he does ("il se leve"). He briefly takes

---

73. Bonnet, *Histoire générale,* 64: "La crainte a des pas lents dans les approches, & précipitez dans la retraite, une démarche tremblante & suspendue, une vue égarée, les bras embarassez, & une contenance incertaine."

74. Magri/Skeaping, 73–74; Magri, *Trattato,* 1:38.

75. Weaver, *Loves,* 28: "The stretching out the Hands downwards toward the Knees, is an Action of *Entreaty,* and suing for *Mercy,*" "To hold out both the Hands joyn'd together, is a natural Expression of *Submission* and *Resignation.*"

76. Weaver, *Loves,* 28: "To extend and offer out the Right Hand, is a Gesture of *Pitty,* and Intention of *Forgiveness.*"

her hand again (the note "il lui [?] la main" is illegible but the notation again shows him taking his wife's hand in both of his own perhaps for a second kiss) and then prepares for the solo ("il se prepare a dancer") with which he is to begin the following *pas de deux*. There is no notation for his wife after her smile ("elle sourit"). Ferrère does not indicate how the painter prepares for his solo, but his wife probably withdraws to another part of the stage as he walks to the center to take up his opening pose. The ensuing duet expresses their joy at their reconciliation but has no gesture and will not be discussed in this essay.

This extended *pas de deux,* with its three linked dances, thus forms a *pas d'action* tracing the course of the quarrel between the painter and his wife through dancing with gestures, dancing with no gestures, and gestures with no dancing. Each dance is structured differently, with gestures at the end, or at the beginning, integrated with or separated from the dance steps, but they form a linked sequence, as the gesture at the end of the first dance continues into the second, and the sequence of solos with gestures follows from the second into the third. These duets use gestures to imitate actions, to represent speech, and to express passions — as Weaver did in *The Loves of Mars and Venus* — so it is not entirely surprising to find that some of those notated by Ferrère can be recognized as those described by Weaver. The notations also show how gestures were integrated into dances, by being performed immediately after a *pas marché*, or at the same time as taking a step, and with complex and expressive steps before or after them. All of Ferrère's gestures are performed within a single bar of music, sometimes at the beginning, sometimes at the end, and sometimes throughout the whole bar, so where they are used with steps they are fully integrated choreographically, and where they form separate sections they are fully integrated musically. Ferrère did not need to make either a choreographic or a musical distinction between steps and gestures, since both could be accommodated within the same musical structure at the same tempo. Steps and gestures are both fundamental to the continuous narrative expressed by the three dances which form the extended *pas de deux* within *Le Peintre amoureux de son modèle.*

## Les Bûcherons et les sabotiers

Ferrère's *Les Bûcherons et les sabotiers* deals differently with the integration of dance steps and gestures. This *ballet-pantomime* is a series of loosely linked episodes, without the unifying narrative of *Le Peintre amoureux de son modèle* (see the synopsis in chap. 7).

It opens with woodcutters cutting wood and stacking up logs. A *sabotière* arrives in her wooden shoes, collecting wood chips, and dances a *pas de trois* with two woodcutters; only this *pas de trois*, for which I reconstructed and danced one of the woodcutters, will be considered here.[77] Despite its use of gestures imitating actions and representing speech, this dance is in many respects closer to the nonrepresentative dancing found in *divertissements* than to a "danse pantomime." Ferrère used Feuillet notation to record part of it, but there is also much verbal annotation (see fig. 8.5). The men perform a duet for most of the dance, with dance steps rather than gestures, but Ferrère routinely recorded the steps on only one side with the track (occasionally with bar lines or other signs) and the annotation "contre pas" on the other. Although the two men undoubtedly performed the same dance steps on opposite feet, this may not always have been true of their gestures.

The music is in 6/8 with the musical structure AABBAB (both the A and B sections have eight bars of music). All three dancers come onto the stage at the same time; the two men arrive on each side downstage as the *sabotière* enters from upstage left, carrying a basket. The men dance a four-bar phrase, which culminates in a *tour en l'air,* and then repeat it to end on either side of the woman (first A section). As they dance, she walks across the stage, acknowledging them ("salue de la tête") and going about her business as she puts down her basket and happily begins to fill it with woodchips ("elle met son panier à terre," "dit c'est bon," "elle met des copeaux dans son panier"). The trio thus begins with two very different sorts of movement performed simultaneously. As the *sabotière* continues to fill her basket (second A section), the men signal her presence to one another ("il montre la femme," "il l'appelle," "l'autre dit oui"). Ferrère provides verbal instructions and notation for the left-hand man only, so it is uncertain whether they do exactly the same gestures at the same time or whether one calls and the other responds. After two bars of gestures, the men perform a four-bar phrase of steps and then take the woman's hands and run forward with her downstage. Throughout these opening

77. The other woodcutter was danced by Jennifer Thorp; the *sabotière* was danced by Madeleine Inglehearn. My account draws on the reconstruction work we did together, as well as my own analysis of the notation. As with the *pas de deux* from *Le Peintre amoureux de son modèle,* the reconstruction was significantly helped by a transcription of the notation from the original manuscript by Carol Marsh, which again has been used to assist the analysis in this essay (Photo, Bibliothèque Nationale de France, Paris).

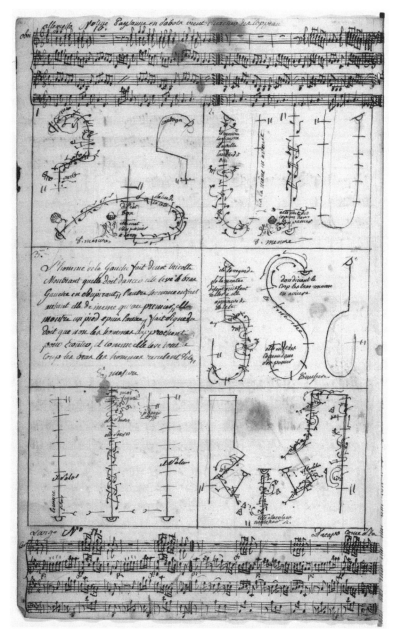

Figure 8.5: The choreography of this *pas de trois* from *Les Bûcherons et les sabotiers* in the Ferrère manuscript (p. 38) mixes Feuillet notation, sketches, and verbal description. In the first box the woman is shown entering from upstage left with a basket over her arm, while the two men dance symmetrical figures downstage.

sections the choreography for the men is lively and jaunty, in contrast to the woman, whose actions imitate the ordinary movements of real life. The humor of the scene arises from the men's determination that the *sabotière* will dance with them, although they are sure that her wooden shoes will prevent her from emulating their fancy footwork.

Ferrère provides no notation for the first B section, which is almost entirely gestures, instead writing out in words the sequence performed by the three dancers. Each man in turn performs two "tricotte" to the woman, inviting her to dance with them ("montrant qu'elle doit dancer"), to which she responds by lifting her left arm and sighing ("elle leve le bras gauche en soupirant"). It is difficult to interpret the term "tricotte," which does not correspond to any of the known step names. It may perhaps be related to the Italian term "intrecciare," which can be translated as "interweaving," and it would not be unreasonable for the men to perform a *capriola* which involved the interweaving of the feet.[78] The woman continues by indicating first one foot and then the other, signaling no with her finger ("elle montre un pied et puis l'autre, fait signe du doigt que non"; she is presumably pretending that her wooden shoes make it impossible for her to dance). The two men approach her, but retreat when she suddenly raises her arms ("les hommes s'approchent pour écouter et comme elle lève tout à coup les bras les hommes reculent vîte"). Ferrère does not notate their actions, but they perhaps use Weaver's astonishment: "Both Hands are thrown up towards the Skies; the Eyes also lifted up, and the Body cast backwards."[79]

At the beginning of the second B section, the *sabotière* slips out from between the men and goes back upstage to continue gathering woodchips, but the two men signal each other to follow her ("il la regarde," "il la montre," "disent qu'il faut aller à elle," "approuve de la tête") and dance upstage to either side of her. In the third A section they again take her hands and run forward downstage with her. This time she does not refuse, but smiles ("elle sourit") and gestures her agreement to dance ("je danse aussi"). In the final B section, she curtsies to each man in turn and withdraws upstage ("elle recule en marchant") while the men, who are to each side of her, perform a duet. The following dance begins with the

---

78. For references to the interweaving of the feet in *capriole*, see Magri/Skeaping, 157; Magri, *Trattato*, 1:121. Edmund Fairfax, in a letter to Carol Marsh, suggests that the "tricotte" is in fact an interweaving gesture of the hands very similar to that still performed by ballet dancers today (in the older works still in repertoire) as an invitation to dance. I am grateful to Carol Marsh for passing this information on to me.

79. Weaver, *Loves*, 21.

*sabotière* performing a lively solo full of beats, turns, and stamping steps, so she is presumably taking up her opening position as the men bring the *pas de trois* to a close. The audience, recognizing the dancer who took the role, would have known from the beginning of the trio that the *sabotière* would show up her two would-be dancing partners as soon as she began to dance.

This trio is very different from the duets in *Le Peintre amoureux de son modèle*. Although the two woodcutters use gesture, usually to represent speech, at certain points of the *pas de trois*, they mostly just dance. Their gestures are grouped together into phrases and are preceded and followed by phrases of dance, rather than being fully integrated into the dance vocabulary. Most of their steps are technically demanding, incorporating jumps and beats — *contretemps battu, brisé, assemblé battu*, and beaten *chassé* (Magri's *chassè battuto*) — which contrast strongly with their speechlike gestures. The *sabotière* hardly dances at all, instead performing a series of gestures which imitate real actions and represent speech. There are virtually no gestures expressive of strong emotions in this *pas de trois* and very little narrative. Nevertheless, this trio is a small-scale *pas d'action* which presents a choreographed version of everyday life, imitating its actions, representing its verbal exchanges, and expressing the affections rather than the passions of the three characters.[80] Ferrère's notation of *Les bûcherons et les sabotiers* provides us with a complete example of the danced entertainments based on everyday occupations that were a staple of the popular theaters in Paris, London, and elsewhere during the eighteenth century.

## Magri, Ferrère, and John Weaver

Despite the differences in time and place which separate them, Weaver, Magri, and Ferrère were recognizably working within the same tradition and employing many of the same gestures and steps for expressive purposes. Weaver provides the only detailed descriptions of the gestures used by dancers, and these can still be seen in Ferrère's notations. The steps described by Magri can be recognized in Ferrère's manuscript, and Ferrère's use of Feuillet notation provides a link to the theatrical dances

---

80. Weaver distinguishes between the "Passions, as *Love; Hatred; Grief; Joy; Despair, Hopes, Fear, Anger*, &c. and others of a lesser Degree, which may be call'd Affections; as *Tranquility* [*sic*]; *Grace; Civility; Gentleness;* and the like," *Anatomical and Mechanical Lectures*, 144–45.

recorded in Weaver's day. It is thus possible to compare and contrast some of the choreographic conventions familiar to each dancing-master. The dancing that Ferrère was notating had changed considerably since the early eighteenth century; both style and technique differed from the dances for which Feuillet notation was devised. Jumps and extensions were probably much higher than in the early 1700s, although the notation cannot indicate this. The phrasing in the dances (which can be understood only through the process of reconstruction) differs considerably from the earlier dances; by Ferrère's day, dancers seem to have been working in dance phrases as their basic units rather than bar by bar, as the notations of the early 1700s suggest. This change may reflect not only higher jumps and extensions, but also the combination of steps into longer sequences used in a variety of dances, and the increased use of repetition, all of which require steps to flow in a sequence over a musical phrase. Early-eighteenth-century dances did not ignore phrases or avoid longer sequences of steps, but they avoided exact repetition and gave greater emphasis to the differing rhythmic subtleties of steps in successive bars, since these were important aspects of their smaller-scale style and technique.

There is no surviving evidence to show how gestures, and the integration of gestures with dance steps, changed between John Weaver and Gennaro Magri. Weaver's scenario for *The Loves of Mars and Venus* and Ferrère's notations suggest that there was continuity as well as change, just as there was in the dance vocabulary. Weaver does not provide enough detailed information to tell us for certain how dance steps and gestures were brought together in his works, but his insistence on the expressive possibilities of dancing is one of a number of indications that he did not separate the two. Ferrère's notations show how easily dance and gestures could be brought together by the second half of the eighteenth century; the fluency of the choreographies he records indicates that he was working with long-established and fully accepted conventions. Taken together, Magri, Ferrère, and Weaver provide us with new and important evidence about the vitality and variety of expressive theatrical dancing during the eighteenth century.

# 9

# Putting Together a
# Pantomime Ballet

## CAROL G. MARSH AND REBECCA HARRIS-WARRICK

The genre of pantomime ballet constitutes a generous category, one that
encompasses many movement styles and various levels of narrative development. The goal of this chapter is to use the models provided by the
Ferrère manuscript—the only works known to have survived with such
extensive choreographic and musical information—in order to eluci-
date the structures and component parts of the lighter types of pantomime ballet, those performed by dancers such as Gennaro Magri,
Cosimo Maranesi, or Auguste Ferrère, who specialized in grotesque or
comic styles. Four of the eight works in the Ferrère manuscript fall into
the category of pantomime ballet: *Le Peintre amoureux de son modèle*, *Les
Galants villageois*, *La Réjouissance villageoise, ou Le Sabotier*, and *Les Bûcherons et
les sabotiers* (see the synopses in chap. 7). These four form the principal objects of study, which are then compared with information derived from
other ballet scenarios, musical scores, and Magri's *Trattato*, in order to
extract general principles regarding the works of this type that were performed around Europe.

One of the first points that emerges from both the Ferrère works and
the scenarios included in appendices 2–5 is that narrative coherence is
not a requirement. Some of the works do tell stories—*Le Peintre amoureux*

*de son modèle* among the Ferrère ballets and Magri's own *Alla ricerca di un tesoro* (In Search of a Treasure) among them. But others simply provide a colorful framework — often via a setting such as a fish market or a village festival — that allows for character dances and comic actions. Among the Ferrère works, *Les Bûcherons et les sabotiers* is of this type, as is Magri's *Arrivo di viaggiatori nella posta di Vienna:* "The post-stage near Vienna is shown, with the arrival of various travelers, and the ballet follows with festivities and joy."[1] Clearly, works such as these are a long way from the mythology-based ballets that often followed the first act of operas performed in Italy (see app. 2), or even more so from the tragedies of Angiolini and Noverre, which drew upon the dance traditions of the *serio* or noble style and sought by taking on serious subjects to raise pantomime ballet to a higher aesthetic plane.

Even so, the models of light ballets provided by Ferrère can help bring the issues involved in recreating more serious works into sharper focus. The genre of pantomime ballet carries within itself a tension between its narrative elements and those parts that might be called pure dance. Even in the works of the foremost exponent of the *ballet d'action*, Jean-Georges Noverre, scenes of pantomime alternate with *divertissements;* for him the operative model appears to have been the French *tragédie lyrique*, where in every act the narrative is interrupted by a visually sumptuous mixture of choral singing and ballet. In act 3 of Noverre's *Médée et Jason*, for instance, during the wedding festivities of Jason and Créuse, "the populace shows its approval of Créon's choice through its dances."[2] Here the forward momentum of the story stops and celebratory dancing takes over, in a *divertissement* that could have come out of any number of operas. Other scenes in *Médée et Jason*, such as the athletic contest or one in which Médée conjures up creatures from the Underworld, also have operatic analogues, the only difference being that in a *tragédie lyrique* solo and choral singing would supplement the dances. Thus even in tragic ballets, where narrative continuity is fundamental, audiences did not want to see gestures alone and choreographers always found ways to work moments of spectacle into their works.

The same distinction between narrative carried out in pantomime and moments of pure dancing appears in the lighter ballets that choreographers such as Ferrère and Magri produced. In *Le Peintre amoureux de son*

---

1. These two Magri ballets were both composed for Naples; see app. 4, nos. 5 and 2.

2. "Le peuple applaudit par les danses au choix de Créon"; scenario from the Vienna production, published in *Denkmäler der deutscher Tonkunst* (Wiesbaden: Breitkopf und Härtel, 1958), 43–44:lii.

*modèle,* for instance, a scene in which the painter's jealous wife vents her rage by breaking a painted canvas across her husband's head is followed shortly by a *pas de deux* that demonstrates through dance that a reconciliation has been effected. The distinction between modes of movement is even made explicit in a scenario for one of the ballets Dehesse composed for the Comédie Italienne in Paris, *L'Opérateur chinois* (1748): "The invention and arrangement of the pantomime, as well as the dances, were composed by Monsieur Dehesse."[3] And it was to continue in the nineteenth century: Lisa Arkin and Marian Smith have estimated that in a ballet such as *Giselle* (1841), half of the elapsed time was occupied by pantomime, half by dance.[4] But whereas in some kinds of scenes the dancing is compartmentalized from the pantomime, because it represents the kind of situation (such as a wedding) in which dancing would have been done in real life, ballet scenarios in general suggest that these two modes of movement often blended into each other — a point that emerges repeatedly in earlier chapters of this book. Anger might, for example, be conveyed purely through gestures of the hands and arms, or it might involve the whole body, or it might be expressed through an affective choice of dance steps — or a combination of all three. On the basis of a ballet scenario alone, however, it is very difficult to move from the printed word to the action, so the models Ferrère supplies are extremely precious, even for this one issue alone: as Moira Goff demonstrates in chapter 8, Ferrère supplies several different models for how dance and action get integrated.

But Ferrère's concrete models also provide guidance on many other topics fundamental to understanding ballet and its history: step vocabulary and step combinations within the context of actual choreographies; how solo, small ensemble, and group dances are constructed; how music and the dance go together, and so forth. This chapter examines such topics, looking both for general principles and at individual case studies. The synthesis presented here rests on study of the Ferrère manuscript as a whole and, very importantly, on reconstructions that have been done of

3. "L'invention & la disposition de la pantomime, ainsi que les danses, sont de la composition du Sieur Dehesse." This scenario is included in a four-volume anthology of printed librettos of works performed in the Théâtre des Petits Appartements in the château of Versailles between 1747 and 1750, F-Po C. 2768.

4. "First of all, mime and action scenes typically constituted as much as half of an entire ballet: indeed, it was not unheard of for entire scenes of a ballet (sometimes two in a row) to be devoid of dancing. . . . The ratio of dance to mime and action scenes in the original *Giselle,* for instance, was roughly equal." Lisa C. Arkin and Marian Smith, "National Dance in the Romantic Ballet," in *Rethinking the Sylph: New Perspectives on the Romantic Ballet,* ed. Lynn Garafola, Studies in Dance History (Hanover, NH: Wesleyan University Press, 1997), 11–68 (20–21).

parts of it. As more of the works in this manuscript are reconstructed and performed, a more nuanced understanding of the workings of pantomime ballets and their component parts will undoubtedly emerge.[5]

## Overview

Although the structural details of each of Ferrère's pantomime ballets are different, the overall shape is the same: group scenes frame the opening and closing, while the "action" of the ballet is delegated in between to a small number of individual characters. When the curtain rises, the audience sees a group of people, either engaged in some kind of activity, such as cutting trees, as in *Les Bûcherons et les sabotiers*, or dancing together, as in *Le Peintre amoureux de son modèle*. Sometimes both things happen, in that the group's labors may give way to a dance before the soloists enter. In either case, the audience gets introduced to the locale and its inhabitants through a kind of animated tableau. Both of these opening gambits can be seen in Dehesse's ballets for the Théâtre Italien as well: *L'Opérateur chinois, Les Bûcherons, ou Le Médecin de village* (see synopsis in app. 5), and *Le Pédant* all open with some kind of group activity, whereas *Le Mai* begins with a group dance. Although Magri's scenarios are much less detailed, they too have a similar shape; even a one-sentence scenario such as the one already quoted for *Arrivo di viaggiatori nella posta di Vienna* appears to follow this pattern. Similar conventions apply to the ballets of this type performed in Vienna.[6]

At the end of the work the group returns, accompanied by the solo dancers, in a scene of general rejoicing. Such dances, usually referred to as *contredanses générales*, not only conclude Ferrère's ballets but had long served across Europe, not just in France, to end a variety of theatrical genres including spoken comedies, *opéras-comiques*, and even some serious operas. From a choreographic perspective, the *contredanse générale* does have points in common with contemporary social contredanses, but it is by no means identical, the use of the same word notwithstanding (the point is discussed toward the end of this chapter). From a dramatic perspective

5. See the acknowledgments for a list of colleagues who have reconstructed excerpts from the Ferrère manuscript. These reconstructions have been enormously helpful in gaining an understanding of Ferrère's choreographic style.

6. See the discussions by Salvatore Bongiovanni and Bruce Alan Brown in chaps. 3 (73–76 and 86–88) and 4 (93–97), along with the scenarios in the corresponding appendices.

the *contredanse générale* serves to bring the work to a rousing conclusion with the entire cast on stage. In Ferrère's four ballets the number of *figurants* (those who perform in the group dances) varies from six to twelve,[7] a range that is in line with Magri's Neapolitan ballets. Noverre's pantomime ballet *Les Fêtes chinoises* required thirty-two *figurants* when it was performed at the Opéra Comique in Paris in 1754, a number large enough to provoke special comment.[8] The Italian ballets also generally end with group dances: see, by way of example, Magri's *Alla ricerca di un tesoro*, which closes with an "allegrissima contraddanza" (see app. 4, no. 5), or many of the entr'acte ballets from northern Italy included in appendix 2.

The events between these framing groups vary but always feature dances for the main characters, who appear as soloists, in duets, or in trios; there are generally additional group dances. Ferrère's works require from two to five soloists, and one ballet, *Le Peintre amoureux de son modèle*, includes roles for two characters — a servant and the painter's model — who only mime and do not dance. Depending on the needs of the story, the soloists may communicate through gestures, which, as Moira Goff has shown in chapter 8, may be done either in conjunction with dance steps or as purely mimed actions. These actions can be simple, such as asking another character to dance, or they can form part of an extended mimed sequence. But even the most narrative story features a large proportion of dance for its own sake, and the story lines are clearly contrived with many opportunities for the soloists to showcase their abilities. Some of Ferrère's works feature what might be called "novelty" dances, in which the dancer uses a prop such as a long pole or wears wooden shoes. These pieces put special demands on the dancer's technical abilities and must have been especially popular with audiences, judging by their frequency on European stages.

Ferrère's ballets are comprised of a series of discrete choreographic components accompanied by closed musical forms. As can be seen from the pages of the manuscript reproduced in figures 9.1–2, the notation for

---

7. Ferrère often refers to the *figurants* collectively as "le ballet."

8. "Il est terminé par une contredanse à trente-deux personnes dont les mouvemens forment une prodigieuse quantité de figures nouvelles & parfaitement dessinées, qui s'enchainent & se dégagent avec la plus grande facilité." ([The ballet] was concluded by a contredanse of thirty-two persons, whose movements formed a prodigious quantity of new and perfectly designed figures that intertwine and undo themselves with the greatest of ease.) *Almanach des Spectacles de Paris* (1754; this series, whose title varied, is generally known as *Les Spectacles de Paris*), 136–37. Magri also composed a *contraddanza* for thirty-two, but for the ballroom not the stage; see Magri/Skeaping, 227–31 and folio 21; Magri, *Trattato*, 2: 87–93 and plate 39.

Figure 9.1: This, the first page of the Ferrère manuscript, includes music for both the overture and the first dance, which is followed by choreographic notation for the twelve dancers, who enter from the sides in two groups of six. The sketches show the floor patterns, while the steps are listed by name; box 3, for example, calls for "4 chassé à 3 pas." (Photo, Bibliothèque Nationale de France, Paris)

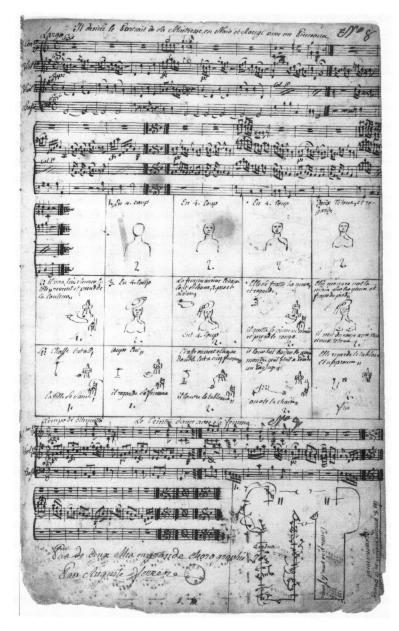

Figure 9.2: In this pantomime from *Le Peintre amoureux de son modèle* (Ferrère manuscript, p. 3) the music at the top of the page accompanies the actions described and sketched in the fourteen boxes beneath. The painter's actions are carefully coordinated with the musical score. The first figure of the subsequent *pas de deux* appears in the lower right-hand corner in Feuillet notation. (Photo, Bibliothèque Nationale de France, Paris)

each choreography is preceded by the entire music for that dance. This format differs from that of Feuillet notation, in which each page of the dance contains only the segment of melody accompanying the figure on that page. Ferrère's arrangement has the benefit of indicating how he conceptualized the choreographic units that make up each ballet. For ease of identification in discussing these components, we have numbered each one beginning with the overture, whether or not it accompanies movement. In the great majority of cases each choreographic unit (a group dance, a *pas de deux*, etc.) corresponds to a discrete musical unit, such as a binary or rondeau form. Furthermore, these units usually co-incide with the entrance or exit of one or more characters. The audience thus receives both an aural and a visual sense of the structure of the work.

Ferrère's four ballets contain anywhere from six to eleven component parts; because the music for each part can be repeated many times, par-ticularly in the *contredanses générales*, the units vary in length from 24 to 254 bars. When Ferrère departs from this organizational system he does so in one of two ways: either he strings together several closed musical forms to accompany a single choreographic unit, as happens, for example, in the *pas de trois* for the two soldiers and the village woman from *La Réjouis-sance villageoise;* or he uses the same music to accompany two different choreographic units, as he does in the dance for the townspeople, fol-lowed by the soloists, from *Le Peintre.* In such cases we identify these sub-divisions with letters: 10a, 10b, etc.

Before turning to tables 9.1 and 9.2, which outline the structural ele-ments of two of the ballets in Ferrère's manuscript, it would perhaps be useful to say a word about his various systems of notation. Although Fer-rère's usage is not entirely consistent, he does utilize different notation styles, depending on the kind of dance he is notating. The "Notation" column in the outline indicates in brief the system(s) prevailing in that particular number. Examples of the notation are shown in figures 9.1–2; these represent pages 1 and 3, respectively, of the manuscript and show the four basic systems in use.

1) Feuillet notation: This system, which dates back to the late seventeenth century, is used for most of the soloists' dances. The steps are indicated by means of a set of symbols notated along a track showing the floor pat-tern; see in the lower right-hand corner of figure 9.2 the first figure of a *pas de deux*. (In this example Ferrère took a short cut by notating only the man's part and then indicating in words — "contrepas pour la femme" — that the woman does the same steps on the opposite foot.) In

some instances the Feuillet notation is augmented by small sketches and/or written descriptions of the action; see figure 8.3, part of another *pas de deux* from *Le Peintre*. At the beginning of the first frame a little sketch of the portrait shows that it is still behind the wife's back; during the next four measures she brings it forward to show to her husband and then smashes it over his head. The little box with the dot in the middle on the right-hand side of the frame shows the painter's head in the middle of the portrait. In the third frame of the same dance Ferrère writes "elle frappe des mains haute" (she claps her hands over her head) and notates this as well.

2) Floor patterns and step names: Ferrère's group dances are notated by showing the approximate floor patterns along with the names of the steps (see figure 9.1). The notation appears in a series of frames, each of which usually contains four or eight bars of choreography; hollow circles represent men, filled-in circles represent women. Each frame contains a number indicating how many measures of music that particular figure requires. In the fourth frame, for example, all twelve dancers are in motion. The annotation gives the names of the steps ("glissade à 3 pas," "assemblé," and "cont," which, in this context, probably means "contretemps de gavotte"); the number "4" in the lower right-hand corner indicates that this figure requires four bars of music.

3) Sketches and descriptions: For his purely pantomimic scenes Ferrère provides sketches illustrating the action that is taking place, supplementing his drawings with short descriptions. In figure 9.2 a series of frames shows the progress of the painter's portrait of his model, with annotations as to how many brush strokes he uses; for example, in the first frame "en 4 coups" indicates that four strokes — a half-note of music for each — are used to outline the model's head and upper torso.

4) Description alone: At one point in the *pas de trois* for the *sabotière* and the two woodcutters in *Les Bûcherons*, Ferrère abandons notation completely for eight bars, and simply describes the pantomimic action (see fig. 8.5).

Table 9.1, the outline of *Le Peintre amoureux de son modèle*, shows how these notational distinctions map onto the work's structure and onto the type of action or dance occurring. (See chap. 7 for synopses of both this ballet and the one outlined in table 9.2.) The three group dances (nos. 2, 10a, and 11) represent dance for its own sake, and Ferrère provides floor patterns and step names, his standard group dance notation. This style of notation is also used for number 3. In two dances (nos. 9 and 10b) the painter and his wife dance together, and the Feuillet notation conveys only the steps. However, in the *pas de deux* set to three consecutive pieces of music (nos. 6–8), their dancing mixes with gestures of various kinds,

Table 9.1: *Outline of* Le Peintre amoureux de son modele

| Heading | Key/Meter | Instrumentation | No. of bars/Form | Notation | Performers | Manuscript annotations, comments* |
|---|---|---|---|---|---|---|
| 1. Ouverture: Simphonie allegro | G; 2/4 | hn 1,2 vln 1,2 bass | 34; AA + coda | none | none | Sur la fin de l'ouverture le rideau se lève et représente la salle du peintre; plusieurs peuples arrivent chez le peintre en dansant. (At the end of the overture the curtain rises on the painter's studio; many people arrive dancing.) |
| 2. — | G; ₵ | hn 1,2 vln 1,2 bass | 48; AABB | floor patterns, step names | *figurants:* 6 men, 6 women | Pas de deux pantomime d'Italie; le peintre entre en dansant avec sa femme et continue sa pantomime. (*Pas de deux* in Italian pantomime; the painter enters dancing with his wife and continues his pantomime.) |
| 3. Allegretto | G; 6/8 | vln bass | 50; AABBCC ABCC' | floor patterns, step names | painter wife | |
| 4. Staccato | D; 3/4 | hn 1,2 vln 1,2 bass | 41; ABCDE | sketches, descriptions | painter servant model | Le peintre fait ranger son chevalet pour peindre sa maîtresse qui arrive dans l'intervalle; il la salue et la fait asseoir. (While the painter arranges his easel, in preparing to paint his mistress, she arrives; he greets her and seats her.) |

| 5. Largo | G; C | hn 1,2 vln 1,2 bass | 28; ABAC | sketches, descriptions | painter model wife servant | Il dessine le portrait de sa maîtresse en noir et rouge avec un pinceau. (He draws her portrait in black and red with his brush.) |
|---|---|---|---|---|---|---|
| 6. Tempo di minuetto | G; 3/8 | hn 1,2 vln bass | 64; AABACABA | Feuillet notation plus sketches, descriptions | painter wife | Le peintre danse avec sa femme. Pas de deux mis en grande chorégraphie par Auguste Ferrère. (The painter dances with his wife. *Pas de deux* notated by Auguste Ferrère.) |
| 7. Largo; Allegro | G; ¢ [2/4] G; 2/4 | ob 1,2 vln 1,2 bass | 4; A 20; B | Feuillet notation plus sketches, descriptions | painter wife | Elle lui montre le portrait et [le] lui casse sur la tête. Colère de la femme. Le mari se sauve avec le portrait à travers la tête sur le 2ième air suivant. (She shows him the portrait and smashes it over his head. The wife's rage. The husband exits with the portrait around his head to the second tune.) |
| 8. Andante | G; 3/4 | hn 1,2 vln 1,2 bass | 48; ABCABD | Feuillet notation plus sketches, descriptions | painter wife | Il arrive cherchant à s'excuser. (He enters seeking to apologize.) |
| 9. Andante | D; 2/4 | vln 1,2 bass | 56; AABACCA | Feuillet notation | painter wife | Ils dansent ensemble; l'homme commence. (They dance together; the man begins.) |

Table 9.1: *continued*

| Heading | Key/Meter | Instrumentation | No. of bars/Form | Notation | Performers | Manuscript annotations, comments* |
|---|---|---|---|---|---|---|
| 10a. Allegro | D; 2/4 | ob 1,2 vln 1,2 bass | 40; ABCDA' | floor patterns, step names | *figurants:* 4 couples | Plusieurs peuples entrent pour féliciter en dansant. (Many people enter dancing to congratulate the painter.) |
| 10b. | d; 2/4 | vln bass | 32; EEFE | floor patterns, step names | painter wife | Mineur pas seul. (Minor-mode section, solo for the wife.) |
| | D; 2/4 | ob 1,2 vln 1,2 bass | 40; ABCDA' | Feuillet notation | | L'homme seul sur le majeur de l'air. (Male solo to the major-mode section.) |
| | d; 2/4 | vln bass | 32; EEFE | | | Mineur la femme seule. (Solo for the woman to the minor-mode section.) |
| | D; 2/4 | ob 1,2 vln 1,2 bass | 46; ABCDA' + coda | | | Pas de deux. |
| 11. Contredanse générale | G; 2 | hn 1,2 vln bass | 144; AA [BBACCA] x4 | floor patterns, step names | *figurants:* 6 couples painter wife | Cette contredanse se joue toujours en rondeau jusqu'à ce qu'elle soit finie. (This contredanse is played in rondeau form until the dance is finished.) [The soloists enter at bar 81.] |

* These annotations appear as headings for the respective numbers; there are many additional annotations in the dance notations, particularly in the pantomime scenes. Ferrère's French has been modernized; translations are in parentheses.

and Ferrère combines Feuillet notation with various sketches and descriptions to communicate the pantomimic elements. The two remaining units (nos. 4–5) have almost no dancing per se, with the action communicated primarily via pantomime. The table also includes information about the musical structure, plus those annotations that appear in the manuscript as headings for the respective numbers. Ferrère's misspellings and grammatical errors have been corrected.

Table 9.2 outlines Ferrère's *Les Bûcherons et les sabotiers,* the work in which Cosimo Maranesi performed in Paris, probably with Bettina Buggiani (see chap. 7). The cast consists of a *sabotière* (a woman in wooden shoes), two men also dancing solo roles, and six couples in the roles of woodcutters and their wives. This ballet has less narrative content than *Le Peintre amoureux de son modèle;* what little there is (in nos. 1 and 4) serves primarily as a scaffolding for the competitive dancing between the main couple, both of them wearing wooden shoes (nos. 5–6). It was this kind of dance that Maranesi and Buggiani took on the road, as they performed across Europe.

Each ballet begins with an overture, during which, or at the end of which, the curtain rises.[9] The timing of the curtain signals a difference as to what happens next. If the curtain comes up during the overture, as it does in *La Réjouissance villageoise* and *Les Bûcherons,* it reveals a scene taking place in pantomime. If, on the other hand, the curtain rises after the overture is completed, as in *Le Peintre,* it reveals an empty stage that rapidly fills, as the *figurants* dance onto the stage. In works that start with pantomime, a group dance immediately follows, so that the function of the second piece of music — the one following the overture — is always that of a group dance. The Ferrère manuscript contains only four pantomime ballets, but if this small sample shows us the workings of two distinguishable dramatic conventions, then they are ones that anyone trying to put a ballet scenario together with its music should bear in mind.

Once the curtain rises, the succession of scenes proceeds without a break. Even though the music consists of a series of closed pieces, the emphasis is on continuity; Ferrère indicates movement of some sort for almost every bar of music. With one exception (the opening eight-bar phrase of the first duet in *Le Peintre*) the stage is never completely empty; there is always at least some overlap when characters enter and leave the stage in sequence. When the *figurants* enter from the wings, choreographed

---

9. In all four ballets Ferrère includes the rubric "le rideau se lève" to indicate precisely when the curtain rises, thus showing that these works were intended for a proscenium stage.

Table 9.2: *Outline of* Les Bûcherons et les sabotiers

| Heading | Key/Meter | Instrumentation | No. of bars/Form | Notation | Performers | Manuscript annotations, comments |
|---|---|---|---|---|---|---|
| 1. Ouverture | D; ¢ | hn 1,2 vln 1,2 bass | 64; AABB | sketches, descriptions | 12 *figurants*: 6 woodcutters 6 women | On lève le rideau sur la fin du 1er commencement; 12 mesures. (The curtain rises at the end of the first strain; 12 measures.) [Entire piece is in pantomime.] |
| 2. Andantino | G; 2/4 | vln 1,2 bass | 52; AABACA | floor patterns, step names | 12 *figurants* from no. 1 | [at end of choreography:] L'air suivant est encore pour le ballet et va tout de suite après celui-ci. (The following music [i.e., no. 3] is also for the *figurants* and comes immediately after this music.) |
| 3. Allegro | D; 2/4 | hn 1,2 vln 1,2 bass | 40; ABABA | floor patterns, step names | 12 *figurants* from no. 1 | |
| 4. Allegretto | G; 6/8 | ob 1,2 vln 1,2 bass | 48; AABBBAB* | Feuillet notation plus sketches, descriptions | soloists: 2 men 1 woman | Une paysanne en sabots vient chercher des copeaux. (A peasant woman in wooden shoes comes looking for wood shavings.) |
| 5. Largo | D; 2/4 | hn 1,2 vln 1,2 bass | 48; ABABAB | Feuillet notation plus sketches, descriptions | 1 woman 1 man (both from no. 4) | La sabotière danse seule. [Woman's solo, 32 bars; duet, 16 bars; both dancers are wearing wooden shoes.] |

| | | | | | | |
|---|---|---|---|---|---|---|
| 6a. Allegro | G; 3/4 | vln 1,2 bass | 48; AABABA | Feuillet notation plus occasional sketches and descriptions | same as no. 5 | Pas de deux. Il salue de la tête. Il demande la main; elle la donne; elle passe sous son bras; il la pousse. (He greets the woman by nodding. He asks for her hand; she gives it to him and passes under his arm; he pushes her.) |
| 6b. | g; 3/4 | ob 1,2 vln 1,2 bass | 64; [CCDD] x2 | | | Mineur; la femme seule. Mineur; l'homme danse seul. [Woman's and man's solo, each 32 bars.] |
| 6c. | G; 3/4 | vln 1,2 bass | 48; AABABA | | | Majeur; ils dansent ensemble. [At end]: Salue de la tête, les bras en guirlande. ([They] greet by nodding, arms intertwined.) |
| 7. Contredanse générale | D; 2/4 | hn 1,2 vln 1,2 bass | 136; AA [BACA] x3 BBA | floor patterns, step names | 12 *figurants* from no. 1 2 soloists from no. 5 | [Soloists enter at measure 81.] |

*In nos. 4 and 5 Ferrère has neglected to provide his usual meticulous indications showing how the choreography and dance go together — for example, the phrase "la 1ère reprise" might appear in the choreography to signal a *da capo* repetition of the music. In the score for no. 4 each strain has a repeat mark, and there is a *dal segno* sign at the end of the B section, so the solution shown above seems the most logical. However, since both A and B strains end on the tonic, the form could also be AABBAA, or even AABABA. In the score for no. 5 the A strain does not have a repeat sign, although it has an internal four-bar repeat. The B section does not have a repeat sign, which, when taken with the annotation "Da capo come sta," seems to indicate a repeat of the entire piece, as is shown in the table.

entrances are the norm; that is, they dance, not walk, onto the stage one couple at a time or in small groups. After the opening dance, the "protagonists" appear — or at least some of them, given that the episodic nature of several of these works means that more individuals may enter later. Ferrère does not normally notate the entrances of the solo dancers; their first notated steps coincide with the first beat of the music for their dance, which suggests that they walk into position — or get there in a manner that does not need to be choreographed — during the closing measures of the preceding piece.[10] Thus it is not clear from where within the performing space their entrance is made, although Ferrère frequently choreographs the exits of the soloists to one or the other sides of the stage at the end of a dance. Similarly, the ends of the group dances are also notated, either as a dance off stage, or as a choreographed retreat to the sides of the stage in order to free up the center.

Whereas the *figurants* often remain on stage to watch the soloists — and their presence provides a sense of continuity in these episodic ballets — the soloists may make frequent exits and re-entrances. In general they come on stage only to perform their dances and leave when they have finished. This, at least, is the case when they are performing formal dances; action scenes have a more fluid structure. But the choreographed exits into the wings mark a notable difference from the ends of earlier choreographies in Feuillet notation, when the dancers tend to retreat backward into their starting positions at the end of the dance. The exits in Ferrère's ballets do not always make dramatic sense (that is, an exit is not necessarily motivated by the plot, such as it is), but the exit of one dancer may serve to highlight the solo of the other and also provide an opportunity for the exiting dancer to take a breather out of the eyes of the audience. The paucity of choreographic documentation makes generalizations risky, but at the very least it can be said that this kind of behavior on the part of the solo dancers seems more in line with nineteenth-century ballet than with the one earlier ballet that survives in its entirety (from 1688), in which all the performers remain on stage during the entire duration of the work.[11]

10. In cases when the soloists were already on stage, the notation does occasionally indicate that they take up their positions during the last few bars of the previous dance, as in no. 8 in *Le Peintre*, where Ferrère wrote "il se prépare à danser" (he gets ready to dance).

11. See Rebecca Harris-Warrick and Carol G. Marsh, *Musical Theatre at the Court of Louis XIV: "Le Mariage de la Grosse Cathos"* (Cambridge: Cambridge University Press, 1994), especially 59–66. This mascarade was, however, performed in a large room, not on a proscenium stage, which may have affected how the performers used the space.

# Ferrère's Choreographic Style

The purpose of this section is to highlight the most salient features of Ferrère's choreographies, relative to what has been preserved in the notated works of other eighteenth-century choreographers. One problem, however, is that there is a large temporal gap between Ferrère's manuscript (1782) and the earlier theatrical choreographies in Favier or Feuillet notation, which date from 1688 to ca. 1725.[12] Moreover, whereas most of the earlier notations preserve dances in the noble style with only a small number from the comic realm (such as a few dances for peasants, three chaconnes for Harlequin, and, in Favier notation, one drunk dance), Ferrère's dances come from a different genre, the comic pantomime ballet, which has its own traditions that are not necessarily fully comparable. That said, Ferrère's notations do turn out to be legible to students of Feuillet notation and show a good deal of continuity with choreographies from the past, while at the same time exhibiting a number of features not present in the earlier preserved works. Our point of comparison is of necessity to the dances that were notated, but absence of notation does not mean that dance practices visible in Ferrère did not already have a long history. Lambranzi's 1716 book, with its many plates showing mostly grotesque dancers in the midst of performing, attests to the variety and ingenuity of comic dancing in the earlier part of the eighteenth century, even if it remains relatively imprecise as to the movements per se.[13] The remarks that follow do not aspire to anything like a complete comparison of the earlier theatrical notations with Ferrère, but aim to flag the general tendencies. Moreover, earlier chapters have already discussed many of the changes apparent in dance technique over time or between styles.

To what extent does Ferrère's choreographic style resemble that of Magri? Given the absence of notated dances by the Italian choreographer, any answer can only be partial. Ferrère's step vocabulary does appear to include many steps described by Magri, although their execution

---

12. A number of choreographies in Feuillet notation were published in the second half of the eighteenth century, but they are for the ballroom rather than the theater. See, for example, the dances in Magny's *Principes de chorégraphie* (Paris, 1765) For more details about these and the earlier notated choreographies, see LMC.

13. Gregorio Lambranzi, *Neue und curieuse theatralische Tantz-Schul* (Nuremberg: Johan Jacob Wolraub, 1716); trans. Friderica Derra de Moroda as *New and Curious School of Theatrical Dancing*, ed. Cyril W. Beaumont (New York: Dance Horizons, 1966). See illustrations from Lambranzi throughout this book, including figure 9.3.

may not have been identical. Ambiguity arises from the fact that Magri names his steps and describes their execution in words, whereas Ferrère either notates steps or names them but does not say anything about how they are done. Given the changes in dance technique between the era around 1700 when Feuillet's *Chorégraphie* was compiled and the third quarter of the century when Magri and Ferrère were active, the same terminology cannot be assumed to indicate the same movements. Moreover, not all the steps used by professional dancers had names; Magri himself alludes to the existence of unnamed steps and combinations,[14] besides the many to which he does give names. Appendix 7 indexes all of the steps Magri discusses in his *Trattato,* in addition to the other dance terms he mentions.[15]

Ferrère's fondness for beaten steps and virtuosity for its own sake seems in keeping with Magri's preferences and with the Italian practices described by Kathleen Hansell in chapter 1. Magri gives numerous examples of steps to which *battimenti* may be added, and Ferrère's notations also show that steps familiar from earlier in the century were often enriched with added technical challenges;[16] for instance, almost every cadential *pas assemblé* in Ferrère is notated with a beat, and many other steps include beats as well. As Magri himself points out, "We moderns do not measure the cadence with the steps as did the ancients, for whom each step occupied one bar. [We sometimes take several bars for one step, and sometimes put several steps into one bar.] One *ambuettè* used to be done in one bar of ternary time; in our time there is nobody who does not repeat two or three in one bar. In two bars, also of ternary time in *chaconne* tempo, one *jeté,* three *battements* and an *assemblé sur place,* were done; now in the same time with the sequence of the same steps, up to eight or ten *battements* are repeated."[17] Moreover, *entrechats* are frequently employed,

14. Magri/Skeaping 131; Magri, *Trattato,* 1:95.

15. Two books by Edmund Fairfax, *The Styles of Eighteenth-Century Ballet* (Lanham, MD: Scarecrow, 2003) and "The Technique of Eighteenth-Century Ballet" (in preparation), pull together a great deal of information found in primary sources from across Europe and across the century.

16. This is not to say that earlier dancers did not enrich their steps as well. Some Feuillet notations even hint that the notation has been simplified from the way the dance was performed.

17. Magri/Skeaping, 61; Magri, *Trattato,* 1:23–24: "Noi moderni non misuriamo la cadenza co' *passi,* come gli antichi, che ogni passo occupava una battuta. Noi facciam correre più battute in un passo, e mettiamo più passi in una battuta. Facevansi que' un' *Ambuettè* in una battuta di tempo trinario, a tempi nostri non v'è chi in una battuta, non ne raddoppia due, et tre. In due battute di tempo pur ternario, in tempo di *Ciaccona,* si faceva un *Jettè,* tre *battiment,* un' *assemblé sotto al corpo* ; ora nell'istesso tempo con la ligazione de' medesimi passi i battimenti si raddoppiano fino ad otto, a dieci." (We have corrected the translation of the second sentence.)

by women as well as men, and by the *figurants* as well as by the soloists.[18] *Entrechats quatre* or even *entrechats six*, for example, appear in a number of Ferrère's dances for women, whereas only one baroque choreography gives even a *demi-entrechat* to a woman.[19] This is only one aspect of the change in the technical demands placed on the women, who now perform steps that had been assigned to men in the earlier repertoire. The men's solo dances underwent a parallel development, and Ferrère's dances for men remain more virtuosic than the solos for women. These notations support the many comments from the period (some of them disapproving) that dancing had grown flashier as the eighteenth century progressed and that dancers were being judged more and more by their technical prowess.

The nature of grotesque dancing sometimes put additional technical demands on the dancers. Wooden shoe dances were a staple of the period, and there are two such in Ferrère, for men and women both. These dances capitalize on the noise that the shoes make, incorporating stamps and shuffle steps that bear some relationship to Appalachian clogging as it is practiced today (see chap. 6, where Linda Tomko discusses one of these dances). Both also use the *tortillé* step, which weaves the foot in and out, perhaps as a way of calling attention to the dancers' footwear, and both incorporate a step using bent knees. In *La Réjouissance villageoise* the performer not only wears wooden shoes but uses his three-foot-long pole as a baton, twirling it, throwing it in the air, tossing it from one hand to the other, and beating it on the soles of his shoes. However, during the most difficult passages involving the baton, the dancer has either very simple steps or else stands still. Two other novelty dances are found in the Ferrère manuscript. The tambourine dance, a male solo that occurs in the second intèrmede of *Les Trois Cousines*, is similar to the *sabotier* dance in that the dancer uses the tambourine as a prop with which to do tricks while he is dancing—beating it in quick succession against his free hand, his elbows, knees, heels, and toes, and also throwing it into the air and catching it. The tambourine antics are not continuous, but alternate with passages of difficult footwork. In the "Turkish Slave" the dancer enters with chains on his hands and feet, and during

18. *Entrechats* are an example of how ballet terminology has changed over the centuries. The *entrechats* notated by Ferrère are what Feuillet called the "entre-chat droit" (though Ferrère uses a shorthand version of the notation), which is very similar to the modern *entrechat quatre* (or *six*), beginning and ending in closed position. What Feuillet calls the "entre-chat à 4" is the modern *échappé battu*.

19. L'Abbé's "Passagalia of Venus and Adonis" (LMC 6580).

the first thirty-two bars of the choreography he explores the limits of his movements while chained. After the chains are removed the movement quality changes as the dancer revels in his new freedom with outstretched arms, leaps to wide second position, and *entrechats*.[20]

The way steps are built into phrases represents another point of difference from early-eighteenth-century choreographies. Although no thorough study of choreographic phrase structures in either period has as yet been carried out, dancers who have reconstructed parts of the Ferrère manuscript have remarked that Ferrère's *enchaînements* (the way he combines individual steps into longer sequences) feel more like nineteenth-century ballet than baroque dance, as does his tendency to perform a sequence twice, using opposite feet on the repeat. Another characteristic of Ferrère's style is that he may repeat the same step several times in a row, something that also appears in nineteenth-century ballet, but almost never in the surviving baroque theatrical dances. In some cases, the fact of repetition is itself an aspect of the virtuosity. For example, in one of the *pas de deux* for the painter and his wife, each dancer has a solo that includes extensive repetitions; the painter does a sequence involving a *pas tombé* with jumps seven times in a row, and in her solo the wife has a six-measure passage in which she performs multiple *entrechats*. (See an outline of the entire *pas de deux* in table 9.5. The passages in question occur in secs. 3 and 4.) Magri alludes to step repetitions as well, mentioning, for example, both the *jetté battuto* and the *brisé* as steps that may be repeated "as many times as one wishes." As with other features of Ferrère's choreographies, one wonders if this kind of repetition came out of Italian traditions, or whether it had long belonged to the *lingua franca* of ballet as it was practiced across Europe, but simply had been not been notated earlier.

Ferrère's floor patterns have a number of points in common with those familiar from Feuillet. The orientation is frontal and symmetrical, operating around an invisible line that bisects the stage from front to back; although individual figures within a dance may use diagonal lines, the imaginary axis for the orientation of a dance never goes from an upstage corner to the one diagonally opposite, as was to happen in the next century. This general spatial principle applies to the group dances as well as to the solos, *pas de deux,* and *pas de trois.* The usual kinds of symmetry still apply and in the "formal" dances the dancers do the same steps at the same time: there is no differentiation in this kind of *pas de deux* be-

---

20. Lambranzi's book (see n13) also shows dancers with poles or in chains; see, for example, pt. 2, plates 21 and 40.

tween steps for the man and steps for the woman when they are dancing simultaneously. In scenes involving action, however, whether expressed via pantomime or danced steps, the drama overrides formal considerations and the dancers may perform different movements simultaneously or use the space more freely. In *Les Galants villageois*, for instance, the shepherdess has a solo and is then joined by the shepherd, who dances in such a way that she cannot see him. During the time he is attempting to hide from her, they are both dancing, but are doing different steps and are not using symmetrical floor patterns. In *Le Peintre amoureux de son modèle*, during the dramatic confrontation between the painter and his wife (see the discussion in chap. 8 in this volume), there are several instances in which one person dances while the other gestures or performs particularly expressive (and different) dance steps. The floor patterns adhere to the demands of the action.

Near the opening of the same ballet, when the painter and his wife dance together for the first time and before her suspicions have been aroused (no. 3 in table 9.1), Ferrère gives the dance the heading of "Pas [de] deux pantomime d'Italie." What Ferrère means by "pantomime from Italy" is not at all clear, especially since this is the only place he uses such a designation and this particular scene does not appear different in character from the other scenes that involve gestures in various ways.[21] At one end of the spectrum the characters mime and do not dance at all, as happens in numbers 4 and 5 of *Le Peintre*, when the painter sets up his studio and begins the portrait. More commonly, the mime and/or gestures are integrated with dance (as in the unit labeled "pantomime d'Italie); this can happen in one of several ways. Sometimes the two modes of expression happen consecutively, as in the rage scene from the same ballet where there are five bars of mime followed by dancing. In another instance the two are simultaneous, as when one character dances while the other mimes (as at the end of the minuet, no. 6). It also happens that one person may gesture or express a strong emotion while simultaneously dancing, as when the wife in *Le Peintre* waves a clenched fist over her head to express anger or when the shepherdess in *Les Galants villageois* appears sad when she cannot locate her sweetheart (Ferrère wrote "elle est triste" into the manuscript at this point). Not all the emotions need be negative:

---

21. One hypothesis is that in "Italian pantomime" gestures were more important than precise floor patterns, and so Ferrère chose to use a particular notation style — sketches and step names — in order to reflect a particular movement style. This dance is not, however, the only one in the manuscript to be so notated.

the *sabotière* in *Les Bûcherons* waving her hat over her head is apparently expressing her confidence in her dancing. A more subtle kind of expressive gesture seems to be indicated by Ferrère's sketches of face silhouettes that frequently accompany the soloists' dance notation; here the implication seems to be that the dancer turns to stare (or glare) at his or her partner in a way that goes beyond the normal interaction between soloists.

Another type of gesture that Ferrère mentions, but whose content he does not specify, is the greeting. Many manuscript annotations indicate that one character "salue" another, something that happens particularly between the soloists and the *figurants* when someone enters or leaves the stage. Such a greeting may serve as a transition between numbers, as when in *Le Peintre* the *figurants* enter, framing the soloists, following which they all greet each other (transition from no. 10a to 10b). A similar event takes place in *La Réjouissance villageoise* after the two Savoyards have danced. Here the *figurants* move from their "observation posts" on the sides of the stage to form a curved line upstage, framing the soloists, who then move downstage. Next comes a choreographed two-bar greeting by the *figurants:* the manuscript reads, "Ils saluent des pieds, puis des mains," and the sketch shows the *figurants* stepping sideways toward the center and then backward on the diagonal, presumably indicating that they are bowing and gesturing. Making the onstage social interactions visible to the audience in the theater was clearly important for Ferrère.

# The Music

As was the case in the dance notations preserved from earlier in the century, there is a close correspondence in Ferrère's works between music and dance. However, styles had evolved since the start of the eighteenth century, as had practices in regard to how the two arts related to each other. This section looks at the music in the Ferrère manuscript; the next examines how the music fits with the dancing.

One of the most valuable features of the Ferrère manuscript is that music is provided for all of the choreographies. The music for each dance immediately precedes the dance notation, and Ferrère has taken great pains to indicate precisely the correspondence between dance figures and strains of music. Another welcome feature is that unlike earlier Feuillet notations, in which only a melody is supplied, almost all of Ferrère's dances have a bass line, and the majority have additional parts as well. For the four ballets, his preferred scoring (sixteen of thirty-three pieces) has two violin parts, unfigured bass, and two horns. Eight pieces are scored for two violins and bass, without horns, and in five pieces oboes replace the horns. Elsewhere, Ferrère includes parts for flute and for viola. Ferrère does not indicate whether any of the parts were doubled — that is, whether this music was intended for orchestra or for a chamber ensemble. Records from the Parisian theaters with which Ferrère Senior had contact when he was in Paris in the early 1750s, however, provide an idea of the instrumental forces Ferrère probably had in mind. In 1751, the Théâtre Italien in Paris had at its disposal seven violins, one cello, one oboe, one flute, one bassoon, two horns, and one *tambourin* (drummer). The violins were undoubtedly divided into two sections and may also have included violas (the term "violon" often refers to the entire violin family). In 1752 the Opéra Comique had nine violins, three basses (cellos, *contrebasses,* or a mixture), two oboes, and two bassoons.[22] Forces such as these would be perfectly adequate to the demands of Ferrère's scores, which show that he varied the scoring of the wind instruments from piece to piece (see the instrumentation column in tables 9.1 and 9.2).

No composers are identified in the manuscript, but at least some of the music was borrowed from pre-existing works. This pasticcio technique — stringing together pieces from a variety of sources by a variety of composers — was accepted practice for theatrical dance music in the mid-eighteenth century and was to remain so well into the nineteenth century, so it is no surprise to encounter it here.[23] In the case of the entr'acte dances that Ferrère provided for Florent Dancourt's play *Les Trois Cousines,* he reused some of the music Jean Claude Gillier had composed for the play's premiere in 1700, but other pieces came from elsewhere. To date, three of the pieces from his four ballets have been identified: the *contredanse générale* in *Le Peintre amoureux de son modèle* was borrowed from Jean-Philippe Rameau's opera-ballet *Les Fêtes d'Hébé* (1739), a tambourin comes from the same composer's *Castor et Pollux* (1737), and the *sabotière* in *Les Bûcherons* dances to a mid-century vaudeville tune;[24] it is

22. *Almanach des spectacles de Paris* (1752), 72, and *Nouveau Calendrier des spectacles de Paris* (1753), 150.

23. Regarding pasticcio technique in other ballet repertoires, see Bruce Alan Brown, *Gluck and the French Theatre in Vienna* (Oxford: Clarendon, 1991), 163–64; Kathleen Kuzmick Hansell, "Theatrical Ballet and Italian Opera," *Opera on Stage,* vol. 5, The History of Italian Opera (Chicago: University of Chicago Press, 2002), 220; and Marian Smith, *Ballet and Opera in the Age of Giselle* (Princeton, NJ: Princeton University Press, 2000), 101–21.

24. The *contredanse* concludes the third entrée of Rameau's opera-ballet; Ferrère transposed the music from E major to G major. Bruce Alan Brown recognized the vaudeville tune as coming from Favart's *opéra-comique Raton et Rosette* of 1753, where it is identified by the title (*timbre*) "Dans un bocage frais."

possible that more such borrowings will come to light. Among the music that remains unidentified, some of it looks to have been composed in all its instrumental parts by a trained composer, whereas some looks as if the melody line alone might have been composed or acquired, and then a bass and harmonization supplied by someone with lesser musical skills. It is possible that Ferrère himself either composed or harmonized some of the music, as many dancers — Angiolini among them — were trained in music. However, if Ferrère was the one who oversaw the music that appears in the manuscript, then it must be said that his musical skills were not highly developed.[25]

Given the subject matter of Ferrère's ballets, it is not surprising to find that the music is, in general, lighthearted and cheerful. Three contrasting melodic styles appear frequently. In what might be described as an instrumental style, the violin part is full of triple and quadruple stops alternating with sixteenth-note runs or arpeggiated figures. This style is used for the overtures and for some of the choreographies for the soloists (see mus. ex. 9.1a). Melodies for the group dances are less virtuosic and use a narrower range of notes; they tend to be singable, or at least have an easily remembered melodic structure, factors that suggest they might have been borrowed from the vast supply of vaudevilles with which Ferrère would have been familiar (see mus. ex. 9.1b). Other pieces adhere to the *galant* instrumental style prevailing at mid-century (see mus. ex. 9.1c). In all three styles regular four- and eight-bar phrases predominate; modulations other than to the dominant or relative major are rare. The predominance of major keys is typical of early classical music and the key choices are conservative: each ballet is restricted to two or three major keys, with excursions to their parallel minors, and nearly half of the pieces are in G major. In general there is no attempt to use keys to suggest affect; instead, characterization and emotion are suggested by musical gestures and motives. As an example, consider the *colère* scene in *Le Peintre,* where the wife smashes the painting over the painter's head. Instead of moving to G minor, as one might expect for such a dramatic moment, the music stays in G major, the key of the preceding piece. The wife's anger is expressed in a number of musical gestures, including the

---

25. Although Ferrère's melodies are quite serviceable, and occasionally even memorable, his bass lines seem to have been constructed by someone with no musical imagination and only a rudimentary knowledge of harmony. They seldom leave the safety of the chord's root, and rarely participate in any motivic interchanges with the melody. In addition, a number of notes in the bass line are simply wrong. Similarly, Angiolini's talents favored choreography over musical composition; see Hansell, "Theatrical Ballet," 224.

Musical example 9.1a: Ferrère, *La Réjouissance villageoise*, no. 8, mm. 20–28

Musical example 9.1b: Ferrère, *La Réjouissance villageoise*, no. 9, mm. 1–8

Musical example 9.1c: Ferrère, *Les Bûcherons et les sabotiers*, no. 4, mm. 1–8

upward rushing scales, the rapid arpeggiated chords, and the irregular and unbalanced phrases. If, in fact, Ferrère did not compose this piece he must have commissioned someone to write it specifically for this ballet.[26]

Conspicuous by their absence from Ferrère's four pantomime ballets are pieces labeled as generic French dances—rigaudons, passepieds, and the like. Most of the pieces have Italian tempo markings (Allegro, Andante, etc.) regardless of musical style. Only one piece mentions a French dance, and even there the heading is in Italian: this is the Tempo di minuetto in *Le Peintre* (see no. 6 in table 9.1), which is part of a *pas de deux* for the painter and his wife. Another triple-meter piece, this one in *Les Bûcherons*, can also be seen as a minuet, even though it is marked Allegro. Like the Tempo di minuetto it makes use of an occasional minuet step, but both choreographies are dominated by the difficult and varied step vocabulary typical of Ferrère's dances for soloists. Nor does either dance make use of the floor patterns typical of the ballroom minuet. Other parts of the manuscript do have a few French dances, most notably two tambourins—a dance type that occurs frequently in the works of Rameau. In fact, one of the two tunes Ferrère uses was borrowed from *Castor et Pollux*. Both of these dances are virtuoso male solos; they are the only surviving examples of theatrical tambourin choreographies.[27] Fer-

---

26. The same assumption can be made for the painting scene, where the musical gestures perfectly match the pantomime gestures; see musical example 9.2.

27. There is one other tambourin notation, a ballroom dance by Pécour from the annual collection for 1719: LMC 1380.

rère's preference for Italian tempo markings for his dance pieces was shared by other composers of pantomime ballet music during this period. See, for example, the Mannheim ballets from the 1760s and 1770s by Christian Cannabich, Georg Joseph Vogler, and others, where French dance types such as the chaconne are included, but where the majority of the pieces are identified by Italian tempo markings — even though the choreographers were mostly French.[28] Magri also alludes to dances identified by their tempo marking in his chapter on meter.[29] This preference for tempo markings means, alas, that the titles of the dance pieces tell us nothing about the choreography; the examples from Ferrère of how dances are set to such music are thus extremely valuable.

They are also valuable on structural grounds: the Ferrère manuscript, which allows us to see exactly what music goes with every part of each choreography, reveals that the formal structures of the dance music were much more flexible than anyone would guess by looking at the score alone. By today's conventions, a musician would expect to play a binary dance piece as AABB, by taking both its repeats, or a rondeau as ABACA or AABACA. Ferrère's dances show both that there is no such thing as a standard repeat structure for the familiar formal patterns (a rondeau might be played AABACCA or AABACABA) and that short strains of music can be combined in ways that build other kinds of structures. Straightforward binary and ternary forms (AABB, AABBCC) occur in only four of his thirty-three pieces, and simple rondeaux are also infrequent; instead, Ferrère often repeats the initial strain of a piece somewhere within it and again at the end — somewhat in the manner of a rondeau — but does not follow a predictable pattern. Ferrère also includes through-composed pieces, but usually these are comprised of a series of eight-bar strains; in this case the regularity of phrase structure creates the effect of a rondeau minus the repetition of the refrain. In addition, there are more complex formal structures in which two binary or rondeau sections are joined together with a *da capo* of the first section; and for his longest choreographies he strings several of these *da capo* pieces together. Some of Ferrère's structures are outlined in table 9.3; other examples may be seen in tables 9.1 and 9.2. These show not only that there

---

28. Chief among the French choreographers who worked at Mannheim were François André Bouqueton (fl. 1754–ca.1771) and Etienne Lauchery (fl. 1772–78). Regarding the scores of these ballets, see n34.

29. Chapter 6; Magri/Skeaping, 60–62; Magri, *Trattato*, 1:22–26.

Table 9.3: *Musical structure in selected Ferrère dances*

| No. | Form | Bars per strain | Total bars | Description |
|-----|------|-----------------|------------|-------------|
| 1. [I/3] | AABBCCABCC' | 8/4/4 [i.e., A=8, B=4, C=4] | 50 | *Pas de deux* for the painter and his wife |
| 2. [I/10] | [ABCDA'EEFE] x2 ABCDA' + coda | All strains are 8 bars; coda is 6 bars | 190 | *Figurants* followed by *pas de deux* for the painter and his wife |
| 3. [II/2] | AABACABA | 8/8/8 | 64 | Dance for *figurants* from *Les Galants villageois* |
| 4. [IV/2] | [AABAAC] x2 | 4/8/8 | 64 | Dance for *figurants* from *La Réjouissance villageoise* |
| 5. [IV/5] | ABABABCCDDABA EEFFF' GHIG'I' JJKKJLLJ + coda | 8/8/8/8 8/16/4 8/8/8/16/8 8/4/4/2 | 254 | *Pas de trois* from *La Réjouissance villageoise* |

are more repeats than one might expect but that the patterns of what gets repeated are unpredictable.

An important observation results from identifying Ferrère's musical structures: if only the music — minus the dance notation — had survived, we would have little inkling either of the complexity of his formal structures or of the lengths of the pieces. The 160-bar *pas de deux* in *Les Bûcherons et les sabotiers* is built from only four eight-bar strains of music, repeated according to the following formula: AABABA CCDD CCDD AABABA (the A and B strains are in G major, the C and D strains in G minor). The *contredanses générales* are particularly prone to expansion, where, for example, 16 bars of music can be expanded by means of repeats to 144 bars of dance.[30] Repetition is, of course, an economical way of expanding a limited amount of music to meet the needs of the choreography, and Ferrère's additive approach to musical structure suggests that practical considerations took precedence over regularity in formal designs. Presumably if Ferrère had mounted one of his works in a large theater, where he

30. The dance in question, the *contredanse générale* in *Le Peintre*, consists of three strains of music — A, B, C — which are eight, four, and four bars in length. The repeat scheme for the dance is as follows: AA [ BBACCA] x4.

needed more music to get people around the stage, he could simply have added another repeat of one of the eight-bar phrases.[31] At the very least, his examples provide a useful reminder that middle- to late-eighteenth-century theatrical dance music (by composers such as Rameau, Cannabich, or Gluck) might have lasted considerably longer than it appears in the score.

## The Relationship of Dance and Music

For people interested in understanding pantomime ballets from the past, one of the problems they encounter is how to put the scenario together with the score — assuming both such documents survive in the first place. The survival issue has to do with the circumstances of a work's performance: if anything at all was published for the benefit of the audience (by no means always the case), it was a scenario. With only a few exceptions, ballet music remained in manuscript,[32] for use in the theater, and much of it has been lost. Only a little of what survives has been published in modern editions, such as Gluck's music for Angiolini's reform ballets *Sémiramis* and *Don Juan* or Jean Joseph Rodolphe's music for the Stuttgart premiere of Noverre's *Médée et Jason* (1763),[33] although there are encouraging steps underway toward making more ballet music available. The ongoing series *Ballet Music from the Mannheim Court,* for example, includes scores by Christian Cannabich, Carl Joseph Toeschi, and others composed during the 1760s and 1770s.[34] But even when a modern researcher

---

31. Already in the dances in Feuillet notation there are numerous instances of music needing to be repeated in order to accommodate the choreography, as, for instance, "La Mariée" by Pécour (LMC 5360), which must be played AABBAABB. Similarly, Lambranzi's annotations for the dances shown in his plates often suggest that multiple repetitions were necessary: "Two peasant boys begin to dance. When the air has been played once, two peasant men enter and laugh at them." The description continues for another three sentences (pt. 1, plate 11, translated by Derra de Moroda; see n13).

32. The most notable exception is the six volumes of ballet music, composed for the Théâtre Italien in Paris, that Jean-Joseph Mouret published during the 1730s; for a list of their contents see Renée Viollier, *Jean-Joseph Mouret: Le Musicen des Grâces* (Paris: Librairie Fleury, 1950), 221–25.

33. Both Gluck ballets were edited by Richard Engländer and published in ser. 2, vol. 1, of Christoph Willibald Gluck, *Sämtliche Werke* (Kassel: Bärenreiter, 1966). Facsimiles of the scenarios, along with Angiolini and Ranieri di Calzabigi's *Dissertation sur les ballets pantomimes* (Vienna, 1765), appear in a separate volume: ser. 7, supp., vol. 1 (Kassel: Bärenreiter, 1995). *Médée et Jason*, edited by Hermann Abert and revised by Hans Joachim Moser, was published in vols. 43–44 of *Denkmäler der deutscher Tonkunst*; the scenario is on li–liii, the score on 243ff.

34. The volumes are part of *Recent Researches in the Music of the Classical Era* published by A-R Editions; to date, nine ballets have been published in four volumes (45, 47, 52, and 57). Five more bal-

has access to both a scenario and a score, it is often problematic to fit the two together. How does a one-paragraph description of the action map onto a dozen short pieces all marked Allegro or Andante? A scenario never provides any remark as concrete as "the village children play hide-and-seek to a lively Allegro in G major filled with 16th-note arpeggios," and only occasionally does a score have a descriptive heading ("Air for the shepherds") or an annotation in the music as to the action. When scenarios or score annotations do survive, as is the case for several of the Mannheim ballets, it is at least possible to see the correspondences between music and story line in a general way. When the music is descriptive enough, it may become possible to construct plausible and more specific hypotheses as to which actions it accompanied; see, in this context, Bruce A. Brown's discussion of some of Gluck's ballet music in chapter 3.[35] But even those occasional musical passages that can be anchored to the action still leave many others in doubt.

One very great virtue of the Ferrère manuscript is that it is possible to see exactly what music goes with which dance steps and gestures. It thus provides useful principles that can be brought to bear on ballets for which no choreography survives. Whereas Ferrère's models do not by any means provide a template for resolving all the music-dance relationship problems that come up in pantomime ballets — not least because their musical and dramatic range is quite limited — they do help on both the large and small levels.

Even a cursory look at the manuscript reveals that Ferrère considered it important to specify what actions go with which music. This is not just a matter of matching structural points in the music to structural points in the dance, although that kind of connection was crucial to Ferrère, but his concern operates on the smaller level as well. At least some of what Ferrère was up to has a long history: in Feuillet notation the correspondence between each measure of music and each measure of dance is clear, and conventions governed the rhythm of the steps within the measure. But Ferrère notates this level of correspondence for the pantomime as well. For instance, when the artist paints his model, the little sketches in the manuscript showing the progress of the portrait are keyed very precisely to the music (see fig. 9.2). Most of the gestures require two bars

---

lets are in preparation. An important article by Sibylle Dahms, "Ballet Reform in the Eighteenth Century and Ballet at the Mannheim Court," appears in volume 45, ix–xxiii.

35. See also Brown's discussion of how the scenarios and scores of *Sémiramis* and *Don Juan* may fit together in *Gluck and the French Theatre in Vienna*, 317–21 and 338–41.

Musical example 9.2: Ferrère, *Le Peintre amoureux de son modèle*, no. 5, mm. 1–4

of music, two of them require one, and one longer sequence takes four. (The music is in common time with a tempo of Largo.) The fact that every time the painter wields his brush he is said to make four strokes on the portrait, when taken into account with the nature of the musical line in these measures, strongly suggests that his brushstrokes are operating on the level of the half note, two per bar, in an even rhythm (see mus. ex. 9.2). This kind of literal connection between gesture and musical rhythm also appears in Dehesse's pantomime ballet *Les Bûcherons* for the Théâtre Italien (see app. 5), where the curtain rises on a scene showing woodcutters sawing trees in time to the music.

In the cases just cited, what seems to be required of the music is that it provide the right kind of rhythmic frame, both allowing the gestures to be synchronized with the music and supplying the right phrase structure for changes in the action. In the painting scene, the start of the portrait operates across eight measures, that is, the first statement of the A music. When the painter goes to adjust the angle of his model's head and get a new color ("il va lui [ar]ranger la tête, revient et prend de la couleur"), these actions occupy the four bars of the B music. He returns to his painting where the A music repeats, but after two measures his wife enters and begins to get suspicious, stamping her foot at the end of the strain. A key point in the action—the fear of the model who runs offstage—coincides with the start of the C section; as this phrase continues the painter hides the portrait beneath a landscape and his wife now appears appeased. But whereas the important actions coincide with structural points in the music, the music's character does not reflect the change in the emotional climate. Rather, it retains the same affect as when the painter first began his portrait, still moving in a period of eight measures divided into balanced antecedent and consequent phrases. It seems that for Ferrère, musical and choreographic structure need to be coordinated (as a further example, when the painter and his wife switch out of pantomime mode and begin to dance together, a new piece of music begins), but there appears to be no requirement that the music paint the action—at least not as a general rule. The character of a piece needs to be appropriate to the overall context, but its melody and harmony do not express the action on a measure-by-measure basis. Nor does Ferrère's music reflect different simultaneous actions; during the Tempo di minuetto of the extended *pas de deux* that follows the pantomime scene just mentioned, the painter continues to dance while his wife switches into pantomime. Perhaps a sophisticated composer could have used contrapuntal lines to suggest the difference in the actions by the two protagonists: some of Rameau's dance music suggests that there may be more than one thing happening either simultaneously or in rapid succession, and the pantomime ballet scores of composers such as Gluck and Starzer contain passages that aim to paint action in a considerably more expressive way.[36] However, this level of explicitness between melodic or harmonic construction on the one hand and action on the other does not feature in the music Ferrère provided—or had at his disposal—for these particular pantomime ballets.

By and large Ferrère makes use of musical structures that have built-in repeats of various kinds (see table 9.3), but such a structure does not preclude progression in the action. In other words, the structure of the music matters, but a musical repeat does not stand in the way of continuing the forward motion of the action; a repetition of a phrase of music does not bring about a literal repetition in the choreography. (This practice dates back at least as far as the theatrical dances notated starting in 1688, which are generally set to binary music but always through choreographed.) The principle applies whether the dance is for its own sake (e.g., the dance of reconciliation between the painter and his wife at the end of the ballet) or whether it is pantomimic, and it means that there is no impediment to setting action scenes to binary or other types of pieces that repeat. To take but one example, in *La Réjouissance villageoise* a pantomime scene in which two soldiers hunt frantically for their stolen wine bottles, accusing various people of having taken them, is set to a standard binary piece (see table 9.4). Moreover, among the pantomime ballet music that survives, much of it consists of binary pieces, as in Gluck's

36. Toward the end of the program accompanying his ballet *Le Festin de pierre* (also known as *Don Juan;* see n33), Angiolini praised the expressivity of Gluck's music: "Gluck has grasped perfectly the awfulness of the action. He has sought to express the passions that enter in and the horror that reigns during the catastrophe. Music is essential to pantomimes; it is the music that speaks, we only gesture . . . It would be almost impossible to make ourselves understood without the music, and the more it is appropriate to what we wish to express, the more we make ourselves intelligible." ([Gluck] a saisi parfaitement le terrible de l'Action. Il a tâché d'exprimer les passions qui y jouent, & l'épouvante qui regne dans la catastrophe. La Musique est essentielle aux Pantomimes: c'est elle qui parle, nous ne faisons que les gestes . . . Il nous serait presque impossible de nous faire entendre sans la Musique, & plus elle est appropriée à ce que nous voulons exprimer, plus nous nous rendons intelligibles.)

Table 9.4: *Structure of the* pas de trois *for two soldiers and a woman from* La Réjouissance villageoise

| No. | Music | Form | Total bars | Performers | Comments |
|-----|-------|------|-----------|-----------|----------|
| 1a. | Allegretto D; 2/4 | ABABAB 8/8/8/8/8/8 | 48 | 2 soldiers | Soldier 1 solo (16 bars); solo repeated by soldier 2; duet. |
| 1b. | | CCDD 8/8/8/8 | 32 | As no. 1a | Drinking scene: pantomime. |
| 1c. | | ABA | 24 | 2 soldiers woman | The soldiers continue their duet and the woman enters. |
| 2 | Andantino d; 3/4 | EEFFF′ 8/8/16/16/4 | 52 | 2 soldiers woman | Soldiers discover that bottles and glasses are missing; accuse the villagers of taking them; woman reenters. |
| 3 | Andante G; 2/4 | GHIG′I′ 8/8/8/16/8 | 48 | As no. 2 | Formal dance. |
| 4 | Allegro D; 2/4 | JJKKJLLJ + coda 8/8/4/4/8/4/ 4/8/2 | 50 | As no. 2 | Formal dance continued. |

music for the ballet *Les Corsaires*, some pieces from which are discussed by Bruce Alan Brown in chapter 3.

Musicologists working with ballet scores from the second half of the eighteenth century often assume that through-composed pieces were intended to accompany pantomime and that binary forms signal dance for its own sake. Ferrère's examples disprove such a simplistic view, as does the sheer quantity of structured dance music composed in binary or rondeau forms for ballets whose scenarios are action packed. That said, when a piece of music is through composed, there does seem to be action going on. In *Le Peintre*, the only two pieces that are through composed (nos. 4 and 7 in table 9.1) accompany scenes that are, in the first instance, entirely in pantomime (the arrival of the model as the painter gets every-thing set up) and, in the second, the dramatic high point of the ballet, during which the wife discovers the nude portrait of the model, smashes it across her husband's head, and — in dance steps — chases him out of the room. Thus a more accurate view of the relationship between musi-cal structures and action in a ballet would acknowledge that whereas a through-composed piece *does* indicate that some kind of action is happening, a piece with a regular structure may do so as well.

However, as this last example and many others in the Ferrère manuscript show, the reality of these ballets is still more complicated, in that action does not necessarily equate to pantomime alone. One of the most important observations that can be made from a study of Ferrère's ballets is that dance and pantomime are not two distinct modes of performance that are confined to separate sections of the ballet; rather, there is often a fluidity of movement styles within a single dance. A clear distinction between dance and pantomime may have existed in Noverre's serious mythological ballets (although there is no dance notation to show what happened in practice), but it is decidedly not the case in Ferrère's works. In this and in previous chapters we have already encountered several instances where two characters are engaged in different simultaneous activities or go in and out of dancing within a single piece of music.[37] In yet another example, this one from *La Réjouissance villageoise*, the *sabotier* and four village women move primarily in pantomime but with some dance steps included; the jaunty 6/8 music in rondeau form with regular phrases would be equally appropriate for a contredanse.

The 254-bar *pas de trois* from *La Réjouissance villageoise*, in which the two soldiers are enjoying a drink together until a village woman steals their wine, may serve as an example of how this fluidity works in practice. The action moves easily between pantomime and dance until the final all-danced section, after the three have made peace. The entire dance is notated by rough sketches for the floor patterns and a corresponding list of steps and/or pantomimic gestures for each sketch.

This *pas de trois* is set to four different pieces of music, each with its own repeat structure. As is generally the case in Ferrère's dances, the structural points of dance and music mostly coincide, although there is some flexibility on this point. At the start of the dance the first soldier enters with a bottle in his hand and performs a sixteen-bar solo to the two strains AB; when the second soldier enters with his own bottle, he does the same solo to the same music while the first one watches. (This is a rare

---

37. Some examples of this phenomenon include in *Le Peintre* the minuet in which the wife goes into pantomime mode while her husband continues dancing; in the same ballet the "begging for forgiveness" scene which combines dance and gesture, with the entire last figure in pantomime; in *Les Galants villageois* the second *pas de deux*, during which the woman looks for her partner who dances in such a way as to remain out of her line of vision; and in *Les Bûcherons* the *pas de trois*, where the mixture of pantomime and dance is performed to eight-bar strains with regular antecedent/consequent phrases.

instance in Ferrère of the same music being used for the same choreographic phrase; there is, however, a change in performer.) The music is
played yet again as they embrace and then join in a duet; this unit (1a)
serves to introduce the two characters to the audience. When a new section of music is heard (1b), the soldiers retrieve glasses from the brims of
their hats, pour wine, toast each other, and drink — actions performed
entirely via gestures. Their movements are broken down into short two-
or four-bar segments: for example, "they drink, saying that it's good"
(four bars), and "they place their glasses on the ground" (two bars). After
finishing their drinks, they resume their dance to the "dance music"
(ABA). During the B strain a village woman, unnoticed by the two soldiers, dances to the bottles and glasses, picks them up, and exits on tip-
toe. The oblivious soldiers continue to dance.

The music of section 2 stands in sharp contrast: the change of meter
and tempo and particularly the switch to the parallel minor reveal that
the soldiers have finally discovered the theft of their wine. The music
here parodies the baroque lament topos; the descending chromatic bass
line and the sighing motives in the melody would be more appropriate
for the death of a mythological heroine such as Dido than for the loss of
wine bottles. The choreography mixes pantomime and dance steps as
the soldiers question the villagers on the sides of the stage, accuse each
other of playing a trick, and run into the wings searching for the missing
wine. Five bars into the second strain (F) the woman returns, carrying the
bottles and glasses; her entrance is exceptional in that it comes in the
middle of a strain rather than at the start. The remainder of section 2
consists entirely of pantomime; the woman refuses to let the soldiers have
their wine unless they dance with her, and after some bantering they
agree to do so. The last phrase of this section constitutes a *petite reprise* of
the last four bars of the F music, during which the three dancers move
upstage into position for the dance to follow.

For the remainder of the *pas de trois* (secs. 3 and 4) the now reconciled
protagonists engage in dancing, rather than in any kind of action. The
choreography, which is set to two pieces of music that contrast with each
other in key and tempo, consists as much of short solos or duets as it does
of trios. Interestingly, only the woman is a soloist; the soldiers always
dance together. As we have come to expect from Ferrère, the changes in
the number of dancers coincide with structural points in the music, although some of them come close in time to each other, with the shortest
dance phrases being only four bars long. The pattern over both pieces of
music is for solos and duets to alternate until, toward the end of each

dance, all three dancers join together. Overall, the *pas de trois* exhibits a variety of movement styles, yet the changes between them, not to mention the changes in the number of performers in motion, are carefully coordinated with the music.

## Solo Dances and Small Ensembles

The above *pas de trois* also serves as an example of the ways that the set pieces feature the solo dancers who figure in every ballet. Each of Ferrère's ballets accords a large place to dancing by soloists — the protagonists, so to speak, of these simple works; in fact, many of the "plots" serve as flimsy frames on which to hang flashy or comic solos, duets, or trios. The absence of ensemble dances for larger numbers of soloists (*pas de quatre* or *pas de cinq*) from Ferrère's manuscript may be an artifact of the small sample, but on the other hand, the listings of performers' names in scenarios by other choreographers suggest that *pas de deux* for a mixed couple were the dominant ensembles in this type of work.[38] In Ferrère's four pantomime ballets there are eleven *pas de deux*, all for a mixed couple, as opposed to only two *pas de trois*, and one solo. There are, however, solo passages embedded within the ensemble dances, and other parts of the manuscript, such as the *agréments* for the spoken plays, include solos.

Of the eleven *pas de deux*, only two of them (nos. 3 and 6 from *Le Peintre*) consist of a dance set to a single piece of music in which both performers dance throughout. The rest extend over more than one piece of music and/or involve an alternation in the number of performers. We have chosen to apply the words "pas de deux" and "pas de trois" to Ferrère's choreographies for two or three dancers, not only because Ferrère himself uses the terms but because in these regards the choreographies have more in common with later ballet *pas de deux* than they do with the duets set to a single piece of music familiar from Feuillet notations. In terms of style they vary from pure pantomime, with no dance steps specified, to formal abstract dances with no narrative content. But most of the ensembles include a mixture of styles, usually beginning with abstract dance and shifting to pantomime, or at least incorporating various gestures, at some point during the number. Despite their variety, a number of general observations can be made:

---

38. Italian librettos tend to list the solo dancers primarily by couples, with much less frequent mention of larger ensembles; see apps. 2 and 4.

- pas de deux are generally notated in Feuillet notation, but in addition to the notated dance steps they may contain pantomime or gesture, as indicated by drawings and verbal instructions;
- in the sections of the dances that do not involve pantomime, the floor patterns are symmetrical in ways not dissimilar to theatrical duets of the baroque period;
- Ferrère's pas de deux are frontal, that is, the dancers' orientation is primarily toward the audience, especially when they are performing virtuosic steps;
- the pas de deux tend to be set off from their surroundings in that the performers usually enter specifically for this choreography. Furthermore, unlike the group dances, in which the performers normally remain on stage after they have finished, the performers almost always exit at the end; these exits are usually choreographed;
- with only two exceptions, each dancer in a pas de deux has at least one solo section, usually back-to-back with a solo by the other dancer; a dancer sometimes exits temporarily following a solo, but not always;
- a pas de deux may begin with a solo, but always ends with both dancers moving simultaneously, even though the a2 section may be quite short;
- overall the dances range in length from 24 to 160 bars; the solo sections range from 8 to 49 bars;
- changes from solo to duet (or vice versa) are often accompanied by a new section of music along with a change in mode (e.g., from major to minor — in which case the woman always gets the music in the minor mode);
- repeated choreographic passages (for example, when the man and the woman dance the same sequence in succession) are usually performed to repeated music, but such passages are relatively infrequent and, as discussed earlier, a repetition in the music does not require a repetition in the choreography;
- when the partners are dancing together they perform the same steps simultaneously more often than not, but it is also possible for them to do different steps at the same time; such differences occur, however, only when the story line means that the two are engaged in different activities, as when one person hunts for another (both of them dancing), or one mimes while the other continues to dance.

Since Ferrère's *pas de deux* exhibit such variety, it is not possible to point to any particular one as typical. *Le Peintre* alone has six *pas de deux*, each of them very different. (In table 9.1 these correspond to nos. 3, 6–8, 9, and 10b.) Moira Goff discusses the second one in chapter 8, 217–25; here we look at number 10 (outlined in table 9.5), which is of particular interest

Table 9.5: *Outline of nos. 10a and 10b from* Le Peintre amoureux de son modèle

| Section | Music | Form | Bars | Performers | Comments |
|---------|-------|------|------|------------|----------|
| 1 [10a] | Allegro D; 2/4 | A | 8 | *figurants:* 4 couples painter wife | Choreographed entrance for the *figurants;* the soloists remain stationary upstage. |
| | | BCD | 24 | as above | Soloists exit during B music. |
| | | A' | 8 | *figurants* (and wife) | Wife enters during the A' music, remaining stationary upstage. |
| 2 [10b] | d; 2/4 | EEFE | 32 | wife (*figurants* remain on sides throughout) | Formal dance; wife exits upstage left at end of her solo. |
| 3 | Allegro D; 2/4 | ABCDA' | 40 | painter | Formal dance; painter exits stage right at end of solo. |
| 4 | d; 2/4 | EEFE | 32 | wife | More formal dancing; wife moves downstage left at end. |
| 5 | Allegro D; 2/4 | ABCDA' + coda (6 bars) | 46 | painter wife | *Pas de deux;* the dance begins downstage with the painter on the right of his wife; they exit downstage right. |

because of the way in which it integrates the soloists and the *figurants*. It also provides one model for how solo and duet sections may alternate.

Prior to this scene the painter had begged his wife for forgiveness, which she finally granted; the couple had then danced a *pas de deux* to celebrate the reconciliation (no. 9). At this point a group of eight people enter, to wish the couple well (Ferrère tells us that they come "pour féliciter"). The normal practice in Ferrère's ballets is for the soloists to leave the stage before the following group dance begins. Here, however, they remain during the eight-bar entrance of the *figurants,* and after mutual greetings the painter and his wife dance off upstage left while the group dance continues. During the last eight bars of the group dance the wife returns alone; the *figurants,* in two columns, dance to the sides of the stage and watch as the *pas de deux* proper gets underway with a thirty-two-bar solo for the wife set to minor music (sec. 2). Following this dance she exits again, upstage left.

The dance notation changes from floor patterns and step names to Feuillet, signaling a technically more difficult choreography, and the music repeats the major tune used for the *figurants'* dance,[39] as the painter enters and performs a forty-bar solo (sec. 3). Like so many of Ferrère's male solos it is almost entirely frontal — that is, the dancer remains facing the audience whenever possible — and is designed to show off the technical skill of the performer. He leaves the stage and his wife returns; her thirty-two-bar solo (sec. 4) is performed to the minor section of the music to which she had already danced. Although her dance differs from his (it includes, for instance, passages traveling to the sides), both dancers have extended passages in which they repeat the same steps multiple times. For example, in section 3, bars 9–15, the man does the same step combination (which involves a *pas tombé,* hops, and beats) seven times. In the woman's solo, section 4, bars 9–16, she repeats two steps over and over, and in bars 25–30 she does three sets of three *entrechats quatre* interspersed with two iterations of a brief sequence involving a *tombé* plus a jump — all this done within six bars of 2/4 time. After these two flashy solos, the husband and wife finally dance together; a third repeat of the major music accompanies their forty-six-bar duet. As is usual in Ferrère's duets, the partners perform the same steps in symmetrical floor patterns, and except for one short passage where they face each other, pass, and dance toward the sides of the stage, the choreography remains frontal; their focus is directed toward the audience, not toward each other. During the six-bar musical coda the dancers exit downstage right.

This formal, abstract choreography stands in sharp contrast to the other *pas de deux* for the painter and his wife, four out of five of which contain pantomimic elements to a greater or lesser degree — although they, too, put technical demands on the dancers. Here, however, the painter and his wife do not even share the stage for much of the time: the three consecutive solos (wife, painter, wife) are done in the absence of the other partner, before the two finally round off this unit by dancing together. At this point in the ballet, all the tensions have been resolved and action gives way to dance for its own sake, something Ferrère emphasizes by using the *figurants* as an onstage audience.

In the first of the two *pas de deux* in *Les Galants villageois,* the alternation between the soloists happens with a different rhythm that seems to par-

---

39. There is one other instance of the same music being used for a group dance and a *pas de deux,* which occurs in the *agréments* for *Myrtil et Lycoris.*

ticipate in the construction of the admittedly minimal story line. This is
a formal dance in Feuillet notation, but it incorporates some pantomimic
gestures. As the ballet opens, a shepherd enters alone, dancing to a forty-
nine-bar Andantino in A major. He departs and a shepherdess arrives;
the mode changes to A minor for her thirty-two-bar solo. Up to this point
neither dancer appears to be aware of the existence of the other. But as
a new piece of music begins, the shepherd returns. The shepherdess is
immobile, standing downstage right facing the audience, where she cannot see the shepherd. In the fourth bar of his brief solo he stares at her;
two bars later he gets her attention and they greet each other. For the
next ten bars the two engage in what appears to be a choreographed flir-
tation: she dances away from him for two bars, then stands as he moves
toward her, then dances away again, as the two continue to respond to
each other every two bars. Unlike the baroque dance repertoire in which
such passages are usually echoes, with each dancer performing the same
steps in alternation, in this passage the shepherd's steps are different
from — and harder than — the shepherdess's. The asymmetrical floor
pattern — an "S" shape that travels upstage — is reminiscent of the floor
pattern in the *colère* duet from *Le Peintre* (see the second diagram in fig.
8.3), but here it seems to signal the growing attraction between the two,
as the shepherd follows the shepherdess. In a very brief climax the two
finally dance simultaneously and even perform the same steps, but only
in the final four bars of the dance. In this duet the alternation between
performers is not aimed (at least not exclusively) at providing dazzling solos for the audience to applaud, but serves the interests of the story. Similarly, in the second *pas de deux* from the same ballet the story line trumps
conventions: when the shepherd tries to play a trick on the shepherdess
by dancing in such a way that she cannot see him, the two use different
steps, even though dancing simultaneously, and their floor patterns are
not symmetrical.

If the *pas de deux* in the Ferrère manuscript impress through their variety, the *pas de trois*, which number only two, provide but a small sample
of the choreographic possibilities that must have been used for such a
combination at the time. Nonetheless, we must be grateful that these
dances exist at all, as they are the only two choreographies of theatrical
*pas de trois* that have survived from the eighteenth century, even though
opera librettos and ballet scenarios suggest that this combination was not
rare. *Pas de trois* and other dances for an odd number pose problems of
symmetry, which apparently remained an important principle of choreographic construction, if Ferrère's *pas de deux* can be seen as exemplifying

general conventions.[40] In the best-known early example, the "Balet de neuf danseurs" (published in 1700), Feuillet avoided the problem by having his groups of four or eight dancers alternate with the soloist, but never asking that the nine dancers move at the same time.[41] In the *pas de cinq* from *Le Mariage de la Grosse Cathos* (1688), the only other baroque theatrical choreography for an odd number, Favier *l'aîné* kept the movements of the four women symmetrical and positioned the man for most of the dance as its center axis, allowing him slightly different steps and figures.[42] In both these choreographies, the extra dancer is thus set apart in some way from the other members of the group. This is also the case for the *pas de trois* pictured in Lambranzi's book (1716), which always define two of the dancers as the same, the third as different: two old women and a young boy (pt. 1, plate 15—see fig. 9.3); Bacchus and two of his followers (pt. 2, plate 20); or two witches and a ghost (pt. 2, plate 50).

The two Ferrère *pas de trois* make the same kind of distinction, both in the ways the dancers' roles are defined and in the choreographies themselves. Both are for two men and a woman and only rarely do all three perform the same steps at the same time. Frequently the two men will dance in mirror-image symmetry while the woman performs a different sequence of steps, or a short male duet will alternate with a female solo, the latter either echoing the men's dance or providing contrasting material. The purely danced section of the *pas de trois* for the drunken soldiers and the village woman from *La Réjouissance villageoise*, which follows a long pantomime scene for the same three characters, comprises ninety-eight bars (secs. 3 and 4 in table 9.4), of which twenty-eight bars are solos for the woman (in four- or eight-bar segments) and twenty bars are male duets. The three dance together for fifty bars, but in half of these tutti

40. Most baroque choreographies for a couple, both ballroom and theatrical, begin and end in mirror-image symmetry; the axis of symmetry is vertical, and the dancers perform the same steps on opposite feet. Parallel symmetry occurs when both dancers perform the identical figure using the same feet; it is most common in ballroom minuets and passepieds, since the minuet step always begins on the right foot. Many choreographies include one or two short passages that deviate from these principles, usually in one of the following ways: a passage, in which one dancer circles around the other one, who turns in place; or a figure in which the couple holds inside hands and travels sideways. But these exceptions represent only a small proportion of the total number of bars in a given choreography, and their presence in a dance serves to reinforce the notion of symmetry as the norm.

41. LMC 1320. The dance was set to music from Lully's *Bellérophon*. In the bourée section of "An Ecchoe" (LMC 2560), a dance by Groscort for three women, the echo structure of the music is reflected in the choreography. Two women, moving in mirror-image symmetry, initiate each phrase and then rest while the third woman dances to the musical echo. However, her steps and figures do not always imitate those of the duet.

42. See Harris-Warrick and Marsh, *Musical Theatre at the Court of Louis XIV*, 153–61 and 275–80.

Figure 9.3: A *pas de trois* for two old women and a youth. (Lambranzi, *Neue und curieuse theatralische Tantz-Schul* [1716], pt. 1, plate 15)

passages (twenty-four bars) the men perform the same steps in mirror-image symmetry while the woman is either performing steps different from the men's or does the same steps but with a different floor pattern. In only a quarter of the formal dance (twenty-six bars) does Ferrère confront the problem of symmetry created by an odd number of dancers. He resolves it in one of three ways: the most common solution is for the men to move in parallel motion, with the woman between them moving in mirror image to both men (fourteen bars); for example, while all three are facing downstage the two men do a *chassé* to the right while the woman does a *chassé* to the left. A second solution is for the men to move in mirror image on a horizontal axis, while the woman does the same figure on a vertical axis (ten bars). Finally, Ferrère includes a very short (two-bar) passage in which all three dancers are in parallel motion.

The trio for the two woodcutters and the woman in wooden shoes from *Les Bûcherons et les sabotiers* has been discussed by Moira Goff in chapter 8 in terms of how it integrates gesture with the dancing. It may also be useful in this context to mention some of its points of difference with Ferrère's other small ensemble dances. Unlike Ferrère's *pas de deux* and the *pas de trois* for the two soldiers and the village woman, this trio contains no solos. When they are dancing, the two men move in mirror-image symmetry throughout; during the eight-bar pantomime sequence in the middle of the dance they perform sequentially at two-bar intervals — that is, in temporal rather than spatial symmetry. The role of the woman soloist stands in sharp contrast. Confined to the center of the stage between the two men, she walks or runs and uses various pantomime motions: greeting the men, picking up wood chips and putting them in her basket, and so forth. (In musical terms, this trio could be described as a male duet with female *obbligato*.) In the penultimate figure the men stop their fancy steps and join hands with the woman, the three running downstage together; however, during the final eight-bar figure the woman retreats upstage alone, in preparation for a solo dance to follow, while the men revert to their previous mode of dancing with each other. As in the other *pas de trois*, the woman's position is generally in the center of the formation, with the men moving symmetrically in relation to her. This same spatial relationship between the matched pair and the third, different person is shown in all of Lambranzi's plates that include three dancers (see, by way of example, fig. 9.3).[43]

---

43. French opera librettos sometimes list dancing roles for groups such as the three Graces. One supposes that they performed *pas de trois*, and the fact that all three played the same role may well have made for a different kind of choreographic construction.

# Group Dances

The group characters in this type of ballet generally consist of the inhabitants of whatever place provides the setting, performed by dancers identified as "figurants" ("figuranti" in Italian) or sometimes simply as "le ballet." In Ferrère's works (as in the Magri scenarios found in app. 4) the *figurants* numbered between six and twelve individuals. In Ferrère's choreographies it is possible to see that all of them did not necessarily dance each time a group was called for, but that a subset might be involved. Ballet scenarios show that the *figurants* could engage in pantomime as well as dance — see, for example, in appendix 4, Magri's *Assalto di corsari lapponesi,* in which Lapp pirates attack a village. Two pantomime scenes by group characters occur in Ferrère's ballets, both taking place during the overture. In *La Réjouissance villageoise* a group of villagers sits around a table, demanding food and wine from the innkeeper. These particular characters never dance but thereafter remain on stage, watching the proceedings. (Such a division of labor calls to mind Dehesse's ballet *L'Opérateur chinois* [Théâtre Italien, 1749], whose cast list distinguishes between roles for dancers and for those who mime.) Ferrère's *Bûcherons* opens with a woodcutting scene of fifty-two bars; the six men are chopping and stacking wood as their wives wind their way down the mountain in the background, carrying baskets of food. As was pointed out earlier, initial pantomime scenes such as this one are set in Ferrère's ballets to the music of the overture (see table 9.2, no. 1). During the last four bars the men propose a dance, to which the women readily agree. Once the dance begins (set to the Andantino, no. 2), the pantomime ceases.

Group dances frame each of Ferrère's ballets and may occur in the middle as well. The opening and intermediary dances are considerably shorter than the *contredanses générales* that conclude each work, lasting from 40 to 64 bars compared with from 136 to 176 bars for the final dances. They may also involve a reduction in the number of dancers from the total number of *figurants* available, whereas the concluding *contredanse générale* is performed not only by the entire group but also by the soloists. Ferrère notated all nineteen of the group dances in the manuscript (including the eight *contredanses générales*) using floor patterns, with the names of the steps written in the frame (see fig. 9.1). Ferrère's format may have been inspired by the standard notations for contemporary *contredanses françaises,* dances for four couples arranged in a square formation, which were published in large numbers beginning in 1762. Each of these had a four-page format consisting of a title page, a page of dance notation with each figure in an individual frame (not dissimilar to Ferrère's group dance notation), a page describing each figure verbally, and, on the back page, the music, usually treble and bass.[44]

Since part 2 of Magri's treatise includes notations and explanations for thirty-nine *contraddanze*, it would be gratifying if we could draw parallels between his group dances and those in the Ferrère manuscript. But Magri makes it clear that his dances are for social occasions, and most of them are intended for an indefinite number of dancers (similar to the "longways for as many as will" formation of contemporary English country dances), whereas Ferrère's dances have a defined number of dancers (varying from six to sixteen) and in their spatial organization have more in common with the square or round formations of the *contredanse française*.[45] However, Ferrère's group dances are much more complex than the typical social contredanse of the period, both in terms of floor patterns and step vocabulary. In the contemporary *contredanse française* only a few steps are prescribed, primarily the *demi-contretemps* (the main traveling step), the *pas de rigaudon*, and the *chassé*, whereas in some of Ferrère's group dances as many as fifteen different steps are required, many of them performed in a variety of ways. For the most part these steps are familiar from the baroque ballroom dance vocabulary of the early eighteenth century: *pas de bourée, pas de sissonne, échappé*, etc. However, Ferrère relies on the *chassé à trois pas* and the *chassé à quatre pas* as his primary traveling steps; in the *contredanse générale* of *Le Peintre amoureux de son modèle* these two steps account for one-third of the total steps used. Even *entrechats* are occasionally called for, although the number of times the feet are to cross is not clear, since the steps are named and not notated. Not all of Ferrère's group dances call for such a rich step vocabulary; two of the four dances in *La Réjouissance villageoise*, for example, rely almost exclusively on the *pas d'allemande*. But even in the dances with a larger step vocabulary, the emphasis is on creating interesting and constantly shifting floor patterns, rather than on a virtuosic display of technique.

And, in fact, an even greater contrast between the social contredanses of the period and Ferrère's choreographies can be found in the floor patterns. The social dances are in rondeau form, with a choreographic re-

---

44. See the four volumes published by de La Cuisse, *Le Répertoire des bals, ou Théorie-pratique des contredanses* (Paris, 1762–65). A digitized copy can be accessed at the Library of Congress "American Ballroom Companion" Web site: http://memory.loc.gov/ammem/dihtml/dihome.html.

45. Magri's *contraddanza* for thirty-two (see n8) could work as a theatrical piece.

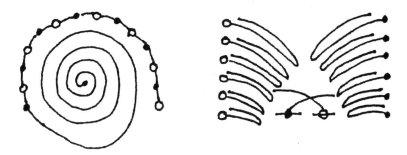

Figures 9.4a–b: These two drawings show patterns the dancers trace on the floor in two group dances from the Ferrère manuscript.

frain that is unique to each individual dance. In between the refrains, the dancers perform a prescribed sequence of nine figures common to all *contredanses françaises,* such as the *ronde* or *moulinet.* Ferrère, on the other hand, dazzles us with his choreographic inventiveness. Each group dance is composed of a unique series of figures and floor patterns from his apparently limitless imagination. The choreographic refrains of the social contredanse are completely absent: the music may repeat, but the dance does not. And although some of the individual floor patterns are drawn from contemporary social contredanses, most of them are more elaborate. In the final contredanse of *Les Trois Cousines,* for example, the line of fourteen dancers travels inward along ever smaller concentric circles to form a tight spiral (see fig. 9.4a), a figure Ferrère calls a *colimaçon* (snail). In Ferrère's contredanses the number of dancers may contract or expand as the figures shift, rather in the manner of a kaleidoscope: every four- or eight-bar musical phrase corresponds to a turn of the lens and a new design emerges.

In the *contredanses générales* that conclude Ferrère's four ballets, the group is enlarged via the addition of the soloists, who enter shortly after the halfway point of the dance and perform a short passage on their own while the *figurants* watch. Thereafter they all join forces, but the soloists may still have different floor patterns and steps from the *figurants.* In one such dance, from *Les Bûcherons et les sabotiers* (see fig. 9.4b), the twelve *figurants,* with men on the left, women on the right, move from their positions along the sides of the stage to form a kind of "V" shape that encloses the two soloists and then retreat to the positions on the sides, using four *contretemps de gavotte;* during this four-bar passage the soloists move toward and then away from each other using different steps from the *figurants.* Twelve bars later the soloists perform an eight-bar sequence of steps (including a *cabriole à l'italienne*) in the center of the stage while the *figurants* travel from one side to the other in a curved line behind the soloists.[46] When it is a play or *opéra-comique* that ends with a *contredanse générale*, the dancing generally involves the actors or singers as well. In the concluding *divertissement* that Ferrère supplied for *Les Trois Cousines*, songs and dances alternate, the grand finale being supplied by a strophic *vaudeville*, followed by a *contredanse générale* set to the same tune, in which the actors join the *figurants*. Ferrère's complex dances reveal that it would be a mistake to be misled by the term "contredanse générale" into assuming that these grand finales looked much like ballroom contredanses.

The great virtue of the Ferrère manuscript is that it gives us access to the conventions of pantomime ballet with a specificity well beyond what can be learned from a ballet scenario alone. In this chapter we have sought to abstract these conventions from the works themselves in order to make them available as a lens through which to look at other works for which less information survives. Thus far we have primarily compared Ferrère's practices to those discernible in earlier notated dances and to the works of some of his contemporaries. Whereas we hope that others will extend the work on eighteenth-century choreographic conventions that has only just begun here, we would also like to point out that what can be learned from Ferrère has the potential to illuminate later practices as well.

The most famous pantomime ballet of the late eighteenth century, as far as dance lovers are concerned, is Jean Dauberval's *La Fille mal gardée*, first given in Bordeaux on 1 July 1789 under the title *Ballet de la paille*.[47] Dauberval's ballet has been seen as marking a new departure, away from the mythological ballets preferred at the Paris Opéra, and in fact, with its young lovers, its mixture of dancing and pantomime, its harvest-time *divertissement*, and its final scene of general rejoicing, it has much in common with the works recorded by Ferrère just a few years previously. Ferrère's manuscript thus becomes an obvious source for those seeking to recreate Dauberval's popular ballet.

Ferrère also has potential as a tool for exploring continuity and

---

46. Ferrère's *cabriole à l'italienne*, which he mentions only in words and does not notate, might be the same as Magri's *capriola all'italiana*, an *entrechat* that begins and ends in second position; see Magri/Skeaping, 156; Magri, *Trattato*, 1:119–20.

47. For an account of the ballet and its early performances, see Ivor Guest, *The Ballet of the Enlightenment* (London: Dance Books, 1996), 386–89.

change in theater dancing during the nineteenth century. Sandra Noll Hammond has explored the steps and structures of four *pas de deux* created between 1820 and 1835 by leading choreographers and recorded by Michel St. Léon during the 1830s.[48] She pointed out the similarities between their structures and those of the *pas de deux* in the Ferrère manuscript, in particular the apparent convention of opening with a solo for the woman, the alternation of solos by the woman and the man, and placing of duets at the end of sections within the *pas de deux*. These features, together with their accompanying musical structures, merit further comparison with the *pas de deux* surviving from later periods. Sandra Hammond also drew attention to the link between the dances recorded by St. Léon and those to be found in the ballets of August Bournonville, who worked in Paris and Berlin early in his career. Bournonville's own ballets, with their blend of pantomime and dancing, and use of *divertissements*, are also worth comparing with works from the eighteenth century—particularly those of Dehesse, Ferrère, and Magri.[49]

The structures recorded by Ferrère even survive, albeit in much altered form, into the late nineteenth century. Perhaps the most famous of the classical ballets created by Marius Petipa are those he made to the music of Tchaikovsky, and above all *The Sleeping Beauty* first performed in St. Petersburg on 15 January 1890. This work self-consciously recalls the court ballets of Louis XIV and the court entertainments of his successors. It is one of the few ballets from this period to have been written down, with the help of a system devised by the dancer Vladimir Stepanov that comprises written descriptions, floor plans, and notation for some of the dances—a mixture that immediately calls to mind Ferrère's own notational systems.[50] *The Sleeping Beauty* cannot be directly compared with the small-scale pantomime ballets of Ferrère, but some of his structures can still be seen within the later large-scale work. For example, the *divertissements* generally begin with a group dance, which is followed by a series of solos, duets, trios, and still more group dances. The third and final act culminates in a group dance (in this case a mazurka) for all the dancers,

---

48. Sandra Noll Hammond, "Windows into Romantic Ballet: Content and Structure of Four Early Nineteenth-Century *Pas de Deux*," in *Reflecting Our Past; Reflecting on Our Future: Proceedings of the Society of Dance History Scholars, Twentieth Annual Conference, Barnard College, New York City, NY, 19–22 June 1997* (Riverside, CA: Society of Dance History Scholars, 1997), 137–44.

49. For Bournonville, particularly the surviving sources for his ballets, see Knud Arne Jürgensen, *The Bournonville Tradition: The First Fifty Years, 1829–1879*, 2 vols. (London: Dance Books, 1997).

50. See Roland John Wiley, *Tchaikovsky's Ballets: Swan Lake, Sleeping Beauty, Nutcracker* (Oxford: Clarendon, 1985).

including the soloists—surely a direct descendant of the *contredanse générale* of Ferrère's time. In this same act the well-known bluebird *pas de deux* adheres to a structure that is recognizably related to the *pas de deux* recorded by both Michel St. Léon and Ferrère. The similarities and differences between works spanning a period of more than one hundred years invite closer analysis.

# Appendix 1

# Grotteschi in Italy, 1750–1800
## A Preliminary Tabulation

### COMPILED BY KATHLEEN KUZMICK HANSELL

The names below are taken mainly from the following sources, roughly in order of frequency:

- opera librettos
- ballet scenarios
- published theater chronologies (such as Wiel for Venice,[1] Bouquet for Turin,[2] Girardi and Rossi for La Fenice,[3] Tintori for La Scala,[4] etc.)
- *Indice de' spettacoli teatrali* (Milan and other cities, 1764ff.).

Librettos and scenarios used are in part original and in part cited from other sources, such as Claudio Sartori, *I libretti italiani a stampa dalle origini al 1800: Catalogo analitico con 16 indici* (Cuneo: Bertola & Locatelli, 1990–95); the online RISM libretto catalogue; and various published libretto catalogues.

1. Taddeo Wiel, *I teatri musicali veneziani del Settecento* (Venice: Visentini, 1897).
2. Marie-Thérèse Bouquet, *Il teatro di corte, dalle origini al 1788*, vol. 1 of *Storia del Teatro Regio di Torino*, ed. Alberto Basso, 5 vols. (Turin: Cassa di Risparmio, 1976–88); vol. 5, *Cronologie*, ed. Alberto Basso.
3. Michele Girardi and Franco Rossi, *Il Teatro la Fenice: Cronologia degli spettacoli, 1792–1936* (Venice: Albrizzi, 1989).
4. Giampiero Tintori, *Cronologia: Opere, balletti, concerti 1778–1977*, vol. 2 of *Duecento anni di Teatro alla Scala*, ed. Carlo Gatti (Gorle: Grafica Gutenberg, 1979).

279

Dancers included are those who are cited as a *grottesco/-a* in at least one published (or occasionally manuscript) source. The majority of them also danced in *serio* or *mezzo-carattere* roles. The starting date of 1750 was chosen so as to include the entirety of Magri's career and also to reflect the fact that Italian librettos tended not to name individual dancers until about 1760.

*Grotteschi* who also worked as choreographers are italicized.

## MALE DANCERS

Accorsi, Giuseppe
*Agostini* (Agostino), *Pietro* di
    Madrid
*Albertini, Pasquale* di Lucca
Alfini, Felice
*Ambrosiani, Giovanni*
Ambrosini, Sebastiano
Ambrosini, Stefano
*Andreoni, Nicola* (Niccolò)
    *detto lo Spezieria*
Andreoni, Pietro detto (lo)
    Spezieria
*Anelli, Giuseppe* di Roma
*Angiolini, Nicola* (Niccolò)
Angiolini (Angelini),
    Pasquale di Firenze
*Angiolini, Pietro* di Firenze
Anguelli, Antonio di
    Firenze
Antonelli, Paolo
Antonelli, Pietro
Arosio, Gaspare

Baccanti, Venceslao
Bac(c)anti, Vincenzo
Bacchini, Giuseppe
Bacilei, Giuseppe
Balbi, Guido
Baldacci, Luigi
Balle, Lodovico
Baloc(c)hi, Giuseppe di
    Roma
*Banchelli, Leopoldo*
Banchetti, Giovanni di
    Modena

Banfieri, Lorenzo
Banti, Carlo di Milano
*Banti, Guglielmo* (Billi)
*Banti, Zaccaria*
Banti Pazzini, Francesco
Baratti, Antonio
*Barat(t)i, Innocente*
    (Innocenzio) di
    Bologna
Barat(t)ozzi, Ferdinando
Baratozzi, Francesco
Barberis, Carlo
Barberis, Giovanni di
    Torino
*Bardotti, Luigi* di Firenze
Bartolomic(c)hi, Luigi
Barufaldi, Carlo
Basili(o), Andrea di Roma
*Bassi, Francesco*
Bassi, Giovanni
*Bassi, Pietro* di Cremona
Battaglia, Antonio
Battaglia, Vincenz(i)o
Battini, Antonio
Bedotti, Camillo di Genova
*Bedotti, Filippo* di Genova
*Bedotti, Francesco* di Roma
Bedotti, Pietro
Bellini, Nicola
Belluc(c)i (Belluchi), Luigi
    detto il Portoghesino
Belor, Felice
Benghili, Gregorio
*Benvenuti, Giuseppe*
Benvenuti, Luigi

Bergonzoni, Gioachino →
    *see:* Borgonzoni,
    Gioac(c)hino
Bernabei, Petronio
Bernardi, Giovanni
*Bernardini, Antonio*
*Bertarelli* (Bertorelli,
    Bertorello), *Agostino*
Bertelli, Filippo
Berteul, Sig.
*Berti(ni), Antonio* di
    Piacenza
Berti(ni), Francesco
Bertoni, Filippo di Roma
Bertorelli → *see:* Bertarelli
Betti(ni), Antonio
Bettini, Camillo
*Betti(ni), Giuseppe*
Bettini, Giuseppe
Bianchi, Francesco
Bianciardi, Giovanni
Bidò, Giovanni
Bidò, Pietro
*Big(g)iog(g)ero, Antonio*
Bimbi, Gennaro
Bini, Francesco
*Biscioni, Luigi*
Bis(s)erelli, Antonio
Biz(z)arelli, Giacomo
Blake (Blach), Henry
    (Enrico)
*Blake* (Blech, Bleck),
    *Richard* (Riccardo)
    Irlandese
Blasi, Fortunato

Bocchino, Giuseppe
Boccio, Antonio
Boggina (Boggini), E.
Boggini, Antonio → *see:*
   Buggini, Antonio
*Bolognini, Domenico*
Bolla, Fortunato
*Bolla, Giuseppe*
*Bonardi, Francesco*
Bondanelli, Vincenz(i)o
Borgiot(t)i (Burgioti),
   Gaetano
Borgonzoni (Borgonzone,
   Bergonzoni),
   Gioac(c)hino
Borgonzoni, Giovanni
Borri, Giovanni
Borri, Serafino
Bos(s)i, Antonio di
   Venezia
Bosi, Giovanni
*Bos(s)i, Giuseppe* di Livorno
Brac(c)esi, Gaspero
   (Gaspare)
Bracci, Francesco di
   Roma
*Brambilla, Antonio*
Brambilla, Carlo
*Brugnoli, Paolo*
Brunetti, Giacomo
Brunetti, Gioachino
   (Giovacchino)
*Buggini* (Boggini), *Antonio*
*Burc(h)i* (Bursi), *Gasparo*
   (Gaspero) di Firenze
Burgioti, Gaetano → *see:*
   Borgiotti, Gaetano
Bursi → *see:* Burc(h)i
Buselli, Giuseppe

Caccialupi, Angelo
Calabresi, Angelo
*Calabresi, Cam(m)illo*
Calcina, Domenico
Calvarola, Antonio detto
   Tognino
*Calvi, Carlo*

*Calvi* (Calzi), *Giuseppe*
*Campigli* (Campilli), *Leopoldo*
Campioni, Giovanni
*Campolmi, Gaetano*
Campolmi, Giuseppe
Campolucci, Gaetano
*Cantori* (Cantoni), *Domenico*
Cappellari, Giuseppe
*Cappelletti, Giuseppe* di
   Firenze
Caprara (Caprari), Pietro
Caramelli, Gioachino
   (Giovachino)
Cardosi, Cipriano
Caritori, Domenico
Carrero, Giuseppe
Casabona, Vincenzo di
   Venezia
*Casazza* (Casazzi, Casacci,
   Casassa), *Giuseppe* di
   Torino
*Caselli, Francesco*
*Caselli, Pasquale*
Casoli, Giacomo
Caspani, Luigi → *see:*
   Gaspani, Luigi
*Castagna, Giuseppe* di Torino
Castiglioni (Castioni),
   Luigi
Cat(t)enari (Cattinari),
   Antonio
Cattoli, Gaetano
Cat(t)oli, Giacomo
Cattoli, Vincenzo
Cavalieri, Lorenzo di
   Roma
Cedrati, Lorenzo
Cedroni, Candido
Cellai, Francesco di
   Firenze
Celli, Rinaldo
Cenni, Gaspero (Gaspare)
*Cerut(t)i* (Curotti), *Felice* di
   Torino
Cesari (Ceseri), Filippo
*Cesari* (Ceseri), *Gaetano* di
   Firenze

*Cherubini, Stefano*
Chiari(ni), Giovanni
Chiaveri, Antonio
Chiaveri, Leatar [?]
*Chiaveri, Luigi*
Chimerli, Antonio
Chimerli, Francesco
Chiusetti (Cus[s]etti,
   Cossetti), Carlo
Christofani, Gioachino
Cianfanelli → *see:*
   Gianfanelli
Cicci, Benedetto di Roma
Cieserino, Sig.
Cingheria (Cingherli,
   Cinghorli), Giuseppe
Cipriani, Antonio di
   Modena
*Cipriani, Francesco* di
   Firenze
*Cipriani, Gaetano*
*Cipriani, Giovanni*
Cipriani, Onorato
Cipriano, Giuseppe
   Giovanni
*Citterio, Francesco*
Ciuffi, Giovanni
Clos(uè), Antonio
Clozzi, Antonio
Codacci, Antonio → *see:*
   Cus(s)ani, Antonio
   detto Codacci
Codacci, Gaetano
Codacci (Codazzi),
   Giovanni
Colleoni, Lorenzo
Col(l)ina, Francesco
*Col(l)ina* (Collino), *Giuseppe*
   *detto Pavaglione*
Colombi, Giovanni
Colombi, Pietro
Consegnato (Consegnati),
   Francesco → *see:*
   Nastasio, Giovanni
   Francesco detto
   Consegnato di Napoli

Consegnato (Consegnati),
Giovanni
Consegnato (Consegnati),
Lorenzo
*Conti, Giuseppe detto (il)*
*Prussia* di Venezia
Conti, Pietro
*Coppini, Antonio*
*Coppini, Giuseppe*
Corsi, Girolamo detto
Ferrara
*Cortesi, Giuseppe*
Corti, Giovanni Battista
*Corticelli, Luigi* di Milano
Cos(s)ani, Antonio → *see:*
Cus(s)ani, Antonio
Cosazzo, Santo
Cossetti, Carlo → *see:*
Chiusetti, Carlo
Costa, Carlo
Costa, Francesco
*Costa, Luigi*
Costantini, Gaetano
*Costantini, Giuseppe* di
Firenze
Cozzi, Cesare
Crisostomi → *see:*
Grisostomi
Cristofani, Gioacchino di
Roma
Croce, Alessandro
Cuffiat, Carlo
Cuneo, Eligio
Cuper, Angelo
Curioni, Francesco di
Milano
Curotti, Felice → *see:*
Ceruti, Felice
Cus(s)ani (Cossani,
Gussani), Antonio
detto Codacci
Cus(s)etti, Carlo → *see:*
Chiusetti, Carlo
Cus(s)etti, Luigi

Dal Lungo → *see:* Del
Lungo

Damiani Colombo, Pietro
Dante, Antonio
Danunzio, G.
Danunzio, Pietro Antonio
(Petronio) di Roma
De Caro, Paolo
De Domenicis, Giuseppe
Dedreis, Antonio → *see:*
Detrais, Antonio
*Del Lungo* (Dal Longo, Dal
Longe), *Gaspare*
(Gaspero)
Del Signore, Giacomo
De Martini, Paolo
Detrais (Dedreis), Antonio
*Diani, Pietro* (Colombo)
Domenichini, Michel(e)
Angiolo
Dominech, N.
D'Oploo (D'Oplò),
Giacomo → *see:* Oploo,
Jakob van

Erin, Guglielmo

*Fab(b)ri* (Fabris), *Luigi*
*Fabris, Francesco*
Federighi, Angelo di
Lucca
*Ferlotti, Raffaele* (Raffaelo)
Ferrara, Girolamo
Ferrari, Francesco
Ferrari, Giovanni
Ferrari, Giuseppe
*Fer(r)ini, Giacomo* di Lucca
*Fer(r)oni, Gaetano detto*
*Ferroncino* di Bologna
Ferroni, Giuseppe
*Fidanza, Raimondo*
Fini, Luigi
*Fiorelli, Evangelista*
*Fissi, Gaetano*
Flambò, Gaetano
Flori, Giuseppe
*Focosi* (Fogosi), *Luigi*
*Fontanella, Francesco* di
Milano

Fontanella, Stefano
Fontanesi, Pietro
Foresti, Antonio di
Venezia
Foresti, Gerolamo
(Girolamo) di Venezia
Foresti, Giacomo
Formic(c)hi (Formica),
Giuseppe
Fornaretto, Antonio
Fornari, Vincenzo
Fracassi, Giuseppe
Franceschi(ni), Antonio
Franchetti (Franchetto),
Pietro
Franchi, Angiolo
Franchi, Antonio
Franchi, Giuseppe
Franchi (Franco), Pietro di
Torino
Francolini, Giovanni
Frassi, Pietro
*Fras(s)i, Vincenz(i)o*

*Gabrielli, Ranieri* (Rainero)
di Roma
*Galantini, Giovanni Battista*
di Firenze
Galli, Giuseppe di Parma
Gallina, Vincenzo
Gambini, Marco
Garbagnati, Giuseppe
Gaspani (Caspani), Luigi
Gelati, Antonio
Gentili(ni), Filippo
*Gentili, Giacomo*
Ghedini, Cesare
*Ghedini, Domenico* di
Bologna
Ghelardini → *see:*
Gherardini
*Gherardini* (Ghelardini),
*Gaetano*
Gherardini (Ghelardini,
Ghilardini, Gilardini),
Luigi
Gherardini, Stefano

Gheri, Giovanni Battista
Gher(r)i, Giuseppe
Ghilardini → *see:*
    Gherardini
Ghinazzi (Ghinassi,
    Ghinazzo), Michele
Giacinto, Sig.
*Gianfaldoni, Pietro*
*Gianfanelli* (Cianfanelli),
    (Giovanni) *Antonio* di
    Firenze
Gianferi, Antonio
Giannini, Angelo
    (Angiolo)
Giannini, Gaspero
*Gian(n)ini, Lorenzo detto*
    *Cachena* di Lucca
Gilardini → *see:*
    Gherardini
*Gioja* (Gioia), *Gaetano*
Girodini, Luigi
Giunti, Angiolo (Angelo)
    detto Boccio
Giustini, Giuseppe
*Golfini, Agostino* di Lucca
Goresi, Antonio
Goresi, Giuseppe
*Gori, Luigi*
Gorla, Pietro
Grasettini (Grassellini),
    Giovanni di Lucca
Graziola, Luigi
*Grazioli, Giovanni Battista*
    *detto Schizza* di Roma
Green (Grini), William
    (Guglielmo)
Grendez, Guglielmo
Grini, Guglielmo → *see:*
    Green, William
Grisostomi (Crisostomi),
    Gregorio di Roma
Guaccio, Giuseppe
Gucci, Giuseppe di
    Firenze
*Guglielmi, Alessandro*
    (Alessio) di Roma
Guglielmi, Antonio

Guidetti, Giovanni detto
    Costantino
Gussani, Antonio → *see:*
    Cus(s)ani, Antonio

Iustini, Giuseppe

Lacomba, Lorenzo
Lamsoschi, N.
*Landini, Antonio*
Landini, Carlo di Bologna
*Landuc(c)i, Pietro*
La Ros(e) (Laros),
    Salvadore
Lazzari (Laz[z]eri), Pietro
Lena, Giuseppe
Len(n)a, Luigi di Livorno
Lodi, Giuseppe
Lolli, Domenico
Lombardi(ni), Gaetano di
    Milano
Longhi, Paolo
Lorenzi, Vi(n)cenz(i)o
    detto Bocchino di
    Firenze
Lucasini, Giacomo
Lucchesi, Francesco
Lucchi, Luigi
Luchini, Domenico
Lucidi, Carlo
Lucidi (Lucini), Nicola
    (Niccolò)
*Luzzi* (Luzio), *Eusebio* di
    Roma

*Magagnini, Stefano* di Roma
Maggini, Andrea
*Magni, Domenico*
*Magni, Giuseppe* di Firenze
Magnoni, Giuseppe
*Magri, Gennaro detto*
    *Genariello* di Napoli
Malazampa, Antonio
Mancini, Antonio
Maneti, Pasquale → *see:*
    Monet(t)i, Pasquale

Maranesi, Cosimo di
    Firenze
*Marassi* (Maraffi), *Antonio*
*Marchesi(ni), Giovanni*
    *Battista*
Marchesini, Pietro
*Marchetti, Paolo* di Venezia
Marchisi, Francesco
*Marchis(s)i(o)* (Marchesi),
    *Pietro*
Marconi, Antonio
*Marconi, Giuseppe*
Marcucci (Marcuzzi),
    Francesco di Lucca
*Marcucci, Giovanni* di Lucca
Marcucci, Pietro
*Mari, Gioachino*
    (Giovacchino)
Mariatti, Andrea → *see:*
    Mariotti, Andrea
Marinati, Girolamo
*Marinelli, Francesco* di
    Firenze
Mar(i)oni, Giuseppe
    [=Marconi?]
*Mariotti(ni)* (Mariatti),
    *Andrea*
Marrani, Giuseppe
Martini, Alessandro
*Martini, Francesco*
Marucci, Alessandro
Masà → *see:* Massan
*Massai* (Mazzai), *Andrea*
Mas(s)an, Angiolo
*Mas(s)an* (Masà, Masari),
    *Felice*
Mas(s)an (Mas[s]à),
    Gaetano
Mas(s)an, Luigi
Massini, Gaetano di
    Firenze
Matteucci, Angelo
Mattioli, Giuseppe
Matucci, Natale
Mazzai → *see:* Massai
Medina, Antonio

*Mei, Silvestro detto Pisello* di
Roma
Mendici, Alessandro
Menicucci, Antonio
*Menicucci, Vincenzo*
Mercuri, Felice
Mersi (Merci, Merzi),
Paolo
Michel, Giovanni
Michel, Pierre Bernard
Francese
*Migliorucci, Giacomo*
*Migliorucci* (Miglioruzzi),
*Vincenzo* di Roma
Milani, Carlo
*Minghi, Antonio* di Firenze
Mingotti, Odoardo
Moia, Giuseppe
Molinari, Nicola
Mol(l)er, Giuseppe
Monaretti (Monoretti,
Munaretti), Gaetano
Monari (Monati), Lorenzo
Monati, Lorenzo → *see:*
Monari, Lorenzo
*Monet(t)i* (Manet[t]i),
*Pasquale*
*Montani, Francesco* di
Milano
*Montani, Luigi*
Monterumisi, Pietro
Monti, Camillo
Monti, Gaetano
*Montignani, Francesco*
*Montignani, Gaetano* di
Bologna
Montignani, Lorenzo
*Montignani* (Montignari),
*Vincenzo* di Bologna
*Morelli, Domenico* di Torino
Morini, Bernardo
Morini, Felice d'Imola
Munaretti *see:* Monaretti

Narici (Nericci), Antonio
di Bologna
Narici, Francesco

*Nastasio, Giovanni*
*Francesco detto*
*Consegnato*
(Consegnati) di Napoli
Neri, Francesco
Neri, Giuseppe
Nericci, Antonio → *see:*
Narici, Antonio

Ongarelli → *see:* Ungarelli
*Oploo, Jakob van* (=
D'Oploo [D'Oplò],
Giacomo di Maastricht
Orlandi, Giovanni detto
Brigola
*Orti, Giovanni Battista*
(Giambattista) di Roma
*Ostici, Giacomo* di Bologna

*Pac(c)ini, Gaetano* di Firenze
Paccini, Ranieri → *see:*
Pazzini, Ranieri
Paccò, Amadeo
*Paccò, Carlo*
Paccò, Giovanni
Padovani, Giovanni di
Roma
Pagani, Giuseppe
Pagnani, Lorenzo
Paladini, Antonio
*Paladini, Luigi* di Lucca
*Paladini, Pietro*
*Pallerini, Filippo* di Pisa
Pallerini (Pallarini),
Girolamo (Gerolamo)
Panzani, Gaetano
Panzani, Gaspero di
Firenze
*Panzieri, Lorenzo*
Panzieri, Vincenzo
Panzini, Nicola
*Pap(p)ini, Antonio* di Firenze
*Pap(p)ini, Giuseppe*
Pappini, Pietro
*Paracca, Giuseppe*
Paris, Pietro
Parisini (Paresini), Nicola

Pasini, Francesco
Passaponte (Passaponti),
Giuseppe
Passaponte (Passaponti),
Pietro
Passerini (Passarini),
Giuseppe
Passerini, Luigi
*Pazzini* (Paccini), *Ranieri*
(Neri, Rainero) di Pisa
Pecci, Antonio
*Pen(n)etti, Giuseppe*
Pera, Giovanni
*Perez, Nicola* di Napoli
Perez, Silvestro [= Peri?]
*Peri* (Perri), *Silvestro*
Perini, Vittorio di Firenze
Pesci, Antonio
Pesci, Carlo
Pesci, Vincenzo
Piattoli, Francesco
*Piattoli, Vincenz(i)o* di
Firenze
*Picchi, Francesco*
Picconi, Filippo
Pieri, Pietro
Pieri, Vincenzo
Pinucci (Pinuzzi), Pietro
(Piero)
Pioni, Antonio
Pirola (Piroli), (Antonio)
Francesco
Pirotti, Lorenzo
Poetiù, Giuseppe
Ponci, Giovanni Battista
*Porri* (Porro), *Antonio* di
Firenze
Porri, Giovanni
Pozzi, Francesco
Pozzi, Luzio
Provasio, Giuseppe

Quattrini, Francesco
Quattrini, Ignazio

Radaelli, Giuseppe detto il
Bello di Milano

Rainoldi (Rainaldi), Paolo
*Ramac(c)ini, Simone*
Ramo, Antonio
*Rasetti, Francesco* di Torino
Razatti, Innocente
*Reg(g)ina* (Reg[g]ini),
   *Giuseppe* di Monaco
Restani, Lorenzo
Riboli, Luigi di Parma
Ricci, Francesco di Lucca
Ricci, Luigi
Ricci, Pietro di Roma
Ricci, Vincenz(i)o
Ricci, Vincenzo
Ricciolini (Ricciolino),
   Gaetano
Rinaldi, Luca
Rizzati, Francesco
Rizzi, Angelo
Rizzi, Giuseppe
Romagnoli, Giuseppe
Romani, Luigi
Romanino, Camillo
*Ronzi, Gaspare* (Gaspero) di
   Bologna
*Ronzi, Giorgio* di Bologna
Rossari, Gaspare
Ros(s)etti, Marco detto
   Schizza
Rossi, Antonio
Rossi, Biaggio
Rossi, Filippo
Rossi, Pietro
*Ros(s)ino* (Rossini), *Giuseppe*
   di Milano
Rottiliani, Camillo
Rub(b)ini, Gaetano di
   Bologna
*Ruggieri, Bortolo*
   (Bartolomeo) di
   Bologna
Rutini, Giuseppe

*Sab(b)atini* (Sabbadini,
   Sabatino), *Carlo*
Sacco (Giovanni), *Antonio*
Sala, Giuseppe

Sala, Paolo
Salomoni, Pietro di
   Bologna
*Sanquirico, Antonio* di
   Milano
Santambrogi(o)
   (Sant'Ambrogio),
   Giuseppe
Saraceni, Michele
Sarmetti, Paolo → *see:*
   Sermet(ti), Paolo
Sarro, Antonio → *see:*
   Ser(r)a, Antonio
Sartori(o), Giulio
Sartorj, Mariano
Savoni, Vincenzo → *see:*
   Tavoni, Vincenzo
Sbrocchi, Luigi detto
   Sanino
*Scalesi* (Scalese), *Giuseppe*
Schiera, Antonio → *see:*
   Sichera, Antonio
Schlanfofshy, Francesco
Secchioni, Antonio
Secchioni, Luigi di
   Firenze
Sereni, Luigi
Sermet(ti) (Sarmetti),
   Paolo
Ser(r)a (Sarro), Antonio
*Ses(s)oni* (Sesconi), *Carlo*
Sichera (Sighera, Schiera,
   Schero), Antonio
Sichera, Giuseppe
Simi, Giuseppe
*Sirletti, Antonio*
*Sirletti, Giovanni*
Sirletti, Pietro
*Sorbolini, Giuseppe*
Soster, Paolo di Parma
Spadoni, Gioachino
Sucidi, Nicola
Suga, Cosimo

*Taglioni* (Taglione), *Carlo* di
   Torino
Tamagni, Luigi

Tarabattoni *see:*
   Trabat(t)oni
Tarapattan, Innocente
Tassani, Giuseppe
Tavoni (Tavani), Luigi
Tavoni (Savoni),
   Vincenzo
Testa (Testi), Carlo
*Testini, Nicola*
Tiberti, Giovanni
*Tinti, Angelo* di Bologna
Tomasini, Alessandro
Tomasini, Francesco
Tomboloni, Rafaello
Torelli (Torello, Turello),
   Antonio
Torelli, Gaetano
Torres, Antonio
Torri, Gaetano
Tor(r)i, Gennaro di
   Napoli
*Tortori* (Tortoli), *Marco* di
   Firenze
Trabat(t)oni (Trapatoni,
   Tarabattoni), Giacomo
*Traf(f)ieri, Giuseppe* di
   Firenze
*Trentanove, Francesco* di
   Bologna
Trento, Antonio
*Trento, Domenico*
Trento, Santo
*Turchi, Domenico*
*Turchi, Giuseppe*
Turello, Antonio → *see:*
   Torelli, Antonio

Ungarelli (Ongarelli),
   Antonio

Valli, Pietro
Vedovani, Giuseppe
Veneti, Francesco
Venna, Carlo → *see:*
   Vien(n)a, Carlo
*Venturini, Filippo* di Lucca
*Venturi(ni), Francesco*

Verzellotti, Giuseppe
Vetrioli, Francesco
Vezzosi, Pietro
Vieni, Angelo
Vieni, Francesco
Vieni, Pietro
Vienna, Antonio
Vien(n)a (Venna, Vienni),
    Carlo
*Viganò, Giovanni* (Gianni) di
    Milano
*Viganò, Onorato* di Milano

Vignola, Stefano
Vilioli, Andrea
Villa, Antonio di Milano
Vimercati, Giovanni
    Battista di Milano
Vitali, Luigi
Vittori, Antonio

Zacc(h)arini, Mauro di
    Bologna
Zampettini (Zampetrini),
    Niccola

*Zampieri, Pietro* di Venezia
Zanetti, Gaetano
Zanotti (Zanetti), Angelo
    di Bologna
Zanti (Zante), Antonio
Zanti (Zante), Gaetano
Zappa, Francesco
Zoccoli, Vincenzo
Zucchelli, Alessandro
Zucchelli, Tommaso di
    Bologna
Zurli, Luigi

## FEMALE DANCERS

Acerbi, Luigia → *see:*
    Monari Acerbi, Luigia
Accorsi Acerbi, Luigia (?)
Accorsi Arosio, Chiara
Adoni, Francesca di
    Milano
Agostinelli, Luigia (Luisa)
    di Venezia
Agostini, Cristina [= De
    Agostini?]
Agostini, Ortensia
Airoldi (Ajroldi), Antonia
Albermir, Giovanna
Albertazzi, Teresa
Alberti, Teresa
Albertini, Annunziata
    (Nunziata)
Albertini, Margarita
    (Margherita)
Albertini, Maria di Lucca
Alessandri, Violante
Alippi, Teresa → *see:*
    Mattioli Alippi, Teresa
Allegretti, Antonia
Allegro, Anna
Allegro, Elisabetta
Amati, Margarita
Ambrosi, Giuseppa
Andriani Santoli,
    Geltrude di Bologna

Angiolini, Fortunata →
    *see:* Corti Angiolini,
    Fortunata
Arosio, Chiara → *see:*
    Accorsi Arosio, Chiara
Asner, Anna
Astori, Antonia

Bagato, Chiara
Ballari, Margherita
Banchelli Mazzolini,
    Maria Anna
    (Marianna) di Parma
Banchetti, Isabella di
    Modena
Banchetti, Luigia
Bandettini Galletti,
    Margherita di Lucca
Banti, Clementina
Banti, Felicita
Banti Pazzini (Paccini),
    Francesca di Milano
Banti, Maria
Banti, Teresa di Milano
Baratti Cappelletti,
    Carolina
Bardotti, Elisabetta → *see:*
    Stellato Bardotti,
    Elisabetta
Barlassina, Giuseppa di
    Milano

Bartolamei
    (Bartolom[m]ei), Clara
    (Chiara) di Roma
Beccacini, Luigia
Beccari, Colomba → *see:*
    Montani Beccari,
    Colomba
Bedeschi, Maddalena
Bedotti, (Anna) Maria di
    Roma
Belazine, Marianna
Bellazzi, Angela
Bellazzi, Marianna
Belli, Fiordalisa
Benaglia, Aurora di
    Milano
Benvenuti, Felicita → *see:*
    Ducot Benvenuti,
    Felicita
Bergomi, Anna
Bergomi, Caterina
Bergonzi, Anna
Bernabei, Costanza
Bernardi, Anna Maria
Bernardi, Geltrude
    (Gertrude) di Milano
Bernasconi, Chiara
    (Clara)
Bertini, Lucia
Besesti (Bisesti) Simonetti,
    Teresa

Bettina, Giocomina
Bettini, Camilla
Bettini Mazzolà, Maria
Bianchi, Coralinda
Bianchi, Rosa → *see:*
Cremonini Bianchi,
Rosa
Bianchi Brizzi, Teresa
Bianciardi, Carolina
Bidò, Anna
Bielman, Maria
Biggiani Mei, (Maria)
Maddalena di Firenze
Big(g)iogero (Bigiogera),
Annunziata (Anna) di
Firenze
Big(g)iog(g)ero, Antonia
Bignotti, Maria → *see:*
Brovellina Bignotti,
Maria
Bini, Teresa
Bisesti, Teresa → *see:*
Besesti Simonetti,
Teresa
Boggi, Teresa → *see:*
Boggi(o), Teresa
Boggini (Boggina),
Eugenia *see:* Buggini,
Eugenia
Boggini, Lucrezia
Bog(g)io, Chiara (Clara) di
Torino
Boggio, Laura → *see:*
Carlini Boggio, Laura
Boggi(o) (Boggi, Poggi,
Pozzi), Teresa
Bolla, Sara
Bol(l)ini, Teresa → *see:*
Dolci Pitrot Bollini,
Teresa
Bolognini, Maddalena
Bondanelli, Anna
Bondanelli, Giacinta
Borsari, Elisabetta
(Bettina) → *see:*
Mancini Borsari,
Elisabetta

Boschis, Maria
Bos(s)i Lombardi, Elena
→ *see:* Storni Bossi,
Elena
Bossi, Maria
Bossi, Teresa
Bracci, Francesca di
Firenze
Bragaglia, Luigia (Luisa)
Bragaglia, Maria
Brancher(e) (Bragher),
Carolina
Brendi Silei, Maddalena
di Napoli
Brendi, Maria
Brendi, Teresa
Brizzi, Teresa → *see:*
Bianchi Brizzi, Teresa
Brovellina Bignotti, Maria
Brugnoli (Brognoli),
Giuseppa
Brugnoli, Maria (Marietta)
Brunetti, Maria
Brunetti, Teresa
Buggiani, Maddalena
Buggini, Antonia → *see:*
Per(r)ani Buggini,
Antonia
Buggini (Boggini,
Boggina), Eugenia
Bugiani, Elisabetta
Burazzini, Gertrude di
Bologna
Burci, Maria Anna
Burello, Rosalinda
Bussi, Teresa
Buttini, Elena
Buzzi, Caterina

Calvi, Teresa
Campigli, Giovanna
Cappelletti, Brigida di
Firenze
Cappelletti, Carolina →
*see:* Baratti Cappelletti,
Carolina
Cap(p)elli (Cappello),

Maria → *see:* Gnudi
Cappelli, Maria
Cappello, Rosa
Caprotti, Teresa
Carboni, Caterina
Carlin(i) (Chiarini) Boggio,
Laura
Carraresi, Caterina
Carraresi Regini (Reggi),
Teresa detta Fornaina
Carrero, Francesca
Casali, Luigia
Casassa (Casassi), Maria
Casati, Anna
Casazzi (Casassi), Teresa
Caselli, Gaetana
Casolina, Carolina
Caspani, Maria → *see:*
Gaspani, Maria
Casselli, Maria
Castagna, Giovanna
Castagna, Orsola di
Torino
Castelli, Angiola → *see:*
Lazzari Castelli,
Angiola
Castiglioni, Maria
Cavazza, Rosa
Cavazzi, Geltrude
Cebrari, Caterina
Cel(l)ini (Stellini) Cipriani,
Caterina di Firenze
Cellini Fiorilli, Luigia
(Luisa)
Cellini, Stella di Firenze
Ceruti, Francesca
Ceruti, Vittoria → *see:*
Chenni Ceruti, Vittoria
Cerut(t)i, Anna Maria
(Maria)
Cerut(t)i, Marta
Cesari (Ceseri), Angiola →
*see:* Ricci Cesari,
Angiola
Cesari, Anna
Cesari (Ceseri), Teresa
Chedini → *see:* Ghedini

Falchini, Margarita
Fantini, Teresa
Ferrari Pappini, Petronilla
Ferrari Testini, Rosa →
see: Ferroni Testini,
Rosa
Ferrari, Teresa
Ferraria, Maria
Ferrari(s) (Ferraria,
Ferreri), Giuseppa
Ferri, Anna
Ferri (Ferro), (Maria)
Domenica
Ferroni, Anna → see:
Chiarini Ferroni, Anna
Ferroni, Chiara
Ferroni, Geltrude
Ferroni, Maddalena
Ferroni Testini, Rosa →
see: Ferrari Testini,
Rosa
Filzer, Marianna
Fiorelli, Nunziata
Fiorilli, Antonia
Fiorilli, Luigia (Luisa) →
see: Cellini Fiorilli,
Luigia
Fiorilli Pac(c)ini,
Marianna
Focosi, Francesca → see:
Perfetti Focosi,
Francesca
Focosi, Luigia
Fontanella, Teresa
Foresti, Anna
Foresti, (Maria) Rosa
Foresti, Teresa
Formigli (Formilli),
Annunziata (Nunziata)
Forti, Anna
Forti, Rosa
Fortina (Fortuna),
Marianna
Fracassi (Fracasso),
Marianna
Franceschi Consegnato,
Laura di Firenze

Franchi, Giuseppa → see:
Olivares Franchi,
Giuseppa
Franchi, Marianna
(Maria Anna) di
Venezia
Franchi, Rosa
Franchini, Teresa
Fresca, Rosa
Fusi, Antonia
Fusi, Elena di Milano
Fusi Scardavi Cipriani,
Margarita detta la
Carrozziera di Milano

Gabuti, Anna di Bologna
Galaffi, Geltrude → see:
Galassi, Geltrude
Galantini Grassini,
Aurora di Firenze
Galassi (Galazzi, Galaffi),
Geltrude (Gertrude)
Galassi (Galazzi),
Gesualda di Bologna
Gallerina, Angiola
Galletti, Margherita → see:
Bandettini Galletti,
Margherita
Garbagnati, Giuseppa
Garibotti, Benedetta
Gasoni, Teresa
Gaspani, Francesca
Gaspani (Caspani),
Maria
Gelmi, Anna
Gemmi, Camilla
Gentili, Carolina → see:
Ronzi Gentili,
Carolina
Ghedini (Chedini)
Pen(n)etti, Anna di
Bologna
Ghedini (Chedini),
Domenica di Bologna
Ghedini (Chedini),
Giuliana

Ghedini (Chedini),
Giuseppa → see:
Santambrogio
Ghedini, Giuseppa
Ghedini, Marianna
[= Anna?]
Ghelardini → see:
Gherardini
Gherardini, Annunziata
(Annonziata, Nonziata)
Gherardini (Ghelardini),
Luigia
Gherardini (Ghelardini),
Violante (Viola) → see:
Pinzani Gherardini,
Violante
Ghezzi, Maria
Ghizzola, Marianna
Gianfanelli Poggi, Rosa di
Milano
Gian(n)elli, Maria Ester
Giannetti, Teresa
Giannini, Maddalena
Gigoria, Basilea
Gingoli, Marianna di
Parma
Gioiale (Giojale, Gioiali)
Colla, Giuseppa
Gnudi (Niudi) Cappelli,
Maria
Goiorani, Assunta
Goresi, Antonia
Goresi, Maria
Goresi, Orsola → see:
Rossi Goresi Sirletti,
Orsola
Granati, Anna
Grandis Mariotti(ni),
Teresa → see: De
Grandis Mariottini,
Teresa
Granetti, Teresa
Grassini, Cecilia
Greca, Luigia
Grimaldi, Caterina
Grimaldi, Maria

Grisostomi Montignani,
Agata di Roma
Grisostomi, Gertrude →
see: Pac(c)ini Grisostomi,
Gertrude (Geltrude)
Grossi, Luigia
Gucci, Anna di Firenze
Guglielmi, Antonia (Anna)
→ see: Heymin-
Guglielmi, Antonia
Guidetti, Maria
Gussani, Sabina → see:
Cus(s)ani, Sabina

Heymin-Guglielmi,
Antonia (Anna) di
Vienna

Isola, Benedetta

Lanzoni, Petronilla
Lasagna (Lesagna), Anna
Laurenti, Gaspera
Lazzari (Lazzeri) Castelli,
Angiola di Bologna
Leoncini, Giacomina di
Venezia
Leoni, Francesca
Lesagna → see: Lasagna
Lodi Chiaveri, Francesca
Lolli, Giuditta
Lombardi, Elena → see:
Bossi Lombardi, Elena
see also: Storni Bossi,
Elena
Longhi(na) (Longhini),
Giuseppa
Longo, Chiara → see: Dal
Lungo, Chiara
Lorenzini (Lorenzani),
Anna
Lumicisi, Marianna

Maffei, Anna di Lucca
Magagnini, Maddalena →
see: Porci Magagnini,
Maddalena

Magistretti, Teresa di
Milano
Majer → see: Mayer
Mancini Borsari,
Elisabetta (Bettina)
Manna, Caterina
Manni (Manna), Teresa di
Milano
Mantegazzi, (Maria) Anna
→ see: Orti
Mantegazzi, Anna
Manzoli, Teresa
Marchi, Barbara → see:
Monterumisi Marchi,
Barbara
Mariatti, Teresa → see: De
Grandis Mariotti(ni),
Teresa
Marinelli, Barbara di
Firenze
Mariotti, Maria
Mariotti(ni), Teresa → see:
De Grandis
Mariotti(ni), Teresa
Marliani, Massimilla
Martelli, Carlotta
Martelli, Teresa di
Venezia
Martinelli, Marianna
Martini, Anna
Masà → see: Mas(s)an
Masari, Giuseppa
Masini, Giuditta
Masnieri, Rosa di Brescia
Massa (Mazza), Teresa
Mas(s)an (Massà, Masson,
Mazzà), Camilla
Mas(s)an (Masà, Masán),
Rosa di Napoli
Massini, Anna
Mas(s)ini, Giuditta
Matteucci, Caterina
Mattioli Alippi, Teresa
Mayer, Elisa
Mayer (Majer), Marianna
Mazza, Teresa → see:
Massa, Teresa

Mazzei, Maria
Mazzolà, Maria → see:
Bettini Mazzolà, Maria
Mazzolini, Maddalena
Mazzolini, Marianna →
see: Banchellli
Mazzolini, Maria Anna
Mazzoni, Teresa di
Bologna
Mei, Maddalena → see:
Biggiani Mei,
Maddalena
Mei, Maria
Mejer → see: Meyer
Meocicca, Eufemia
Meroni, Maria di Milano
Meyer, Benedetta
Meyer (Mejer), Teresa
Milani, Clementina
Minarelli, Rosa di
Bologna
Mira, Teresa
Mogni, Annunziata
Moller, Giuseppa
Monari, Geltrude di
Bologna
Monari, Lucia → see:
Fabris Monari, Lucia
Monari Acerbi, Luigia
Monari, Maria di Bologna
Montani Beccari,
Colomba di Lucca
Montani, Rosa → see:
Costa Montani, Rosa
Monterumisi
(Monteromis) Marchi,
Barbara
Monti Pap(p)ini,
Marianna (Maria
Anna) di Bologna
Monti, Rosa
Monticini, Antonia
Montignani, Agata → see:
Grisostomi
Montignani, Agata
Montignani, Beatrice
Moraglia, Rosa

Radaelli, Agostina
Radaelli, Angiola
Radaelli, Giuseppa → see:
    Pontiggia Radaelli,
    Giuseppa
Ramac(c)ini, Caterina →
    see: Piattoli Ramac(c)ini,
    Caterina
Ramo, Anna
Rassi, Angiola [= Raffi?]
Ravarina, Teresa
Ravasini, Rosa
Reggi, Teresa → see:
    Carraresi Regini,
    Teresa
Regini Cortesi,
    Margherita
Restani, Maria (Marietta)
Ribalti, Teresa
Riboli, Maria
Ricci Cesari (Ceseri),
    Angiola di Bologna
Ricci, Francesca
Riga, Rosa
Riga, Santa
Rinaldi, Teresa
Ronzi, Antonia
Ronzi Gentili, Carolina
    (Carlotta)
Rossi, Anna
Rossi Deville, Giuseppa
Rossi Tor(r)elli,
    Margherita (Margarita)
    di Venezia
Rossi Goresi Sirletti,
    Orsola di Bologna
Rossi, Stella
Rossi, Teresa
Rossignoli, Teresa di
    Parma
Rub(b)ini Corradini, Anna

Sala, Anna
Salamoni, Beatrice
Salamoni, Costanza → see:
    Tinti Salamoni,
    Costanza

Sammartini, Maria
Sanromeri, Giovanna di
    Parma
Santambrogio (S. Am-
    brogio) Ghedini,
    Giuseppa (Gioseffa)
Santambrogio, Giustina
Santini, Caterina
Santini, Gaetana
Sarajfoghel (Seraifoghel),
    Teresa
Sarmetti, Paolina → see:
    Sermet(ti), Paola
Sarmetti, Teresa
Scap(p)ini, Annunziata
    (Nunziata)
Scappini, Rosa
Scardavi Cipriani,
    Margarita → see: Fusi
Scardavi Cipriani,
    Margarita
Scattai (Scattaja, Sgattai,
    Scattaglia), Rosa di
    Venezia
Serafini, Antonia
Serio, Maria
Sermet(ti) (Sarmetti),
    Paola (Paolina)
Serra, Francesca
Serra, Maddalena
Serra, Marianna
Serrandrei, Brigida
Ses(s)oni, Assunta
    (Assonta)
Sessoni, Maria
Signorini, Marianna di
    Milano
Silei, Maddalena → see:
    Brendi Silei,
    Maddalena
Simonetti, Caterina
Simonetti, Giovanna
Simonetti, Teresa → see:
    Besesti (Bisesti)
Simonetti, Teresa
Simonetti, Vittoria

Sirletti, Orsola → see:
    Rossi Goresi Sirletti,
    Orsola
Sirletti, Vincenza
Sputoni (Spontani), Santa
    di Bologna
Stella, Anna
Stellato Bardotti,
    Elisabetta (Bettina)
Stellini Cipriani, Caterina
    → see: Cellini Cipriani,
    Caterina
Storni Bossi, Elena → see:
    Bos(s)i Lombardi,
    Elena
Storni, Maria
Strada, Orsola

Tad(d)ei, Luigia
Taglioni, Maria
Tantini, Anna di Firenze
Tarabattoni → see:
    Trabattoni
Tarapatona, Vienna
Tassani Col(l)ina, Antonia
Terrades, Anna → see:
    Nadi De Sales
Terrades, Anna
Terrades, Antonia → see:
    Tom(m)asini
Terrade(s), Antonia
Testini, Rosa → see:
    Ferrari Testini, Rosa
    see also: Ferroni Testini,
    Rosa
Tiberti, Giovanna
Tinti Salamoni, Costanza
Tomasini, Domenica
Tomasini, Giuseppa
Tom(m)asini Terrade(s),
    Antonia
Tom(m)as(s)ini, Regina
Toni, Marianna
Tor(r)elli, Margherita →
    see: Rossi Tor(r)elli,
    Margherita
Torri Trento, Antonia

# Appendix 2

## Scenarios of Selected Ballets Performed in Northern Italian Theaters

COMPILED AND TRANSLATED BY

BRUCE ALAN BROWN AND

KATHLEEN KUZMICK HANSELL

Call numbers are those of copies consulted; in initial headings, name of librettist precedes that of composer (of opera). For cast lists, format of original is generally reproduced, with translations following, as necessary.

1. Turin, Regio Teatro, Carnival 1761: ballets
(all by Vincenzo Saunier) for the opera *Artaserse* (Artaxerxes; Metastasio/J. C. Bach), premiere 26 December 1760

1st ballet:  *La morte, ed il rinascimento del Pastore Adone* (The Death and Rebirth of the Shepherd Adonis)

2nd ballet:  *Ridotto di Maschere di varie Nazioni* (Ball of Masks from Various Nations)

3rd ballet:  *Di persiani adoratori del sole* (Of Persian Sun-Worshippers)

Libretto: Schatz Collection, Music Division, Library of Congress, Washington, DC, 532 (reel 12)

ARTASERSE / DRAMMA PER MUSICA / *DA RAPPRESENTARSI* / NEL REGIO TEATRO / DI TORINO / NEL CARNEVALE DEL MDCCLXI. / ALLA PRESENZA / *DI* / S. S. R. M. / TORINO. / Presso GIACOMO GIUSEPPE AVONDO / Stampatore, e Librajo della Società de' Signori Cavalieri.

ARTAXERXES / DRAMA IN MUSIC / *TO BE PERFORMED* / IN THE ROYAL THEATER / OF TURIN / DURING THE CARNIVAL OF MDCCLXI. / IN THE PRESENCE / *OF* / H. S. R. M. / TURIN. / By GIACOMO GIUSEPPE AVONDO / Printer, and Bookseller of the Society of Noble Gentlemen.

MUTAZIONI DI SCENE.

CHANGES OF SCENERY.

ATTO PRIMO. . . .
*Per il Ballo [primo]*
Bosco in lunga, e stretta Valle con Colline praticabili in fondo, il quale poi si trasforma in delizioso Giardino della Reggia di Venere adorno di Fiori, Statue, ed Amorini.

FIRST ACT . . . .
*For the [first] Ballet*
A wood in a long and narrow valley with traversable hills in the background, which then changes to a delightful garden in Venus's palace, bedecked with flowers, statues, and Cupids.

*ATTO SECONDO.* . . .
Gran Sala del Reale Consiglio tutta circondata da Tribune praticabili per il Popolo. Trono da un lato, Tavolino, e Sedia a fianco del medesimo. Sedili dall'altro per i Grandi.

*SECOND ACT.* . . .
Great hall of the Royal Council Chamber, the whole surrounded by traversable galleries for the people. Throne to one side, little table and chair next to it. Chairs for the grandees on the other side.

ATTO TERZO. . . .
Magnifico, e grandioso Tempio del Sole, il di cui simulacro vedesi in alto circondato da gran luce, festivamente apparato per la Coronazione d'Artaserse. Trono da un lato; Ara nel mezzo accesa.

THIRD ACT. . . .
Magnificent, grandiose Temple of the Sun, a statue of whom is seen on high, surrounded by a great light, festively adorned for the coronation of Artaxerxes. To one side a throne; lighted altar in the middle.

*Inventori, e Pittori delle medesime.*

*Designer, and painter of the same.*

Li Signori Fratelli Galliari Piemontesi. . . .

The Brothers Galliari of Piedmont. . . .

BALLI.

BALLETS.

*Inventore, e Direttore de' medesimi.*

*Inventor, and director of the same.*

Il Signor Vincenzo Saunier.

Mr. Vincenzo Saunier.

*Compositore delle Arie de' medesimi.*

*Composer of the music of the same.*

Il Signor Giuseppe Antonio Le Messier Musico Suonatore di Cappella, e Camera di S. R. M.

Mr. Giuseppe Antonio Le Messier Instrumental Musician of H. R. H. Chapel and Chamber

La morte, ed il rinascimento del Pastore Adone.

LA Scena rappresenta un Bosco in lunga, ma stretta Valle con alture praticabili in fondo, ove segue una caccia, la quale poi si trasforma in delizioso Giardino adorno di fiori, e statue trasparenti.

Si legge nella Storia favolosa, che il Pastore Adone inseguendo alla caccia un Cinghiale per opera di Diana ad istanza di Marte, fu da quella Belva feroce ucciso, e che il suo corpo alle preghiere di Venere fu trasformato in un Fiore.

Per dar lieto fine al Ballo si è ideato di farlo nascere dalla pianta medesima per opera della stessa Dea, sopra del qual soggetto è stato formato il seguente Ballo.

Alzata la tela vedrassi Adone con seguito di Cacciatori, e Cacciatrici, Venere, che viene al di lui incontro, ed egli, che prosiegue la sua Caccia, dove incontra il Cinghiale, che atterra il Pastore, e lo uccide.

Venere scende dal Cielo, e trasforma il Corpo d'Adone in un Fiore; Marte geloso arriva, e vedendo le premure di Venere per quella pianta, s'affatica invano per ispellerla dal suolo. Qui Venere implora il soccorso di Giove, si veggono lampi, s'ode il fragore del tuono, sparisce il Fiore, e ne rinasce Adone, e qui la Scena si cambia in una deliziosa adorna di Fiori, e Statue trasparenti; Venere scende dalla sua Reggia, ed accoglie Adone, il quale proccura [sic] in ogni modo d'esprimerle la sua riconoscenza. Verranno le azioni suddette frammischiate dai Passi a due del Cacciatore del Falcone, di due Pastori, e da quello di Adone, e di Venere. Segue la Contradanza finale di tutte le Ninfe, Cacciatori, e Pastori, colla quale si termina il Ballo.

The Death and Rebirth of the Shepherd Adonis.

The stage shows a wood in a long but narrow valley with traversable hills in the background, where a hunt takes place, which [scene] then is transformed into a delightful garden adorned with flowers, and transparent statues.

We read in mythology that the shepherd Adonis, while on a boar hunt for Diana, at the instigation of Mars, was killed by that ferocious beast, and that due to the pleas of Venus his body was transformed into a flower.

In order to provide a happy ending for this ballet it was decided to have it arise from the plant itself through the office of the same goddess, on which theme the following ballet was formed.

When the curtain is raised, we see Adonis with his retinue of hunters and huntresses, and Venus who comes to meet him; he, pursuing his hunt, meets with the boar, which knocks the shepherd down, and kills him.

Venus descends from heaven, and transforms the body of Adonis into a flower; the jealous Mars arrives, and seeing Venus's attentions to that plant, struggles in vain to pull it out of the ground. At this point Venus implores the aid of Jupiter, and lightning is seen, the noise of thunder is heard, the flower vanishes and out of it Adonis is reborn, and here the scene changes to a garden adorned with flowers and transparent statues; Venus comes down from her palace, and greets Adonis, who attempts in every manner possible to express his gratitude to her. The above actions will be intermingled with *pas de deux* by the falconer, by two shepherds, and by Adonis and Venus. Then follows the final contredanse of all the nymphs, hunters, and shepherds, with which the ballet ends.

BALLO SECONDO.

Ridotto di Maschere di varie Nazioni.

LA Scena è la stessa, che serve al gran Consiglio d'Artaserse.

Sendosi bastantemente veduti sulle moderne scene li ridotti di maschere del Teatro Italiano, si è pensato di prendere per soggetto di questo Ballo il concorso di varie nazioni straniere ad una pubblica festa di Ballo, e siccome non è possibile il descrivere le varie accoglienze, che ivi si fanno tra loro gli concorrenti alla festa, e le altre picciole Pantomime, le quali come non sono di essenza del Ballo, e possono esser soggette a variazioni, non si sono quì accennate: epperò saravvi dopo la solita introduzione fatto luogo alli passi a due, di Pollachi, di Tedeschi, e di Spagnuoli, i quali uniti alli varj corpi di Ballo, e contradanze formeranno tutta l'idea propostasi in una festa di ballo, o sia ridotto di maschere, e di varie, e diverse nazioni.

BALLO TERZO.

Di Persiani adoratori del Sole.

LE azioni del Dramma essendosi tutte passate nella Città di Susa capitale della Persia, ed essendo stato culto principale de' Persiani quello del Sole, tanto più che la scena rappresenta il Tempio col simulacro di esso, quivi si è introdotto per soggetto del Ballo un grande del Regno con corteggio di numeroso Popolo di vario sesso, il quale accorre al Tempio per quivi adorare il Nume tutelar della Persia, e quivi dopo varj atti di venerazione, e d'ossequio si darà principio al Ballo de' Persiani, nel quale saranno frammeschiati li passi a due d'una coppia grottesca, di un'altra di mezzo carattere, e finalmente dalla Giacona della prima cop[p]ia seria, e questa verrà seguita dalla generale contradanza, colla quale si darà fine allo spettacolo.

SECOND BALLET.

Ball of Masks from Various Nations.

The setting is the same as for the great Council Chamber of Artaxerxes.

Since balls with masks from the Italian theater are commonly seen on the modern stage, we decided to take as a subject for this ballet the gathering of different foreign nations at a public gala ball, and as it is not possible to describe the various greetings that the participants in the ball make to each other, and the other little pantomimes, which by nature are not danced, and which are subject to variation, they are not mentioned here: nevertheless after the usual introduction there follow the *pas de deux* for Poles, for Germans, and for Spaniards, which together with various group dances and contredanses will form the whole idea that is proposed in a gala ball, or *ridotto* of masks and of various diverse nationalities.

THIRD BALLET.

Of Persian Sun-Worshippers.

Since all the actions of the [opera] take place in the city of Susa, capital of Persia, and since sun worship has been the main religion of the Persians, and all the more since the stage shows the temple with a statue of it [the sun], at this point we introduce as subject of the ballet a grandee of the realm with his large retinue of people of both sexes, who hasten to the temple in order to worship the tutelary god of Persia, and then, after various acts of veneration and respect, the ballet of Persians will begin, in which will be intermingled the *pas de deux* of a grotesque couple, another one of a *mezzo-carattere* couple, and finally the chaconne of the first serious couple, and this will be followed by the contredanse for all, with which the spectacle will come to a close.

## 2. Milan, Regio Ducal Teatro, 1768–69 season: ballets (all by Vincenzo Galeotti) for the opera *Alceste* (Alcestes; Calzabigi, rev. Parini/Guglielmi), premiere 26 December 1768

1st ballet:    *La favola di Phsiche* (The Fable of Psyche)

2nd ballet:    *La fiera d'Amsterdam, con ballo intrecciato di Provenzali, e d'Olandesi; ed introdotto da una pazza ec.* (The Amsterdam Fair, with a dance joined in by Provençals and Dutch; and a crazy woman is introduced, etc.)

3rd ballet:    *di carattere uniforme, detto Ciaccona* (of uniform character, called Chaconne)

Libretto: Schatz 4233 (reel 85)

ALCESTE, / DRAMMA TRAGICO / DA RAPPRESENTARSI / NEL REGIO-DUCAL TEATRO DI MILANO / Nel Carnovale dell' Anno 1769. / DEDICATO / A SUA ALTEZZA SERENISSIMA / IL / DUCA DI MODENA, . . . / IN MILANO, ) ) MDCCLXVIII. / Nella Regia Ducal Corte, / per Giuseppe Richino Malatesta Stampatore / Regio Camerale. . . .

ALCESTES, / TRAGIC DRAMA / TO BE PERFORMED / IN THE ROYAL-DUCAL THEATER OF MILAN / In the Carnival of the Year 1769. / DEDICATED / TO HIS MOST SERENE HIGHNESS / THE / DUKE OF MODENA, . . . / IN MILAN, ) ) MDCCLXVIII. / At the Royal Ducal Court, / by Giuseppe Richino Malatesta Royal Chamber / Printer. . . .

*MUTAZIONI DI SCENE.*

*CHANGES OF SCENERY.*

SCENE PER IL PRIMO BALLO.
Luogo delizioso ec.
Orrida Montagna nella Lapponia.
Reggia d'Amore.

SCENERY FOR THE FIRST BALLET.
Delightful garden etc.
Horrid Mountain in Lapland.
Palace of Love [Hymen].

BALLO SECONDO.
Veduta della Fiera nella Città d'Amsterdam ec.

SECOND BALLET.
View of the Fairground in the City of Amsterdam etc.

*Inventori, e Pittori delle Scene.*

*Designers, and Painters of the Scenery.*

Li Signori Fratelli Galeari.

The Brothers Galeari.

PRIMO BALLO.
RAppresenta la Favola di Phsiche, Principessa di una bellezza tale, che l'Amore medesimo, Cupido volle farsi suo Sposo, laonde impose a Zefiro, che la trasportasse in un Lungo delizioso ec.

    Si dà principio al Ballo da varie Ninfe, che aspettano la venuta di Phsiche, la quale portata da Zefiro, festevolmente ac-

FIRST BALLET.
Presents the fable of Psyche, a princess of such beauty that Love himself, Cupid, wishes to become her husband, and therefore imposes on Zephyrus, who transports her to a delightful garden etc.

    The ballet begins with various nymphs, who are awaiting the arrival of Psyche, whom, carried in by Zephyrus, they wel-

colgono, e diconle dover'ivi attendere lo Sposo, e partono.

Si fa notte; compare l'Amante, le scherza d'intorno; timorosa la rassicura, e seco si addormenta sopra Sedile di Verdura.

Phsiche risvegliatasi, vuole riconoscere lo Sposo ancor dormiente: Corre a prendere una Fiaccola, e vede allo splendore di essa, in vece d'un'orrido Mostro, che dall'Oracolo erale stato presagito, il bel Cupido, il cui vago sembiante, e la bionda Capigliatura lo rendevano il più amabile degli Dei; e mentre vicina lo vezzeggia, disgraziatamente gli abbruccia un'Ala.

Scuotesi disdegnoso Cupido, l'abbandona; e nel tempo stesso vien giorno, e quell'ameno soggiorno si tramuta in orrida Montagna della Lapponia, dalle cui Grotte veggonsi uscire que' rabbuffati Abitatori per rapire Phsiche, dalle mani de' quali, mentre in vano tenta involarsi, ecco aprirsi quel Monte, e comparire Borrea, che posti avendo in fuga i Lapponi, aspira violentemente al possesso della medesima, la quale per liberarsene si precipita fra que' dirupi, tramutati sul momento dal compassionate Cupido nella Reggia d'Imeneo, in cui da Venere accoppiata viene la fortunata Phsiche al figlio Cupido in Matrimonio, festeggiato da que' Genj ec.

BALLO SECONDO.
Rappresenta la fiera d'Amsterdam, con Ballo intrecciato di Provenzali, e d'Olandesi; ed introdotto da una Pazza ec.

BALLO TERZO.
Di Carattere uniforme, detto Ciaccona*

come joyfully; they tell her she must there await her bridegroom, and depart.

Night falls; the lover appears and makes merry with her; he dispels her fears and she falls asleep with him on a seat of verdure.

Psyche, reawakening, wants to identify the still sleeping bridegroom: she runs to fetch a torch, and sees in its gleam instead of a horrid monster, whom the oracle had predicted for her, handsome Cupid, whose lovely visage and blond hair render him the most lovable of the gods; and while she comes close and caresses him, she unfortunately burns one of his wings.

Scornful, Cupid wakes up and abandons her; at the same time day breaks and that pleasant abode is changed into a horrid mountain in Lapland, from the grottos of which its unkempt inhabitants are seen to emerge in order to steal away Psyche; while she is trying in vain to flee from their clutches, behold, the mountain opens up, and Boreas appears; he having put the Laplanders to flight, likewise fiercely aspires to be the possessor of her [Psyche], who, to free herself leaps into the ravine, which is transformed in an instant by the compassionate Cupid into the Palace of Hymen, in which the fortunate Psyche is joined by Venus to her son Cupid in matrimony, celebrated by the nymphs, etc.

SECOND BALLET.
The Amsterdam Fair, with a dance joined in by Provençals and Dutch; and a crazy woman is introduced, etc.

THIRD BALLET.
Of uniform character, called Chaconne*

[* A generic designation for a common sort of *terzo ballo* in Milan, either tenuously or not at all connected to the subject of the opera, and without specified characters.]

COMPOSITORE DE' BALLI / COMPOSER OF THE BALLETS
SIG. VINCENZO GALEOTTI,
ED ESEGUITI / AND PERFORMED

| Dai Signori / By Messrs. | E Signore / And Mlles. |
|---|---|
| Vincenzo Galeotti. | —Antonia Guidi Galeotti. |
| Carlo Russler. | —Annunciata Casari. |
| Antonio Busida. | —Rosa Campora. |
| Adamo Fabroni. | —Rosa Tinti. |
| Giuseppe Radaelli. | —Anastasia Radaelli. |
| Vincenzo Tinti. | —Cattarina Baffa. |
| Antonio Canquirico. | —Rosa Pitrai. |
| Girolamo Greco. | —Paola Terranea. |
| Antonio Clerico. | —Elena Signorini. |
| Giuseppe De Maria. | —Angela Gallerini. |
| Antonio Tangassi. | —Angela Capredona. |

Violante Pitrai.

Fuori de' Concerti / outside the company dances

Signor Carlo Sabbatini.                     Signora Anna Sabbatini,

Virtuosa di S.A.S. il Duca di Modena ec. ec. /
Virtuosa of H.R.H. the Duke of Modena etc. etc.

## 3. Mantua, Regio-Ducal Teatro Vecchio, Carnival 1770: ballets (both by Cosimo Morelli) for the opera *Demofoonte* (Demophoön; Metastasio/Traetta), premiere 1758

1st ballet:        *Il ratto di Proserpina* (The Abduction of Proserpine)
2nd ballet:       *Una festa cinese* (A Chinese Festival)

Libretto: Schatz 10408 (reel 211)

DEMOFOONTE / DRAMMA PER MUSICA / DEL *SIGNOR ABATE* / PIETRO METASTASIO / POETA CESAREO, / Da rappresentarsi nel Regio-Ducal Teatro Vecchio di Mantova il Carnovale dell'anno 1770. / DEDICATO AL MERITO SUBLIME / DELLE / NOBILISSIME DAME / DI DETTA CITTA'. / IN MANTOVA, / Per l'Erede di Alberto Pazzoni, Regio-Ducale Stampatore. . . .

DEMOPHOÖN / DRAMA IN MUSIC / BY THE *SIGNOR ABATE* / PIETRO METASTASIO / IMPERIAL POET, / To be performed in the old Royal-Ducal Theater of Mantua during Carnival of the year 1770. / DEDICATED TO THE SUBLIME MERIT / OF THE / MOST NOBLE LADIES / OF THAT CITY. / IN MANTUA, / By the heir of Alberto Pazzoni, Royal-Ducal Printer. . . .

IL VESTIARIO
Sarà di ricca, e bizzarra invenzione del Sig. Giuseppe Vitali di Milano.

THE COSTUMES
Is the rich and fascinating design of Mr. Giuseppe Vitali of Milan.

INVENTORE, E DIRETTORE DE' BALLI /
INVENTOR AND DIRECTOR OF THE BALLETS

Sig. Cosimo Morelli,

Eseguiti da' seguenti: / Performed by the following:

| | |
|---|---|
| Sig. Cosimo Morelli suddetto. | Signora Anna Salamoni Morelli. |
| Sig. Vincenzio Piattoli. | Signora Giuditta Falchini Piattoli. |
| Sig. Vincenzio Tinti. | Signora Rosa Tinti. |
| Sig. Angiolo Zànotti. | Signora Antonia Negri. |

LO SCENARIO

Sarà del rinomato Sig. Cavaliere Antonio Galli Bibbiena, Architetto all'attual servigio delle Loro Maestà Imperiali.

THE SCENERY

Is by the renowned Cavalier Antonio Galli Bibbiena, Architect currently in service to Their Imperial Majesties.

LE DECORAZIONI DE' BALLI

Saranno del Sig. Gaetano Crevola, Architetto Teatrale.

THE DECORS OF THE BALLETS

Are by Mr. Gaetano Crevola, Theatrical Architect.

SPIEGAZIONE DEL PRIMO BALLO.

STa Cerere in una vasta pianura alle falde del Monte Etna unita alla figlia Proserpina insegnando a numerosa quantità di Villani, e Villane la maniera di coltivare le Terre: nella premura di trasferirsi altrove all'effetto stesso raccomanda a questi la detta sua figlia; si congeda con un bacio dalla medesima, e parte.

Affine di consolare Proserpina afflitta per la partenza della Madre, s'industriano i Villani coll'intreccio di danze di tenerla sollevata.

Scoppia improvvisamente dal Monte un gran lampo, che tutti sgomenta, e confusamente li riduce a fuggire. La sola Proserpina rimane, che, mentre agitata qua, e là s'aggira, s'avviene in Pluto, il quale, disceso dal suo carro, le viene incontro. Essa tutta tremante lo fugge, Egli amoroso l'insegue fin a che, stanco di farlo senza frutto, l'afferra, e trattala a forza sul proprio carro la guida all'Inferno.

Rinvenuti i Villani dallo spavento sortono con fiaccole accese in traccia di Proserpina, e, non veggendola, all'indizio

EXPLANATION OF THE FIRST BALLET.

Ceres is in a vast plain at the foot of Mount Etna, together with her daughter Proserpine, teaching a large number of peasant men and women how to cultivate the earth: in her haste to go elsewhere she commends her daughter to them for this same purpose; she takes leave of her with a kiss, and departs.

In order to console Proserpine, who is saddened by her mother's departure, the peasants endeavor to raise her spirits by forming dances.

A great bolt of lightning unexpectedly bursts forth from the mountain, and causes [the peasants] to flee in confusion. There remains only Proserpine, who while agitatedly wandering to and fro encounters Pluto, who having exited his chariot, comes toward her. All a-tremble, she flees him; he, full of love, pursues her until, tired of doing so fruitlessly, he grabs her, drags her forcibly to his chariot and drives her to Hell.

Having recovered from their fear, the peasants emerge with lighted torches, looking for Proserpine, and not seeing

del fumo s'accorgono, che sia stata rapita. Compiangono quindi una tanta disgrazia, quando sopravviene Cerere, e richiede la figlia. La dimostrano questi rapita, e ne additano quel più che sanno. Ella forsennata d'amore risolve d'andar a rintracciarla, e presa la via del Monte, vi sale fino alla sommità, dalla quale, dato un addio a' suoi fidi seguaci, si scaglia, e precipita nell'Inferno.

Stupidi, e dolenti partono questi, ed ecco sul momento comparire la Reggia di Pluto, e questo Nume con Proserpina assiso in Trono. Lo scaccia la Giovane, e sopravvenendo Cerere tra quegli orrori, fugge tra le bracccia della Madre. Pluto la segue, e contrassegnano Madre, e figlia il rispettivo amor loro, e lo sdegno loro concorde verso Pluto, che senza pregiudizio del suo potere cede solo al materno, ed al figliale vicendevol amor delle Dee, e tutto affettuoso concerta colla Madre, cui riconosce di non poter resistere, di lasciarle sei mesi dell'anno la figlia, e gli altri sei ritenerla presso di se. Resta Pluto contento, e lascia consecutivamente la figlia in poter della Madre. Sortono entrambe da quel luogo d'orrore, ed uscite appena, scoppia un fulmine, dietro il quale comparisce la Reggia di Giove, tutta circondata di nubi, tra le quali vedesi Giove stesso, colle sfere celesti, che le fanno cerchio. Cerere, e Proserpina vi si portano, e genuflesse l'adorano, e le rendono le dovute grazie dell'ottenuto favore. Frattanto scoperte queste da' loro seguaci, veggonsi questi comparire, e con una maestosa marchia [*sic*] attaccano il concerto.

[beween Acts II and III:]

*IL SECONDO BALLO.*
*Rappresenterà una festa Cinese.*

her, realize from the traces of smoke that she has been abducted. They are bemoaning that misfortune when Ceres appears and inquires about her daughter. They indicate that she has been abducted, and point out what little they know. Ceres, insane with love, resolves to go find her, and taking the path up the mountain, climbs to the summit, from which, having bid farewell to her faithful followers, she leaps into Hell.

Stunned and mournful, these last leave, and at this moment Pluto's palace appears, and the god himself seated on the throne with Proserpine. The young girl chases him away, and when Ceres appears among these horrors, she flies into her mother's arms. Pluto follows her, and mother and daughter give signs of their love for one another, and of their mutual disdain for Pluto, who without compromising his power cedes only to the reciprocal maternal and filial love of the goddesses, and full of emotion he decides along with her mother, whom he realizes he cannot resist, that he will leave her daughter with her for six months of the year, and for the other six keep her with him. Pluto is content, and he then leaves the daughter in her mother's power. Both of them leave that place of horror, and as soon as they exit, a bolt of lightening explodes, behind which appears the palace of Jupiter, all surrounded by clouds, among which we see Jupiter himself, with the celestial spheres circling him. Ceres and Proserpine go over to him, and kneel before him in adoration, and give thanks for the favor they had been granted. Their followers, having found them in the meantime, come on and with a majestic march begin the company dance.

*THE SECOND BALLET.*
Represents a Chinese festival.

## 4. Milan, Regio Ducal Teatro, Primavera 1770: ballets for the opera *Il regno della luna* (The Realm of the Moon; ?/Piccinni)

1st ballet: *Aci, e Galatea* (Acis and Galatea; by Antonio Campioni)
2nd ballet: *Ballo di Americani* (Ballet of Americans; by Vincenzo Monari)

Libretto: Schatz 8106 (reel 167)

IL REGNO / DELLA LUNA. / *DRAMMA GIOCOSO* / DA RAPPRESENTARSI / NEL REGIO DUCAL TEATRO / DI MILANO / Nella corrente Primavera, / DEDICATO / A SUA ALTEZZA SERENISS.<sup>MA</sup>/ IL / DUCA DI MODENA, / REGGIO, MIRANDOLA ec. ec. . . . / IN MILANO, MDCCLXX. / Appresso Gio: Batista Bianchi Regio Stampatore. . . .

THE KINGDOM / OF THE MOON. / *COMIC DRAMA* / TO BE PERFORMED / IN THE ROYAL DUCAL THEATER / OF MILAN / During the present Spring, / DEDICATED / TO HIS MOST SERENE HIGHNESS / THE / DUKE OF MODENA, / REGGIO, MIRANDOLA etc. etc. . . . / IN MILAN, MDCCLXX. / By Gio: Batista Bianchi Royal Printer. . . .

INVENTORE DELLE SCENE.
*Il Sig. Cavaliere Antonio Galli Bibbiena, primo Architetto, ed Ingegnere attuale delle LL. MM. Imperiali.*

DESIGNER OF THE SCENERY.
*The Cavalier Antonio Galli Bibbiena, first Architect, and Engineer in the service of Their Imperial Majesties.*

INVENTORE DEGLI ABITI.
*Li Signori Francesco Motta, e Giovanni Mazza, Allievi del fu Sig. Francesco Mainino.*

DESIGNER OF THE COSTUMES.
*Messers Francesco Motta and Giovanni Mazza, Students of the late Mr. Francesco Mainino.*

BALLO PRIMO / *ACI, E* / *GALATEA.*

FIRST BALLET / *ACIS AND* / *GALATEA*

ATTORI DANZANTI.
ACI, Amante corrisposto di Galatea.
*Il Sig. Antonio Campioni, all'attual Servigio di S.A.R. l'Infante Don Ferdinando, Duca di Parma ec. ec.*

DANCING ACTORS.
ACIS, reciprocated lover of Galatea.
*Mr. Antonio Campioni, presently in the Service of H.R.H. the Infante Don Ferdinando, Duke of Parma etc. etc.*

GALATEA, Amante di Aci.
*La Signora Giustina Campioni Bianchi, all'attual Servigio, come sopra.*

GALATEA, Lover of Acis.
*Madame Giustina Campioni Bianchi, presently in the Service, as above.*

POLIFEMO, Ciclope, Amante ricusato di Galatea.
*Il Sig. Vincenzo Monari.*

POLYPHEMUS, Cyclops, spurned lover of Galatea.
*Mr. Vincenzo Monari.*

TETI.
*La Signora Antonia Torri.*

THETIS.
*Madame Antonia Torri.*

NETTUNNO.
*Il Sig. Giuseppe Casazzi.*

NEPTUNE.
*Mr. Giuseppe Casazzi.*

ANFITRITE.
*La Signora Maria Casazzi.*

AMPHITRITE.
*Madame Maria Casazzi.*

| | |
|---|---|
| IMENEO. | HYMEN. |
| *Il Sig. Giuseppe Clara.* | *Mr. Giuseppe Clara.* |
| SEGUITO / DI PASTORI, E PASTORELLE / CON | SUITE / OF SHEPHERDS AND |
| ACI, E GALATEA. | SHEPHERDESSES / WITH ACIS AND GALATEA. |

|  |  |
|---|---|
| | { Sig. Francesco Picchi. |
| *Pastori / Shepherds* | { Sig. Gio: Batista Vimercati. |
| | { Sig. Carlo Dondi. |
| | { Sig. Vincenzo Bardella. |

|  |  |
|---|---|
| | { Signora Giustina Castelli. |
| *Pastorelle / Shepherdesses* | { Signora Anna Padulli. |
| | { Signora Maria Dondi. |
| | { Signora Elena Signorini. |

SEGUITO DI POLIFEMO. / FOLLOWERS OF POLYPHEMUS.

|  |  |
|---|---|
| | { Sig. Bartolomeo Benaglia. |
| | { Sig. Gio: Batista Ajmi. |
| *Ciclopi / Cyclopes* | { Sig. Francesco Sedini. |
| | { Sig. Francesco Parravicini. |
| | { Sig. Giuseppe Nanini. |
| | { Sig. Giuseppe De Maria. |

SEGUITO DI NETTUNNO, E DI TETI. / FOLLOWERS OF NEPTUNE AND THETIS.

|  |  |
|---|---|
| | { Sig. Bartolomeo Benaglia. |
| | { Sig. Gio: Batista Ajmi. |
| *Tritoni / Tritons* | { Sig. Francesco Sedini. |
| | { Sig. Francesco Parravicini. |
| | { Sig. Giuseppe Nanini. |
| | { Sig. Giuseppe De Maria. |

|  |  |
|---|---|
| | { Signora Lucia Monti. |
| | { Signora Angiola Gallarina. |
| *Nereidi / Nereids* | { Signora Angiola Capredoni. |
| | { Signora Paola Terranea. |
| | { Signora Rosa Palmieri. |
| | { Signora Maria Manna. |

DIRETTORE DEL BALLO. / DIRECTOR OF THE BALLET.

Il Sig. Antonio Campioni ec.

| | |
|---|---|
| *ACI, E GALATEA* | *ACIS AND GALATEA* |
| SCENA I. / Marina. | SCENE I. / Seashore. |
| ACI viene solo, in atto di ricercar | Acis enters alone, looking for Galatea, |
| Galatea, inquieto per la sua lontananza. | uneasy because of her absence. He takes |
| Prende, e suona il suo flauto. La Ninfa, | up his flute and plays it. The nymph, |
| riconoscendolo, appar sulla Scena. | recognizing him, appears on stage. |

SCENA II.

GAlatea fa sembiante di ricercar qualcun altro fuor d'Aci. Se ne mostra impaziente. Cerca di evitar Aci. Egli la insiegue.

SCENE II.

Galatea pretends to be looking for someone other than Acis. She shows impatience. She tries to avoid Acis. He follows her.

SCENA III.

UNa Sinfonia annunzia l'arrivo dei Pastori, e delle Pastorelle. Aci invita Galatea a vedere i loro trastulli. La Ninfa vi acconsente, e siede con Aci. Festa Campestre, interrotta da una vivace Sinfonia. Galatea fa cenno a tutti i Pastori, ed alle Pastorelle, che si ritirino. Partono, e seco conducono Aci.

SCENE III.

A symphony announces the arrival of the shepherds and shepherdesses. Acis invites Galatea to watch their amusements. The nymph agrees, and sits with Acis. Country festival, interrupted by a lively symphony. Galatea signals to all the shepherds and shepherdesses to withdraw. They leave, leading Acis away with them.

SCENA IV.

POlifemo entra furioso, cercando par ogni lato i Pastori, e le Pastorelle, che ha colà intesi.

SCENE IV.

Polyphemus enters in a fury, looking everywhere for the shepherds and shepherdesses he had heard there.

SCENA V.

GAlatea si mostra sulla Scena. Polifemo, in veggendola, si raddolcisce. Danza avanti la Ninfa studiando tutte le grazie per piacerle. Si getta a' suoi piedi. Galatea sembra di accarezzarlo, nel tempo stesso, che ne deride, e ne insulta l'amore. Polifemo incantato dalle mal credute carezze chiama i Ciclopi.

SCENE V.

Galatea appears on stage. Polyphemus, seeing her, grows more tender. He dances before the nymph, trying to show all possible graces in order to please her. He throws himself at her feet. Galatea seems to caress him, at the same time that she mocks and insults his love. Polyphemus, enchanted by the feigned caresses, calls the Cyclopes.

SCENA VI.

I Ciclopi vengono a rendere omaggio a Galatea. Polifemo si frammischia con loro. Danza con la Ninfa. Indi si ritira col suo seguito. Galatea resta un momento sola.

SCENE VI.

The Cyclopes come to pay homage to Galatea. Polyphemus joins in among them. Dance with the nymph. Then he withdraws with his retinue. Galatea remains alone a moment.

SCENA VII.

ACI ritorna, e rimprovera alla Ninfa d'aver mostrato di corrispondere all'amore di Polifemo. Galatea si discolpa. Aci attesta, che va disperatamente a gettarsi in preda alle furie del suddetto. Galatea lo trattiene, e gli addita di ricorrere ad Imeneo, essendo pronta a farlo suo Sposo. Aci fa trasparire l'eccessiva sua goija. In questo si vede un lampo, che accenna l'arrivo d'Imeneo.

SCENE VII.

Acis returns, and reproaches the nymph for having shown interest in Polyphemus's love. Galatea defends her actions. Acis vows that out of despair he is going to throw himself to Polyphemus's fury. Galatea restrains him, and encourages him to appeal to Hymen, since she is ready to make him her husband. Acis shows his great joy. At this point a bolt of lightning is seen, which signals Hymen's arrival.

SCENA VIII.

IMeneo, che scende nel suo Carro, a cui le due Amanti porgono le loro preghiere. Esso li rende felici, incoronandoli di fiori, ed unendo le loro destre. Succede a questo un' entrata di Pastori, e Pastorelle, che danzando festeggiano gli Sposi: nel mezzo di questa festa si sente un romore cupo, e lontano.

SCENA IX.

POlifemo vien fuori della sua Caverna, e si fa vedere in vetta della Rupe. Minaccia, e s'infuria, vedendo i due Sposi. Tutta la schiera dei Pastori, e delle Pastorelle intimorita fugge, e si mette in salvo. Galatea, pregando Aci di salvarsi, si precipita nel Mare. Aci vuole raggiungerla; ma Polifemo lanciandogli contro dall'alto un masso, lo fa cader morto, e stiacciato sott'esso. Polifemo discende dalla Rupe, contempla con piacere l'estinto Rivale e con un tratto di ballo fa vedere caratterizzato il piacer, che gli cagiona la vendetta.

SCENA X.

UNa Sinfonia dolce subentra a quella, sulla quale ha danzato Polifemo. Galatea esce dal Mare, e veggendo succedere la calma, e la tranquillità all'orrore, ed al tumulto, che aveva messo l'arrivo del suddetto, si mette in cerca d'Aci. I suoi passi la guidano appiè della Rupe, dove il suo Amante poco dianzi spirò. Ella esprime il suo dolore, e la sua disperazione. Si getta con le ginocchia a terra sul lido del Mare, e indirizza la sua preghiera a Nettunno, a Teti, e ad Anfitrite.

SCENA XI.

NEttunno, Teti, ed Anfitrite appajono sopra una Conca tirata da' Cavalli Marini. Uno Stuolo di Nereidi, e diTritoni appoggiati sull'Urne circondano i due lati del Carro. Nettunno col Tridente tocca il masso, sotto cui Aci oppresso si giace.

SCENE VIII.

Hymen, descending in his chariot, to whom the two lovers direct their prayers. He makes them happy, crowning them with flowers, and uniting their right hands in marriage. There follows an entrée of shepherds and shepherdesses, who dance in celebration of the spouses: in the middle of this celebration a deep and distant noise is heard.

SCENE IX.

Polyphemus comes out of his cave, and appears at the top of the cliff. Seeing the two spouses, he threatens and rages. The whole crowd of shepherds and shepherdesses flees in fear, and seeks safety. Galatea, beseeching Acis to save himself, leaps into the sea. Acis wishes to follow her, but Polyphemus throws a boulder at him from on high, making him fall dead, crushed beneath it. Polyphemus descends from the cliff, and contemplates his dead rival with pleasure and shows with a dance step the pleasure that vengeance causes him.

SCENE X.

A gentle symphony follows the one to which Polyphemus had danced. Galatea comes out of the sea, and seeing calm and tranquility follow upon the horror and tumult caused by the arrival of the aforesaid, goes in search of Acis. Her steps lead her to the foot of the cliff where a short while ago her lover had expired. She expresses her grief and despair. She falls to her knees at the seashore, and directs her prayers to Neptune, Thetis, and Amphitrite.

SCENE XI.

Neptune, Thetis, and Amphitrite appear on a shell drawn by seahorses. A throng of nereids and tritons leaning on urns surrounds the two sides of the chariot. With his trident Neptune strikes the boulder

Questo si trasforma in un'Urna, dalla quale scaturiscono le acque, formatrici d'un Fiume, di cui Aci è il Dio, e che compitamente esprime la Favola.

under which Acis lies crushed. It is transformed into an urn, from which flow waters forming the river, whose god is Acis, thus perfectly telling the story.

SCENA XII.
ACI esce dall'Urna, vestito da Fiume. Galatea appena lo ravvisa, che rapidamente corre fra le sue braccia. Le Nereidi, ed i Tritoni, vengono a render loro i dovuti omaggi. Anfitrite danza da sola. Nettunno, e Teti in seguito danzano insieme. Aci, e Galatea si uniscono a loro. Una danza generale termina il Ballo.

SCENE XII.
Acis comes out of the urn, dressed as a river god. As soon as Galatea sees him she quickly runs into his arms. The nereids and tritons come to pay them homage. Amphitrite dances a solo. Neptune and Thetis then dance together. Acis and Galatea join them. A general dance ends the ballet.

*BALLO SECONDO*

*DI AMERICANI*

SECOND BALLET

OF AMERICANS

ATTORI
I medesimi Danzanti sopra nominati.

ACTORS
The same above-named dancers.

DIRETTORE DEL BALLO.

DIRECTOR OF THE BALLET.

Il Sig. Vincenzo Monari.

SCENA I. / Campagna Americana.
VEdesi tutto il Popolo spaventato alla vista della Luna, che va ecclissando, secondo la superstizione di alcuni Popoli dell'America Settentrionale.

SCENE I. / American Countryside.
We see all the people frightened at the sight of the moon in eclipse, according to the superstition of some peoples of North America.

SCENA II.
SOpraggiungono i Capi della Nazione, e determinano di sagrificare uno Schiavo Europeo, dianzi caduto nelle loro mani.

SCENE II.
The chiefs of the tribe arrive, and decide to sacrifice a European slave who had just fallen into their hands.

SCENA III.
VIene questi condotto, e strascinato al Sacrifizio sovra una picciola Collina.

SCENE III.
The latter is brought on and dragged to the place of sacrifice atop a little hill.

SCENA IV.
Appare la Moglie d'esso piena di dolore, e di disperazione in vista del pericolo, a cui vede esposto l'oggetto del suo amore, senza potergli prestare ajuto.

SCENE IV.
His wife appears full of grief and despair at the sight of the peril to which the object of her love is exposed, yet not being able to give him any aid.

SCENA V.
L'Ecclissi finisce, primachè [sic] il sacrifizio sia incominciato. I capi della Nazione credono perciò di dover riservare ad altra occasione la morte dell'Europeo.

SCENE V.
The eclipse ends before the sacrifice can begin. Accordingly the chiefs of the tribe decide to put off the death of the European until some other occasion.

SCENA VI.

DIscendono tutti lieti dalla Collina.
Grande si mostra singolarmente il giubilo
della Donna Europea, veggendo salvato il
suo Consorte. Essa offre de' doni ai Capi,
per redimere se stessa, e il Marito dalla
schiavitù.

SCENA VII.

LA Donna parte, e ritorna col seguito di
molte persone, cariche di cose Europee,
le quali riuscendo per la novità
sommamente dilettevoli, e care ai Capi
della Nazione, vagliono ai due Europei il
prezzo della libertà.

SCENA VIII.

SI mischia un ballo generale di
allegrezza, con cui termina la
Pantominica [sic] Azione.

SCENE VI.

All descend from the hill joyfully. The
European woman especially shows great
jubilation, seeing her consort saved. She
offers gifts to the chiefs, with which to buy
her and her husband's way out of slavery.

SCENE VII.

The woman leaves, and then returns
followed by many persons carrying
European objects whose great novelty
renders them delightful and precious to
the chiefs of the tribe, earning the two
Europeans the price of their freedom.

SCENE VIII.

All join in a joyful general dance with
which the pantomimic action ends.


## 5. Genoa, Teatro da S. Agostino, Carnival 1783: ballets (both by Francesco Clerico) for the opera *Erifile* (De Gamerra/Giordani), premiere 1780

1st ballet:        *Zorei e Ozai* (Zorei and Ozai)
2nd ballet:        *Una mascherata* (A Mascarade)

Libretto: Schatz 3844 (reel 76)

ERIFILE / DRAMMA PER MUSICA / *DA
RAPPRESENTARSI* / NEL TEATRO DA S.
AGOSTINO / Il Carnovale dell'Anno
1783. / *DEDICATO* / ALLE NOBILISS. DAME /
*E* / NOBILISS. CAVALIERI. / GENOVA /
STAMPERIA GESINIANA . . .

ERIFILE / DRAMA IN MUSIC / *TO BE
PERFORMED* / IN THE THEATER OF S.
AGOSTINO / During Carnival of the Year
1783. / *DEDICATED TO* / THE MOST NOBLE
LADIES / *AND* / GENTLEMEN / GENOA / IN
THE GESINI PRINTSHOP . . .

INVENTORE E COMPOSITORE DE' BALLI /
INVENTOR AND COMPOSER OF THE BALLETS
*Il Sig. Francesco Clerico.*

*Primi Ballerini Serj. / First Serious Dancers.*
Il Sig. Francesco Clerico suddetto.        La Sig. Rosa Clerico.

*Primi Grotteschi. / First Grotesque Dancers.*
Il Sig. Gregorio Grisostomi.        La Sig. Geltrude Grisostomi.

*Mezzi Caratteri. / Dancers of Middle Character.*

Il Sig. Gaetano Clerico.      La Sig. Maria Bielmon.

*Quarti Ballerini. / Fourth Dancers.*

Il Sig. Gaetano Lombardini.      Il Sig. Giuseppe Calvi.
La Sig. Maria Barbieris.      La Sig. Clara Boggio.

*Primi Grotteschi fuori de' Concerti / First Grotesque Dancers Outside the Company Dances.*

Il Sig. Agostino Bertorelli.      La Sig. Violante Gherardini.

*Con numero 16. Figuranti. / With 16 others dancing.*

| | |
|---|---|
| Le Scene tanto della passata Opera come della presente e de' Balli ancora sono inventate e dipinte dal Sig. Antonio Balia di Milano. | The scenery of the [first Carnival] opera, as well as of the present one and of the ballets too have been designed and painted by Mr. Antonio Balia of Milan. |
| Direttore del Palco Scenico il Sig. Paolo Isola. | Stage director Paolo Isola. |
| Il Vestiario tutto nuovo sarà di vaga e ricca invenzione de' Sigg. Pietro Baraggino Milanese, ed Antonio Oliva Genovese. | The completely new, beautiful and rich costumes are designed by Messers Pietro Baraggino of Milan and Antonio Oliva of Genoa. |
| Ricamatore degli Abiti il Sig. Andrea Isola. | Embroiderer of the costumes Mr. Andrea Isola. |

ZOREI E OZAI / BALLO PANTOMIMO / IN QUATTRO ATTI / *COMPOSTO E DIRETTO* / DA / FRANCESCO CLERICO.

ZOREI AND OZAI / PANTOMIME BALLET / IN FOUR ACTS / *COMPOSED AND DIRECTED* / BY / FRANCESCO CLERICO.

PERSONAGGI / CAST

KAMIR Principe Tartaro / Tartar Prince.
Sig. Agostino Bertorelli.

ISIO Re de' Genj / King of the Genies.
Sig. Gaetano Clerico.

NIRSA Fata / Fairy.
Sig. Geltrude Grisostomi.

ZOREI Indiana / Indian girl.
La Sig. Rosa Clerico.

OZAI Indiano / Indian youth.
Sig. Francesco Clerico

MAZIF Servo di Ozai /Servant of Ozai.
Sig. Gregorio Grisostomi.

Schiera di Ninfe, e Piaceri.

Mostri.

Mori.

Soldati Tartari.

La Scena nei primi due atti si finge nel Regno di Kamir, e i consecutivi in un'Isola incantata.

Scena prima. Orrida grotta.

Scena seconda. Gabinetto Chinese.

Scena terza. Giardino incantato.

Scena quarta. Magnifica Reggia incantata.

ESTRATTO

I Climi dell'Oriente credavansi in altri tempi popolati da' Genj, e Fate, che secondo il capriccio delle loro passioni, esercitavano fra' Mortali tirannia e beneficenza. Zorei, e Ozai ne provarono gli effetti: nacquero questi in un'Isola dell'Indostan, ove cresciuti in età s'accesero l'un verso l'altro del più puro ardore; Kamir Principe Tartaro, invaghito di Zorei, col favor d'un incanto gli riesce rapirla? [sic] Nirsa famosa Fata presa d'amore per il giovane Ozai lo trasporta in un'Isola incantata, e in virtù d'una benda aspersa d'acqua d'obblio gli fa scordare la sua diletta amante. Isio Re de' Genj protettor di Zorei, e dell'innocenza uccide Kamir, ridona la memoria ad Ozai coll'acqua di reminiscenza, punisce la Fata, scioglie ogni incanto, e premia i due amanti unendoli in dolce nodo.

Sopra tali accidenti si raggira l'azione del presente Ballo, quale benchè immaginario non tralascia d'esser appoggiato al genere di que' fatti, che più Autori hanno descritti in varj racconti di simile materia. Chi ha l'onore d'esporlo non ha mancato di zelo per renderlo dilettevole, e molto felice si chiamerà, se dalla bontà e clemenza di questo Rispettabilissimo Pubblico gli verrà concesso un benigno compatimento.

Crowd of nymphs and pleasures.

Monsters.

Moors.

Tartar Soldiers.

The scene in the first two acts is set in the kingdom of Kamir, and the next ones on an enchanted island.

First scene. Horrid cave.

Second scene. Chinese cabinet.

Third scene. Enchanted garden.

Fourth scene. Magnificent enchanted palace.

EXTRACT

In former times it was believed that the Orient was peopled by genies and fairies who according to the whims of their passions exercised both tyranny and benevolence among mortals. Zorei and Ozai felt the effects of this: they were born on an island in Hindustan, where as they grew to maturity they were inflamed by the purest ardor for each other; Kamir, a Tartar prince, in love with Zorei, with the aid of a spell succeeds in abducting her. Nirsa, a famous fairy, lovestruck for the young Ozai, transports him to an enchanted island, and by means of a band sprinkled with water of oblivion makes him forget his beloved. Isio, king of the genies and protector of Zorei and of innocence, kills Kamir, restores Ozai's memory with water of reminiscence, punishes the fairy, undoes every spell, and rewards the two lovers, uniting them in sweet bonds of marriage.

Upon such events turns the action of the present ballet, which though imaginary does not stray from those sorts of facts that many authors have described in various accounts of similar material. He who has the honor of displaying [this material] has not lacked zeal in rendering it pleasurable, and he will deem himself very happy if the goodness and clemency of this most respectable public will concede him a benign indulgence.

BALLO SECONDO / UNA MASCHERATA

La Musica tanto di questi due Balli quanto di quelli della prima Opera è del Sig. Francesco Clerico suddetto. [no description]

SECOND BALLET / A MASCARADE

The music of these two ballets, as well as that of the first opera, is by the aforesaid Mr. Francesco Clerico.

# Appendix 3

## Gumpenhuber's Descriptions of Ballets Performed in the Kärntnertortheater during 1759 (excluding end of 1758–59 season)

COMPILED AND TRANSLATED
BY BRUCE ALAN BROWN

Translations of titles are followed by the name of the choreographer and the date of first performance; "Kr" numbers refer to catalogue numbers of corresponding sets of orchestral partbooks that survive in the former Schwarzenberg archive at Český Krumlov, Czech Republic.

| *La Foire* | *The Fair* [Turchi, 16 April] |
|---|---|
| Le Theatre represente une grande place avec plusieurs boutiques, qui sont fournis de marchandises, et representent une Foire. Les Gens de la Ville aussi bien que de la Campagne y acourent de toutes cotés pour marchander. Cela cause diverses Pantomimes, qu'on fait en dansant. Un Garçon qui est dans une Caffée invite un Passager au jeu: Celui-ci l'accepte, et il perd plus d'argent, qu'il n'a sur lui. Pendant qu'on lui maltraite à cause du payement, y arrive sa compagnone, et voyant qu'il est maltraité, | The stage represents a large square with several shops, which are furnished with merchandise and represent a fair. The people from the city as well as from the countryside rush on from all sides to haggle. That causes various pantomimes, which are done while dancing. A boy in a café invites a passerby to gamble: the latter accepts, and he loses more money than he has on him. While he is being abused on account of the payment, his female companion arrives, and seeing him being abused, pays for him, and rescues |

paye pour lui, et le delivre; et le Ballet se finit fort divertissant.

him; and the ballet ends in a most entertaining manner.

## Le Port dans une Isle de l'Archipel

Le Theatre represent l'arrivée d'un Vaiss[e]au Irlandois dans le Port d'une Isle de L'Archipel. On voit les Matelots occupés à transporter à la terre des Tonneaux à vin, et d'autres marchandises, et ces accidens propres en telles occasions causent le commencement aussi bien que quelque pas de deux. Puisque ce Vaisseau est destiné à faire voile, d'abord après avoir acheté le vin, cela met en tête à un jeune homme de ce Païs de ravir son amoureuse, et de se retirer avec elle dans le Vaisseau. Il decouvre son dessein à quelques Matelots, et il les persuade avec des presents de la prendre avec, d'abord qu'ils entreroient dans le Vaisseau, mais par leur malheur il arrive, que leur[s] Païsans le decouvrent, et prennent prisonniers tous les deux. Ils tachent en vain de gagner leur[s] gardes; c'est pourquoi les Matelots tout à la fois animés surprennent ceux, qui ont fait la prise, et mettent en liberté les deux amoureux, qui après avoir montré leur joïe, montent avec les autres dans le Vaisseau, et on finit le Ballet avec toute la joïe possible.

## The Port on an Island in the Archipelago [ Turchi, 16 April]

The stage represents the arrival of an Irish ship in the port of an island in the Archipelago. Sailors are seen occupied in transporting to land some barrels of wine, and other merchandise, and these events that are suited to such occasions provoke the beginning [of the ballet] as well as some *pas de deux*. Since the ship is about to set sail as soon as the wine is bought, a young man of this country gets the idea of abducting his beloved, and stowing away with her on the ship. He discloses his plan to some sailors, and with gifts persuades them to take her with them, as soon as they board the ship, but to their misfortune it happens that their countrymen discover him, and take both of them prisoner. They [the lovers] try in vain to win over their guards; this is why the sailors, all acting at once, surprise those who have taken them captive, and set free the two lovers, who after having shown their joy, board the ship with the others, and the ballet ends with all the joy possible.

## Les Turcs

Le Theatre represent une Campagne en Turckie, où plusieurs esclaves travaillent, à quoi viennent quelques jeunes esclaves, qui tachent de se sauver par la fuite des Corsaires, qui les ont pris; et parceque elles apperçevoient leurs persecuteurs, elles se cachent dans un Moulin. Les Turcs, qui les poursuivent, ne trouvant

## The Turks
### [Bernardi, 30 May; Kr 80]

The stage represents a countryside in Turkey, where several slaves are working, and where some young slave girls come, who are trying to flee from the pirates who had taken them; and because they see their persecutors, they hide in a mill. The Turks who are pursuing them, not finding anyone, leave without stopping.

personne, s'en vont sans s'arreter. Après ça les jeunes Esclaves quittent le lieu de leur retraite, et temoignent leur reconnoissance à ceux qui leur ont donné cette retraite. Cependant [*sic*] cela donne l'occasion au com[m]encement du Ballet. y [*sic*] arrivent deux autres Turcs, qui ont été expediés des Corsaires à cause de leur fuite: ceux-ci en appercevant les jeunes Esclaves forcent les autres Turcs où [*sic*] de les leur rendre, ou de les acheter, et après qu'on accorde le dernier, il[s] recom[m]encent à se divertir, à quoi suit un pas de Trois et un pas de Deux, qui representent differents accidents, qui arrivent en ce païs-là, de sorte que ce Ballet est non seulement bien arrangé, mais il a aussi une parfaite connexion, dont la Conclusion est neuve, et fort divertissante.

After that the young slaves leave their hiding place, and show their gratitude to those who have given them this refuge. In the meantime that occasions the start of the ballet. Two other Turks arrive, who have been sent by the pirates on account of their [the slaves'] flight: these [Turks], on seeing the young slaves, force the other Turks [to choose] either to give them to them, or to buy them, and after the latter [course] has been agreed upon, they again start to divert themselves, whereupon there follow a *pas de trois* and a *pas de deux*, which show various events that happen in this country, so that the ballet is not only well arranged, but also has a perfect connection [between its parts], of which the conclusion is novel, and very entertaining.

## Les Savoiards

## The Savoyards
### [Bernardi, 30 May; Kr 80]

Ce Ballet represente le retour des Savoiards dans leur Patrie. Le Theatre démontre le precip[ic]e de la montagne Montcenis en Savoïe, où les Femmes sont occupées avec des preparatifs pour un festin au retour de leurs maris: ce qu'à leur arrivée donne l'occasion à un grand divertissement, qui est accompagné du chant, et de la danse. Après ça toute la Compagnie s'aprete pour faire un repas à la mode du Païs, mais il est interrompu par un Savoiard, qui pour se moquer d'eux, leur fait ac[c]roire, que le Village brule, à quoi suit un pas de deux, et un pas de trois, qui represente parfaitement la maniere, et la vivacité de ces gens là, et puisque chacun prend part à la joïe, qui regne entre eux, ce Ballet sera fort divertissent [*sic*] aux jeux [*sic*] des Spectateurs.

This ballet represents the return of the Savoyards to their homeland. The stage shows the mountain Mont-Cenis in Savoy, where the women are occupied with the preparations for a feast for the return of their husbands: their arrival occasions a large entertainment, which is accompanied by song and dance. After that the whole company gets ready to eat a meal in the manner of that country, but it is interrupted by a Savoyard who, in order to mock them, makes them think that the village is burning, whereupon there follows a *pas de deux*, and a *pas de trois*, which perfectly show the manner and the vivacity of these people, and since everyone participates in the joy that reigns among them, this ballet will be most entertaining to the eyes of the spectators.

## La Guinguette

## The Cabaret [Bernardi, 26 July]

Le Theatre represente un beau jardin, où il est permis à tout le monde de se promener, et on y voit le divertissement de toute sorte de gens en diverses façons. Cela cause differens accidents, qui arrivent ordinairement en tels endroits, où d'autres jouent aux quils, d'autres mangent, et d'autres se divertissent en dansant. A' cela vient une jeune Fille, la quelle s'accorde à danser, et après que quelques hommes dans le jardin souhaitent de s'accompagner à elle, arrive une querelle, la quelle interrompe le divertissement, et met tous en confusion. Pendant la querelle vient un Officier pour fair[e] la paix. Chacun se montre paisible à son arrivée, et la jeune fille lui fait croire, que ce n'étoit que raillerie. L'Officier devient d'abord amoureux d'elle; et à fin qu'il puisse rester plus long tems en cet endroit en pleine liberté, il và changer ses habits, et danse avec elle. Après cela un Postillon commence à danser avec une pauvre fille, la quelle y est venue pour jouer à la harpe. Ce Ballet est fort divertissant, et se finit avec une Danse Allemanne [*sic*].

The stage represents a beautiful garden, where everyone is permitted to promenade, and one sees all sorts of people being entertained in various ways. That causes different sorts of actions that ordinarily happen in such places, where some are playing skittles, others are eating, and others are diverting themselves by dancing. Thereupon a young girl comes on, who agrees to dance, and after some men in the garden wish to accompany her, a quarrel arises, which interrupts the entertainment, and puts everything in a confusion. During the quarrel an officer comes to make peace. Everyone acts peaceably upon his arrival, and the young girl makes him believe that it was only a joke. The officer at once falls in love with her; and in order to be able to stay longer in this place in complete liberty, he goes to change his clothes, and dance with her. After that a postillion starts to dance with a poor girl, who has come to play the harp. This ballet is most entertaining, and ends with a German dance.

## Le Port de Marseille

## The Port of Marseilles
[Bernardi, 26 July]

On voit la Mer couverte de Vaisseaux, et de l'autre coté quelques Galeres. Au bord de la Mer on voit plusieurs Boutiques, et à Chacune des matelots en chaines, qui s'occupent à quelque travail. Plusieurs filles, qui se promenent, prient l'Intendant des Matelots de les delivrer pour pouvoir danser avec eux. Celui-çi se laisse persuader, et les met en liberté. Les matelots après avoir dansé avec ces filles, s'enfuient, sur quoi l'Intendant mis en desespoir arrête le[s] filles, et les enchaine à la place des matelots: Au même tems le Capitain vient d'arriver d'une Galere, et

One sees the sea covered with ships, and on the other side some galleys. On the seashore one sees several shops, and in each one some sailors in chains, who are busy with some sort of work. Several girls who are promenading plead with the quartermaster of the sailors to free them so they can dance with them. He allows himself to be persuaded, and sets them free. The sailors, after having danced with these girls, flee, whereupon the quartermaster, in despair, arrests the girls, and puts them in chains in place of the sailors; at the same time the captain arrives from

reconnoissant la faite de son Intendant, le veut chatier, mais les prieres d'une jeune Fille de ce païs, la quelle y vient, l'oblige à lui pardoner sa faute. A' cela suit un pas de trois d'un Tonnelier, de son Garçon, et de sa Servante: après une [sic] air tambourine du Capitain, et de cette fille qui l'a prié auparavant de pardonner à l'Intendant: et cependant on accompagne la danse des tambours, et des flûetes de la Galere. Enfin reviennent les Matelots: Ils obtiennent le pardon, et le Ballet se finit.

a galley, and seeing what the quartermaster has done, wants to chastise him, but the entreaties of a young girl of this country, who comes on, obliges him to pardon him for his mistake. Thereupon there follows a *pas de trois* of a cooper, of his apprentice, and his serving girl: then a tambourine air by the captain and the girl who had earlier pleaded for the pardon of the quartermaster: and during this time the dance is accompanied by drums, and flutes from the galley. Finally the sailors return: they obtain a pardon, and the ballet ends.

## Les Perruquiers

## The Wigmakers
## [Bernardi, 3 October]

Le Theatre represente l'aportement [sic] d'un Peruquier, On y voit beaucoup d'hommes et de filles, qui sont occupés à divers travaux de ce métier: ce qui fait une vuë fort agreable. Les Amants de ces filles qu'y travaillent, se glissent dans cette maison sous divers pretextes, et cela cause plusieurs jalousies, et des accidens particuliers, sur quoi tous les intrigues de ce Ballet se fondent. La Pantomime est fort gaye, et accompagné[e] du commencement jusqu'à la fin de la même façon.

The stage represents the apartment of a wigmaker. There one sees many men and girls busy with various tasks of this profession, which makes a most agreeable sight. The lovers of these girls who are working there slip into this house under various pretexts, and that causes several jealousies, and particular events upon which all the intrigues of this ballet are founded. The pantomime is very cheerful, and accompanied in the same manner from the beginning to the end.

## Le Marché aux poissons

## The Fish Market [Bernardi,
## 3 October; = Kr 77?]

Ce Ballet represente le marché aux poissons en Hollande. La Decoration theatrale est fort agreable, et cha[r]mera les yeux des Spectateurs. De jeunes gens dansent avec les filles à la mode du Païs, la quelle est fort divertissante. Les accidents qui arrivent ordinairement en tels endroits causent plusieurs changements divertissants qui seront exprimés dans la

This ballet represents the fish market in Holland. The theatrical décor is most agreeable, and will charm the eyes of the spectators. Some young men dance with girls in the manner of that country, which is very entertaining. The events that ordinarily happen in such places cause several entertaining changes that are expressed in the dance. The invention of this finale

danse. L'invention de ce final est toute neuve, fort vive, et bien pensée.

is completely novel, very lively, and well thought out.

## La Reccolte des fruits

## The Fruit Harvest
[Bernardi, 21 October]

Le Theatre represente une grande Campagne; qui est remplie de toutes sortes d'Arbres de fruits. Les Païsans s'occupent en recueillant des fruits, mais ils sont interrompus par de tels accidents, qui causent differentes Pantomemes [*sic*], les quelles seront exprimées par le Ballet, et attachées à l'intention principale. Ce Ballet est bien gay, et divertissant du commencement jusqu'à la fin: La Conclusion en sera fort gaye, et ridicule.

The stage represents a vast countryside, which is full of all sorts of fruit trees. The peasants busy themselves in picking fruit, but they are interrupted by such events as cause different pantomimes, which will be expressed by the ballet, and attached to the principal intention [of it]. This ballet is quite cheerful, and entertaining from the beginning to the end: its conclusion will be very jolly, and ridiculous.

## Le Suisse

## The Swiss [Bernardi, 17 November; = Kr 70]

Le Theatre represente un petit Village, ou Province en Suisse, où on celebre le jour de naissance d'une femme la plus riche du Païs. Ce Ballet commence en representant dans un Tableau tout ce qui arrive ordinairement au lever du Soleil en tels endroits. Une jeune fille s'eveille la premiere joue quelques coups divertissants aux autres Païsans pour se divertir. Peu à peu ils sortent tous de leurs Maisons, sur quoi suit une Danse generale, dont ils sont detournes [*sic*] par l'Arrivée du Maitre de ce Lieu. Il y a plusieurs accidents fort divertissans en ces ceremonies, dont on se sert en celebrant ce Festin. Ce Ballet est fort bien arrangé, et d'une maniere grotesque: La fin est fort gaye, et se finit avec un Diné, où tout le monde est plein de joïe, et de contentement.

The stage represents a small village or province in Switzerland, where the birthday of the richest woman in the land is being celebrated. This ballet begins by representing in a tableau everything that ordinarily happens at sunrise in such places. A young girl wakes up first and plays several amusing tricks on the other peasants in order to entertain herself. Little by little they all come out of their houses, whereupon there follows a general dance, from which they are diverted by the arrival of the master of this place. There are several very entertaining events in these ceremonies that one makes use of in celebrating this feast-day. This ballet is very well arranged, and in a grotesque manner: its end is most jolly, and it ends with a dinner, where everyone is full of joy and contentment.

## Les Corsaires

## The Pirates [Bernardi, 26 December; = Kr 82]

Le Theatre represente une Isle deserte, où on observe un homme auprès de sa cabanne, qui après un naufrage y ayant passé sa vie depuis long tems tout seul, ressemble à sa mine un sauvage. Par hazard quelques Anglois y abordent qui en Compagnie de son Amante avoient resolû de le chercher, et par les quels il a le bonheur de quitter ce desert, et de partir avec eux. Pendant que les Anglois s'arretent dans cette Isle, prennent prisonier après un grand Combat un Corsaire Turc avec sa compagnone, le quel vient de passer avec son vaisseau, et les enchainent; mais au moment de leur extreme dèsespoir, arrive un autre Corsaire, qui les delivre, et prend prisoniers tous les Anglois, mais ceux-ci reçoivent la liberté par l'Argent, qu'ils donnent au Corsaire, et alors se trouvant tout le monde en liberté, vont après ce Ballet dans le Vaisseau, chaque partie pour prendre sa course vers son Païs. Les caracteres y sont exactement observés, et ce Ballet est bien exprimé et arrangé.

The stage represents a deserted island, where one observes a man next to his hut, who after a shipwreck having for a long time spent his life entirely alone, looks like a savage. By chance some Englishmen land, who along with his lover had resolved to search for him, and through whom he has the good fortune to leave this deserted place, and to depart with them. While the Englishmen are staying on this island, they take as prisoners, after a large battle, a Turkish pirate and his [female] companion, who had just passed with his [the pirate's] ship, and put them in chains; but at the moment of their greatest despair, another pirate arrives who rescues them, and takes all the Englishmen prisoner, but the latter gain their freedom by means of money that they give to the pirate, and then all of them finding themselves at liberty, after this ballet they go on board the ship, each party taking its course towards its own country. The characters are exactly observed, and this ballet is well expressed and arranged.

## Le Prix de la Danse

## The Dance Contest [Bernardi, 26 December; = Kr 82]

Le Theatre represente un[e] Campagne Flamande, où il y a beaucoup de Monde, qui celebre un Festin. Après s'être diverti au jeu, on commence la danse, dans la quelle on voit plusieurs emporter le prix par differentes manieres. Il y a principalement à observer les Castagnettes, les Sabots, et les Tambourins. Pour obtenir le prix chacun tache de surpasser l'autre, de sorte que tous les pas de Deux sont les plus fortes. Ce Ballet est d'une nouvelle invention, et la fin fort gaïe.

The stage represents a Flemish countryside, where there are many people celebrating a feast. After having entertained themselves by gambling, they begin the dance, in which one sees several people take the prize through their different manners. There is principally to be observed in this ballet the castanets, the wooden shoes, and the tambourines. In order to gain the prize everyone tries to surpass the others, so that all the *pas de deux* are extremely strong. This ballet is of a novel invention, and its end very jolly.

Addendum: During 1759 Magri may well have danced in the following "petits ballets," all by Gumpenhuber (premiere dates not known):

| | |
|---|---|
| Les Turcs en serail | The Turks in the Seraglio |
| La Mascarade [= Kr 69] | The Masquerade |
| Les Jardiniers | The Gardeners |
| Les Païsans de[s] montagnes | The Peasants of the Mountains |
| Les Moissonneurs [= Kr 93?] | The Reapers |
| L'Hôpital des foux | The Insane Asylum |
| Les Vendanges [= Kr 50 or 98?] | The Grape Harvest |
| Les Mineurs | The Miners |

# Appendix 4

## Scenarios of Selected Ballets Performed at the Teatro San Carlo, Naples

COMPILED BY SALVATORE BONGIOVANNI,
TRANSLATED BY BRUCE ALAN BROWN

Call numbers are those of copies consulted; in initial headings, name of librettist precedes that of composer (of opera).

For title pages and descriptions, Italian is given on left and English on right; for cast lists, format of original is generally reproduced, with translations following, as necessary.

1. 1765–66 season: ballets for the opera *Il re pastore*
(The Shepherd King; Pietro Metastasio/Niccolò Piccinni),
premiere 30 May 1765

1st ballet:  *Mercato del pesce in Amsterdam* (The Fish-Market in Amsterdam)
2nd ballet: *Ritorno di soldati piemontesi alle loro case* (The Return of Piedmontese
Soldiers to Their Homes)

Libretto: I-Bl, Lo. 4149

Il Re Pastore / Dramma per musica / da
rappresentarsi nel Real Teatro di S.
Carlo / nel dì 30 Maggio 1765 /
festeggiandosi il nome / della S.R.M. /

The Shepherd King / Drama in music /
to be performed in the Royal Theater of
San Carlo, the 30th of May 1765 / in
celebration of the name-day / of his

di / Ferdinando IV / nostro clementissimo sovrano / ed alla medesima S.R.M. / dedicato. / In Napoli MDCCLXV / Per Francesco Morelli impresso.

Serene Royal Majesty and our most clement sovereign Ferdinand IV / and likewise dedicated to his Serene Royal Majesty. / In Naples MDCCLXV / Printed by Francesco Morelli.

MUTAZIONI DI SCENE
*Per il primo ballo:*
Mercato del pesce in Amsterdam, situato su le sponde del Reno [!].

CHANGES OF SCENERY
*For the first ballet:*
Fish market in Amsterdam, situated on the banks of the Rhine [!].

*Per il secondo ballo:*
Veduta di una parte del Mosenise dall'alte cime del quale si vedranno calare i soliti [recte: soldati] Piemontesi, che ritornano alle loro Case, ove sono attesi dalle loro famiglie.

*For the second ballet:*
View of a part of Mont-Cenis from the high peaks of which one sees the Piedmontese [soldiers] descending, returning to their homes, where they are awaited by their families.

Scene D['] Antonio Iolli / Modanese

Scenery by Antonio Iolli / of Modena

NOTA DE' BALLI
*Primo ballo*
Nel mercato del Pesce in Amsterdam, situato su le sponde del Reno, si vedranno sbarcare alcuni Scozzesi, che uniti all'altre genti concorse in detto luogo, formeranno allegro concerto, al quale succederanno altri diversi balli, che finalmente termineranno con un grazioso finale.

NOTE ON THE BALLETS
*First ballet*
In the fish market of Amsterdam, situated on the banks of the Rhine, some Scotsmen disembark, who, along with other people who have congregated in that place, will form a lively group dance, which will be followed by various dances, which will finally be terminated by a gracious finale.

*Secondo ballo*
Nell'atto che diverse donne Savojarde sono intese ai loro femminili travagli, veggono calare dall'alte cime del Monsenise i loro mariti, che ritornano alle proprie case, ove sono accolti dalle mogli, e da' loro figlioli; ed in segno di allegrezza si canta un'arietta intrecciata colla danza, alla quale sieguono altri graziosi balli, e si termina l'allegria con un bizzarro concerto.

*Second ballet*
While various Savoyard women are seen to be occupied in their womanly tasks, one sees descending from the high peaks of Mont-Cenis their husbands, who are returning to their homes, where they are received by their wives, and by their children; and in token of happiness an aria interwoven with dance is sung, after which follow other gracious dances, and the joy is terminated with a whimsical group dance.

NOTA DE' BALLERINI / NOTE ON THE DANCERS

*Ballerine [Dancers (female)]*
Sig. Elisabetta Morelli
Sig. Anna Bellucci

*Ballerini [Dancers (male)]*
Sig. Gennaro Magri
Sig. Giuseppe Bellucci

*Ballano ne' concerti, terzetti, e quartetti / Dancers in group dances, trios, and quartets*

Sig. Rosa Granazzo

Sig. Domenico Morelli

*Figurano / Also dancing*

| | |
|---|---|
| Sig. Anna Provenzale | Sig. Francesco Beltramo |
| Sig. Andreana Giraldi | Sig. Francesco Roberti |
| Sig. Maria Magiolini detta | Sig. Francesco Giannattasio |
| [called] la Romanina | Sig. Giuseppe Magri |
| Sig. Marianna Jovino | Sig. Gio. Antonio Braganza |
| Sig. Antonia Corona | Sig. Gennaro Candelora |

Inventore e direttore de' balli il suddetto / Inventor and director of the ballets, the
aforesaid Signor Gennaro Magri Napolitano [Neapolitan]

La Signora Giacomina, e [and] Signor Giuseppe Forti
*Ballano fuori de' concerti / Dance outside the company dances.*

## 2. 1765–66 season: ballets for the opera *Creso* (Croesus; Gioacchino Pizzi/Antonio Sacchini), premiere 4 November 1765

1st ballet:  *Arrivo di viaggiatori nella posta di Vienna* (Arrival of Travelers at a Viennese Post-Stage)
2nd ballet: *Assalto di corsari lapponesi* (Attack of the Lapp Pirates)
3rd ballet: *Di diversi caratteri* (Of various characters)

Libretto: I-Rsc, Libr.XVII.46

Creso / Dramma per musica / da
rappresentarsi nel Real Teatro di S.
Carlo / nel dì 4 novembre 1765 /
festeggiandosi il glorioso nome / della
S.R.C.M. / di / Carlo III / monarca
delle Spagne / ed alla S. R. M. / di /
Ferdinando IV / nostro clementissimo
Re / dedicato. / In Napoli MDCCLXV /
Per Francesco Morelli / Impressore del
Real Teatro.

Croesus / Drama in music / to be
performed in the Royal Theater of San
Carlo / the 4th of November 1765 / in
celebration of the name-day / of his
Serene Royal Imperial Majesty / Charles
III / monarch of Spain / and dedicated
to his Serene Royal Majesty / and our
most clement King / Ferdinand IV. / In
Naples MDCCLXV / By Francesco
Morelli / Printer of the Royal Theater.

MUTAZIONI DI SCENE
*Per il primo ballo:*
Portico dell'osteria, e della posta in
vicinanza della Città di Vienna.

CHANGES OF SCENERY
*For the first ballet:*
Portico of the inn, and of the post-stage
near the city of Vienna.

*Per il secondo ballo:*
Spiaggia di Mare con varie abitazioni
rustiche sorprese, e poste a sacco da corsari Lapponesi.

*For the second ballet:*
Seashore with various rustic habitations,
set upon and sacked by Lapp pirates.

Inventore, Dipintore e Architetto delle scene D. Antonio Jolli Modanese, aiutante della Real Foriera di S.M.

Inventor, Painter and Architect of the scenery D[on] Antonio Jolli of Modena, adjutant of the Royal Herald's Office of His Majesty.

NOTA DE' BALLI

*Primo ballo*

Si rappresenta la posta vicino Vienna coll'arrivo di vari viaggiatori, e con feste, ed allegrie siegue il Ballo.

NOTE ON THE BALLETS

*First ballet*

The post-stage near Vienna is shown, with the arrival of various travelers, and the ballet follows with festivities and joy.

*Secondo ballo*

Da corsari Lapponesi si dà un assalto ad un villaggio su le sponde del mare, in cui siegue con altri oltremontani fiero combattimento, e dopo questo i vincitori mossi a pietà danno la pace ai vinti, e gli mettono in libertà, onde in segno di allegria si intreccia il ballo.

*Second ballet*

Lapp pirates attack a village on the shore of the sea, in which there follows a fierce combat with other foreigners, and after this the victors, moved to pity, make peace with the vanquished, and set them free, whence in token of happiness they form a dance.

*Terzo ballo*

In applauso della pace stabilita tra Ciro e Creso si forma allegro ballo di diversi caratteri.

*Third ballet*

Applauding the peace established between Cyrus and Croesus, a joyous dance of various characters is formed.

NOTA DE' BALLERINI / NOTE ON THE DANCERS

*Ballerine [Dancers (female)]*
Sig. Elisabetta Morelli

*Ballerini [Dancers (male)]*
Sig. Gennaro Magri

Li Sig. Domenico Morelli, Anna e [and] Giuseppe Bellucci

La Signora Rosa Granazzo
*Balla ne' terzetti, quartetti e concerti / Dances in trios, quartets, and in company dances.*

*Figurano / Also dancing*

Sig. Anna Provenzale
Sig. Andreana Giraldi
Sig. Maria Magiolini detta la Romanina
Sig. Marianna Jovino
Sig. Antonia Corona

Sig. Francesco Beltramo
Sig. Francesco Roberti
Sig. Francesco Giannattasio
Sig. Giuseppe Magri
Sig. Gio. Antonio Braganza
Sig. Gennaro Candelora

Inventore e direttore de' balli il suddetto / Inventor and director of the ballets the aforesaid Signor Gennaro Magri Napolitano [Neapolitan].

*Ballano fuori de' concerti / Dance outside the company dances.*

La Signora Rosa Marchiani ed [and] il Signor Giuseppe Forti

## 3. 1766–67 season: ballets for the opera *Il gran Cid* (The Great Cid; Gioacchino Pizzi/Niccolò Piccinni), premiere 4 November 1766

1st ballet:     *Di Spagnoli e Mori* (Of Spaniards and Moors)
2nd ballet:    *Di Zingari e Scozzesi* (Of Gypsies and Scots)
3rd ballet:     *Dagli amici di Rodrigo* (Of the friends of Rodrigo)

Libretto: I-Rsc, Libr.XVII.70

Il Gran Cid / Dramma per musica / da rappresentarsi nel Real Teatro di S. Carlo / nel dì 4 novembre 1766 / festeggiandosi il glorioso nome / della S.R.C.M. / di / Carlo III / monarca delle Spagne / ed alla S.R.M. / di / Ferdinando IV / nostro clementissimo re / dedicato. / In Napoli MDCCLXVI / Per Francesco Morelli / Impressore del Real Teatro.

The Great Cid / Drama in music / to be performed in the Royal Theater of San Carlo, / the 4th of November 1766 / in celebration of the name-day of his Serene Royal Imperial Majesty / Charles III / monarch of Spain / and dedicated to his Serene Royal Majesty / and our most clement King, / Ferdinand IV. / In Naples MDCCLXVI / By Francesco Morelli / Printer of the Royal Theater.

MUTAZIONI DI SCENE
*Atto primo:*
Logge interne dalla parte più rimota del Palazzo Reale con vedute di campagna.

CHANGES OF SCENERY
*Act one:*
Internal loggias in the most remote part of the Royal Palace with views of the countryside.

Aspetto esteriore delle mura di Siviglia con porta, e ponte alzato vicino al piano, altra porta in prospetto anche con ponte alzato, che poi si cala, e si unisce all'antico ponte di fabbrica in parte diruto, ed atterrato, sotto al quale passa il fiume Gualdaquiver, che bagna colle sue acque le mura suddette. Da un lato rovinosi edifici intrigati di piante selvagge.

Exterior view of the walls of Seville with gate, and raised drawbridge near the plain, another gate in the background, likewise with raised drawbridge, which later is lowered, and joins with a partially ruined and fallen-down old bridge, underneath which the Guadalquivir River passes, bathing the aforesaid walls with its waters. To one side ruined buildings entangled with wild plants.

*Per il primo ballo:*
Resta la medesima scena.

*For the first ballet:*
The same scenery remains.

*Per il secondo ballo:*
Rustico, e rimoto ritiro con grotta, e tenda, ove si adunano i Zingari presso le sponde del mare nelle vicinanze di Siviglia.

*For the second ballet:*
Rustic and remote retreat with cave, and tent, where the Gypsies gather near the seashore in the vicinity of Seville.

Scene di Antonio Jolli.

Scenery by Antonio Jolli.

*Primo ballo*

Da una delle porte della Città di Siviglia vengono diversi Spagnoli, che traggono in catene alcuni mori prigionieri. Calati al piano vogliono i vincitori passare per il fil di spada i vinti; nel qual atto accorrono diverse more, che gittandosi a' piedi de' Spagnoli con lagrime intercedon la vita di quelli, alle quali lagrime si uniscono anche i prieghi di alcune donne Spagnole, che ottengono finalmente grazia per i mori, onde s'intreccia allegra danza, alla quale sieguono diversi altri balli di caratteri adattati alle sudette nazioni.

*Secondo ballo*

Si vedrà una truppa di Zingari radunata sotto tende, ed in una grotta presso le sponde del mare nelle vicinanze di Siviglia, ed alla punta del giorno fanno costoro diversi furti a passaggieri. Intanto si vedrà una barca approdare, d'onde caleranno diversi Scozzesi, che portano una donna di riguardo, cercando segreti per guarirla dalle convulsioni. Si accostano a' Zingari, e domandano loro di qualche specifico. Si offre il capo di questi per la cura, e con graziosa maniera si guarisce la donna; onde per allegrezza della ricuperata salute, si forma allegro concerto, al quale sieguono diversi altri balli con piacevoli pantomimi.

*Terzo ballo*

Dagli amici di Rodrigo, o sia del Gran Cid, si forma ballo in attestato di giubilo per le sue nozze con Climene.

*First ballet*

From one of the gates of the city of Seville come various Spaniards, who are leading some Moorish prisoners in chains. Having descended into the plain the victors wish to put the vanquished to the sword, at which various Moors come running, throwing themselves at the feet of the Spaniards, and with their tears intercede for the lives of the others; to their tears the entreaties of some Spanish women are joined, and these finally obtain mercy for the Moors, which occasions a joyful dance, followed by various other dances of characters appropriate to the aforesaid nations.

*Second ballet*

One will see a troupe of Gypsies gathered under a tent and in a cave near the seashore in the vicinity of Seville, and at dawn they try their various ruses on passersby. Meanwhile one will see a bark land, from which various Scotsmen will descend, carrying a woman of quality, seeking secrets with which to cure her convulsions. They approach the Gypsies, and ask them for a remedy. The head of the [Gypsies] offers his services for the cure, and with a gracious manner he heals the woman; whence a joyous company dance is performed out of happiness at the [woman's] recovered health, and is followed by various other dances with pleasing pantomimes.

*Third ballet*

The friends of Rodrigo, or the Great Cid, form a dance expressing jubilation at his marriage with Climene.

NOTA DE' BALLERINI / NOTE ON THE DANCERS

Sig. Elisabetta Morelli                    Sig. Gennaro Magri

Signori Domenico e [and] Margarita Morelli, e [and] Cosimo Maranesi.

La Signora Rosa Granazzo

*Balla ne' terzetti, quartetti, concerti, e finali / Dances in trios, quartets, company dances, and finales.*

*Figurano / Also dancing*

| | |
|---|---|
| Sig. Andreana Giraldi | Sig. Francesco Beltrano |
| Sig. Marianna Jovino | Sig. Francesco Cimmino |
| Sig. Maria Rosa Intronti | Sig. Franc. Giannattasio |
| Sig. Antonia Corona | Sig. Antonio Gioja |
| Sig. Francesca Toriello | Sig. Domenico Figliolini |
| | Sig. Gennaro Candelora |

Inventore, e direttore de' balli il sudetto / Inventor, and director of the ballets the aforesaid Signor Gennaro Magri Napolitano [Neapolitan].

La Signora Caterina Stacchini, ed [and] il Signor Mauro Zaccherini
*Ballano fuori de' concerti / Dance outside the company dances.*

## 4. 1766–67 season: ballets for the opera *Bellerofonte* (Bellerophon; Giuseppe Bonechi/Joseph Mysliveček), premiere 20 January 1767

1st ballet:   *Un Bassà Turco* (A Turkish Pasha)
2nd ballet:   *Pantomimo tra Pulcinella, Arlecchino e Coviello* (A Pantomime between Pulcinella, Harlequin and Coviello)

Libretto: I-Rsc, Libr.XVII.24

Bellerofonte / Dramma per musica / da rappresentarsi nel Real Teatro di S. Carlo / nel dì 20 Gennaio 1767 / in cui si festeggia la nascita / della S.R.M.C. / di / Carlo III / Monarca delle Spagne / ed alla S.R.M. / di / Ferdinando IV / suo amabilissimo figlio, / e nostro clementissimo re / dedicato. / In Napoli MDCCLXVII / Per Francesco Morelli / Impressore del Real Teatro.

Bellerophon / Drama in music / to be performed in the Royal Theater of San Carlo, / the 20th of January 1767 / in celebration of the birthday / of his Serene Royal Imperial Majesty / Charles III of Spain / and dedicated to his beloved son, our most clement king Ferdinand IV. / In Naples MDCCLXVII / By Francesco Morelli / Printer of the Royal Theater.

MUTAZIONI DI SCENE
*Nell'atto primo:*

CHANGES OF SCENERY
*In the first act:*

Logge a vista del Fiume Xanto nella Reggia dei Re di Lycia.

Loggias with a view of the Xantus River in the Palace of the Kings of Lycia.

Galleria negli appartamenti Reali adornati di trofei militari.

Gallery in the royal apartments, decorated with military trophies.

Gabinetto con sedie.

Cabinet with chairs.

*Per il ballo:*

*For the ballet:*

Resta la suddetta scena e poi

The same scenery remains and then

Vasto solitario recinto di antiche e maestose fabbriche rovinate.

Vast solitary enclosure of ruined antique and majestic buildings.

*Nell'atto secondo:*

*In the second act:*

Camera terrena.

A ground-floor room.

Portici contigui alle carceri.

Porticos adjacent to the dungeon.

Orrida ed oscura valle formata dal recinto di erti e rovinosi monti con ingressi di vaste caverne.

Horrid and dark valley formed by the enclosure of steep and ruinous mountains with entrances to vast caverns.

*Per il ballo:*

*For the ballet:*

Resta la suddetta scena e poi

Remains the same scenery and then

Piazzetta con diverse case praticabili ed osteria.

Little square with various practicable houses and an inn.

Inventore, Dipintore e Archit. il S. D. A. Jolli.

Inventor, Painter and Architect, S[ignor] D[on] A. Jolli.

Inventore e direttore del battimento il S. Pietro Capone M[aestro] Di Spada Napoletano.

Inventor and director of the combats S[ignor] Pietro Capone M[aster] of Swords, Neapolitan.

NOTA DE' BALLI
Sul principio dell'opera si forma una festa di ballo intanto che si canta il coro.

NOTE ON THE BALLETS
At the beginning of the opera a festive dance is formed while the chorus is sung.

*Nella fine dell'atto primo*
Un Bassà Turco non vedendosi corrisposto da una sua schiava, sdegnato, la condanna colle sue compagne ad essere divorata da certi mostri, che tiene rinchiusi in un luogo solitario. Sono queste condotte alla morte; ma diversi schiavi disarmando le guardie vanno a darle soccorso. Cosicchè cangiandosi la scena si trovano le suddette donne esposte a detti mostri, i quali nell'atto che vogliono esercitare la loro ferocia, vengono assaliti dai suddetto schiavi, ed uccisi, onde salvate le donne, in segno di giubilo formano allegra danza, alla quale succedono altri graziosi balli.

*At the end of the first act*
A Turkish pasha, enraged at not seeing his love for his slave reciprocated, condemns her and her companions to be devoured by certain monsters that he keeps enclosed in a solitary place. They are led to their death; but several slaves come to their aid and disarm the guards. The scenery being changed, the aforesaid women are exposed to the said monsters, which while in the act of exercising their ferocity are attacked and killed by the aforesaid slaves, whereupon the women, having been saved, perform a gay dance in token of their jubilation, which is followed by other gracious dances.

*Nella fine dell'atto secondo*
Siegue pantomimo tra Pulcinella, Arlecchino e Coviello colle loro donne vestiti da pellegrini i quali dando in un mago soffrono spaventosi incontri; ma

*At the end of the second act*
There follows a pantomime between Pulcinella, Harlequin and Coviello with their women, [all] dressed as pilgrims, who meeting up with a magician, suffer fearful

| finalmente conferita a Pulcinella dal mago suddetto l'arte della magia a volo passano tutti nella città, ove riconosciuti dalle loro vecchie madri e da' figli siedono a mensa e nell'atto che vogliono mangiare Pulcinella fa una urla ad Arlecchino ed a Coviello e terminando il pantomimo con giocosa danza, si formano altri balli in susseguenza di graziosi caratteri. | encounters; but the art of magic being in the end conferred upon Pulcinella by the aforesaid magician, they all fly into the city where, recognized by their aged mothers and by their children, they sit down to eat, and as they are about to eat, Pulcinella gives a shout to Harlequin and to Coviello and, ending the pantomime with a joyous dance, other dances of gracious character are subsequently formed. |

NOTA DE' BALLERINI / NOTE ON THE DANCERS

Sig. Elisabetta Morelli                               Sig. Gennaro Magri

*Ballano fuori concerto / Dance outside the company dances*

Sig. Margarita Morelli                                Sig. Caterina Stacchini
Sig. Domenico Morelli                                 Sig. Mauro Zaccarini

La Signora Rosa Granazzo

*Balla ne' terzetti, quartetti, concerti e finali / Dances in trios, quartets, company dances and finales.*

*Figurano / Also dancing*

Sig. Andreana Giraldi                                 Sig. Francesco Beltrano
Sig. Marianna Jovino                                  Sig. Francesco Cimmino
Sig. Maria Rosa Intronti                              Sig. Franc. Giannattasio
Sig. Antonia Corona                                   Sig. Antonio Gioja
Sig. Francesca Toriello                               Sig. Domenico Figliolini
                                                      Sig. Gennaro Candelora

Inventore e direttore dei balli il suddetto / Inventor and Director of the ballets the aforesaid Signor Gennaro Magri Napolitano [Neapolitan].

5. 1773–74 season: ballets for the opera *Il trionfo di Clelia*
(The Triumph of Clelia; Metastasio/Giovanni Battista Borghi),
premiere 30 May 1773

1st ballet:    *Rinaldo e Armida* (Rinaldo and Armida; by Le Picq)
2nd ballet:    *Alla ricerca di un tesoro* (In Search of a Treasure; by Magri)

Libretto: I-Rsc, 15377

| Il Trionfo / di Clelia / Dramma per musica / da rappresentarsi nel Real Teatro di S. Carlo / nel dì 30 Maggio 1773 solennizzandosi / l'augusto, e real nome / del / re nostro signore, / ed alla / | The triumph / of Clelia / Drama in music / to be performed in the Royal Theater of San Carlo / the 30th of May 1773 to celebrate / the august and royal name-day / of / our lord, / and |

Maestà sua / dedicato / In Napoli
MDCCLXXIII / Per Francesco Morelli /
Impressore del Real Teatro.

dedicated to / his Majesty / In Naples
MDCCLXXIII / By Francesco Morelli /
Printer of the Royal Theater.

NOTA DE' BALLI

NOTE ON THE BALLETS

*Mutazioni di scene pel primo ballo*

*Changes of scenery for the first ballet*

Bosco con isoletta formata dal Fiume
Oronte, alla cui sponda Colonna con
iscrizione &c.

Wood with small island formed by the
Orontes River, on the shore of which is a
column with inscription &c.

Reggia di Armida, ch'indi vien
trasformata nella sua deserta abitazione.

Armida's Palace, which is then
transformed into her desert abode.

*Primo ballo*
Sdegnata Armida contro Rinaldo, per
aver questi da' di lei incanti liberati alcuni
Guerrieri, ne giura vendetta; onde posta,
sul sentier di Rinaldo, presso all'Oronte,
una colonna, ov'era scritto, *Qui discendi, e
vedrai Cosa non vista mai*, alletta l'incauto al
tragitto. Non trovando che solitari orrori,
vuol egli ripassar la riviera; ma l'onda si
divide, e ne sorge una Najade, che gli
contrasta l'uscita, come pure fanno due
Ninfe, ond'è vano ogni tentativo del-
l'Eroe per sottrarsi al cimento, prigio-
niero tra molli lacci. Vinto alfine dalle
piacevoli ripulse, e lusinghe, da sopor
dolce sorpreso, sovra fiorito sedil si abbandona. Corron le Ninfe a darne avviso
ed Armida, che armata di stile viene per
sacrificarlo alla sua vendetta. Ma nel mi-
rarlo, si arresta, le cade il ferro di mano, e
s'invaghisce della sua preda. Trasforma
in carro il sedile ed in quello son' ambi
trasportati in delizioso soggiorno. Esce
dal superbo edificio tutto il lusinghiero seguito della aga, intrecciando liete carole.
Tenta pur qui la fuga il Guerriero; ma
offrendogli Armida col Regno anche il
cuore, si accende anch'esso d'uno scam-
bievole affetto; e ne festeggia contento il
coro. Partono alfin tutti; ed ecco Carlo,
ed Ubaldo, che superato ogni ostacolo
cercan Rinaldo. Va da un lato Ubaldo; e
mentre Carlo vuol gir dall'altro, vien' im-
pedito da vaga Ninfa. Accorre in suo soc-

*First ballet*
Armida, incensed at Rinaldo on account
of his having liberated various warriors
she had enchanted, swears vengeance; for
which reason she places a column in
Rinaldo's path, near the river Orontes,
where was written, *Stop here, and you will
see / That which never before was seen*, enticing
the incautious one on his way. Finding
nothing but solitary horrors, he wishes to
cross the river, but the waves divide, and a
naiad arises, who blocks his exit, as do also
two nymphs, so that every attempt of the
hero to extract himself from the combat is
in vain; [he becomes] a prisoner in tender
snares. Defeated at last by the pleasant re-
pulsions and allurements, and overtaken
by a sweet drowsiness, he lies down on a
flowery seat. The nymphs run to advise
Armida of this, and she comes armed with
a dagger to sacrifice him to her
vengeance. But in looking upon him, she
stops, the blade falls from her hand, and
she falls in love with her prey. She transforms his seat into a chariot and both of
them are transported in it to a delightful
place. From the magnificent edifice the
entire alluring retinue of the sorceress exits, forming merry dances. Here, though,
the warrior attempts to flee; but Armida,
offering him her heart along with her
realm, inflames him with a reciprocal
affection; and the chorus happily cele-
brates. All finally leave; and Carlo and

corso ben' opportuno Ubaldo, che con verga incantata pone in fuga la Ninfa, e n'esce orrida Furia, che contende il varco a' campioni dentro il Giardino. Vuol combatter Carlo; ma Ubaldo colla verga fuga il Mostro, ed entrano inosservati dentro il verziere. Tornan fra tanto Rinaldo, ed Armida; indi avvertita questa esser già l'ora delle sue magiche operazioni, si divide con dispiacere dal caro Amante. Allor si scoprono i due Guerrieri: Attonito Rinaldo, va per abbracciarli, ma Ubaldo gli presenta il terso scudo, in cui ravvisa la sua effeminatezza. N'arrossisce l'Eroe; e quelli gli porgon lo scudo, e il brando, per partire. Ritorna Armida; si affanna indarno per trattenere il fuggitivo, e vien meno. Accorre Rinaldo, e se le getta a' piedi; ma i Compagni lo svellon quindi a forza, e seco alfin lo conducono. Rinviene la Maga, e fremendo abbandonata, chiama in soccorso la Gelosia, l'Odio, e la Vendetta. Sovraggiungono insieme tutte le Seguaci d'Armida, a cui le Furie danno istigamento di distruggere l'incantato edificio; indi comparendo un carro tratto da Mostri, sen fugge la Maga colle Furie a volo, e tutto il Seguito pien di terrore si dilegua.

Ubaldo, who have overcome every obstacle, appear in search of Rinaldo. Ubaldo goes to one side; and while Carlo wants to turn to the other, he is impeded by a fair nymph. Ubaldo opportunely runs to his aid, putting the nymph to flight with an enchanted wand, and out comes a horrid Fury, who blocks the champions' path into the garden. Carlo wants to fight; but Ubaldo with his wand flees from the monster, and they enter into the orchard unobserved. Meanwhile Rinaldo returns, along with Armida; then she, advised that this is the hour of her magical operations, separates with displeasure from her beloved. Then the two warriors reveal themselves: Rinaldo, astonished, moves to embrace them, but Ubaldo shows him the reflective shield, in which he recognizes his effeminacy. The hero blushes at this; and the warriors present him his shield and his sword, [and prepare] to depart. Armida returns; she endeavors in vain to retain the fugitive, and falls in a faint. Rinaldo runs to her, and throws himself at her feet; but his companions grab hold of him, and lead him away. The sorceress returns, and trembling at being abandoned so, calls to her aid Jealousy, Hate, and Vengeance. All the followers of Armida arrive, and the Furies incite Armida to destroy the enchanted edifice; then appearing on a chariot drawn by monsters, the sorceress flees into the air with the Furies, and all her retinue disperses full of terror.

*[Mutazioni di scene] Pel secondo ballo*
Selva con prospetto d'orrida Grotta, in cui si asconde un tesoro, che poi si scopre, e trasformasi in una Montuosa con molte rustiche case, ch'indi si trasformano in una Fortezza, e tutto il Monte in militare accampamento.

*[Changes of scenery] For the second ballet*
Wood with view of a horrid cave, in which a treasure is hidden, which afterward is discovered, and [the scene] changes into a mountainous [landscape] with many rustic houses, which then are transformed into a fortress, and all of the mountain into a military encampment.

*Secondo ballo*
Verso montuosa Caverna van due Stranieri, con astrolabio, bussola, e carta

*Second ballet*
Two strangers go toward a mountainous cave, with astrolabe, compass, and map, to

regolatrice per rinvenire un tesoro, ed i Servi, col lume, hanno instrumenti per iscovarlo. Trovano il segno indicato; ed aspettando l'ora dell'attesa Stella, e lieti insieme sedendo, sprofondasi un sasso, e ne sbucano più Mostri, del tesoro custodi. Si atterriscono i Servi, ma già comparsa la Stella, e cominciando un di questi a rompere il muro, sentesi percosso. Fra vari equivoci, contrasti e paure de' Servi, atterra finalmente il muro un de' Padroni. Comune è il giubilo; ma bruciando negligentemente i Domestici l'indicante foglio, se ne sdegnano i Padroni, che dopo loro perdonano; ed essendo per tramontar già la Stella, vanno ad ultimare l'impresa; ma da strano Augello replicatamente spaventati, nulla ottengono; anzi ingoiati da voragine i Servi, e fuggendo a volo l'alato Mostro, si trovano i Padroni in un villaggio. Ivi all'allegria, ed a bere invitati, non ben per anco rimessi dalla paura, rifiutan l'invito. Ma dopo avvedutisi di due Spose, ivi assise, fan loro ossequi, che son da quelle sprezzati. Accettando però tabacchiera d'oro, ed insieme danzando, sovraggiungono il Padre, e gli Sposi delle Donzelle. Si ritirano i Forestieri; e veggendo gli Sposi il regalo in mano delle Fanciulle, mentre protestano al Padre di non più volerle sposare, accettan pur quelle destramente in nuovo dono un ventaglio. Ciò visto gli Sposi, stracciano i capitoli; e fuggendo le Donzelle, parton quelli ancora. Placato il Genitor dagli Amici, va in traccia de' Generi, e ne segue festivo concerto. Ma tornando i Forestieri, torna a sdegnarsi il Padre, onde quelli di ciò afflitti, tentan d'uccidersi; ma lor comparsa la Fata del tesoro, che porge loro una bacchetta, per ottener ciò, che bramano. Trafugan subito le Donzelle, onde il Padre, e gli Sposi minaccian con armi da fuoco i Rattori, i quali fuggendo a quell'alture colle suddette, fan disparir l'antro, e il Villaggio, che cangiasi in mi-

recover a treasure, and their servants, with torches, have tools with which to uncover it. They find the sign indicated [on the map]; and awaiting the hour of the expected star, and happily sitting down together, a rock falls down, and out of it spring several monsters, custodians of the treasure. The servants are frightened, but as the star has already appeared, one of these [servants] starts to break down the wall, but becomes exhausted. Amid various misunderstandings, disputes, and fears of the servants, one of their masters finally knocks down the wall. There is general jubilation; but the servants accidentally burn the map, and their masters become angry, but afterward forgive them; and as the star is about to go down, they go to finish their task; but repeatedly frightened by a strange bird, they obtain nothing; indeed, the servants being swallowed up by a chasm, and the winged monster flying away, the masters find themselves in a village. Invited there to rejoice and drink, they refuse the invitation, not yet having recovered from their fright. But after noticing two brides sitting there, they pay their respects, and are scorned by them. Accepting a golden snuffbox from them, though, and dancing with them, the father and the bridegrooms of the young women appear. The strangers withdraw; the bridegrooms, seeing a present in the hands of the girls, protest to their father that they no longer wish to marry them; meanwhile, the girls furtively accept a new gift of a fan [from the strangers]. The bridegrooms, seeing this, tear up the [wedding] contracts; and while the maidens flee, they too leave. The father being placated by his friends, goes after his sons-in-law, and there follows a festive company dance. But with the return of the strangers, the father again becomes angry, which distresses them, and they try to kill themselves; but the fairy of the treasure appears, offering them a wand with which to obtain

litare accampamento, ed essi pure, e le
Spose cangian d'aspetto.

whatever they desire. The maidens suddenly flee, whereupon the father and the
bridegrooms threaten the abductors with
firearms, and the latter flee to the hills with
the maidens, make disappear the cavern
and the village, which changes into a military encampment, and both they and the
brides change their appearance.

Si danno alla fuga il Padre e gli Sposi; ma
poi placati, forman quartetto, indi
intrecciano allegrissima contraddanza.

The father and the bridegrooms flee; but
then being placated, they form a quartet,
and then dance a most joyous contredanse.

NOTA DE' BALLERINI / NOTE ON THE DANCERS

Inventore e Direttore del Primo Ballo: /
Inventor and director of the First Ballet:

Inventore e Direttore del Secondo Ballo: /
Inventor and director of the Second Ballet:

Il Sig. Carlo Lepicq

Il Sig. Gennaro Magri Napolitano /
Neapolitan

[Ballerine / Dancers (female):]

[Ballerini / Dancers (male):]

Sig. Anna Binetti
Sig. Veronica Cocchi
Sig. Anna Pallerini

Sig. Carlo Lepicq
Sig. Gennaro Magri
Sig. Gaetano Cesari

*Ballano fuori del concerto / Dance outside the company dances.*

Il Sig. Gaetano Cesari

La Sig. Anna Pallerini

*Figuranti / Also dancing*

Dodici Uomini e dodici Donne.

Twelve men and twelve women.

Inventore, e Direttore del vestiario / Inventor, and Director of the costumes,
il Signor Francesco Marescotti.

## 6. 1773–74 season: ballets for the opera *Romolo ed Ersilia* (Romulus and Ersilia; Metastasio/Joseph Mysliveček), premiere 13 August 1773

1st ballet:   *Ercole e Dejanira* (Hercules and Dejanira; by Le Picq)
2nd ballet:   *La festa delle lanterne* (The Festival of Lanterns; by Magri)
3rd ballet:   *Ballo degli sposi romani con le donzelle sabine, da eseguirsi al principio del drama* (Ballet of the Roman Bridegrooms with the Sabine Women, to be performed at the beginning of the drama; by Le Picq)

Libretto: I-Nc, Rari 10.7.17 (6)

Romolo ed Ersilia / Dramma per musica / da rappresentarsi nel Real Teatro di S. Carlo / nel dì 13 Agosto 1773 / per festeggiarsi la nascita / di / S.M. la Regina, / ed alla real maestà / di / Ferdinando IV / nostro clementissimo sovrano / dedicato. / In Napoli MDCCLXXIII / Per Francesco Morelli.

Romulus and Ersilia / Drama in music / to be performed in the Royal Theater of San S. Carlo, / the 13th of August 1773 / in celebration of the birthday / of / Her Majesty the Queen, / and dedicated to the royal majesty / of / our most clement sovereign / Ferdinand IV. / In Naples MDCCLXXIII / By Francesco Morelli.

NOTA DE' BALLI

NOTE ON THE BALLETS

*Primo ballo*

*First ballet*

Personaggi:

| | |
|---|---|
| Ercole il Tebano | Carlo Lepicq |
| Dejanira | Anna Binetti |
| Jole | Veronica Cocchi |
| Filottete | Francesco Montani |
| Ilo | Filippo Berretti |

Cast:

| | |
|---|---|
| Theban Hercules | Carlo Lepicq |
| Dejanira | Anna Binetti |
| Iole | Veronica Cocchi |
| Philoctetes | Francesco Montani |
| Ilus | Filippo Berretti |

Scene:
Gran Piazza di Tebe.
Gabinetto
Bosco con altare, ed il Fuoco Sacro, indi Nuvole risplendenti sull'alto

Scenery:
Great square in Thebes.
Cabinet.
Wood with altars, and the sacred flame, then shining clouds above

*Secondo ballo*
[Scene:]
Bosco Chinese, alla riva del mare.
Giardino Chinese.
Logge aperte, ed illuminate, festeggiandosi da' Chinesi con solennità il primo Giorno del loro Anno, o sia la Festa delle Lanterne.

*Second ballet*
[Scenery:]
Chinese wood, on the seashore.
Chinese garden.
Open and illuminated loggias, in solemn celebration of the first day of the Chinese New Year, or the Festival of Lanterns.

*Terzo ballo*
Degli Sposi Romani colle Donzelle Sabine, il quale per convenienza del Dramma si eseguisce al principio.*

*Third ballet*
Of Roman Bridegrooms with the Sabine Women, which for the sake of the drama is performed at the beginning.*

[* Presumably this ballet performed at the start of act 1 (during the chorus "Sul Tarpeo propizie e liete") is referred to as "Terzo ballo" because that was the one of the usual three ballets that tended to be linked to the action of the opera (as a *ballo analogo*).]

NOTA DE' BALLERINI / NOTE ON THE DANCERS

Primo Ballerino, Inventore e Direttore del Primo Ballo / First Male Dancer, Inventor and Director of the First Ballet

Inventore e Direttore del Secondo Ballo / Inventor and Director of the Second Ballet

Il Sig. Carlo Lepicq

Il Sig. Gennaro Magri Napolitano [Neapolitan]

Eseguiti dal sudetto, e dalla Prima Ballerina / Performed by the aforesaid, and by the First Female Dancer La Sig. Anna Binetti

colli seguenti altri Ballerini di più del numero stabilito / with the following other Dancers in addition to the regular number.

La Sig. Maria Milongini
Il Sig. Francesco Montani
Il Sig. Filippo Berretti

Eseguiti dal sudetto e / Performed by the aforesaid and by Sig. Veronica Cocchi.

*Ballano fuori del concerto* / *Dance outside the company dances*
Il Sig. Gaetano Cesari, e [and] la Sig. Anna Pallarini.

*Con numero 24 figuranti.* / *With 24 others dancing.*

Inventore e Direttore del Vestiario / Inventor and Director of the costumes
Il Sig. Francesco Marescotti Napolitano.

Scene / Scenery
D[on] Antonio Iolli.

7. 1773–74 season: ballets for the opera *Alessandro nell'Indie*
(Alexander in India; Metastasio/Piccinni),
premiere 12 January 1774

1st ballet:   *Aminta e Clori* (Amyntas and Cloris; by Le Picq)
2nd ballet:   *Pantomimo con maschere* (Pantomime with Masks [i.e., with commedia dell'arte characters]; by Magri)
3rd ballet:   *Da'seguari di Allesandro* (Of the followers of Alexander; by Le Picq?)

Libretto: I-Baf, n.209

Alessandro nell'Indie / Dramma per musica / da rappresentarsi nel Real Teatro di S. Carlo / nel dì 12 Gennaio 1774 / festeggiandosi la nascita / di / Ferdinando IV / nostro amabilissimo sovrano / ed alla maestà sua / dedicato / In Napoli MDCCLXXIV / Per Francesco Morelli imp.

NOTA DE' BALLI
*Aminta e Clori* [description omitted here]

Alexander in India / Drama in music / to be performed in the Royal Theater of San Carlo / the 12th of January 1774 / in celebration of the birthday / of our most beloved sovereign / Ferdinand IV / and dedicated / to his majesty / In Naples MDCCLXXIV / By Francesco Morelli, printer.

NOTE ON THE BALLETS
*Amyntas and Cloris* [description omitted here]

*Primo ballo eroico pastorale*

Personaggi:

| | |
|---|---|
| Aminta | Carlo Lepicq |
| Clori | Anna Binetti |
| Mopso | Francesco Montani |
| Amarilli | Maria Anastasia Radaelli |
| Amore | Veronica Cocchi |

Scene
*Primo ballo*
Campagna deliziosa con alberi
Caverna
Reggia d'Amore

*Secondo ballo*
Piazza con Casino di Pantalone

Grazioso Pantomimo con Maschere

Avendo Pantalone licenziato dal suo servigio Truffaldino, risolve questi di vendicarsene. Entra per servidore con Flaminio, innamorato della Figlia di Pantalone ma già dal Padre promessa in isposa al ricco Pulcinella. L'astutissimo Truffaldino, non tanto in grazia del novello Padrone, quanto in gastigo del vecchio tant'arte adopra, ed inganni, che riduce questo alla necessità d'accettar per genero Flaminio, e lasciar Pulcinella deluso. Fatte le nozze, in segno di giubilo, s'intreccia lietissima danza.

*Terzo ballo*
Da' seguaci di Alessandro si forma nobil Danza, in applauso delle sue reali ed eroiche azioni.

*First heroic-pastoral ballet*

Cast:

| | |
|---|---|
| Amyntas | Carlo Lepicq |
| Cloris | Anna Binetti |
| Mopsa | Francesco Montani |
| Amaryillis | Maria Anastasia Radaelli |
| Cupid | Veronica Cocchi |

Scenery
*First ballet*
Delightful countryside with trees
Cavern
Palace of Cupid

*Second ballet*
Square with Pantalone's Pleasure-house

Gracious Pantomime with Masks

Truffaldino, having been fired from Pantalone's service, resolves to have his revenge on him. He becomes the servant of Flaminio, the beloved of Pantalone's daughter, who however has already been promised in marriage to the rich Pulcinella. The clever Truffaldino, less from consideration for his new master than in punishment of his old one, uses so much skill and deception that he forces the latter to accept Flaminio as his son-in-law, leaving Pulcinella disappointed. Following the wedding, they form a gay dance in token of their happiness.

*Third ballet*
A noble dance is formed by the followers of Alexander, in praise of his regal and heroic actions.

NOTA DE' BALLERINI / NOTE ON THE DANCERS

Primo Ballerino Serio, Inventore, e Direttore del Primo Ballo / First Serious Male Dancer, Inventor, and Director of the First Ballet:

Sig. Carlo Lepicq

Eseguiti dal suddetto e dalla Prima

Primo Ballerino Grottesco, Inventore, e Direttore del Secondo Ballo / First Grotesque Male Dancer, Inventor, and Director of the Second Ballet:

Il Sig. Gennaro Magri Napolitano [Neapolitan]

Eseguiti dal suddetto e dalla / Performed

Ballerina / Performed by the aforesaid and by the First Female Dancer La Sig. Anna Binetti.

by the aforesaid and by Signora Veronica Cocchi.

colli seguenti altri Ballerini di più del numero stabilito / with the following other dancers in addition to the regular number.

La Sig. Anastasia Radaelli
Il Sig. Francesco Montani.

*Ballano fuori de' concerti / Dance outside the company dances*
Il Sig. Gaetano Cesari e [and] la Sig. Anna Pallerini

*Con numero 24 Figuranti / With 24 others dancing.*

Inventore e Direttore del Vestiario / Inventor and Director of the Costumes
Il Sig. Francesco Marescotti Napolitano.

# Appendix 5

## Selected Ballet Scenarios from Three Theaters in Paris

COMPILED BY REBECCA HARRIS-WARRICK,

TRANSLATIONS BY BRUCE ALAN BROWN

*1. Les Bûcherons,*
*ou Le Médecin de village.*

*The Woodcutters,*
*or The Village Doctor.*

Ballet Pantomime, Théâtre Italien, 1750. "L'invention du Sujet et la composition des Danses sont de M. Dehesse."

Pantomime Ballet, Théâtre Italien, 1750. "The invention of the subject and the composition of the dances are by M. Dehesse."

(The scenario transcribed here comes from a four-volume anthology of printed librettos of works performed in the Théâtre des Petits Appartements in the château of Versailles between 1747 and 1750 [F-Po C. 2768]. In these performances, a few courtiers performed alongside the professionals, which accounts for the names of the two nobles in the cast list below. According to the Parfaict *Dictionnaire*, vol. 7, this ballet was performed at the Théâtre Italien starting 17 June 1750, following the play *Le Réveil de Thalie;* the music is by "M. des Rochers, ancien symphoniste de la Comédie italienne" ["retired orchestra member of the Comédie italienne"]. A libretto in the Bibliothèque Nationale de France [F-Pn Th^B 2445] contains a different version of this scenario.)

| Personnages du Ballet | Cast of the Ballet | |
|---|---|---|
| Chirugien: | Surgeon: | M. le Marquis de Courtanvaux |
| Premier Médecin: | First Doctor: | Mr le Comte de Langeron |
| 2e Médecin: | Second Doctor: | M. Dehesse |
| 3e Médecin: | Third Doctor: | M. Vicentini |
| Le Blessé: | The Wounded Man: | M. Piffet |
| Maitres Bucherons et leurs Femmes: | Master Woodcutters and their Wives: | M[essieu]rs La Riviere, Beat, Lepy; Mlles Puvigné, Camille, Reyx. |
| Garçons Bucherons et leurs Femmes: | Apprentice Woodcutters and their Wives: | M[essieu]rs Bourgeois, Berterin, Rousseau, Gougis, Dupré, Barois, Balleti, Marcadet; Mlles Marquise, Dorfeuil, Astraudi, Chevrier, Durand, Foulquier. |

*Le Théatre représente dans le fond une Forêt, & quelques Maisons de Village sur le devant.*

On voit à l'ouverture du Théatre plusieurs Arbres renversés, & comme coupés au pied. Une partie des Bucherons est occupée à les scier, d'autres à les fendre. Des Arbres paroissent encore élevés, sur lesquels on voit des Travailleurs qui en élaguent les branches. Tous les différens Personnages du Ballet paroissent en mouvement, & marquent dans leur travail la cadence du premier air.

Premiere Entrée. Les Maîtres Bucherons & leurs Femmes viennent observer si les Travailleurs font leur devoir; ils en témoignent leur satisfaction en dansant.

Seconde Entrée. Les Femmes des Travailleurs arrivent ensuite avec le déjeuné [sic] de leurs maris, qu'elles apportent dans des Corbeilles. Ils quittent leur travail pour aller au-devant d'elles. Les Maîtres font la distribution du déjeuné, pendant que toutes les Femmes dansent.

Troisieme Entrée. Une partie des Hommes se remet à l'ouvrage, une autre

*The back of the stage shows a forest, and at the front are some village houses.*

The opening of the curtain reveals several toppled trees, as if cut off at the base. One group of the woodcutters is occupied in sawing them, the other in chopping them. Some trees are still standing, on which some workers are pruning off the branches. All the various persons of the ballet appear in movement, and in their work mark the rhythm of the first musical number.

First Entrée. The master woodcutters and their wives come to observe if the workers are doing their duty; they show their satisfaction while dancing.

Second Entrée. The wives of the workers then arrive with their husbands' lunches, which they carry in baskets. They [the husbands] stop their work and go in front of them. The masters distribute the lunches, while all the women dance.

Third Entrée. One group of the men goes back to work, another stays to dance with

reste à danser avec les Femmes. Un des Travailleurs tombe de dessus un Arbre, tous les autres vont à son secours; on le releve, & on le porte sur un siége; il paroît avoir tous les membres brisés, ce qui excite la compassion de ses Camarades.

Quatrieme Entrée. Les Femmes vont chercher un Médecin; les Hommes de leur côté en amenent un autre. Le premier Médecin amené par les Femmes examine le Blessé, & veut se retirer à la vûe de son Confrere dès qu'il le voit arriver; celui-ci marque la même déference. La Femme du Blessé amene un troisiéme Médecin. Différens lazzis entr'eux. On apporte des siéges. Les Médecins priés de soulager le Blessé, paroissent s'entretenir de choses entierement étrangères à cet objet. Sur l'empressement réiteré de la Femme du Blessé, les Médecins envoyent appeller un Chirugien; la Femme y court. On voit arriver le Chirugien habillé comiquement en Barbier. Consultation pantomime entre lui & les Médecins, dans laquelle on ne convient de rien. Enfin, pour se rendre aux clameurs de toutes les Femmes, un des Médecins ordonne au Chirurgien une saignée. Lorsqu'il se met en devoir de la faire, un autre Médecin s'y oppose, & témoigne qu'il veut que l'on coupe un bras: sur quoi un troisieme Medecin conteste, & soutient que c'est la jambe dont l'amputation est nécessaire. La Femme s'oppose également à toutes ces opérations. Le Chirugien fait entendre qu'il a des secrets plus efficaces; il apporte du vin, & en remplit un verre, ce qui produit plusieurs lazzis. Effet merveilleux du vin, le Blessé reprend toutes ses forces, les Médecins l'admirent avec extase, les Bucherons témoignent leur joie.

Cinquieme Entrée. Contredanse générale, dans laquelle on fait danser les Médecins & le Chirugien.

their wives. One of the workers falls out of a tree, all the others go to his aid; they pick him up, and carry him to a chair; it seems that all his limbs are broken, which moves his comrades to compassion.

Fourth Entrée. The women go to fetch a doctor; the men, for their part, bring another. The first doctor brought by the women examines the wounded man, and wants to withdraw from the sight of his fellow doctor as soon as he sees him arrive; the latter shows the same deference. The wife of the wounded man brings a third doctor. Different *lazzi* among them. Some chairs are brought on. The doctors, asked to comfort the wounded man, seem to converse about things utterly unrelated to this. At the reiterated urgings of the wife of the wounded man, the doctors send off for a surgeon; the wife runs for him. The surgeon is seen arriving comically dressed as a barber. Pantomime consultation between him and the doctors, in which they agree on nothing. Finally, in order to give in to the clamoring of all the women, one of the doctors orders the surgeon to bleed him. While they set about doing this, another doctor objects, and declares that he wants them to cut off an arm: at which a third doctor objects, and holds that it is the leg that must be amputated. The wife is equally opposed to all these procedures. The surgeon lets it be known that he has more effective secrets; he brings out some wine, and fills a glass, which produces several *lazzi*. The wine [has] a marvelous effect, the wounded man regains all his strength, the doctors regard him ecstatically, and the woodcutters express their joy.

Fifth Entrée. *Contredanse générale,* in which the doctors and the surgeon are made to dance.

## 2. *La Fête villageoise (The Village Holiday).*

Ballet pantomime by Dourdé, Comédie Française, 1754.
(The discussion and the scenario have been transcribed from Parfaict, *Dictionnaire des théâtres de Paris* [Paris, 1756], 6:229–31.)

Ballet Pantomime exécuté pour la premiere fois au Théatre de la Comédie Françoise, le Lundi 10 juin 1754. Il est de la composition de M. Dourdé, Maître de Ballet à ce Théatre, Musique de M. d'Avennes, ordinaire de l'ARM, à l'exception de celle du premier Pas de deux, qui est de Monsieur Girault, aussi ordinaire de la même Académie, & de celle du Pas de deux du Sieur Maranesi, & de la Dlle Bugiani, qui est d'un compositeur Anglois, & a été apporté par eux. Depuis que les Comédiens François ont rétabli les Ballets à leur Théatre, celui ci est le premier dont nous ayons eu occasion de rendre compte dans les lettres de ce Dictionnaire qui nous restoient à remplir. Il est heureux pour nous qu'il se soit trouvé assez agréable pour mériter l'attention du Public. Nous ne pouvons cependant dissimuler qu'on en a critiqué le titre, & qu'on a prétendu que celui de *Récréation Villageoise* auroit mieux convenu au sujet, le mot de Fête, dans quelque sens qu'on le veuille prendre, ne pouvant signifier un divertissement qui commence par des travaux pénibles. Quoi qu'il en soit de la justice de ce reproche, qui d'ailleurs n'ôte rien à l'agrément du Ballet, même en le supposant bien fondé, nous croyons faire plaisir à nos lecteurs de leur rappeller l'idée d'un spectacle qui a paru les amuser.

Le Théatre représente un bosquet agréable; on y voit divers paysans occupés à différents ouvrages; les uns émondent, les autres coupent des arbres; ceux-ci ratissent des allées, ceux là remplacent des arbrisseaux. De jeunes paysannes arrivent, & veulent faire quitter le travail

Pantomime ballet performed for the first time in the theater of the Comédie Française, Monday 10 June 1754. It was choreographed by M. Dourdé, Ballet Master at this theater; the music is by M. d'Avennes, of the Académie Royale de Musique, apart from that of the first *pas de deux*, which is by Monsieur Girault, also of the same Académie, and that of the *pas de deux* of Sieur Maranesi, and D[emoise]lle Bugiani, which is by an English composer, and has been brought [here] by them. Since the French actors have reinstated ballets in their theater, this is the first one we have had occasion to review in the letters [of the alphabet] of this dictionary still remaining to be filled. It is fortunate for us that it [the ballet] has been found pleasant enough to merit the public's attention. Nevertheless we cannot hide the fact that its title has been criticized, and that people have claimed that the title *Village Recreation* would have fit the subject better, since the word "holiday," in whatever sense one might take it, cannot signify a *divertissement* that begins with onerous work. Whatever the justice of this reproach, which in any case does not detract from the pleasure of the ballet, even if we consider it well founded, we believe we will cause pleasure for our readers in reminding them of the idea of a spectacle that seemed to amuse them.

The stage shows a pleasant grove, where various peasants are busy with different tasks; some are pruning, others are cutting trees; some are raking paths, others are replacing saplings. Some young peasant girls arrive, and wish to make their lovers stop their work; the girls

à leurs Amans qui les rebutent; elles se retirent, mais elles reviennent bientôt en plus grand nombre, & engagent les jeunes paysans à venir danser avec elles. Un Berger & sa Bergere se mêlent parmi les paysans qui leur font place, & leur laissent danser un Pas de deux très-bien éxécuté, par le Sieur Riviere & la Demoiselle Auguste. Deux paysans arrivent chargés de fagots, & s'appercevant que l'on se réjouit, ils posent leur fagots à terre, & vont appeller leurs camarades; ceux-ci, charmés de ce divertissement, veulent que leurs Maîtresses y prennent part, les vont chercher & les aménent, ce qui forme un second corps de Ballet qui se joint au premier. Un autre paysan quitte à son tour le travail, danse seul, & se remet à son ouvrage; mais son Amante en Marmotte, jouant de la vielle, entre en dansant, & ayant apperçu son Amant, elle veut l'obliger à danser avec elle. Après plusieurs agaceries, ils forment un second Pas de deux très brillant, & supérieurement exécuté par le Sieur Maranesi & la Dlle Bugiani. Le Ballet général recommence, dans lequel se mêlent le Berger, la Bergére, la Vielleuse & son Amant, ce qui compose une Contre-danse très vive, très agréable, & très bien dessinée, par laquelle finit le Divertissement.

withdraw, but they soon come back in greater numbers, and get the young peasant men to come dance with them. A shepherd and his shepherdess join in among the peasants, who make room for them, and let them dance a *pas de deux*, very well executed by the Sieur Riviere and the Demoiselle Auguste. Two peasants arrive carrying bundles of firewood, and seeing that people are rejoicing, they put their bundles down and go to call their comrades; these, charmed by this *divertissement*, want their mistresses to take part in it, [they] go looking for them and fetch them, which forms a second ballet ensemble that joins with the first. Another peasant in turn stops working, dances by himself, and goes back to work; but his [elderly] beloved, *en marmotte* [i.e., wearing a typical Savoyard cloth headdress], playing the hurdy gurdy, enters dancing, and having noticed her lover, wants to make him dance with her. After a bit of sparring, they form a second and very brilliant *pas de deux*, superbly executed by the Sieur Maranesi and the D[emoise]lle Bugiani. The general ballet starts up again, in which the shepherd and shepherdess, and the old woman and her lover join in, which makes for a very lively, pleasant, and well designed contredanse, which ends the *divertissement*.

## *3. Les Rejouissances flamandes (The Flemish Celebrations).*

Ballet pantomime by Noverre, Opéra Comique, 1755.
(This scenario has been transcribed from *Les Spectacles de Paris* [Paris, 1756], 158–59.)

*Les Rejouissances flamandes*, Ballet, par M. *Novere*, le 11 Août. Voici l'idée de ce dernier Ballet.

*The Flemish Celebrations*, Ballet, by M. *Nover[r]e*, 11 August. Here is the jist of this last ballet.

Lorsque le rideau est levé, la Décoration offre aux yeux du Spectateur un hameau;

When the curtain is raised, the decor offers the spectators' eyes a hamlet; a hill

une colline en forme le fond; elle est
terminée par un grand arbre, au tour
duquel sont dressées des tables occupées
par des bûveurs. Les deux côtés du
Théâtre sont pareillement garnis de
tables, & celles-ci de Flamands & de
Flamandes qui boivent & se divertissent
sous des treilles. Le Groupe distingué du
Seigneur du lieu & de sa famille,
richement habillés, est placé au milieu de
la Scène. Des valets leur versent à boire,
tandis que les Cabaretiers & les
Cabaretières servent les paysans. Des
Musiciens montés sur des tonneaux
excitent tout le monde à la joye. L'action
est générale jusques-là. Les Paysans & les
Paysannes quittent leurs tables pour jouer
à differens jeux; ceux-ci se font péser;
ceux-là courent la bague, tandis que
d'autres jouent à la boule, aux quilles, &
un Vielleur & un Joueur de Musette leur
font quitter les jeux, & les engagent à
danser. Le Ballet commence après
plusieurs entrées particulieres &
générales. Le Seigneur du Village danse
un pas de quatre avec sa famille, &
ensuite un menuet. Les danses sont
interrompues par une dispute
particuliere; mais tous les hommes
veulent s'en mêler, & toutes les femmes
font leurs efforts pour les en empêcher.
Le Juge du lieu paroît, & rétablit le calme.
Le Ballet est terminé par une contredanse
générale, dessinée d'une maniere
nouvelle & piquante, exécutée par une
foule prodigieuse de danseurs & de
danseuses, sans embarras, sans confusion.

forms the background; it [the decor] is
terminated by a large tree, around which
tables occupied by drinkers are arranged.
The two sides of the stage are both
furnished with tables, and with Flemish
men and women who drink and amuse
themselves under the arbors. The
distinguished group of the local lord and
his family, richly dressed, is placed in the
center of the stage. Some valets pour
drinks for them, while waiters and
waitresses serve the peasants. Some
musicians atop barrels arouse everyone to
joy. The action is general up to this point.
The peasant men and women leave their
tables to play various games; some weigh
themselves; others lance at rings, while
others bowl, [or] play skittles, and a
hurdy-gurdy player and a musette player
make them quit their games, and get
them to dance. The ballet starts after
several individual and group *entrées*. The
village lord dances a *pas de quatre* with his
family, and then a minuet. The dances
are interrupted by a private argument;
but all the men want to join in, and all the
women make an effort to prevent them.
The local judge appears, and restores
calm. The ballet ends with a *contredanse
générale*, designed in a new and piquant
manner, performed by a prodigious
crowd of men and women dancers,
without awkwardness, without confusion.

# Appendix 6

# Table of Contents
of Magri's *Trattato*

## Part 1

The copy consulted of Magri's original treatise is that in the Music Division of the Library of Congress (GV1590.M3). It can be accessed through the Library's Web site at http://memory.loc.gov/ammem/dihtml/dihome.html ("An American Ballroom Companion: Dance Instruction Manuals, ca. 1490–1920").

1. The pages of the *Prefazione* are numbered 7–11; page 12 is blank. The *Avvertimento*, which was interpolated after the book went to press, is separately paginated from 9 to 12, followed by three unnumbered pages.

# Part II

2. The plates in the copy at the Library of Congress are out of order: the final plate, with notation for "L'Amabile," follows "Principj delle Contraddanze" (plate 6 of Magri/Skeaping)

# Appendix 7

## Steps, Other Dance Terms, and People in Magri's *Trattato*, Part I

### COMPILED BY REBECCA HARRIS-WARRICK

The three indexes that follow list movement vocabulary, other dance terms, and names of people found in part I of Magri's *Trattato*.

The first index includes the step names (and a few other dance movements, such as positions of the feet or use of arms) as Magri gave them, in Italian, French, or both, and it preserves his spelling (the one he uses most frequently, in cases of variations). When the entry is for a term to which Magri devotes an entire chapter, the key words of his chapter heading appear in italics, as do the page numbers of the chapter. In the case of the very long chapter regarding caprioles, page numbers are given in italics when Magri dedicates a numbered subunit of the chapter to that particular capriole. Where the word "capriola" appears in parentheses, Magri classified the step as a type of capriole but used the shorter form of the name for it. When Magri discusses variant ways of performing the step (to the front, turning, etc.), the main variants are listed below the main entry. Some terms (*movimento, giro*, etc.) appeared on so many pages of the *Trattato* that it seemed superfluous to index them. Similarly, under the entry for "posizioni" (positions of the feet), only the unusual ones are indexed, not the true positions or the positions in the air, which Magri mentions countless times.

The third column of index 1 shows Skeaping's equivalent of Magri's terms — or, more precisely, the term she uses the most frequently. Because her translation may vary according to the context (e.g., "salto" may be translated as a jump or a spring, or turned from a noun into a verb), the term shown in the third column may not appear in that precise configuration on the pages cited. When nothing appears in the Skeaping column, she has retained Magri's own term. In cases where a term is still in use in ballet, it should *not* be assumed that the step has the same execution as its modern homonym.

Index 2 includes terms such as dance types, which are given in Magri's Italian, and more general concepts, such as use of space, which are listed in English. The entry "style" has several subheadings, for grotesque, serious, theatrical, and other styles.

Index 3 lists the names of people Magri mentions in his text, both historical figures (including himself as a practicing dancer) and fictional character types, such as Coviello. The names are listed as Magri cites them.

Since the page layouts in Magri's *Trattato* and Skeaping's translation are not equivalent, there is not always a direct correspondence between the page numbers in the two columns of these indexes. For example, a term may appear on two consecutive pages in the *Trattato,* but the passage of text that includes both appearances may fit on a single page in Skeaping. Page numbers in the Magri column that appear in parentheses refer to his "Avvertimento" (Warning), which was separately paginated and interpolated into the book after it had gone to press. Anything enclosed in square brackets is editorial.

| Magri's movement vocabulary (his terminology and spelling) | Page(s) in Magri | Skeaping's equivalent | Page(s) in Skeaping |
| --- | --- | --- | --- |
| ale di piccione; see (capriola) ale di piccione | | | |
| ambuettè avanti, in dietro, in fianco, in giro fatto e disfatto, raddoppiato (deublè) | 23, *85–86* | | 61, *122–23* |
| a-plomb [arms, use of]; see *gioco delle braccia* | 20, 91, 105 | aplomb | 57, 128, 143 |

| *Magri's movement vocabulary (his terminology and spelling)* | *Page(s) in Magri* | *Skeaping's equivalent* | *Page(s) in Skeaping* |
|---|---|---|---|
| capriola battuta girando [normal], di sbalzo, afior di terra, intrecciata | *131* | beaten turning capriole | *163* |
| capriole galletti | *133–34* | | *164–65* |
| (capriola) gorgugliè several types | *124–25* | | *158–59* |
| capriola intrecciata | 39, 122, 131 | interwoven capriole | 74, 157, *163* |
| (capriola) jettè battuto in aria | *133* | beaten jeté in the air | *164* |
| (capriola) pistoletta in aria | 50, *132*, 133 | pistolette in the air | 84, *164*, 164 |
| capriola reale | *128*, 136–37 | capriole royale | *161*, 166 |
| capriola ritirata alla francese, all'italiana, alla spagnuola | *122* | | *157–58* |
| (capriola) salto del Basco | *137* | | *166–67* |
| (capriola) salto del fiocco avanti, in fianco | *125* | | *159–60* |
| (capriola) salto dell'impiccato (saut empedù) | *134–35* | saut empendu | *165* |
| (capriola) salto morto sotto al corpo, fiancheggiato | *135* | | *165–66* |
| (capriola) salto ribaltato a fior di terra, alto, rancignato | *126–27*, 137 | | *160*, 167 |
| (capriola) salto tondo sotto al corpo, di fianco, di sbalzo, intrecciato, su d'un piede, su d'un piede di sbalzo, ritirato, rancignato | *128–31*, 137 | | *161–63*, 166 |
| (capriola) sissone battuto avanti, addietro, da fianco, battuto volato, ritirato | *131–32* | beaten sissonne | *163* |

| Magri's movement vocabulary (his terminology and spelling) | Page(s) in Magri | Skeaping's equivalent | Page(s) in Skeaping |
|---|---|---|---|
| (capriola) spazza campagna [normal], fiancheggiata, girando di sbalzo | *127–28* | | *160–61* |
| (capriola) tordichamp in aria saltato sotto al corpo, di sbalzo, in giro, in fianco | *122–24* | tordichamp jumped in the air | *158* |
| capriolata | 67, 101 | | 102, 138 |
| caprioletta | 71 | | 106 |
| *carè* | 71, *107–8* | carré | 107, *146* |
| *chassè;* see *passo scacciato* | | | |
| *contratempo, contratems* semplice (done lots of ways), aperto, di sbalzo volato, contratempo e passo di bourèè disfatto, battuto | 24, 33, 34, 78, *91–95*, 102, 106–7, 121, 124, 125, 128, 129, 130, 131, 135 | contretemps | 61, 69, 114, *129–31*, 132, 140, 145, 157, 158, 159, 161, 162, 163, 165 |
| *coupè, passo tronco* a due movimenti, a tre movimenti | *44–45* | coupé | *79* |
| *courante [step];* see *passo grave* | | | |
| *degagè, passo staccato* | *33–35*, 48, 68, 73, 76, 95, 108, 124, 125, 126, 129, 131, 137 | degagé | *69–70*, 82, 103, 109 112, 131, 132, 146 158, 159, 160, 162, 163, 166 |
| *demi contretems;* see *mezzo contratempo* | | | |
| *[demi coupé];* see *passo mezzo tronco* | | | |
| *demi eschapè;* see *mezzo sfuggito* | | | |
| *demì-jettè;* see *mezzo gettato* | | | |
| *demi tombè;* see *mezzo cadente* | | | |
| *deviluppè* sostenuto, andante, saltato (sautè), battuto | *79–80* | developpé | *115–16* |

| Magri's movement vocabulary (his terminology and spelling) | Page(s) in Magri | Skeaping's equivalent | Page(s) in Skeaping |
|---|---|---|---|
| [entrechats]; see capriola alla francese and other capriole | | | |
| equilibrio [6 types] | 19–21, 28, 31, 41, 42, 47, 52, 53, 58, 60, 66, 69, 74, 78, 79, 80, 83, 88, 90, 91, 92, 110, 128, 129 | equilibrium, balance | 56–57, 64, 66, 76, 77, 81, 87, 89, 92, 95, 98, 102, 104, 110, 114, 115, 117, 119, 126, 127, 128, 129, 148, 160, 161, 162 |
| eschapè; see passo sfuggito | | | |
| fioretto, fleuret semplice (avanti, in dietro, in fianco, in giro), a chassè (avanti addietro, fiancheg-giato, in giro), a jettè (a.k.a. fleuret jettè; can be done in the usual directions), saltato (sautè) | 97–100, 102 | fleuret | 135–37, 140 |
| flinc, flanc in fianco, girando | 94, 105–6, 124 | flinc flanc | 131, 144, 159 |
| fuetè sotto al corpo, girando | 86–87 | fouetté | 124 |
| gioco delle braccia [use of the arms (and head)] in opposizione, rotonde; basse, a mezz'aria, alte, sforzate (les grands bras) | 36, 67, 77, 109–12, 113–18, 128, 129, 134–35 | | 71, 102, 114, 148–50, 151–54, 161, 165 |
| glissata, glissade avanti, addietro, fiancheggiata, in giro, disfatta | 33, 56, 61, 62, 80–81, 97, 98, 108, 109 | glissade | 69, 93, 98, 99, 117–18, 134, 135, 146, 147 |
| gorgugliè; see (capriola) gorgugliè | | | |
| gran gorgugliè; see (capriola) tordi-champ in aria saltato | | | |
| jettè; see passo gettato | | jeté | |

| Magri's movement vocabulary (his terminology and spelling) | Page(s) in Magri | Skeaping's equivalent | Page(s) in Skeaping |
|---|---|---|---|
| jettè battuto in aria; see (capriola) jettè battuto in aria | | | |
| *mezzo cadente, mezzo tombè, demi tombè* | *54*, 66–67, 68 | demi-tombé | *91*, 102, 103 |
| *mezzo contratempo, demi contretems* | 47, 67, 68, 80, *95*, 100, 103, 104, 106–7 | demi-contretemps | 81, 102, 103, 115, *132*, 137, 141, 142, 145 |
| *mezzo coupè; see passo mezzo tronco* | | | |
| *mezzo fuetè* | *87* | demi-fouetté | *125* |
| *mezzo gettato, demì-jettè* | *48–49*, 66 | demi-jeté | *83*, 101 |
| *mezzo passo grave* | *57–58* | demi-pas grave | *94* |
| *mezzo scacciato, demì chassè* | | | |
| semplice, battuto | *77*, 106 | demi-chassé | *113*, 144 |
| *mezzo sfuggito, demì eschapè* | *59*, 87 | demi-échappé | *97*, 125 |
| *mezzo sissone* | 65, *71*, 135 | demi-sissonne | 101, *106*, 165 |
| semplice, rilevato | | | |
| *pas coursè, passo coursè* in fianco, in giro | 73 | pas coursé | *109* |
| *pas de bourèè, passo di bourèè* semplice (many ways), aperto, incrocciato (croucè), girando, fallito, in jettè, tombè, in aria, a quattro passi | *60–68*, 76, 94, 95, 106–7, 109, 132 | pas de bourrée | *98–103*, 112, 130, 132, 145, 147, 163 |
| *pas tombè; see passo cadente* | | pas tombé | |
| *pas trusè* | 65, 67, 94, *103* | pas trusé | 101, 102, 131, *141* |
| *passi* (in general) | 23, 24, 25, *30–31*, 34, 35–*36*, 37, 42, 59, 60, 71, 87 | steps | 61, 62, *66*, 70, 71, 73, 77, 97, 98, 106, 125 |
| *passo bilanciato, pas balancè* | *51–52* | pas balancé | *87–88* |
| *passo cadente, pas tombè* avanti, indietro, fiancheggiato, girando, da lato (All may be done a terra or in aria.) | *53–54* | pas tombé | *89–90* |

| Magri's movement vocabulary (his terminology and spelling) | Page(s) in Magri | Skeaping's equivalent | Page(s) in Skeaping |
|---|---|---|---|
| passo di ciaccona semplice, saltato | 67, 94, *103–5* | pas de chaconne | 102, 131, *142–43* |
| passo di gagliarda, pas de gagliarde | *71–72*, 72, 108 | galliard step | *107*, 108, 146 |
| passo di Marseglia, pas de Mareseilles | *36–37* | pas de Mareseilles[1] | *72* |
| passo di rigodone, rigaudon | *102* | rigaudon | *140* |
| passo di sarabonda | *72–73* | saraband step | *108* |
| passo di sissone, pas de sissonne semplice (avanti, in dietro, fiancheggiato, in giro, disfatto in giro, doublè), rilevato (same possibilities) | 69–71, 123, 126, 127, 131–32, 134 | pas de sissonne | *104–5*, 158, 160, 161, 163, 165 |
| passo gettato, pas jettè, jettè semplice, battuto (Both can be done avanti, in dietro, fiancheggiato, girando, disfatto girando, raddoppiato [doublè].) | 23, *45–48*, 66, 84, 85, 97, 99–100, 104, 106, 108, 109, 126, 133, 137 | jeté | 61, *80–82*, 101, 121, 122, 135, 136, 142, 144, 146, 147, 160, 164, 166 |
| passo grave, courante avanti, indietro, da lato, in giro, a piè fermo, sotto al corpo, in aria; ad una ed a due piegate | *55–57* | pas grave | *92–93* |
| passo marciato, pas marchè | *35–36* | pas marché | *71* |
| passo mezzo tronco, mezzo coupè avanti, in dietro, in fianco, girando avanti, girando in fianco, girando disfatto sotto al corpo | *42–44*, 51, 65, 103 | demi-coupé | *77–78*, 87, 101, 141 |

1. Skeaping was apparently unaware of the "pas de Mr Marcel" described in several eighteenth-century French dance treatises and named after the famous dancer. Magri mentions the dancer, but misspells his name.

| Magri's movement vocabulary (his terminology and spelling) | Page(s) in Magri | Skeaping's equivalent | Page(s) in Skeaping |
|---|---|---|---|
| *passo naturale o semplice* | *31–32*, 35, 74, 77, 95, 98 | simple or natural step | 67, 71, 110, 113, 132, 135 |
| passo nobile | 30–31 | | 66 |
| *passo scacciato, pas chassè* semplice (avanti, in dietro, in fianco, in giro, disfatto girando), aperto (avanti, in dietro), battuto (fiancheggiato, sul collo del piede, in giro, girando disfatto), a quattro passi | 73–76, 97, 99, 102, 106, 108, 109 | chassé | 110–12, 135, 136, 140, 144, 146, 147 |
| *passo sfuggito, pas eschapè* sotto al corpo, girando, sforzato | *58–59* | échappé | *95–96* |
| *passo staccato;* see *degagè* | | | |
| *passo tronco;* see *coupè* | | | |
| *passo unito;* see *assemblè* | | | |
| *pirola, piroùettes* a dritta, a sinistra, disfatta, sotto al corpo sostenuta, forzata incerta, bassa, ritirata, ponta e tacco, tacco e ponta, distesa aperta, incrocciata | *88–91* | pirouette | *126–28* |
| *pistoletta a terra* avanti, in dietro, da lato, in giro | *49–50*, 132 | | *84*, 164 |
| pistoletta in aria; see (capriola) pistoletta in aria | | | |
| *positure (posizioni) de' piedi* | 26–30 | positions of the feet | *63–65* |
| positure false (5) | 27–28, 50 | false positions | 64–65, 85 |
| posizioni forzate (3) | 29, 35, 53, 55, 66, 88, 89, 101, 111, 123, 127 | forced positions | 65, 71, 89, 92, 102, 126, 127, 138, 149, 158, 161 |
| posizioni spagnuoli (5) | 30, 50, 120, 125, 130, 134, 136, 137 | Spanish positions | 65, 85, 156, 159, 162, 164, 166 |

| Magri's movement vocabulary (his terminology and spelling) | Page(s) in Magri | Skeaping's equivalent | Page(s) in Skeaping |
|---|---|---|---|
| quarta capriolata | 67, 101 | | 102, 138 |
| quinta intrecciata | 106 | interwoven fifth | 144 |
| rond de jambe; see *tordichamb* | | | |
| salti (general) | 22, 23, 24, 34, 40, 42, 46, 49, 65, 71, 72, 78, 80, 88, 93, 94, 95, 98, 100, 102, 103, 104, 107, 116, 122ff, 138 | jumps | 58, 61, 69, 74, 76, 80, 84, 101, 106, 107, 114, 115, 120, 130, 131, 132, 135, 137, 140, 141, 142, 145, 153, 158ff, 167 |
| salticello | 40, 46, 49, 58, 72, 73, 75, 78, 80, 83, 85, 86, 87, 92–93, 96–97, 100 | little spring | 74, 80, 84, 95, 108, 109, 111, 114, 115, 120, 122, 124, 129–30, 133, 137 |
| salto del Basco; see (capriola) salto del Basco | | | |
| salto del fiocco; see (capriola) salto del fiocco | | | |
| salto dell'impiccato (saut empedù); see (capriola) salto dell'impiccato | | | |
| salto morto; see (capriola) salto morto | | | |
| salto ribaltato; see (capriola) salto ribaltato | | | |
| salto tondo; see (capriola) salto tondo | | | |
| saut empendù; see (capriola) salto dell'impiccato | | | |
| *sissonne*; see *passo di sissonne* | | | |
| sissone battuto; see (capriola) sissone battuto | | | |
| *soubresaut* | *106–7* | | *145* |
| spazza campagna; see (capriola) spazza campagna | | | |

| Other Dance Terms | Page(s) in Magri | Skeaping's equivalent | Page(s) in Skeaping |
|---|---|---|---|
| dance notation; see segni di corogrofia | | | |
| doublè; see raddoppiato | | | |
| drunk character | 134 | | 165 |
| English dancing or dancers | 27, 50 | | 64, 85 |
| entrata grave | 23 | [entrée grave] | 60 |
| figuranti | 105 | supernumeraries [sic] | 143 |
| follia | 23, 52 | [folies d'Espagne] | 60, 87 |
| French dancing or steps | 10, 23, 56–57, 58, 79, 82, 96, 101, 102, 106, 112, 113, 116, 118–19, 125, 126, 136, 137 | | 44, 60, 92–93, 95, 115, 119, 133, 138, 140, 144, 150, 151, 153, 155–56, 159, 160, 166 |
| Furie | 23, 104, 106, 111–12, 114 | Furies | 60, 143, 145, 149–50 152 |
| gagliarda | 71, 108 | galliard | 107, 146 |
| gavotta | 23 | gavotte | 60 |
| gesti | 18, 36, 111, 116 | gestures | 55, 71, 149, 153 |
| giga | 23, 105 | gigue | 60, 144, 163 |
| Inglesi; see English dancing | | | |
| Italian dancing or dancers | 27, 50, 71, 82, 111–12, 119–20, 121, 136 | | 64, 85, 106, 119, 149–50, 156, 157, 166 |
| lure | 23, 116? [lurnie] | loure | 60, 153? |
| minuetto | 52, 55, 61 | minuet | 87, 92, 99 |
| minuetto scozzese | 52 | minuet ecossais | 87 |
| music; see cadenza | | | |
| oltramontani | 108, 111, 115, 117, 124 | | 146, 149, 152, 153, 159 |
| pantomime | 8–9, 10, 17, [67], 116 | | 44, 54, [102], 153 |
| pas de deux, dances for two | 82, 105, 108 | | 119, 143, 146 |
| paspiè | 52 | passepied | 87 |
| passagagli | 23, 116 | passacaglie | 60, 153 |
| pastoral | 117 | | 153 |
| raddoppiato, raddoppiare, deublè | 23, 24, 47, 48, 49, 51, 65, 70, 71, 86, 97, 101, 102, 109, 130, 133 | doublé, repetition | 61, 81, 84, 86, 87, 101, 105, 106, 123, 134, 138, 147, 162, 164 |
| rigaudon | 102 | rigaudon | 140 |
| *rondeau, rondò* | *108–9* | rondeau | *147* |

| People | Page(s) in Magri | Skeaping's equivalent | Page(s) in Skeaping |
|---|---|---|---|
| Caroso, Signor Fabrizio | 9, 31 | | 44, 66 |
| Cesarini | 41, 129, 135 | | 75, 161, 166 |
| Cicerone, Tullio [Cicero] | 117 | | 154 |
| Coviello | 111 | | 149 |
| Demetrio | 17 | Demetrius | 54 |
| Dufort, Giambattista | 10, 20, 30, 46, 52, 53 | | 44, 57, 66, 80, 87, 89 |
| Ercole | 117 | Hercules | 153 |
| Esopo, commediante | 117 | Aesop, comedian | 154 |
| Euridice | 117 | | 153 |
| Fabris | 116 | | 153 |
| Filibois, Monsieur | 10 | | 44 |
| Iole | 117 | | 153 |
| Ippocrate | 16 | Hippocrates | 54 |
| Lenzi | 116 | | 153 |
| Lepicq, Monsieur Carlo | 86 | | 123 |
| Lucchesi, Francesco | 116 | | 153 |
| Luciano | 17 | Lucien | 54 |
| Luigi il Grande | 55 | Louis le Grand [Louis XIV] | 92 |
| Magri, Gennaro (as dancer) | (9), 37, 40–41, 123, 124, 126–27, 130, 136, 137 | | 46, 73, 75, 158, 159, 160, 162, 166 |
| Mareseilles [Marcel], Mr de | 36 | | 72 |
| Michel, Monsieur | 126 | | 160 |
| Michelangiolo | 18 | Michelangelo? | 55 |
| Mirtillo | 117 | | 153 |
| Mulinaro | 130, 136 | | 162, 166 |
| Muratori, Ludovico Antonio | 8 | | 44 |
| Noverre, Monsieur de | 16, 18, 64–65, 109 | | 54, 55, 101, 148 |
| Orfeo | 117 | Orpheus | 153 |
| Pantomimus | 9 | | 44 |
| Piraut [Pierrot] | 136 | Praut [sic] | 166 |
| Pitrot, Monsieur | 91 | | 128 |
| Planelli, Sign. Cavalier | 14, 16 | | 51, 54 |
| Pulcinella | 130, 134, 136, 137 | | 162, 165, 166 |
| Rigoni, Messer Rinaldo | 9 | | 44 |
| Roscio, tragediante | 117 | Roscius, tragedian | 154 |
| Salomoni, Signor | 17 | | 54 |
| Scaramuccia | 111, 116 | | 149, 153 |

| People | Page(s) in Magri | Skeaping's equivalent | Page(s) in Skeaping |
|---|---|---|---|
| Sgai, Francesco | (9) | | 46 |
| Truffaldino | 116 | | 153 |
| Vestris Fiorentino, Signor | 90 | | 128 |
| Viganò, Signor | 120, 130 | | 156, 162 |

# Contributors

SALVATORE BONGIOVANNI is a dance historian, musicologist, and teacher of Italian literature living in Rome. In addition to writing his 1991 *tesi di laurea* (M.A. thesis) on "Gennaro Magri e il *Trattato teorico-prattico di ballo*," for the Università degli Studi "La Sapienza" (Rome), he has published an essay on the choreographer in *Creature di Prometeo: Il ballo teatrale dal divertimento al dramma* (Florence, 1996). He has also worked as a piano accompanist for several ballet schools.

BRUCE ALAN BROWN is professor of music history at the University of Southern California, Los Angeles. A specialist on eighteenth-century opera and ballet, he has published books on *Gluck and the French Theatre in Vienna* (Oxford, 1991) and Mozart's *Così fan tutte* (Cambridge, 1995), an edition of Gluck's *Le Diable à quatre* (1992), as well as numerous articles. He is a member of the Zentralinstitut für Mozart-Forschung (Salzburg) and the editorial board of the Gluck-Gesamtausgabe and is currently editor-in-chief of the *Journal of the American Musicological Society*.

MOIRA GOFF, a curator of early printed books at the British Library, London, has been researching and reconstructing early-eighteenth-century dance for nearly fifteen years. During that time, she has lectured and published widely and has danced in Europe and the United States as well as throughout the United Kingdom. Specializing in dance on the London stage from the Restoration to the mid-eighteenth century, Goff wrote a doctoral thesis (University of Kent, Canterbury) on the English dancer-actress Hester Santlow and is currently working on a book on Santlow's life and career.

SANDRA NOLL HAMMOND is a dancer and dance historian who was among the first to explore ballet technique and training of the late eighteenth and early nineteenth centuries. She has presented this material in master classes, workshops, lectures, concerts, and articles. Recent publications include "Sor and the Ballet of his Time" in *Estudios sobre Fernando Sor / Sor Studies* (Madrid, 2003) and the fifth edition of her widely used textbook, *Ballet Basics*. She was cofounder of the dance program at the University of Arizona and later professor and director of dance at the University of Hawaii. Her ballet training was at the Juilliard School, the Metropolitan Opera Ballet, and the School of Ballet Repertory. As a performer, she has appeared with Pacific Ballet, Arizona Dance Theatre, and as guest artist in concerts of baroque dance.

KATHLEEN KUZMICK HANSELL is music editor at the University of Chicago Press and managing editor of the critical edition of The Works of Giuseppe Verdi. She is the author of "Theatrical Ballet and Italian Opera" in *Opera on Stage*, volume 5 of The History of Italian Opera (2002); articles on the choreographers Noverre, Gioia, and Le Picq in several encyclopedias; articles on ballet and on Gluck in eighteenth- and early nineteenth-century Stockholm and on aspects of Italian opera in the same era. She has prepared critical editions of Mozart's *Lucio Silla* (1986), Verdi's *Stiffelio* (2003), and Rossini's *Zelmira* (forthcoming).

REBECCA HARRIS-WARRICK is professor of music at Cornell University. She is the author, with Carol G. Marsh, of *Musical Theatre at the Court of Louis XIV: "Le Mariage de la Grosse Cathos"* (1994) and of numerous articles about French baroque music and dance. She has prepared critical editions of Gaetano Donizetti's opera *La Favorite* (1997) and of Jean-Baptiste Lully's *Ballet des Amours déguisez* (2001) and is currently writing a book on the role of dance in French opera during the seventeenth and eighteenth centuries.

CAROL G. MARSH, professor of music at the University of North Carolina at Greensboro, received a Ph.D. in musicology from the City University of New York. Her books include *Musical Theatre at the Court of Louis XIV: "Le Mariage de la Grosse Cathos"* (with Rebecca Harris-Warrick) and *La Danse Noble: An Inventory of Dances and Sources* (with Meredith Little). She has contributed articles and reviews to *Dance Chronicle, Dance Research Journal,* and the *International Encyclopedia of Dance,* and has edited several ballets for the series Ballet Music from the Mannheim Court (A-R Editions).

PATRICIA W. RADER is a cataloger and reference librarian for the Dance Division, New York Public Library for the Performing Arts, at Lincoln Center. She has studied historical dance since 1975 and performed and taught with a variety of ensembles, including the Mannes Camerata and New York Historical Dance Company. Her M.A. in dance research and reconstruction is from City College, City University of New York, where projects included the Renaissance dance video *Il ballarino*, directed by Julia Sutton, and a thesis on the early-eighteenth-century English performer Hester Santlow, supervised by Wendy Hilton. She currently chairs the Early Dance Working Group of the Society of Dance History Scholars.

LINDA J. TOMKO is a historian, dancer, and reconstructor of period choreographies. She holds a Ph.D. in history from UCLA and is associate professor of dance at the University of California, Riverside. She has served as president of the Society of Dance History Scholars and as reviews editor for *Dance Research Journal*, and she currently serves as editor of the Pendragon Press "Dance and Music" series. With Wendy Hilton, she codirected the annual Stanford University Summer Workshop in Baroque Dance and Its Music from the mid-1990s until Miss Hilton's recent passing. Tomko's book *Dancing Class: Gender, Ethnicity, and Social Divides in American Dance: 1890–1920* was published by Indiana University Press in 1999.

# Index